INTRUDER IN MAO'S REALM

An Englishman's eyewitness account
of 1970s China

Richard Kirkby

EARNSHAW
BOOKS

Intruder in Mao's Realm

By Richard Kirkby

ISBN-13: 978-988-8422-04-3

BIOGRAPHY & AUTOBIOGRAPHY / Historical

First printing August 2016
Second printing September 2018

EB077

Published by Earnshaw Books Ltd. (Hong Kong)

FOREWORD

By sheer fluke I find myself writing these opening lines to *Intruder in Mao's Realm* almost fifty years to the day since Mao's "Great Proletarian Cultural Revolution" broke upon the Chinese nation. This memoir has something in common with the Communist Party's own public appraisal of Mao's tumultuous movement: it has seen the light of day only after decades. On the fiftieth anniversary itself – 16th May 2016 – the Party was silent. The following day, though, the *People's Daily* presented the Chinese people with the Party's most unequivocally damning verdict yet:

The Cultural Revolution was wrongly launched by the leaders and exploited by a counterrevolutionary clique. It brought the grave disaster of internal turmoil to the party, country and people of every ethnicity, and the harm it created was comprehensive and severe. History has amply demonstrated that the Cultural Revolution was totally wrong in theory and practice. In no sense was it, or could it have been, revolutionary or socially progressive.

This, then, is condemnation which will be music to the ears of the hundreds of millions of survivors of the great cataclysm, the eleven tumultuous years from 1966 to 1976. But when I launched myself into China in 1974 as it moved the last vicious throes of the Cultural Revolution, I was innocent of Chinese realities, headstrong and perhaps foolhardy.

The handful of foreigners in China at the time inhabited a rarefied world, and of those I came across I cannot recall a single individual who did not find that world a daily trial. This was never a trial of the body, for our Chinese hosts lavished every creature comfort upon us. It was more one of the spirit. Any normal human contact with Chinese people was out of the question. Whether inside or outside our guarded compounds, communication with the great Chinese masses was limited to curt transactional exchanges.

For the well-being of our political consciousnesses, we were, at least, taken out regularly to visit factories, rural communes and schools. On such occasions, communication was limited to formalistic set-pieces by the revolutionary committees - invariably turning on a recent editorial in the *People's Daily*, with stumbling renderings of our ever-present interpreter/ minder. Yes – we consorted to a degree with minders, students, colleagues, some of whom even carried a hint of personal warmth. But in our work and everyday lives, our interlocutors were obliged to behave like ciphers. The foreign world, which strangely we represented, was a vastly dangerous place. Even more galling for us, we were actively discouraged from learning the language, in any other land the *sine qua non* of expatriate assimilation. All in all, it was hugely tempting to simply to surrender to the officials, and moulder in the foreigners' cocoon, always a guarded compound.

Hardly a day went past without an affront to our senses of freedom of choice. Yet young Westerners such as we, children of the Sixties, were hardly likely just to bend to capricious officialdom's decisions about our lives and our work. I found this the greatest ordeal, one which led to constant struggles with the bureaucrats. Our verdicts at the time were entirely unforgiving. We would damn-to-hell the cadres who circumscribed our every move, ignorant of the weight on their shoulders from a danger-laden system. As novices in the matter of traditional Chinese culture we often, too, failed to appreciate that the way people behaved was conditioned not merely by the present, but by the unseen weight of the millennial Chinese past.

'Foreign expert' was our official, uncalled-for (and in most cases, unjustified) title. If I fall into using the term, it will only be for convenience and always tinged with irony. A quasi-ministry in Beijing, the distant State Council Foreign Experts Bureau, monitored our lives through constant reports from our work-unit. Not a few of the wide-eyed foreigners in China at the time found that the reality was more than they could bear. They broke their contracts and left early. Yes, even in those heady days, a one-page contract was offered by the Bureau. Yet others – a tiny few amongst whom I might have been proud to number - were ejected after their political frustrations got the better of them. And perhaps surprisingly, those expelled were usually critics of China from the left rather than the right. It was usually Beijing's self-serving foreign policy which was the straw which broke the camel's back: all too often in that era of official Soviet Union-hating, the People's Republic coincided with, and reinforced, U.S. foreign adventures. But returning home with our tails between our legs was never going to be for us. Whatever the obstacles, we were determined to see out our allotted time and maintain a reasonable measure of sang froid. And our resolve to stay the course, come what may, had firm underpinnings.

Firstly, we daily reminded ourselves of our hugely privileged station: to the envy of all our friends, our political comrades, our bemused families even, we had somehow managed to breach the Bamboo Curtain. To the politically charged Western youth of the Sixties, China was the great unknown, the last great frontier. Yes, Nixon and the U.S. press corps had come and gone, and the occasional Western journalist made a splash by reporting from China while on a brief, chaperoned visit. By and large, though, the outside world scarcely knew a thing about the state of China after years of Cultural Revolution turmoil. Persistence and good fortune had plonked us in the midst of this occluded society. We were determined that whatever the difficulties of life in China, we would never slink home in defeat. In any case, we had burned our home bridges.

Secondly, though our hosts' often paranoid, controlling hospitality was no fun, at heart we knew not to take things too personally. Even covert hostility became understandable. We carried no personal burden of guilt for the actions of our forefathers. Yet we well understood that a century of humiliation at the hands of foreigners – not least the British – could hardly dispose the average Communist Party functionary to think kindly of us.

The Chinese are often said to have long memories. Knowing now far more of Britain's history in China, the Opium Wars, the 1860 razing of the Summer Palace, the bloody aftermath of the Boxer Rebellion, it surprises me that at such a frenetic, xenophobic juncture we were treated with any degree of civility. Despite our hosts' formulaic talk of friendship and goodwill, we nonetheless had few illusions that we had been invited to China for reasons of sentiment. As small cogs in the Communist Party leaders' plans for what they first called 'socialist construction' and later 'modernisation', we were a necessary evil, a plain bloody nuisance which had to be borne for the greater good.

The third thing which stopped us from giving up on China was the gradual realisation that compared with what the Chinese had to bear, our frustrations were as nothing. The multifarious oppression visited on our colleagues, though no longer usually life-threatening as it had been at the height of the Red Guard chaos, was of course never spoken of in our presence. But even in our enforced remoteness, we could sense the pressures which beset our colleagues in their everyday lives. Adding to his 1927 analysis of Chinese classes, Mao Zedong had dubbed the intelligentsia the 'Stinking Ninth' category of class enemy. We knew that despite our soft treatment, as foreign members of that benighted class we belonged to the 'Stinking Tenth'. But next to our colleagues, next to the hundreds of millions of Chinese and their awesome and sometimes awful experiment with history, our own difficulties were but miniscule.

For myself, there were also reasons of a more positive hue for seeing out my allotted time in Nanjing, and later in Shandong. I have to state, in case anyone is in any doubt, that being an adherent of Maoism was never one of them. I went to China as a well-developed anti-Stalinist – indeed with Trotsky's devastating critique of the early course of the Chinese revolution. As a student, I had been caught up by the debates about the nature of political formations which had leapt from national liberation struggles straight to primitive collective systems. China epitomised such societies. Before going to China, I had been keen to study other states which had declared themselves 'socialist'. As a postgraduate, I had even spent some time in Poland at the height of the Gierek repression. When infuriated members of the London public angrily yelled 'get back to Russia' at our anti-Vietnam war demonstrations, we of the anti-Stalinist persuasion merely laughed and waved. Contrary to the belief of the British intelligence services, who interfered with my post-China career (having been in China during Mao's time so I just *had* to be a dangerous Maoist), our interests were sympathetic but never partisan. An understanding of the tragedy of Stalinism had made us firmly into socialists of the 'no country' variety.

Having said that, Maoism did sell its massive societal experiment, the Great Proletarian Cultural Revolution, as socialism with an anti-bureaucratic face. Sitting in London and knowing nothing of the Cultural Revolution's horrors, Beijing's message undoubtedly had some primal appeal to the anti-Stalinist, 'no-country' socialist.

With such a world view, the opportunity to observe the massive experiments of the Mao era was highly seductive. Once I was actually living and working alongside (if not amongst) the Chinese, the abstract constructs of the critique of Stalinism, bureaucracy, 'socialism in one country', the 'stages theory' of the transition to the communist future – all these notions remained at the forefront of my mind. Indeed, I carried to China a pile of tracts on the philosophy and practise of the transition to socialism, and I didn't neglect these often abstruse writings. Of course, on a personal level such theoretical enlightenment was frequently clouded by the tribulations of day-to-day existence. On another level, the Chinese realities confronting me were refracted through the prism of an ancient civilisation, and it did not help that I had arrived in China with only a dim idea of the county's deep cultural traditions.

Finally but perhaps most vitally, I had a specific mission in China, which I had first visited for a month in 1973 – on an official 'study tour'. I was an urbanist of a new variety, which I shall briefly explain. Human settlements cannot be understood through the ambitions of architects or planners – by the formalistic experiments of Renaissance builders or nineteenth century utopians such as Robert Owen and Ebenezer Howard. Rather, they are determined in their general pattern by political and economic conditions of the time. Throughout my residence in Nanjing and Jinan – with Hong Kong squeezed in the middle – I had been intent on uncovering as much as humanly possible about the links between China's collectivist, 'socialist' polity on the one hand, and urban development and relations with the vast countryside on the other. To those interested in so-called Third

World development, China under Mao was a paradox. Alongside a rampant industrial revolution, plain for all to see, where were the uncontrolled migration and urban squalor so familiar in other parts of Asia, Latin America and Africa?

I am grateful for our hosts' attempts to enlighten me on this burning topic, even though what they could reveal was usually sanitized by the latest sloganising of the ever-changing political firmament. Discussions about urban development with supposed practitioners (someone had to be wheeled out to talk to the foreigner) quickly morphed to the very safe plateau of how many trees had been planted that year.

It was a shame that I could not properly disclose my true and not unsympathetic interest in the country's development process. No routine academic research by foreigners was remotely possible until the 1980s, so while resident in Nanjing, and later in Shandong, my snooping for scraps of knowledge here and the wider picture there could easily be misconstrued – and it was. But to confess an ulterior motive for my intrusion into the country would have been to offer a hostage to fortune. As it was, I know now that I kept a large contingent of nervous security officials darkly pondering on why their foreign teacher seemed intent on poking his oversized nose into matters which scarcely concerned him.

Someone close to me read this memoir in earlier draft, and accused me of being too harsh on the Chinese, in danger even of appearing racist. I owed it to her to think hard about this as I worked on completing the book, and what I wish to convey here is the harshness of the *times*. Recently I came across the perceptive work of Anne-Marie Brady: *Making the Foreign Serve China: Managing Foreigners in the People's Republic*, a title which says it all. Brady demonstrates, often hilariously, how our routine experiences as foreign residents of xenophobic Cultural Revolution China followed a definite codification. Oddly, had I come across this eye-opening work earlier, any guilt at my harsh judgments would have been diminished.

It is high time I explained why I have been mysteriously employing the royal 'we'. The body of this book divides into two parts – first Nanjing and then Shandong. The experience was a joint one, for my then-partner Jo was ever-present. Having said that, the reconstruction and interpretation of events in this book are mine alone. And that reconstruction is not only founded on memories and thousands of photographs; throughout I kept diaries, dutifully penned almost daily in a hand impenetrable to anyone but myself.

Our time (late 1974 to early 1977) tutoring groups of ex-Red Guards, now 'worker-peasant-soldier' students at Nanjing University, constitutes the first substantive section (chapters III-XVI). Nanjing was the capital of China during the early Ming dynasty, restored to this position by the Nationalist (Guomindang) government of the late 1920s, overrun by the Japanese in 1937, again becoming the national capital from 1945 on. In 1949, the Nationalists were chased out of China to Taiwan, the Communist Party taking over control of the nation. In spite of its horrendous history (the crushing of the Taiping rebellion in the nineteenth century with significant assistance by Britain's General Charles Gordon commanding the Ever-Victorious Army, the massacres by the invading Japanese in the 1930s), by the 1970s Nanjing was reborn a green and pleasant city. Had it not been for the political maelstrom of the Cultural Revolution, Nanjing would have been a wonderfully liveable place. Hence the flavour of this part of the book: On the shores of the Yangtze – wrong time, right place.

Weary from our daily travails after over two years in Nanjing, we departed for rest and recreation in Hong Kong. It was 1977 and we were en route for home, but in the event never got back to England. Though Hong Kong had always appalled and frightened me in equal measure, from the perspective of the gentle sub-tropical island of Cheung Chau, it now seemed a curious and exciting place. Without really thinking about it, we just stayed. The colour of our skin brought easy money; the melange of Chinese and other cultures made Hong Kong a fascinating place. But soon the glitter palled, and Beijing's agents in the weird colony persuaded us to return, as they put it, to the Bosom of the Motherland. Thus it was that we spent a very strange couple of years in an overgrown village near Jinan, the capital of Shandong province some five hundred kilometers south of Beijing. Though China was beginning to move on from the oppressive atmosphere we had known in Nanjing, impoverished Shandong was an atavistic, unpleasant place. This second long stay in China, chronicled in chapters XVII – XXII, ended in something of a crisis. The Shandong experience (1978-80) I have always considered 'right time, wrong place'.

In late 1979, Jo and our Beijing-born son left China. Jo had become unwell as a result of Yongshan's birth, the latter a novel experience for us as well as for the Chinese involved. I had stayed on in Shandong, from where I made a hurried departure under contrived accusations of malfeasance. Eventually we were reunited in England, my China-born mother, Joanna, helping us get back on our feet.

From the early 1980s on, I became a serial visitor to China, in a confusion of roles: academic researcher, 'diplomat', business-go-between, just plain tourist. My most recent visit found me lecturing once again to wide-eyed Nanjing University students, and visiting my mother's birthplace in Sichuan where Son No.2 now resides. All this will await the sequel to this account, which I plan to call *The Diverse Wanderings of Mr Li Caide*.

The People's Republic today has been longer without Mao Zedong than it was with him. Though the nation's essence is now a strange hybrid of authoritarian capitalism, paradoxically a party calling itself Communist still rules the high ground, and sometimes with draconian force. But China has emerged a far more diverse and complex country than anyone could have imagined a generation ago. Thirty years ago, with China still a land of uniformity, people would pose the inevitable, polite question, 'Do you like China?' I always found it one which defies all sensible response. 'China' is gargantuan in its complexity – a whole galaxy beyond the personal.

I offer in the lines which follow no chronicling of the extraordinary convulsions and political somersaults of the People's Republic in its third decade under Communist Party rule. Many others have illuminated that terrain. Rather, my memoir turns on alien survival, weird happenings, and eccentric individuals observed from my unique perch within the forbidding, intriguing landscape of 1970s China.

Richard Kirkby
May 2016
The Lake District

Contents

I
A CURIOUS PASSAGE

IT HAD ALL BEGUN in London in the depressing greyness of late 1973. Throughout the land, electricity was strictly rationed, and Prime Minister Edward Heath had strangely decreed a three-day working week. Heath was at war with the coal miners. Unlike his successor Margaret Thatcher, whose vicious determination knew no limits, Heath's battle plan in the class war was to switch off the power stations, preserve coal stocks and bring the striking miners to their knees. Instead, his government was soon brought to *its* knees. Huddled around a smoky candle in the narrow passage which served as our kitchen, we gazed out over the massive redbrick chimneys of our neighbour, the notorious Brixton gaol, and dreamt of escape.

Meanwhile, in the brave new world of a parallel universe, struggles were underway on a very much vaster scale. In the latest phase of the Cultural Revolution, Chinese in their countless millions were poring over Chairman Mao Zedong's opaque command to 'criticise Lin Biao and Confucius'. Confucius we thought we knew a little about, mainly from schoolboy jokes. And was not Lin Biao the military man with the un-Chinese big nose and peaked cap who wrote the preface to the Chairman's Little Red Book, the volume of pious readings and earthy sayings which the entire Chinese nation was obliged to recite, day in and day out? You could even get hold of it on the streets of London. But why on earth should he be criticised?

Though certain feelers had been extended, Jo and I had no real expectation that we would soon be joining the toiling masses of the East, as Lenin called the Asian peoples. What we did know was rather more prosaic – that we urgently needed to escape our tormentress, Mrs Orissa Green, who resided below in our terraced house on London's Brixton Hill. The slightest sound carrying through the floor would evoke yelled threats and the frantic banging of a broom handle. Like Mrs Green, we too were becoming neurotic.

It was time for a strategic retreat, and if our silly idea of somehow getting to China was nothing more than a pipe-dream, that retreat had to be a parochial one. Towards Brixton town hall was a leafy side street of solid Victorian villas in obvious decline, their front gardens strewn with rubbish. For some time we had been watching a particularly neglected semi for any sign of life. One dark night, the front door gave to our chisels and we gazed around a spacious hall. We were in, and joy of joys, no one had bothered to turn off the water or electricity. Soon we would be part of that fraternity of politico-squatters which had popped up all over London. Our move down the road from our tortured flat and Mrs Green was imminent.

Until, that is, a small white envelope embossed with the Chinese Embassy's address landed on our doormat:

> *Dear Sutcliffe and Kirkby*
> *With reference to your application to teach English in China, I now have the pleasure of informing you that a positive reply has been received. Could you contact me as soon as possible to arrange an appointment to discuss the matter?*
> *Yours sincerely*
> *Ms Xie Heng, Second Secretary.*

Apart from the way we were addressed, it was impeccable

English, right down to the '?' at the end. Obviously the Embassy had an in-house scribe. But pondering on the English was not where we were at. It was like being chosen from amongst thousands of candidates for a mission to outer space. Unbelievably, we were off to China.

We had practically forgotten about China. It was in November 1973 - ten months earlier - that we had found ourselves in a cavernous eighteenth century drawing room in London's Portland Place, making polite noises about the weather in London and the weather in Beijing. I was well aware that not too long before, the radicals in Beijing had ordered their diplomats the world over to go out and 'make revolution'. The Chinese embassy's occupants had conducted rushed sorties onto the street, where they had threatened surprised passers-by with that Little Red Book. All was now calm and ordered. Jo and I slurped our green tea from lidded mugs under an enormous marble fireplace graced by a portrait of Chairman Mao. Placed around the fireplace was a three-piece suite decorated with lace anti-Macassars. Perched on one of the deep armchairs was a tiny woman with bobbed hair, rounded pink plastic glasses and a neat blue trouser suit.

It was, in truth, my second time at the embassy: as a member of a 'friendship' delegation which had spent a month in China in October 1973, I had been invited to a debriefing reception there. But our present invitation was enigmatic. Could it be something to do with a short conversation with our hostess, Second Secretary Xie Heng, about foreigners and China?

In Xie Heng's mind it clearly was. After a few more faltering exchanges, the diplomat brought our mysterious interview to a close. Dismissing us at the massive Nash terrace door, she mouthed the classic 'Don't call us – we'll call you.' Apparently this had been a job interview, though nothing had been asked about our backgrounds and experience. Nor for that matter were we any the wiser about the nature of jobs available for foreigners in China. Afterwards, we heard not a word from Portland Place, and we got on with our lives. Until the letter arrived.

When I managed at last to get past the embassy switchboard, Xie Heng was alarmingly specific:

'You will be ready to leave for China in two weeks' time. Come to the embassy to receive your visas and to discuss how you will travel,' she informed us in clipped military style.

Clearly any notion of due notice was alien to our new employers. Anxious that our chances would fade if we were hesitant, we humbly begged Xie Heng to stretch out that fortnight: we had jobs to terminate, a landlord to placate and a flat to empty. But this was the least of our worries. A puritanical busybody, a self-declared friend of China, assured us that should we arrive at the border minus a marriage certificate, we would be summarily shown the door. Children of the radical Sixties, we had no intention of conforming to petty notions of couple-dom. But swallowing our principles, we booked ourselves a slot at the Brixton registry office, and got our piece of paper. 'Thanks to that thar Chairman Mayo,' Jo's Yorkshire grandmother sobbed in gratitude.

There were other essential preparations. Like all of the tiny band of foreigners allowed into China, we were being recruited for our supposed skills in our native language. Jo had the advantage of being a qualified teacher of English to foreigners, but I had no idea how I was going to perform in front of an eager class of Red Guards. I quickly got myself enrolled on an English-as-a-Foreign Language cramming course, spending a month practising my imperfect methods on an unsuspecting class of international youth - none, of course, Chinese.

It is a fact that in my earliest memories, China had loomed from close quarters, though I cannot claim that thoughts of that land carved deep furrows in my childish consciousness. As a youngster, I had wondered at the embroidered silks, dolls and shadow puppets which nestled in my mother's 'China drawer' in the mahogany chest in the hall. Born in rural Sichuan province in 1919, just half a dozen years after the fall of the Qing dynasty, Joanna had left her home province on a beleaguered steamboat, fired at from both banks of the Yangtze by the troops of rival armies. Sometimes we would pester her for her childhood memories of a fabled land. All were fearsome: the children chasing her with yells of 'big nose, big feet foreign devil', the snake which rose from a meadow to wrap itself around her ankle, the kidnapping for ransom by roving Tibetan horsemen. When at the age of seven mother arrived in England, she scarcely knew a word of her native language and was amazed to see water running from a tap. Though her Quaker missionary parents had occupied a large villa on Chengdu's downtown Green Dragon Street and were never going to be a real part of that vibrant city's life, they were determined that their four children should try to fit in by speaking nothing but Chinese. For her own children, mother's ability to count to ten in Mandarin seemed the only useful legacy of her China childhood which she could pass on to us. For quite some years, this remained my finest schoolboy party trick.

On my father's side of the family, too, there were strong China links, though at the time I was only dimly conscious of them. I wondered why my paternal grandmother occasionally arrived with Chinese gifts. It turned out that grandmother's brother-in-law – my great uncle – had been posted to Beijing as a diplomat and served there as the personal assistant to the British ambassador from 1919 to 1930. This individual was well-versed in the language, clearly, and was also something of a curio collector. As Sir Eric, he went on to be the secretary to George VI and later Mountbatten's aide during India's shift to independence.

Oddly, it was a chance and tenuous association with China in my early teens which left a deeper impression than my mother's remote tales and my grandmother's Chinoiserie. Like many of my peers, I would earn some Christmas cash by working as a relief postman. From time to time, my postbag would contain a mysterious roll of newspapers emblazoned with Chinese characters and bearing Beijing postmarks. We had a distant aunt in Belfast whom I had never met. For years Aunt Elfrida got us subscriptions to *Reader's Digest*, a publication with a mission to expose the Filthy Commies. The horror stories made their mark and by the age of ten, I was a confirmed anti-communist.

A few years on, with the news media shrieking of the cruelty and mass starvation of Mao's China, the packages in my postman's bag took on a radioactive glow. Always they went to the same nondescript house with its peeling hardboard panelled door and cheap chrome letterbox. This ephemeral intrusion of China into my life aroused strange feelings of a distant, hostile, but intriguing world. I knew even then that one day I would have to enter it myself.

In my formal education China never once appeared. Even as a college student of geography, China was completely off the map. And yet coinciding with my time at Bristol University, where I arrived in 1966, the Chinese were experiencing the most disruptive, strife-riven tumult they had so far had to bear under the capricious rule of Mao. But it was, after all, our Sixties, and the chaos brought to the lives of hundreds of millions of Chinese was on a very dim horizon. The whole, seething world seemed to turn on our own struggles for a new culture and a new politics. When in August 1967 the Chancery of the British Mission in Beijing was burned down by Red Guards we were just about conscious enough of the goings-on in the distant Chinese universe to give a wicked three cheers. Consumed by our own lives, we merely registered with amusement that the popular Embassy brand of cigarettes suddenly dropped their long running slogan 'Light up an Embassy'.

Everything about China in the early 1970s carried a high political charge, and this story would not add up without some further explanation of how my youthful view of the world coalesced, and how the impulse to get to China gradually insinuated itself into my brain. First and foremost, the grand events of the early Sixties, starting with the horrendous Cuban Missile crisis when I ran away from school, were making me a wild political animal. A birthright Quaker, my adolescence brought a passionate pacifism. But being a student in the late Sixties, as for millions of mainly young people throughout the Western world, the Vietnam conflict forced an understanding of naked power. In my Bristol circle of dissidents, we marched, fasted for peace, lobbied MPs, had our teach-ins, sat in on Parliamentary debates at Westminster and had secret contacts with dissidents in the army.

Then a far harsher vision of the world than the pacific Quaker way threw itself in my face. It was a shock to discover the venality of the system, how politicians could deceive. I hated Western policy in Indochina and the bloody play for oil that was the Nigerian Civil War. With the latter, I spent a good year of my life campaigning politically and collecting large wads of aid, my studies at Bristol suffering accordingly. As for the Soviet Union, Moscow had sent its armies to quell the Czechoslovakia uprising, and we held no brief for the Soviet bloc, the 'socialist republics'. As Paris raged in the summer of 1968, and the police horses chased us around London's American Embassy, I was to find a comfortable home among the 'New Left'. West and East – we rejected both. We were certain that the 'socialist' or 'people's' republics - those countries thrust into primitive collectivism before their time, including of

7

course China - would one day be transformed for the better. All that was needed, we simplistically believed, was the infusion of democracy. This would dissolve the self-serving bureaucrats and create our Holy Grail - the Real Thing – democratic socialism.

Two years on from Bristol I was enrolled in a Masters programme - on the face of it in city planning but more truly in political economy. The Planning School at London's Architectural Association was an activists' haven, and it suited me down the ground. I was able now to put my ill-assorted ideas into some kind of coherent order. Politics, economics, and the way human beings contrived their settlements on our planet became a focus of growing fascination. In that context too, my thoughts turned increasingly to China.

From a tender age, I had always been an explorer. At fourteen, my impecunious dad felt it would make a man of me if I worked my passage on a Dutch freighter across the North Sea, through the Kiel Canal and into the Baltic. By the time school was finished, I had hitch-hiked all over northern Europe, and was preparing for longer journeys to the eastern Mediterranean. Even at that stage in my life, my fascination with the 'socialist' countries was strong and I wanted to know more about why the West (and *Reader's Digest*) hated them. Along with best school-mate Martin, within a couple of years of the Berlin Wall being erected, I had crossed East Germany and travelled on into Poland. Our journey came to a sticky end in a ditch, hiding (for no good reason) from a Russian tank convoy. Lacking crucial exit visas, we brazened out the border searches on the Moscow-Berlin train and somehow got through to West Berlin. Though the machine gun-wielding soldiers, the huge, panting Alsatians of the search teams and the drabness of the people and scenery were frighteners and put one strongly in mind of the newly-released James Bond caper, *From Russia with*

Love, my appetite for adventure and my curiosity concerning the 'people's republics' was far from extinguished. In fact, in 1965 and in 1966 Martin and I hitched back to Berlin. Up to no good, our Eastern adventures only ceased after an unpleasant incident at the Checkpoint Charlie crossing between West and East Berlin. We had been taught by a con-man how to smuggle Ostmarks, and were rumbled by the East German border guards, from whom, remarkably, we escaped with nothing more than a rap on the knuckles.

A few years later, and in soberer mood, it was my studies in London which took me back to Poland, by day consorting with officials and by night with a group of youthful rebels. But my Warsaw days now had a serious, an academic, purpose. I was utterly curious about cities, and about land-use decisions in a country where land values and the market were absent. As a young foreign ingénue, and lacking the language, trying to get to the bottom of this enigma led only into an impenetrable bureaucratic morass.

Little the wiser, I left Eastern Europe behind. But the fascinating questions about land and politics still held me captive. And a natural-born perversity was now pointing to towards even more impossible horizons. It was 1971, and in London's Chinatown that I started to pick up opaque propaganda tracts published in Beijing. Periodicals such as *China Reconstructs* and *Peking Review* were, of course, designed to assure the world that the ongoing Cultural Revolution was essentially an anti-bureaucratic and popular movement. I was fascinated, and beginning to masticate on the hard seeds of a plan. Little did I know it, but I was launching myself on what would become almost a lifetime's travail with China.

Meanwhile, in the great world out there, a chasm was opening in the established geopolitical order, one which was to offer me a possible avenue into China. For two decades, the Western powers had demonised and embargoed the China of Mao Zedong but now, ever so suddenly, there came an opening between Washington and Beijing. In early 1971, the U.S. table tennis team was in Japan for a championship competition. Out of the blue, an approach by Chinese officials found the U.S. team transported to China. The world watched with astonishment as young Americans cavorted on Beijing's Square of Heavenly Peace, Tiananmen Square. 'Ping-pong diplomacy!' the headlines proclaimed.

What followed was, of course, a seismic shift in the Cold War triangle. Beijing and Washington were now to make common cause against the Soviet Union, which they both hated even more than they disliked each other. To those of my persuasion, versed as we were in Orwell's 1984 where yesterday's arch-enemy was now the bosom ally, China's was no more than a classic Stalinist betrayal. But that did not put me off. It was not long before that grey eminence Henry Kissinger and his horrible boss Richard Nixon were being driven through the gates of the Zhongnanhai, the Party Central Committee's secretive compound on the western fringe of the Forbidden City. With that famous handshake between Mao and Nixon, the two nations headed slowly towards their 1979 normalisation of relations. And, I thought to myself, if the high and mighty could succeed, lesser mortals might just find a way of creeping under the Bamboo Curtain.

My month-long trip to China of late 1973 was unusual, for Beijing tightly controlled the ingress of foreign souls. In those days, the Chinese government regulated their foreign relations through a tripartite division: 'state-to-state', 'Party-to-Party, and 'people-to-people'. State-to-state meant government officials and diplomats posted to Beijing, obviously no use to me. As a confirmed sceptic, neither could 'Party-to-Party' conceivably be my ticket. According to Beijing's laughable propaganda, the grandly named

Communist Party of Britain (Marxist-Leninist), membership a few dozen stalwarts, stood shoulder-to-shoulder with the 30-million-strong Communist Party of China. The official British 'fraternal party' was not merely political anathema, it was also a joke. The CPB (M-L) 'Chairman', Reg Birch, and his motley entourage were the recipients of regular China freebies, basking in Mao Zedong's personal hospitality, long before Nixon and Kissinger.

So for my plan, only the 'people-to-people' route seemed likely. This brought me swiftly into the dubious realm of *youyi* - 'friendship' - a term which Chinese officialdom deemed the correct sentiment for ordinary foreigners of every hue. And maddeningly, of every class (class politics strangely only seemed to apply within China). We were to hear much about 'friendship between our two peoples' in the coming years. Perhaps perversely, being addressed by Chinese functionaries as 'foreign friend' always aroused in me feelings of intense antagonism.

Nonetheless in my opportunistic quest, I was not above using the *youyi* route. SACU – the Society for Anglo-Chinese Understanding – was the sole UK organisation granted the official 'friendship' imprimatur by the Chinese. SACU had been set up just before the Cultural Revolution's launch in 1966, and for some years even its luminaries (the great Sinologist Joseph Needham was honorary president) had been denied entry to a land raging with faction fighting. By the early 1970s, things had cooled down somewhat and the occasional official friend was allowed to peep behind the screen. Soon SACU was invited to recruit enough 'friends' to make up two or three tour groups a year.

In early 1973, I ascended a dimly lit flight of stairs near London's Warren Street tube station to the SACU offices. In this Oriental outpost nestled a dedicated band of semi-Maoists and ardent Sinophiles - a smattering of ex-missionaries, even - whose purpose was to bring the fabled socialist paradise to a largely agnostic British public. SACU had accumulated a useful library, and produced a regular magazine of wide-eyed travellers' tales and laboured explanations of the latest twists and turns of Chinese Party policy. While this was all more or less of interest, what I was entirely focussed upon was SACU's monopoly of China tourism. Or should I say 'study tourism', for visiting China was a serious business.

The first and easiest step was to pay one's dues and sign up to SACU, a membership which I maintained opportunistically throughout my residence in China. It was only later, in the mid-1980s, that the Maoist loyalists had shrunk away that I agreed to be on the organisation's committee. Back in those early days, the prospective China traveller had to submit to a mild ideological screening. When my turn came, this was conducted by Betty, a no-nonsense woman in her sixties, who with her coiled grey hair, and wire glasses evidently modelled herself on the severe female cadre beloved of Chinese propaganda posters.

I might have tried to sign up for one of the general tours run by SACU, but I had a keener plan. This was to persuade the organisation to persuade whichever organisation it corresponded with in Beijing to organise a special trip for people like me – urbanists, economists, environmentalists. I guessed there might be some mileage in my proposal as only a few months before, in mid-1972, China had surprised the diplomatic world by attending the first-ever global environmental forum – the United Nations Conference on the Human Environment, at Stockholm. The SACU interrogator seemed to warm to my proposal, and I quickly urged half a dozen of my Architectural Association colleagues to sign up and prepare for the trip of a lifetime. This journey, in 1973, turned out to be merely a taster, whetting my appetite for the grand plan – to live and work in China as the only means of finding out what was really happening there.

Why was it that in the early 1970s, with China still rent by struggle and strife, Beijing suddenly started to import a small number of foreign employees? From the earliest days of the People's Republic, a few faithful foreigners had been in the service of the Chinese government, and a couple of dozen or so had remained right through from 1949 until the 1970s. Most were originally connected in some way to the communist movements in their respective homelands. By the early 1960s, they had been joined by a smattering of mainly Western European foreign teachers and propaganda polishers on short-term assignments. When the Cultural Revolution broke out, the younger contingent mostly departed while many of the old timers demanded that they too should have the 'right to rebel', to participate in the mass demonstrations, denunciations and posturing. They were playing with fire and many found themselves behind bars, let out only in 1973.

That very year, 1973, became something of a watershed for China in its recruitment of a new wave of foreign experts - *waiguo zhuanjia*. A less strident faction around the veteran Communist Party leader Zhou Enlai was beginning to gain the ascendancy. Deng Xiaoping, deposed during the Cultural Revolution as China's 'Second Khrushchev', was being stealthily reinstated and a tiny window of moderation was opening. Yet even with this slight change of atmosphere, troublesome, unpredictable foreigners were hardly likely to be welcomed as China residents for their own sake, or for the sentimental 'friendship' reasons which had admitted me under the SACU banner.

The most evident rationale for foreign recruitment was that China needed linguistically competent tour guides. From 1972 onwards, every Western European country, not to mention Canada, Australia and New Zealand, had SACU-like 'friendship' groups eager to visit China. Then there were the Party delegations from the dozens of countries where pro-China leftists were tolerated. Another factor was Beijing's sudden turn to soft diplomacy: the People's Republic was signing up to the foreign aid business. For instance, a huge number of Chinese personnel with skills in English was now demanded by the massive TanZam project – the carving of a new railway hundreds of miles in length, from the copper-belt of landlocked Zambia to the coast of Tanzania, thus by-passing UDI Rhodesia. China was in it for the Third World kudos – and of course for the copper.

Crucial in all this language stuff, but still largely unrecognised outside China, was a deal to import lock-stock-and-barrel no fewer than seventeen one-million-tonne-per-year chemical fertiliser plants. Later, I got to know a lot about this astonishing 'secret' project, as one of the plants was earmarked for Nanjing. Of course, for millennia China had got by quite happily on its own home-made fertilisers. My mother, indeed, once told me a story about the 'shit millionaires' of old China, who would kill for the chance to control the street toilets of cities such as her Chengdu. And once in Nanjing, I saw (and smelt) that even newly-built five-storey blocks of flats in Nanjing had underground tanks nearby into which their flush toilets drained. From every town and city, precious cargoes of human waste were ladled into horse-drawn mini-tankers or canal barges and shipped out to the countryside, to be spread on the land. But now with China's own version of the 'green revolution' underway, fertiliser supplies had to increase significantly.

We should remember that during Mao's era, the very thought of large-scale importation of anything from the capitalist West was utterly taboo. In fact, two decades had passed since factory equipment had been brought in on any scale, and then it had been from 'Elder Brother' - the Soviet Union. In the First Five Year Plan of the1950s, onto willing Chinese soil had been parachuted any number of heavy industrial enterprises – the great steel works at Wuhan and the No.1 Automobile Works at Changchun which turned out copies of 1930s Ford trucks, to name but two. But to rely now on Western sources of equipment? With 'self-reliance' as the ardent cry of the Cultural Revolution, this was outrageously novel, and no wonder the deal of the century had to be kept secret from the population at large, especially as the technical licences belonged to an American company. With the official contract language being English, hundreds, thousands of competent English speakers were suddenly required by the mega-projects. College-educated Chinese who had survived the various purges and were now in their forties and fifties had been taught Russian as their first and only foreign language. Except for a few specialists, English - the language of China's chief oppressors in the century since the First Opium War - had been sidelined. But now in 1970s China, fortunes were being reversed; the Cultural Revolution notwithstanding, English was becoming all the rage.

This is why allowing a few foreigners like us into the country to boost language expertise was no more than pragmatism. But we often wondered, after our polite 'interview' at China's London embassy, how recruits were actually selected. Apart from our tea drinking etiquette, did the embassy staff have some means of vetting supplicants such as us? Was a covert process of investigation at work? If so, how did the embassies go about it? For if the Chinese diplomats I met in London were anything to go by, they were totally at sea in their host communities. We used to joke – maybe too close to the truth - that the London embassy's only means of getting information on us was from British intelligence. Having said that, the U.K. secret services had been simply too idle to catch up with the concept of the New Left, with its unfathomable 'neither East nor West' philosophy. So it is anybody's guess how the Chinese foreign service went about vetting its Westerner recruits – if it bothered to do so at all.

In the years following the U.S.-China rapprochement, prominent Westerners of every political hue seemed to be susceptible to the China's mystique. How did I feel about my first brief taste of the country in 1973? Even as someone incoherently favouring the replacement of the Chinese regime by a purer, anti-bureaucratic socialism, I cannot claim that I was immune from the growing China clamour. For those on the left, disillusioned with their own societies, shocked by the cruel wars against Indochinese peasants, by the harsh repression of dissent from Paris to Chicago, China presented an image of otherness which could be entirely captivating. Left-wing public intellectuals such as Roland Barthes and Joan Robinson were, in the years after Nixon, high on China's invitation list, and a whole bevy made the pilgrimage. And this went beyond the left: for example, Mao's realm even had a kind of ambassador extraordinaire in the American actress Shirley MacLaine. Bizarrely, at a time when internal strife was still at boiling point, these eminences from left and right were able to report a society and people at ease with itself, a workforce dignified, moral and purposeful, a country which was eradicating the harmful divisions of labour, a nation industrialising but without the horrors brought by nineteenth century industrial revolutions. Such was the power of the Cultural Revolution's contrived message.

And then there was Chinese officialdom's ancient skill in handling the foreign visitor. Those charged with receiving overseas delegations were well-schooled in the gentle art of manipulation. Indeed, their jobs and perhaps their very lives depended on it. Arrangements went like clockwork. Cars and buses turned up on the dot, hosts were waiting solicitously on their office doorsteps, hotels were luxurious if charmingly old-fashioned, the food terrific.

Wined, dined and toasted in three varieties of alcohol, and

returned by limousine to one's hotel suite and its satin bed-covers, even the most uncharitable sceptic would weaken. For the privileged China visitor, this was the trip of a lifetime, an impossible dream. Chinese officials knew it. They were trained to make it the most uplifting of experiences, and their charges were all too ready to be uplifted.

So the SACU tour which took me to China in October 1973 was given the full VIP treatment. After a month of courtly progress through model factories, people's communes, and neighbourhood committees I cannot claim that I failed to succumb a little to the blandishments of official China. To complete the picture, every returning SACU delegation was received at that elegant embassy in London's Portland Place. Silent, white-jacketed stewards served up an exquisite buffet, while the attendant diplomats tried out their small talk.

It was then, of course, that I realised that I was presented with an unrepeatable opportunity.

'Is it possible for foreigners to work in China?' I innocently enquired of one of the embassy people as I nibbled on a delectable prawn goujon. My interlocutor was, it turned out, Second Secretary Xie Heng. Years later, when personal tittle-tattle was no longer a state secret, this diminutive woman surprised me by tales of how she had crossed the Yangtze under a barrage of fire to join the capture of Nanjing from the Nationalists.

Xie Heng had quickly shifted the conversation elsewhere and I assumed, very wrongly as it turned out, that my leading question had been lost.

It was by now late 1974, and our China preparations were almost there. Before we left for Nanjing, there were still a couple of urgent matters to sort out. Scarily, the moment it was known we were heading for the Middle Kingdom, the big comrades of our little political group of ultras would not leave us alone. In supreme naivety, they even suggested that we might somehow receive fiery anti-Mao literature and go out and about in Nanjing and recruit a few of the locals. But we had no intention of becoming martyrs to the cause. So in the final weeks, we stubbornly cut all contact with our erstwhile comrades.

The other matter at hand was more prosaic: how were we actually to get to China? Like all travellers, we would need to enter the country over that little railway bridge which marked the border with Hong Kong. Second Secretary Xie Heng did not seem to have a clue. Apparently she had never had to sort out anything like this. In fact, it turned out that she had never even crossed a shop's threshold anywhere in London. We had to use our own initiative.

A Sikh friend's father ran a travel agency, and from him we acquired for a princely sum (I have calculated it as the equivalent in 21st century money of about £1,500) one-way tickets to Hong Kong.

It was December 1974 and it truly felt that we were about to pass through into another realm of existence. To land a Boeing 707 at Hong Kong's old Kai Tak airport demanded special skills. As the plane banked sharply in its descent, it seemed that you could almost pluck the washing from the windows of the high-rise flats which flanked the airstrip. After the bump, bump of landing, the plane taxied along the narrow isthmus of concrete runway flanked by the turgid and odoriferous waters of Hong Kong's ill-named 'fragrant harbour'.

Xie Heng had been unable to offer any definite instructions as to how to proceed once we had arrived in the British colony. 'Find the China International Travel Service' was all she could manage. 'They will know you are coming,' she added enigmatically.

We joined the taxi queue outside Kai Tak, and were soon speeding jerkily through the densely-peopled streets of Kowloon to the Golden Gate Hotel – a dim hostelry which I had understood from my previous trip was somehow connected to the Communists up the road. This seemed to be the right move, as several thin young men in loose dark blue suits and lapel badges proclaiming 'China International Travel Service' were hovering by the hotel reception. One seemed to be expecting us, and introduced himself as our guide to the Chinese border.

Early the following day, we boarded a train at the old, now-demolished Kowloon station, and began our slow progress towards our destination a thousand kilometres to the north. An hour later, we were dragging our luggage over a small bridge, at the other end of which fluttered the Chinese five-star flag. A couple of surly but harmless-looking soldiers in green fatigues nodded us by. Martial music sounded from loudspeakers, and below us, through the trees, school children were practising callisthenics in a playground. After the bustle of Hong Kong, and the filthy ditches which lined the railway up to the border, China seemed a well-ordered haven. But our sojourn in the heart of the country was to prove that Chinese appearances could often be deceptive.

II
THE COSSETED WORLD OF CADRES AND MINDERS

OUR FINE IDEAS ABOUT communing with the Chinese masses had begun to wane within hours of our arrival in Mao's kingdom. It was December 1974, and the final stage of our odyssey was a flight from Guangzhou in the far south. Incredible though it now seems, only illustrious bearers of tribute - presidents and prime ministers - were allowed to fly straight to the Chinese capital far to the north. All lesser mortals entering the country, ambassadors and lords and ladies alike, had to do so by that short walk over the Hong Kong border. As in times past, the unruly barbarian stepped into the Middle Kingdom a safe continent away from its nervous rulers up in Beijing. From the Hong Kong border, the Travel Service guide accompanied us on our train journey up to Guangzhou, where we were met by a cadre from the local Foreign Languages Institute who got us to the city's airport for our flight to our destination.

Soon the Russian Ilyushin with its ear-splitting engines was taxiing to a halt on the concrete slabs of Nanjing's airport. Through the portholes we spied a huddle of figures, swollen in their winter padded jackets. We stepped down the rickety blue ladder onto the runway, and as we did so, the figures lined up as though we too were potentates on a state visit. A podgy-faced character with barely visible eyes drew towards us, both arms outstretched in that Chinese precursor to a handshake. At his side was a diminutive man with a shock of suspiciously black hair.

'This is Party Secretary Li An of the foreign languages department of Nanda,' the small man stuttered in passable English. He was using the universally applied short form for Nanjing University.

'Welcome to our city. You must be very tired,' said the Party Secretary perfunctorily.

With that, he and four other tightly smiling officials climbed into a chrome-bedecked limousine which an aficionado of old spy films would have recognised as a Soviet Zil, a six-litre leviathan which must have arrived in China during happier times with the Soviet Union. The English speaker ushered us into the back of a smaller, lime-green saloon with off-white seat covers and all-round lace curtains.

'I am Comrade Wang. I will look after you here,' he lisped from the bench seat next to the driver.

We took off at high speed after the shiny black Zil limo, dodging waves of cyclists, lunging around ragged teams straining at the harnesses of giant handcarts and racing past lurching trucks, to all appearances straight out of 1930s Detroit.

'Where are we going?' I ventured to Comrade Wang, but he seemed deaf to my enquiries. Was this because he was savouring the novelty of the car ride, or was he rendered speechless by his awesome responsibilities? For amongst all his colleagues, he alone had been chosen as minder to the first foreigners allowed in the city for years.

It seemed from the dim winter sun that we were traversing the city roughly from south to north. Suddenly we were at our destination, and from a tree-lined boulevard we careered through the inner cycle lane heedless of the flood of riders, a gaggle of whom ended up in a messy pile of tangled wheels. I was appalled at this rude introduction to the people of Nanjing, but not a fist was raised. Comrade Wang looked on with dispassion.

The car swung into a gatehouse hung with two giant red lanterns. Here, we were casually scrutinised by a pair of People's Liberation Army youths armed to the teeth but - I noticed with surprise – lacking laces in their grubby plimsolls. We swept past an incongruous Art Deco frontage and came to a shuddering halt behind the Zil, under the canopied entrance to a large cement-rendered building. A great billboard depicting a bridge with red stars and flags aloft loomed over a rime-covered lawn. Through the swing doors of the building I spied a vestibule lavishly carpeted in crimson, the walls hung with two huge paintings of mountain pines. Journey's end, and the University had thoughtfully arranged for us to rest up in some comfort before we settled in on the campus. Or so we thought...

With much bowing and gesturing, our hosts funnelled us down a long corridor and through the door at the end which took us into an airy room half-filled by a sofa and two capacious armchairs, draped in the same starched covers and anti-Macassars as in the car. So far so good. Through a double door, we spied a pair of lacquered bedsteads, each with green satin quilts encased in embroidered covers. Our London recruiters had promised us Spartan quarters at the University, and we had actually demanded nothing less: from a comfortable cocoon we could learn little about China. No doubt this luxurious abode was merely a temporary R & R stop en route for our cold dormitory.

The journey via Bangkok, Hong Kong, and Guangzhou had taken a full two days, and what with the stressful attentiveness of our hosts we were now feeling pretty much exhausted. At last there was a chance to relax while we slowly took stock of our new surroundings. The first door on the right from the corridor led into a bathroom of familiar hotel design, with a deep enamelled tub, and plenty of hard, off-white towels. The plumbing stank of chlorine, and as I slaked my thirst, the tap-water tasted strongly of it. The lavatory cistern hissed and dribbled, resisting my efforts to put it out of its misery by poking the unfamiliar mechanism. In those days, dribbling toilet cisterns, products of some central dribbling toilet plant, were the signature tune of China's hotel industry.

On the glass-topped sideboard in the living room stood an oversized aluminium flask painted with peonies, alongside a tin-plate caddy and some lidded mugs decorated with swooping magpies. We were to cherish the Chinese vacuum flask - whether the posh aluminium model like ours or the rattan-bound variety of the masses – not to mention the practical and capacious mugs. It seemed the right moment to have a little brew-up; making ourselves comfortable in the deep armchairs, we strained the bloated leaves through our teeth while we awaited the next move.

Before long, there came padding feet and a tap at the door. It was Minder Wang and Li An of the heavy eyes, along with the two other airport greeters. With a show of dissimulation they finally seated themselves in the required pecking order: Li An on the sofa next to us, the two other cadres flanking in the deep armchairs, and Wang adopting a modest, woebegone expression from an upright chair outside the magic circle.

'The Nanjing University Revolutionary Committee hopes that our foreign friends like their new home,' announced Li An, Minder Wang translating. Li An was unmistakably referring to our present quarters, which surely could not be part of a college campus.

'I thought we were going to live at the University,' I stuttered. 'That's what Second Secretary Madame Xie Heng told us at your country's embassy in London.'

'Our foreign friends must give us their comments and criticisms,' responded Li An enigmatically.

Our cadres rose as one, and with the ritual game of who-should-go-through-the-door- first over, off they trooped up the corridor. Our first lesson in the social behaviour of Mao's Communist cadres was disconcerting. Knowing little of the weight of Chinese culture, we had somehow expected a robust, proletarian, no-nonsense way of doing things. Instead our hosts seemed to be immersed in the comic opera of bygone manners – deferential and brimming with false modesty.

But we had other things on our mind, chiefly our actual location. Oddly, our hosts still had not seen fit to tell us and in our dazed state we had omitted to ask. This was not going to be the last of our exposure to the need-to-know habits of the Chinese bureaucracy. I searched around for signs, and soon a drawer of one of the two enormous lacquered desks in the corner of the living room revealed the answer. 'Nanking Hotel, China' declared a flimsy pad of red-printed writing paper with helpful indented lines. The other item in the drawer was a round pot of opaque glue – which turned out to be an essential accoutrement. Chinese envelopes and stamps were always glue-less.

The only tourist information we had been able to find back in London was a late 1950s edition of *Nagel's Encyclopedia-Guide*, an erudite tome of over a fifteen-hundred pages packed with archaeological insights which, given both the Cultural Revolution's ravages and the tight restrictions on foreigners' travel were now largely irrelevant. Almost all China's provinces had been closed to foreigners, and in the tiny slices of the country where outsiders could go, ancient history was generally off the itinerary. Old things had been condemned as part of the 'feudal past' and had no place in the happy socialist present. Apart from the newly created exhibition celebrating the Taiping uprising of a century earlier, Nanjing's great museums remained locked and barred.

It turned out that our new home was in the city's northwest, just a short stretch from the old station district and the shores of the Yangtze. *Nagel* helpfully added that the main hotel building had been created in the 1950s for the Russian technicians, sent to China in their thousands to spark the country's dramatic First Five Year Plan. When we asked about this our Chinese hosts always, understandably, were obliged to deny that the place had anything to do with the Russians. This, after all, was now the era of official Soviet hating. Nor, it turned out, could our hosts speak of the odd modernist building with its curved glass frontage which stood near the hotels' entrance from the street. Our trusted guide book informed us that before the Communist takeover, this had been the American officers' club. In the totally different world which had ended so abruptly just a couple of decades earlier, Nanjing had been the capital of the *ancient regime*, and the leafy boulevards of this northern part of the city were the government and embassy district. Where our teenage PLA guards now unconvincingly wielded their Kalashnikovs, not long before all had been starched uniforms, bourbon and jazz.

Whatever the earlier incarnations of Nanjing Hotel, we were soon to realise that as almost its only guests, it was now our very own gilded cage. This chapter hopes to convey how it was to be the only foreigners in Nanjing – our awkwardness to place and people, to our minders and guardians, our thwarted efforts to fit in by learning the language. Little did we suspect that our time in the great city would see the dramatic endplay of Mao's Cultural Revolution, and though there were many experiences which I would not have missed for the world, very little was to chime as familiar, comforting and congenial.

It was Saturday, our first morning, and we were back in our quarters after an exploratory breakfast. Without warning, the foursome of the previous day appeared at our door. With protests of false modesty – which we had already dubbed the 'seating game' - Party Secretary Li An was finally on our sofa and ready to pronounce.

'Mr Ke-ke-bi and Miss Su-ke-li-fu, you will start to teach on Monday morning," Wang helpfully translated. 'Today is a work day and we hope that by Monday our foreign friends will be able to give us their detailed teaching plans for the next six months.'

'How detailed do you mean, Comrade Li An,' I blanched.

'Comrade Wang will tell you,' he replied jauntily. At that, the four visitors rose and got themselves out into the corridor. Gasping at this unlikely order, we set about unpacking the English teaching materials we had brought with us in our large brown fibre suitcase. There was clearly going to be little sleep before Monday night.

Over the weeks that followed, the cadre entourage would often materialise – usually when I happened to be semi-comatose after a rough morning's teaching, or soaking in our great enamel bathtub. Apart from the need to remind us of their authority, we soon understood that our leaders relished the excuse to step through the forbidden portals of the Nanjing Hotel. And once in the compound, there was nothing to stop them from a little detour to the hotel store. While its shelves seemed to us to have nothing out of the ordinary, we had not yet learned to read the signs. Those were not just any cigarettes – they were Peony brand; that was no common bottle of white spirits – it was our province's best sorghum hooch, rarely seen in the stores of the great *qunzhong*, the masses.

Our abode held other attractions to the University leaders. At the Spring Festival, which came not long after our arrival, it seemed that the entire Party leadership of the region found the presence of two foreigners an excuse for a sumptuous banquet. Little by little we came to recognise some of these nattily turned-out habitués of the hotel compound who clearly saw the place as their private club. Long after our own cadres had paid their respects to us and clasped our mugs of welcoming tea to their breasts (always unsettlingly left un-drunk – we soon understood that the etiquette is in the giving rather than the consuming), I would spy them hanging around the lobby or wandering amongst the shrubs. Cultural Revolution politics was as highly secretive as it was volatile, and the snakes and ladders of glory and disgrace were endlessly played out. The hotel with its chauffeurs, waiters and room girls was the city's finest rumour-mill, and it was here that a middle-ranking cadre might tease out tidbits on the waxings and wanings of the political firmament. With a bit of luck, our University bosses might too have the chance for a little schmoozing with the higher beings of the province.

If our cadres had one duty above all others, it was to distract us from the realities beyond our compound. As the weeks and months wore on, we came to realise that our luxurious accommodation, our cars, the soft-class rail compartments which we were only very occasionally allowed to grace, served a much more vital purpose than hospitality. All these things were intended to mask the realities, the ceaseless pressures and struggles which were the daily lot of the ordinary folk.

From time to time, we would be given the afternoon or even a day or two off work, with no explanation. According to Minder Wang, everyone at the University was 'busy' with something or other. Was it a series of mass meetings to salute the latest decision of the Central Committee, or was it something more sinister? It was only later that we discovered that the Workers' Stadium just down the road from the University was the regular venue for public executions. Work units were called to send their staff to witness these spectacles and certainly our smiling colleagues were on the gruesome rota. But confined to the hotel, we remained in comfortable and ignorant bliss of such goings-on, and that is how the officials wanted matters to remain. They had not bargained for our wilfulness in peeping over the parapet.

We gradually came to realise that some of the functionaries who determined our fate were for us, while others were angrily opposed to our presence. Essentially, there were the openers-up who wanted a small degree of engagement with the Western world - provided it was on China's terms. This group had come to national influence after the ping-pong rapprochement with the United States a couple of years before, but there was still a powerful element who wished to keep China in the purity of isolation. With this 'struggle between two lines' raging beneath the surface, it slowly dawned that any foreign residents, regardless of their behaviour, would be caught between the two factions and used by each whenever the opportunity arose. So despite ourselves, regardless of anything we said or did, we were irretrievably the trophies of the 'openers-up'. Adherents of this grand faction would protect us, while their foes would do all in their power to frustrate our lives. We lived in ignorance of the scheming but merely suffered the consequences; only years later were our true allies in Nanjing able to explain some of the events surrounding us.

As time went on, with Mao on his deathbed, the faction fighting throughout China was reaching a crescendo and the murky plotting around us became more naked. The room telephone would ring and a voice would announce: 'Your call to the Reuters News Agency in Beijing is now through – please speak.' We knew enough to drop the receiver like a hot brick, for a single word was all that was needed to implicate us. More insidious, half-a-dozen times our letters arrived with extras. Folded within our correspondence we would find a lurid mimeographed sheet defaming the Chinese Communist Party and purporting to be from this or that democratic cell. My Chinese was by then improving sufficiently to know how to use a dictionary, half the battle with the infuriating language. I struggled deep into the night with the characters of an unfamiliar political lexicon, knowing that in the morning I would have to hand over the incriminating document. Such leaflets could have been the work of genuine oppositionists, but we doubted it. While tempted to keep this 'counter-revolutionary' ephemera for posterity, we took it that this was some kind of loyalty test. Fear rather than good sense meant we handed them over to our poor minder. He would take one sideways glance and pale, for this meant yet another meeting with the Public Security.

While most of our undeclared defenders must have been acting merely in fealty to their particular faction in the great 'struggle between the two lines', it turned out that a few individuals were motivated by less self-serving considerations. I think kindly even now of rotund, balding and Buddha-like Duan, Party Secretary of the English section, and of the good Comrade Yang, who on the quiet tried to help me with my Chinese. Of the functionaries most closely involved with us in Nanjing, these two turned out to be covert allies simply because they were good and kindly human beings. The terror through which the Chinese had survived, at least since the anti-Rightist movement of 1957, had failed to dissolve all decency.

Comrade Wang, the man appointed our first minder, was altogether another matter. There was no mistaking that he was a 110-percenter - the first peasant son of his village who had ever had much of an education, let alone a university one. When we had to forgive Minder Wang for some misdeed against us, which was quite often, we told ourselves that his lack of scruples in doing his masters' bidding spoke of a psyche of extreme gratitude. It was not merely fear. Like tens of millions, Wang owed his life chances to the Party, and never would he question its capricious authority.

Little by little we got the measure of Wang and his ulterior programming. In the days after our arrival, with orders to produce a mountain of teaching material in a very short time, the first Sunday saw us immersed in the struggle, for the following day we would have to present them to the University. We were surprised when Minder Wang turned up alone and made himself comfortable in prime place on our sofa. He fidgeted with his mug of tea and finally broached the matter which had brought him.

'How many *jin* of wine can you drink in an evening, Ke-ke-bi?' he asked, addressing me by my phoneticised name. The Chinese seemed to call anything alcoholic 'wine', but I guessed Wang meant was *baijiu* - the white lightning which most foreigners liken to aircraft fuel. And a *jin* was half a kilo – about a pint.

'I don't expect I can drink more than a glassful,' I replied.

Comrade Wang looked relieved.

The next time we had Party Secretary Duan to ourselves, I got the conversation round to the matter of *baijiu* capacity. We were to discover that Duan was a person who tried his best to be gratifyingly candid with us.

'Before the Cultural Revolution there was a teacher here from France who went into the classroom with a bottle of wine in one hand and his book in the other,' he explained, reddening. 'And when he left to go back to his country we found a room of empty bottles, especially under his bed.'

So was this a posting liable to drive one to drink? I quickly assured Duan that I had not come to China to bolster the ancient stereotype of the wild Western barbarian, even if with my red hair, blue eyes and big nose I was a dead ringer.

Yet you could hardly blame our hosts. Few of the people with whom we dealt had ever witnessed a Westerner at close quarters. Nanjing, a major metropolis with over a million inhabitants, had seen no other Western residents and for years only a handful of foreigners had passed through the city. In the whole of our Jiangsu province, population fifty millions-plus, it turned out that there was only one other Westerner – an Australian woman attached to the Suzhou Silk Institute. The officials did all they could to prevent us meeting her, or any other foreigners for that matter. Such liaisons between aliens on their soil seemed to fill them with an irrational fear. But occasionally an encounter was unavoidable. It was usually the case that the first point of conversation would be our respective minders. We were comforted to find that strained relations were pretty much the rule.

Individualistic Westerners, whatever their degree of sympathy for the regime, were constitutionally programmed to resist the corralling to which their minders were dedicated. This was a recipe for low-level warfare, and though the issues at stake were often trivial, the poor minder was always squeezed from both sides. His only consolation was that the powers-that-be decreed only a short secondment from ordinary duties, this presumably to limit the likelihood of his going native. Of course, to their colleagues tied to the drudgery of the classroom, our minders' association with the *waiguoren* - the foreigners - implied an elevation to an exalted lifestyle. But in reality, the chance to travel to distant provinces during our summer vacation paid-for tour, to dine occasionally alongside their charges at the table of lofty provincial leaders so remote from ordinary mortals that their names were mere rumours, the incomparable opportunity to improve one's English – all this was dwarfed by the occupational hazards of minder-ship. In short, to be a buffer between the unpredictable and fractious foreign devil and the quirkish hierarchy was a dangerous privilege.

'It's very easy to make a mistake when it comes to foreigners' one of our colleagues whispered in a candid moment. To 'make a mistake' carried a dark meaning in Cultural Revolution China, when the most tenuous of connections with the foreign world could be your undoing. Though the Red Guard frenzy was now over, societal tension was palpable and the quest for scapegoats still unquenched. Take our fellow teacher who much later confided that he had been endlessly persecuted because he refused to give up his ancient 'imperialist' bicycle, a genuine 1930s Nottingham Raleigh. Not until Mao had long gone 'to see Marx' – as he always hopefully put it - did another of our colleagues dare disclose the existence of an uncle who had emigrated to Taiwan years before the Communist victory of 1949. If such a connection had been known, our friend's minor Party career would never even have started, and more than likely he would have fallen by the wayside in one of the many *yundong* – the unpredictable political campaigns periodically unleashed from on high.

Undoubtedly, our minders' trips with us to model factories, to the city's scenic corners or to a political variety show hardly excited the envy of their colleagues. But there were more auspicious dates on our social calendar and we would await with some anticipation the elaborately inscribed invitations to those special banquets. Observing the leaders at close quarters was always interesting, while the food and drink were beyond belief. But our minders must have faced these occasions with a sense of dread, for it propelled them straight into the danger zone.

The large circular table of Chinese banqueting is in reality a European import, symbolically transmuted to local custom. While the host invariably faces the entrance with the most honoured guest to his right, the most humble of the company is seated opposite the host, back to the door, the natural target for any unbidden dagger. It was at this lowly and vulnerable position that our minder instinctively knew to place himself.

Translating the small talk of the foreign devil emboldened by alcohol was a duty which I guessed the minders most dreaded. I was always sorry that the exquisite morsels of banquet food hardly seemed to pass their lips. Neither could they drink away their misery, though this was hardly due to any puritanical urge. For some long forgotten reason, a formal banquet demanded three glasses to each table setting - one for sweet red wine, one for beer, and a thimble-sized glass for the dreaded *baijiu*. While we and the cadre-hosts would invariably get into heavy competitive toasting, never did I witness a minder taking even the smallest sip from any of his glasses.

The ever-present possibility of calamity caused by his new charges meant that Comrade Wang, our first minder, went about the place like a condemned man. Even after his duties were over and we had long departed for home, trouble could still be brewing. Most of the tiny number of Westerners allowed into China after 1949 imagined they had a story to tell, and on returning home, not a few of them published accounts of their experiences, inevitably implicating minders, guides, colleagues. In several instances which came to my ears, the aftershock of such publicity reached Chinese shores, with disastrous results for those who had been associated with the foreigner..

Increasingly frustrated by Wang's nervous intransigence, I could not help taunting him with questions which I knew he would find hard to answer. You could almost feel his pain as he struggled to find a way through. With anything slightly unusual, he would just repeat the question, mimicking my intonation, and then turn away.

Sometimes I was just plain cruel. 'Are you a Communist Party member, Comrade Wang?' I enquired, my demeanour all innocence. Like all Party matters, this was going to be a State Secret, and the dilemma ricocheted around Wang's brain in search of a non-committal solution. After a few moments came the weakly intoned response: 'I do not know.'

When pressed with an impossible request - such as 'can we

go to Shanghai this coming weekend?' Wang might well take another tack, promising the earth. It was a while before we were properly attuned to this baffling cultural trait of our hosts. Saying 'yes' is both opportune and infinitely polite, even if the answer is manifestly 'no, no, no'.

Uncouth creatures that we were, perhaps the worst thing for our minders was the belief that we had an inalienable right to address the high-ups whenever we wished. In front of me as I write is a thick file of carbon copies, still royal blue. These issued from our sturdy Seagull typewriter and are unnerving evidence of our constant petitioning of the University's Revolutionary Committee, the Jiangsu provincial bureaucracy, and of course of our ultimate masters, the State Council Foreign Experts Bureau in faraway Beijing. Needless to say, a humble Chinese citizen would never dream of engaging with high officialdom, let alone of courting confrontation through outrageous requests for exceptionality. But we were determined to get the most out of our time in China, and confronting the powers-that-be held no fear for us. We were, after all, products of our own anti-authoritarian cultural revolution back home, and had launched ourselves into China from a life punctuated by endless political protests and fiery actions on the streets of London.

Even in this new proletarian China, officials had to be addressed in a certain language. Naturally, the niceties of register were something of which we were ignorant; the minder's unhappy duty was to somehow moderate our barbarian mutterings and confusions into language approximately civil and acceptable. Unfortunately he lacked the advantages enjoyed by the mandarin minders of an earlier English intruder into the Middle Kingdom. Back in the 1790s, George III's plenipotentiary to China, Lord Macartney, had taken with him as his own interpreter, a Chinese Christian convert who, through the Jesuits, had made his way to the Vatican. Once back on his native soil, the interpreter remembered the sanctions taken against Chinese who dabbled with the foreigners, and refused point-blank to render Macartney's untutored missives to the officials. An ingenious device was hit upon: his Lordship's thirteen-year-old pageboy was something of an artist who without any inkling of their meaning could do passable imitations of Chinese characters. The fearful interpreter was only willing to translate Macartney's appeals if the final version was in the youth's hand, so that technically he was not their author.

Shooting the messenger is a long established Chinese tradition, and such was our daily frustration that it was a tradition which had strong appeal.

Every so often in our first months in Nanjing, Minder Wang would announce that another visit had to be made to the central post office in the city centre. It seemed that the flurry of parcels we had sent ahead from England by sea-mail were always the cause of some concern.

'What are ten pecks,' enquired Wang out of the side of his mouth as we sped downtown to collect the first arrival. 'Wang's had his nose in some illicit Shakespeare,' I thought admiringly.

'A peck is an old English measure, no longer used,' was my attempt at erudition, as I fielded his question with a straight bat. The parcel turned out to contain a well-known brand of sanitary wear, of a type utterly alien to Chinese womanhood.

The next arrival was a portable typewriter, a sturdy East German model in a brown leather case. As I unwrapped it, a profusion of broken keys and forlorn springs dropped to the floor. I shoved the bits in the waste paper basket and handed this apparent terminal casualty of the international mails to the two room girls when they came in with the refilled vacuum flasks. I never expected to set eyes on it again until, unkindly, I recalled the story which used to do the rounds about the worn-out sock which a foreign traveller left in a hotel waste-bin. Just before he crossed that Alice-in-Wonderland bridge which divided austere communistic China from rampant capitalistic Hong Kong, an official panted up and presented him with the wretched thing, darned, washed and ironed. Sympathetic political tourists were in the habit of relating this story to prove the honesty of the Chinese proletariat. The actual reason was less heroic: the sock was like a hot coal which no one wanted to handle for a moment longer than necessary in case they were accused of the very serious crime of theft from a foreigner.

Sure enough, a couple of weeks later the typewriter reappeared in perfect fettle. It was doubtless nothing to do with that apocryphal sock tale: some unknown mechanical genius had proved that China was still far from the throwaway society. But though it now worked perfectly again, the little portable typewriter was never going to be up to cutting the blue stencils for the Department's duplicator, and to enhance our productivity Minder Wang soon delivered a shining heavyweight. Somewhere in Mao's kingdom, a cottage industry was turning out hand-built, fully Qwerty-ised Western writing machines. You had to have special clearance to get near any reprographic equipment and though our colleagues looked on it with envy, we had our splendid Seagull *daziji*, our 'beating words machine', all to ourselves.

The teaching materials and novels we had posted in as many as ten heavy parcels caused Minder Wang all kinds of anxieties: in his mind, accusations of aiding and abetting the import of illicit materials were always a possibility.

'Do your books take class struggle as the key link?' he enquired nervously, as our obviously repackaged parcels were handed over to us by a stern-faced postal official. Poor Wang was beginning to give the impression that every visit to the post office would be his last, that he would be confronted by a gaggle of public security men waving the decadent evidence of sedition in his face. Cultural Revolution China was very big on guilt by association. In reality, the worst thing that ever happened to Minder Wang on these trips was that he once got his new blue Dacron Zhongshan jacket smeared with the expectorations of the revolutionary masses. Over the post office portal hung a huge blue padded curtain, there to keep out the wintry draughts. It seemed that someone had taken it for a large and handy kerchief.

Unsurprisingly, Nanjing's post office became firmly associated in our minds with hassle. The most remarkable incident of mutual misunderstanding concerned the case of the long-johns. From time to time we would want to send stuff to relatives, and at first this seemed straightforward and familiar. We would simply wrap our parcels in brown paper and tie them with string, sometimes with the contents scrutinised at the post office beforehand, and sometimes not. One day I arrived with an oddly shaped package of Christmas gifts for the folks back home which had been awkward to wrap. When my turn came at the counter, an officious clerk waved me away. The usual crowd had materialised and a helpful bystander pointed to an illustrated poster. It seemed that there was a new regulation and all parcels should now be swaddled and sewn into a white cotton wrapper.

I swore loudly and given the company, quite fruitlessly. Still, someone produced a needle and thread, but no wrapping material. I suddenly hit on the solution. To the astonishment of the onlookers, now a melee of dozens, I ripped off my baggy blue trousers and my precious Damart thermal long-johns. Into these, I thrust the parcel. I sat down cross-legged on the post office's concrete floor and proceeded to sew up the legs and the waist. The resulting misshapen sack, inscribed in heavy ballpoint, I then delivered triumphantly to the counter. The clerk was probably too shocked to protest, but took in my offering and sent it on its way across the oceans. Decades on, these sturdy under-strides are still wearable, with faint traces still visible of my parent's Durham address.

III
THE CAMPUS

BEFORE WE WERE LET loose on the students, Minder Wang took us to the corner of the campus which was to be ours. The Foreign Languages Department was tucked away in a charming courtyard of two-storey 1920s buildings. Outside, the grass was cropped like an English lawn, and occasionally on Friday afternoons our teaching group was sent out, each person with a pair of sewing scissors to keep it that way.

'We intellectuals must love labour and guard against being divorced from the masses,' Minder Wang lectured as I tore into an obstinate clump of grass with blunt scissors. 'And Chairman Mao tells us that grass is a bad thing because it is the place where mosquitoes grow,' he added with a slightly uncertain look.

Like much of the civic construction of the Republic of China's heyday which was brought to an end with the Japanese invasion of 1937, the foreign languages buildings were topped off by traditional roofs with attractive runnels of grey tiles. As a talisman against the malign influence of we foreign arrivals, the door to our stairwell had been decorated on the outside with a colour portrait of Mao draped with red ribbons – the one where the Chairman stares out in a self-satisfied manner, his chin mole prominent. Minder Wang led us up the concrete steps and showed us into a good-sized room.

'This will be only for you,' he beamed, 'and you can sit here and prepare your lessons and sometimes the teachers will come here to learn from you too.'

Our office had been kitted out with two new lacquered

kneehole desks. New furniture was rare and highly prized, and just as the tables and desks in people's homes, our desks were protected by heavy plate glass covers. Under them, someone had thoughtfully inserted cheerful calendar cards and the term's teaching timetable, reproduced in spidery English on a duplicator. To accommodate an audience, the place had been supplied with a dozen or so heavy upright chairs with sky-blue loose covers. Of more immediate interest to us was a cupboard with thermos and enamel tray where a tea caddy rested between two lidded mugs painted always with magpies. It was January and sitting in the middle of the room, so that you had to walk around it to get from the door to my desk, was a pot-bellied stove, the flue-pipe strung by ceiling wires to a hole cut in one of the window panes. Once they had overcome their shyness, our fellow teachers found plenty of excuses concerning gerunds or past participles to wander into the office and warm their backsides. Because Nanjing lies just south of the Yangtze River, by government decree no public buildings could be heated, unless of course foreign bodies had arrived in town.

Almost opposite the office door was a latrine intended for our private use. Rather than have them walk up to the next floor, we encouraged our colleagues to share this convenience. Even then, they would only do so when they thought no one was looking. The only problem with this sharing was a reluctance, no doubt born of habitual water shortages, to flush the squatter-pans. The stench drifted across the corridor and mingled with the wreaths of noxious gases occasionally emitted from our stove. When once I found the un-flushed newspapers which had been used as sanitary wear, I felt that our gesture towards loo democracy should perhaps be withdrawn, and one hint to Minder Wang was sufficient.

Much later, I found out that each 'foreign expert' meant a

subsidy from Beijing amounting to some tens of thousands of *yuan*. This huge sum softened the blow, I suppose, of having to put up with us difficult beings. Our accommodation at the hotel, our car, our warm and well-furnished office were all signs of the State Council Foreign Experts Bureau's largesse.

So was our new factotum, who went well with the office's somnolent warmth. Lao Fan was a retired countryman, a *lao xiang*, brought into the city on a temporary residence permit with the sole aim of seeing to our extravagant needs. A kind of Chinese batman.

My notebook entry for January 10, 1975 reads:

Meeting Lao Fan, Comrade Wang interpreting: 'I am Fan Dunguang of Yangzhong County, Fongyu People's Commune, Yongku Brigade, Team No.6. I am a poor peasant and before the commune my family had only 2 mu of land. My mother died when I was eight and my father has been dead since 1946. Serve the people!'

While I was sure that Lao Fan would have tied my shoelaces if I asked him, this flourish of a slogan about civic attitudes, visible at every turn, was not all it appeared. The five characters *wei renmin fuwu* ('Serve the People') were emblazoned in red on each of the students' little olive green shoulder bags and, over every shop counter. Yet you could not help noticing that the Chinese generally seemed to recoil from the idea of serving real people. Even for us with our unwanted celebrity status, any request in the stores to inspect more than one size of garment or try on more than one pair of cotton shoes was met with surliness and turned backs. This was not something new, for in Chinese tradition the service trades were generally disdained. So Chairman Mao's 'Serve the People' slogan, the title of his 1944 essay which became part of the 'Little Red Book', was one element of the propaganda barrage which we quite liked.

Though we were the first such creatures he had ever set eyes on, Lao Fan never seemed the least intimidated by our foreignness. He would invariably greet us with a little dance of glee, his small-poxed face lighting up and his gold teeth flashing against our two bare bulbs. Our absurd foreign names were impossible and it was Lao Fan who renamed us. With a broad grin and a cry of 'Zhou laoshi, Li laoshi, cha laile' ('Teacher Zhou, Teacher Li – tea's up!') Lao Fan would deliver the steaming mugs to our numbed hands and then stand over us awaiting approval. He held his head up high when out of the office on some errand. The reflected glory of working for the only foreigners in town made him a person of some note on our Nanjing campus.

Lao Fan spoke in a thick north Jiangsu accent which even our teacher-colleagues found hard to penetrate. Like the Englishman abroad, the less we understood the more he would raise his voice. We were only around the office an hour or two a day, and meagre though his pay must have been, Lao Fan was employed on a full-time monthly salary. China's hundreds of millions of rural dwellers had to rely for their livelihoods on what they produced, and few would turn down the chance of exchanging their fragile stations for the incomparable 'iron rice bowl' of the cities. That is why farming communities were always overjoyed when their land was taken over for some non-agricultural use. It meant cash wages.

We were sure that Lao Fan had arrived at the University through some 'back-door' or other, but we never found out which of the Nanda officials was his distant relative. Whatever, Lao Fan was in clover, and when we were not around he would wield his little hand-brush of yellow reeds for a few minutes, make himself a brew in his old glass jar, and doze the day away by the stove.

Medieval sieges and stormings, student-run armouries producing mortars perilously improvised from cast-iron drain-pipes –

deaths and cripplings – all these were commonplace on college campuses during the bitterest phase of the Cultural Revolution. And where local strife was most severe, as it was upriver from us at Chongqing, a fuller range of military hardware was deployed on the campuses. I heard tell of heavy machine guns, field artillery and even battle tanks looted from the great caches which Mao had commanded to be laid down in anticipation of a Soviet attack. By the time we arrived in late 1974, China's re-opened universities were scarred with neglect, if not actual battles, and Nanjing University – Nanda for short - was no exception.

From the height of the unrest until 1971 - or in some cases until 1972 - the universities had been completely shut down. In the re-opened institutions, everything but the time-honoured rote-learning was new: the rules of enrolment, the curricula in every subject, the over-weaning emphasis on 'political study'.

As for the latter, ignoring quite naturally the core problems of China - the absence of democratic institutions and the emergence of a new class of bureaucrats - the Maoists loudly insisted that the revolution was in imminent danger of being lost to the once-defeated class forces. This was nonsensical, for the Chinese Communists had experienced no trouble at all in their first years in power in eliminating all opposition. And the state's grip was so total that opposition from below stood not the slightest chance. Though the Party constantly exhorted the masses to hunt down the old class enemies, in reality, the battle's real protagonists were the few dozen superannuated cadres who ran the Central Committee in Beijing. The masses played no more than a minor walk-on role.

The universities, however, were still regarded by China's leaders as potential arenas of trouble, and a close watch was kept on them so none might waver from Mao's 'revolution in education'. At Nanda, it was considered that the foreign presence had to be on side too, and from time to time we were called into the

Yellow House to learn about the latest directives. We would sink into the deep sofas, sip the ever-present tea served by a pigtailed and white-jacketed young female, pull on the obligatory saltpetre-laden Zhonghua cigarettes, while Comrade Zhou, cross-eyed Li An, and suave Comrade Zhou of the Nanda Revolutionary Committee would launch into their set pieces. There was usually a fourth person facing us: Professor Chen Jia, who was one of the three elders in our section who mysteriously retained an elevated academic title, and the salary to go with it. The rest of our colleagues, including us, were just 'teachers'. It seemed that the professor had somehow climbed out of his petit-bourgeois disgrace to full membership of the Revolutionary Committee.

'Before the Great Proletarian Cultural Revolution the universities were playgrounds of the bourgeoisie,' Chen Jia declared sanctimoniously during our first briefing session. He was obviously trying his best to outdo the most ardent of Maoists.

'The working people weren't allowed to enter the universities before 1966,' he went on. The sacrosanct *Peking Review*-ese phrases contrasted amusingly with his Ivy League English. Certainly, long before 1949 when this ancient bourgeois academic was himself a student, ordinary citizens had never got anywhere near to the universities. But in the 1950s and early 1960s, there was no doubt that university intake had been democratised. Professor Chen Jia usually got irritated with our minders – his ex-students after all – as they struggled to interpret at these meetings. Only those of a solid working class or poor peasant background were ever going to be appointed foreigners' minders.

'According to our new policies, only those steeled through labour and re-educated by the workers, the poor-and-lower peasants and People's Liberation Army can gain entry into our universities,' the Professor went on.' We have defeated the reactionary revisionist line and strengthened Chairman Mao's revolutionary line in education.'

We heard a lot about these 'poor-and-lower-middle peasants' – you were not allowed to simply say 'peasants' as that would include all the suspect classes of rural dwellers, including the baddies, the ex-landlords and the rich peasants.

'The new way of entering the universities guarantees that the proletarian masses decide who should be educated as their revolutionary successors,' the stately and smooth Comrade Zhou, our main overseer in the Revolutionary Committee, added in his oily voice. 'We don't call the young people students any more – they're worker-peasant-soldier-studiers!'.

Little by little, we discovered the reality was somewhat different from these strident declarations about our students – sorry, our studiers' backgrounds.

This was not the only area in which appearances were deceptive. Authority as far as we were concerned resided with the aforesaid University Revolutionary Committee. A number of little remarks and incidents made us realise that matters were not quite so straightforward. We could not help noticing that around the corridors of Foreign Languages patrolled an elderly chain-smoker in a long blue padded cotton coat and a funny peaked cap. I was curious why this fellow kept turning up. My enquiries eventually revealed that Master Ke – Ke *shifu* as he was respectfully addressed - was the chief of our very own Worker-Mao Zedong-Thought Propaganda Team, a ruinous mouthful of English which came immutably straight from the Chinese characters. These proletarian platoons had been sent into the universities to sort out Red Guard warfare and demolish any last vestiges of ivory towers. Over Nanda's Revolutionary Committee, over its supposedly all powerful Party Committee presided this cabal of gnarled workers, the high and mighty Propaganda Team. Master Ke, it was whispered, was only semi-literate even in Chinese. But in him was vested the ultimate power over both the staff and teaching materials of the Foreign Languages Department.

I am sure Master Ke and his team thoroughly enjoyed the unexpected opportunity to lord it over the untrustworthy and soft-palmed 'intellectuals'. By the second year he and his mates suddenly disappeared – they had been relegated back to whence they came – the Yangtze shipyard. The academics breathed sighs of relief.

IV
THE COMPOUND

NANJING HOTEL WAS CERTAINLY designed to generous Russian specifications. Like all public buildings where foreigners might tread, it boasted an oversized central heating system, the entrance to the glowing boiler house half-hidden by a mountain of glistening coal. High pressure steam pipes fed everywhere in the hotel complex. Thus were we kept snug but smut-covered in the Nanjing winter, when for long periods the thermometer seemed to hover around zero. This was another attraction to our cadres, for south of the Yangtze it was arbitrarily decreed that no public buildings, blocks of flats included, were permitted the comforts of central heating.

At the front of our home of unwanted luxury was an unlikely English lawn flanked by two massive and even more unlikely Christmas trees. The garden's backcloth was a fifty-foot concrete display board depicting the glorious Nanjing Yangtze River Bridge. Hidden behind this huge mural was a tranquil patch where straw-hatted gardeners pottered amongst compost heaps, cloches, and miniature trees. Incongruously, at the back of the compound lurked a square stuccoed villa which would have been more at home in 1930s English suburbia. It stood shuttered and empty.

To every Chinese, Nanjing's Yangtze River Bridge was an instantly recognisable icon of the Great Proletarian Cultural Revolution. This was the first-ever structure over the lower reaches of the river and the bridge was proclaimed as a great victory for Mao's policy of self-reliance. After all, Russian experts in the 1950s and American ones of an earlier era had sworn that no bridge could be built at Nanjing. The defiant construction of the bridge had been one of those mass campaigns for which Mao's China was renowned: half the city, including all our proud University colleagues, had mixed concrete and shifted heavy handcarts at the worksite.

The bridge was inescapably the first place of pilgrimage for any newcomer to the city. When a giant steam locomotive harnessed to an endless line of carriages thundered along its lower deck, smoke billowing through its shaking girders, it became an almost romantic structure. The mile-long elevated approach ramp was not too far from our home and it was a challenge to get to the top without dismounting from our bikes. We liked this ride as few locals ventured onto the bridge on foot, so it was a sanctuary from our molestation by the unceasing crowds on the city's streets. We would climb down to the under-tier and await the terrific spectacle of the next train just feet from our vantage point.

The hotel's lavish complement of staff never seemed idle, though what they actually occupied themselves with during the eight-hour working day dictated by Chairman Mao was a mystery. After all, normally we were the only visible guests in an establishment of over one hundred beds. I was intrigued, and decided to conduct an informal headcount. At the stroke of 11:30 (lunch) or 5:30 (dinner) the whole crew of room boys, clerks, receptionists, cable operators, telephonists, boiler stokers, and sundry other managers and hangers-on could be observed in rapid transit towards the back door of the dining room, enamel bowls and chopsticks at the ready. I seated myself nonchalantly on a low wall around one of the well-tended flowerbeds, and counted ... and carried on counting. We were in the capable hands of nearly one hundred staff. Nanjing Hotel was a self-contained industry, happily self-sufficient. I was always amazed that similar overstaffing throughout China's urban work units could still provide its citizenry with all the basics. It was a signal achievement, and, one might argue, a humane kind of inefficiency compared with the competitive dog-eat-dog society which was to be country's future.

It was to the same newly constructed kitchen and dining hall, high-ceilinged and capacious enough for a hundred guests, that we traipsed three times daily. Here, in eerie isolation, we would take our seats at a small square table with starched white tablecloth. We had been looking forward to a wholesome Chinese diet of copious vegetables, sparse animal protein and an absence of unhealthy things like desserts. But the hotel had other ideas. Cultural Revolution or no, the cooks must have been sent on some kind of training course in Western cuisine – overseen by ageing veterans of the long-gone pre-1949 foreign devil world. Their creations, proudly set before us, consisted mainly of slabs of sinewy meat, usually fried in breadcrumbs, along with a heap of over-boiled cabbage and potatoes. While we masticated on their handiwork, the entire kitchen staff would peep through the curtains which separated us from their domain. For the first week or so we felt obliged to reassure them with false nonchalance. But we had to put a stop to their innovations, even at the risk of appearing ungracious.

'You are Westerners and you eat Western food. We are Chinese and we eat Chinese food,' Minder Wang tried to reason with us. 'And you cannot use chopsticks,' he added as conclusive proof. This was just one of the ideas the Chinese seemed to have about the 'genetic' predisposition of foreigners..

'But why can't we cook for ourselves?' we objected.

'You are our foreign friends and the conditions are not right,' came the opaque reply. So we continued to be fed our supposed native diet, closing our ears to the loud sizzlings from the kitchen as some delectable stir-fry was prepared for the locals.

The suave Comrade Zhou had been introduced to us as our link with the University Revolutionary Committee and we lost no time in tackling him about our special dining arrangements. Half-starved for generations, most Chinese took their food seriously. Even when running a high fever, or in Jo's case prone and gasping for breath in a hospital delivery room, our hosts insisted that we fill our guts. A protest about the wrong sort of food was something to take note of. Eventually Comrade Zhou relented, and to our great relief, one fine day our veal escalopes, water buffalo rump steaks and sponge puddings were no more. In their place, we were served up modest but tasty Chinese meals with plenty of vegetables and a pile of the local gritty grey rice. Just what we had in mind.

In the cavernous dining room, the staff could hardly avoid contact with us, though there was an unseen line over which they stepped at their peril. So we were later to realise. We were told to address our waitress as Lao An, 'Lao' being an honorific and meaning 'respected aged'. She was a no-nonsense woman in her late thirties, her face open and pleasant with an un-Chinese aquiline nose. Lao An dressed carefully and from somewhere she had managed to acquire a pair of strappy court shoes. Such slight attributes of attire - little personal touches – were the norm in this supposed land of the uniform boiler suit. As our Chinese was still almost non-existent, any exchanges with Lao An were monosyllabic and formal.

Quite different was our waiter, a person always ready to confer a pleasant smile. Xiao Zhou (Xiao being another honorific and meaning small – the difference usually being age, but sometimes status) was a good-looking but spotty lad of about twenty - not so far off our own ages - who shuffled and minced around the dining chamber in his grubby white jacket. He was obviously an enterprising soul as he had somehow managed to learn quite passable English. Xiao Zhou concentrated hard on his English tones and I was most impressed by his end-of-question inflections. We always enjoyed a bit of banter. I would bring the frogs legs in our stir-fry to life and hop them over the tablecloth, or teach him a bit of unaccustomed slang when he delivered a plate of exotic indescribables to our table. Each of us would mime the animal it came from, and then which part of that animal. We were always conscious of the danger of compromising Xiao Zhou, but sometimes could not resist turning the conversation to broader matters.

The lad probably owed his exalted position as our waiter to his family background. His father was clearly Someone of Importance at the Yangtze shipyard. From the lofty heights of the great bridge we would peer down at its miniature cranes and toy-like steam engines, the clanging of steel on steel coming to us through the evening air. The lot of most school leavers was hard labour in the countryside, or at least assignment to an urban factory, and Xiao Zhou's mild sentence to the hotel was doubtless due to a bit of influence-wielding. The extraordinary thing was that everything about Xiao Zhou shrieked 'gay'. It was bad enough that he had learned the foreigners' tongue and was daily conversing with us. But in Cultural Revolution China, homosexuality was on the long, unwritten list of capital offences. We feared greatly for our dining room friend, and hoped that in China, people did not read the signs the same way we did.

Our forebodings seemed to be borne out when Xiao Zhou was one day abruptly removed from our sight. I met him again only once soon after his disappearance from the dining room. He looked thin and depressed and his spots had become joined weals down his cheeks. He tried to hurry by in the hotel corridor and his abashed and fearful face said it all. HE HAD BECOME TOO

CLOSE TO THE FOREIGNERS.

Later, Xiao Zhou was no longer around at all; perhaps he had been sent off to some village for a spell of re-education by the peasants. Whatever Xiao Zhou's fate, I fervently hope that he managed to hang on until the gradual easing of sexual mores of the 1980s and 1990s, let alone the possibility of 'coming out' which now exists in 21st century China. We had joked, chatted and laughed with Xiao Zhou without thought to where we were, and in a way never to be repeated with anyone else in our Nanjing period. It was a sad comment on the mindset of fear haunting China that in all our time in Nanjing and in all our encounters, it was this young man who came closest to a real human being.

Beyond the dining hall, perhaps half-a-dozen other hotel people had apparently been instructed that they might communicate with us. There were also a few individuals who obviously had not taken too seriously the briefings on how to deal with the foreigners. The woman with the flowery jacket and sweet smiles who ran the hotel post office was one. Her eagerness to try out some words from her English phrasebook every time we passed by, and her giggles at our corrections, were un-choreographed and a breath of fresh air. On our way home from work we would often stop by to admire a new stamp issue or wield the post-lady's glue pot to seal our letters. The bundles of envelopes neatly tied in ribbons by my mother and now restored to me are surprising reminders that in those pre-email days, the letter writing instilled into me on Sunday evenings at school remained a compulsive habit. The post office occupied a room on the side of the main entrance and the inordinate number of telegrams through the chattering machine by the window made it the hotel's nerve centre. Somewhere deep in the building was a telephone exchange too, where our very occasional phone calls back home were pre-arranged and eagerly listened to. To get an overseas connection needed a week's notice, and more than once, four in the afternoon was confused by the hotel's unseen female operator as four in the morning. Half senseless with sleep, I conducted a now legendary five-minute conversation with my puzzled mother on the subject of what size underpants she should send me.

Others permitted to deal with us, this time merely through bashful smiles and monosyllabic requests, were two pigtailed young women who attended to our room. They took their responsibilities seriously, and in the spirit of socialist egalitarianism, shifted around the dust with dripping mops until there was a more or less even layer throughout the floor. To our surprise, even the ornate and expensive woollen rugs received the treatment. This was China in pre-vacuum cleaner era, though just before we were forced to leave the place, in our honour Nanjing Hotel acquired an experimental cleaning machine which roared like a taxiing aircraft.

After a few weeks our patience with these pleasant daily intruders was somewhat exhausted. We needed our place to ourselves and invoked that ubiquitous Chairman Maoism, 'self-reliance'. Doubtless losing them a fair amount of face, we got the hotel to restrict the young women's duties to daily hot water deliveries.

In the matter of food self-reliance, we soon had to acknowledge that Comrade Wang had probably been correct when he said 'the conditions are not right'. Even if cooking facilities had been available, food shopping would have been well-nigh impossible due to the complicated rationing system which all urban Chinese had to put up with. To keep abreast of the ever-changing array of ration tickets and to get yourself in the right queue at the right time was a major challenge. And in truth, the daily shopping round was all but done while we foreign devils were still tucked in under our satin quilts. For us, it was tough enough having to rise at 6:20 for our 7:30 classes, let alone stand in line from five in the morning to get our hands on fresh vegetables or a few eggs. So on this point, we happily capitulated to China's hotel industry, and the unbreakable 'iron rice bowl' which guaranteed us and the rest of the hotel staff their daily sustenance. Unlike the 'reformed' China of much later, the Mao system at least kept tens of millions of urban Chinese in minimal material contentment, if little ambition.

Some weeks before our ejection from Nanjing Hotel, we could not help noticing a flurry of activity around the little Western-style stuccoed villa in the corner of the compound. Here, a dozen workmen were shifting furniture, clearing debris from the flower beds, and setting about the window frames and shutters with paint brushes. It was an intriguing display which none of our hotel contacts were willing to explain.

Shortly after, I was lounging in the hotel lobby when a maroon Mercedes minibus purred up the drive. There were Western vehicles in the city, true, but they were all ancient hangovers from the pre-1949 era. This Mercedes was modern, an exotic, head-turning novelty. It drew up outside the villa and disgorged a dozen Africans, the men in white robes and skull caps, the women in colourful head scarves and long shifts. Emerging from the minibus after them was a man I recognised. It was Comrade Qiao of the Medical College, a character at once obsequious and derisive whose unusual quiffed hairstyle I regarded as rather risqué. Qiao had briefly attended one of my young teachers' classes, where he antagonised everyone with his know-it-all attitude. At least now I could understand why he had been sent to improve his English.

I caught up with Qiao at the reception desk and asked him what was going on.

'Your new neighbours are from Zanzibar,' he reluctantly

conceded. 'They have come to our province because we are friends and they will be in Nanjing for three years to learn from our advanced medical units.'

By now I was quite used to being hailed by passers-by as a Tanzanian, the aid link between Jiangsu province and this part of Africa being well advertised in the local press. But the last thing I expected was that the isolation of our ghetto would be relieved by some genuine Africans.

'Great,' I responded to Qiao. 'Now we'll have some new people to talk to.'

'Our friends from Africa will be far too busy with their studies,' their minder declared with finality.

So...the foreign population of Nanjing had just increased several-fold. But unlike the other outsiders for whom entry into the secluded kingdom of Mao was a crowning achievement, I was soon to find out that our new neighbours were not in China by choice.

'How did you manage to get here?' I asked excitedly on my first encounter with three of the Tanzanians who were busy exploring the hotel grounds.

'We all wanted to go to London, or at least Moscow for further training, but our government sent us here instead,' a tall bearded character wearily replied, in excellent English.

It had not entered my head that only in the Western countries did the intelligentsia indulge Oriental, rural fantasies. Whatever the socialist pretensions of their homeland, these were the sons and daughters of the elite, and to be sent merely to another developing country for the sake of larger politics was a searing let-down. It was hardly surprising, then, that our new Zanzibari neighbours were to show almost no curiosity about Chinese society.

Under strict instructions from the Foreign Ministry, the provincial hospital in Nanjing which was to train the newcomers was obviously bending over backwards to accommodate them. *Qingzhen* (halal) cooks were sent in from the city's Muslim quarter; the Zanzibaris dined in a heavily-curtained annex, unsullied by the pork eating natives, and well away from our corrupting corner of the echoing dining chamber. We had heard plenty of rumours about the harsh treatment meted out to China's own Muslims: later I was to clandestinely meet some in Yunnan province's capital of Kunming. Amongst other atrocities visited upon them, they told of members of their community having their legs cut off at the knee to stop them praying, So it was even more surprising when we discovered that the African students were encouraged to interrupt their lectures and ward rounds for prayers towards Mecca.

While we were actively discouraged from learning Chinese, for the new arrivals this was a compulsory and even urgent task. In just twelve months, they had to achieve a proficiency in the language which would allow them not only to digest lectures in their complex medical specialisms but, even more challenging, minister to patients on the wards where something of a bedside manner in Chinese would be required. I could imagine the incredulity of their patients, none of whom would ever before have encountered a foreigner, let alone one with a black skin. Apart from linguistic problems, to the ordinary Chinese, generally speaking, the darker the skin the more negative the connotations. I had often wondered at my flock of supposedly revolutionary students - whenever we were sent out to do labour together, I was amazed by their precautions against sunlight. Hats would be drawn down and arms tightly covered.

'Dark skin is a bad thing,' they would tell me. 'Touch black and your heart will go black.' Though China was on a mission to win friends across the post-colonial world, beneath the official hullaballoo of Third World solidarity was a powerful prejudice against those unfortunates with darker complexions than the Chinese.

Our own leaders saw it as their duty to arrange regular trips to model factories, kindergartens and rural communes. We always leapt at the chance to get out and about, for despite the Potemkin Village factor there was always something to learn. The Zanzibaris were offered no such delights, and nor did they demand them. Consequently, their extra-curricular life in the city was limited to short strolls just beyond the gatehouse on Zhongshan Road. Even this meagre recreation lasted only a short time - the streets of Nanjing were just too much of an ordeal. On their first free day, I offered to show a few of them the neighbourhood. The local reaction was daunting. With Jo and I, two Caucasians, the crowds would point, incite their children to stare, though always allowing a certain distance. The Zanzibaris were permitted no such body-space: the throng edged close and became threatening. To the great amusement of the crowd, one daring character pushed forward and grabbed a black cheek, while another tugged at his companion's hair. After this, our new neighbours resigned themselves to the confinement of the hospital, the hotel and the Friendship Store, to which they were securely delivered in their fancy maroon Mercedes bus.

Starved of company for so long, on Sundays we encouraged the Zanzibaris to come over to sip some of our precious coffee from the Shanghai ships' chandlers. This dingy little warehouse near Shanghai's wharves, serving foreigners only, was the only place in China where we could find coffee beans. Our little soirees with the newcomers seemed a mutually pleasant experience, though on the second and subsequent Sundays only a couple turned up.

'We've been told that Africans and Chinese are shoulder-to-shoulder in struggle against the old colonialists and the new Soviet Social imperialists,' declared the only one of our new neighbours who was to keep up a regular appearance, the tall and suave Saleh, his spectacles dangling on a cord and his bedside manner already well-honed. 'Most of my friends don't want to upset anyone, so they're staying clear of you.'

We could not deny that our forefathers had indeed aggressed up and down both the East African and Chinese coasts: objectively, we had to agree that we bore something of the mark of the beast. On a personal level, though, we were about as anti-imperialist as you can get, and to be shunned for our nation's past wrongs was galling.

There were, though, occasions when the officials conveniently forgot their determination to separate us from their Third World Brothers-in-Struggle. Perhaps they believed that only Westerners appreciated the seductions of alcohol. Anyway, I found myself roped in to assist with an embarrassing diplomatic difficulty. Whenever a foreign group came to China in those days, it had to appoint a leader, someone with whom the local officials could negotiate. When it came to the Zanzibaris, there was only one possibility, though it hardly turned out to be the happiest of choices. Suleimann was none other than the eldest son of Zanzibar's ruler, who also happened to be Vice-President of Tanzania. The large and portly young man carried a princely demeanour, but turned out to be neither courtly nor pliable. From Saturday afternoon when lessons ended through to Sunday evening, the gilded youth would be drowning his sorrows. Eventually, Minder Qiao swallowed his pride and begged me to rescue Suleimann from the Friendship Store, where I found him slumped against a glass counter, a bottle of local brandy half empty, regaling the terrified staff in his broken Chinese. I helped him finish the bottle, by which point we were old buddies, and wheedled him into the waiting minibus.

Soon, Suleimann's comrades began to steer clear of him but still the drinking went on. Much humbled, Qiao took to pleading with me to come up with some solution, as his superiors were beside themselves at the diplomatic implications. As ever, it would be the underlings who would carry the blame. In due course, a First Secretary arrived from the Tanzanian embassy in Beijing and ordered the wayward Suleimann to pack his bags. At the eleventh hour, Suleimann realised what a mess he was in.

'Please write to my father,' he pleaded with me, 'and tell him I'm doing well in China and that you'll be taking care of me.'

Of course I had to do so, promising the Vice-President that I would be happy to act as his son's moral guarantor. Suleimann's sentence was suspended and the drinking stopped, at least in public, and eventually he went home with his surgeon's certificate.

The Zanzibari doctors were not the only Africans to hit Nanjing. It was early summer and the stultifying wet heat of July and August was yet to come. Suddenly the hotel corridors were a blitz of sweeping and mopping; I could not resist snooping upstairs: in the dozens of normally empty rooms, dust covers had been removed and curtains drawn back. Important guests were on their way. But we certainly did not anticipate the half-dozen blue and white Nanjing-made buses which drew into the compound, nor their passengers.

From distant Beijing, rumour had reached us of the unusual exploits of the young Zambians and Tanzanians in the Chinese capital. It was an oddity of Cultural Revolution China that all the radios on sale in the department stores had shortwave bands, and yet it was strictly forbidden to listen to foreign broadcasts. Anyone caught doing so, especially to Soviet broadcasts, would be severely punished. Already corrupted by the outside world, we seemed to be exempt, though it probably did nothing for my reputation that I would often find myself tuning in on our 'Red Lantern' valve set to Moscow's Radio Peace & Progress, the foreign station with far and away the strongest signal. With barely disguised glee, the station would report the misadventures of a certain group of Beijing foreigners from Africa. Chinese diplomatic discomfort was always to be relished.

With an eye to Zambian copper, amongst other things, the Chinese had launched themselves into the African continent with the epic task of building a railway from landlocked Zambia to the Tanzanian coast. No Western governments would take on this project and neither would Moscow. As part of the aid deal, two hundred young Africans were in Beijing, at the famous Jiaotong University, to learn everything there was to know about running a railway,

At the best of times, a cultural chasm might be expected between buttoned-up Chinese officialdom and a large crowd of youthful foreign residents. But the last years of Mao were far from being the best of times, and the puritanical stand-offishness of the Chinese was a recipe for misapprehension and trouble. Like us, the railway Africans resented all attempts to confine and ghettoise them. Unlike us, they resisted with brazen escapades in the city, often returning somewhat the worse for wear long after curfew, when they clashed with angry guards as they clambered over their unit's walls. Apart from the surprisingly ubiquitous liquor stores with their rows of lurid bottles, in those days there were few distractions on Beijing's streets–hardly any restaurants, while bars in any form were for the distant future. Nonetheless the city's main shopping street, Wangfujing, and the Friendship Store with its cheap beer, even the International Club opposite (so international that Chinese were barred from entry) held more attractions than the dreary college compound.

Perhaps for very good reason, the association between the alien invader and sexual aggression is deeply lodged in the collective psyche of the Chinese. The repressive Cultural Revolution only heightened the neurosis about the proclivities of foreign men.

Even my own quite innocent behaviour was carefully watched when it came to Chinese females – soon after my arrival I found myself hauled up in front of a political commissar for inadvertently touching a student's forearm. I was only trying to explain some point of English grammar. Predictably in a country which forbade sexual relations between any foreigner and a Chinese, the flashpoints with the African students came when the more adventurous tried to carouse with the supposedly terrified maidens of Beijing. When it came to their women, it seemed that the Chinese on the street shed their usual reserve with foreigners. Verbal skirmishes were commonplace, assaults upon the Africans not uncommon, and at least one serious stabbing was gleefully reported by the Moscow radio station. Yet as Third World brothers in struggle, the officials could hardly forbid association with China's *laobaixing*, its 'old hundred names', the ordinary people.

'The Chinese are sending all the two hundred railway students from Tanzania and Zambia on a tour of their country – and they're paying too,' my friend Saleh explained. 'And they're hoping that by the time they get back to Beijing, things will have calmed down,' he added with a grin.

The modern mandarins were well practised in the ritual arts of hospitality. In years to come, I saw how easily an agitated foreign businessman or diplomat could be pacified by a special trip, an elaborate banquet or a night at the acrobatics. Their hosts reckoned the foreigners to be simple beings, captive of their instincts and appetites. The average foreign devil was easily turned around.

This was not quite the case with the railway students, though on their Nanjing excursion things started off promisingly enough. The hotel management had been ordered to roll out the red carpet in a way I never saw repeated for any other group of guests. The younger members of the hotel staff were kitted out in red silk pyjamas and daubed with bright make-up, and as the students arrived at the entrance they were beaten in with drums and clashing cymbals, with much choreographed waving of large paper flowers. I watched from behind my curtains as the young men and a handful of women stepped off their buses and shimmied appreciatively into the lobby. They were definitely in uncompromising party mood, and dressed to kill. In Beijing there were tailors specially reserved for the foreign community with their many outlandish demands: here were copies of Wrangler shirts in flowery silks, double breasted Motown suits in bright velvet satins with crazily flared trousers.

For a couple of days, our staid hotel became a riotous party; ghetto blasters strung from bedroom windows, the lobby an impromptu dance floor and the lawn strewn with empty bottles. Both we and the Zanzibari doctors thought it in our interests to enjoy the spectacle only from a distance. For myself, I relished the worried expressions of the visiting Beijing minders and our local officials as they did their best to marshal their flock. Several times I caught Mr Ding, chief English interpreter of our local *Luxingshe*, casting about him in despair. So enjoyable was this interruption to our monotony that we easily forgave the visitors for depriving us of our alcoholic rations. After the TanZam party had departed for another unsuspecting city, it was impossible to get hold of a beer, and the little store by the guardhouse no longer stocked sweet white wine or Chinese Vermouth. Months of the hotel's precious booze quota had been consumed in just two days. Far worse, ancient Chinese etiquette and modern cadre power and been flagrantly flouted and humiliation had been witnessed by us to the full

Weeks would go by with no other guests, and then suddenly the silent corridors of Nanjing Hotel would be rent by slamming doors and snatches of foreign voices. We were always kept in ignorance of any imminent comings and goings, discouraged from making contact with any foreigner who happened to pass through the city. Starved of company, we would unashamedly hang around the hotel lobby in the hope of passing a word or two with any newcomer. We got on reasonably well with the local *Luxingshe* travel guides who used the hotel as their base, often seeking us out to test abstruse phrases which they wished to add to their vocabularies. But on such occasions all we got were irritated glances as they tried to hurry their foreign charges quickly past us.

Every so often, a privileged lone traveller would be passing through the city – a foreign dignitary in China at the behest of some Beijing ministry. From the descendants of an old Hong Kong opium *hong* to an eminent international public health specialist, such VIP visitors promised relief from the evenings of tedium, indeed from our own company. A private dinner for these special arrivals would be followed by the obligatory revolutionary entertainment – an incomprehensible film or a song-and-dance performance. By 8:30pm at the latest, the individual concerned would be delivered back to a lonely hotel room, satin-covered quilt turned back in a strong hint that bedtime was nigh. After all, within half-an-hour, throughout the land practically the entire population would be tucked under their own more modest cotton-covered quilts, and anyone who was not was an object of suspicion. But full of the strange discoveries of the day, few travellers would contemplate retiring at such an early hour. Our greed for company of any kind was boundless, and if we managed to intercept one of these rare arrivals, we would drag them back to our quarters. After all, there was nowhere else they could go – in those days, Chinese hotels deliberately lacked bars or lounges. My notebook records the arrival, for example of Daniel Thomas, curator of the New South Wales Art Gallery:

A frightfully arty type, scourge of the ignorant, and
absolutely at home in China where he's treated as a god,
my diary records. It continues: *I untactfully remarked*
'it's flattering being in China, isn't it!'. He didn't agree
at all'. Perhaps he was used to being flattered back home.

It was, of course, rare for any Western artistic offering to
penetrate into China. No doubt this was all part of diplomatic
footsy with Australian government.

'The paintings were strictly vetted by Chinese embassy officials
back in Australia,' Thomas told us gleefully, 'But I still managed to
get in a few nudes under their noses.'

Later in the gallery he surreptitiously pointed out a canvas
with a group of naked aborigines, almost too tiny to be seen. But
his real triumph of subversion was the cover of the exhibition
catalogue, which showed a painting of a termite mound, red and
very phallic.

'And the art gallery was packed daily even though advance
tickets were needed, and do you know what? The biggest crowds
were always around the phallus painting!'

Some fellow guests were distinctly less savoury, and oddly it
was such people that the Chinese always seemed happy to thrust
upon us. We had been asking for ages to visit a hospital to witness
the wonders of surgery under acupuncture anaesthesia, and one
Saturday afternoon Minder Wang turned up to announce that the
moment had come.

'It is convenient for you to visit the Workers' Hospital to see an
operation with other foreign friends,' he told us.

We bethought ourselves of a happy interlude amongst pleasant
company.

That afternoon we waited at the hotel entrance at the appointed
hour, and down the grand staircase which divided half-way up,

came a bevy of males in gold-braided uniforms followed by their lacquered-hair high-heel wives. Mr Ding of the *Luxingshe* hovered solicitously while the strange party climbed into the waiting bus. As we swung out of the hotel gates, bringing the tide of cyclists to a ragged halt, one of the peaked-capped males turned to us with a friendly smile.

'We from Chile in America. Where you come from?' he enquired.

Jo and I looked at each other with astonishment, quickly tinged with disgust. We had been teamed up with a bunch of Chilean fascists, fresh from the torture camps of Santiago. This was only shortly after the CIA-inspired coup against the elected government of Salvador Allende, and leftists the world over were still in a state of shock. Not so the Chinese, who were so blinded by anti-Sovietism and so covetous of Chile's copper, that Beijing was the very first government to recognise the Pinochet regime. To the officials, all 'foreign friends' were equal.

By the evening we had begun to recover from the indignity of our afternoon's company, not to mention the sordid spectacle of a surgeon manhandling a patient's guts as he sipped tea behind a fabric screen. We came across the Chilean party gathered in the lobby, the men in tuxedos and the painted women in long dresses, decked out in jewellery and ready for the opera. No one had told them that a night at one of Madame Mao's acrobatic revolutionary performances in a careworn Chinese theatre was a going to be million miles from the La Scala experience which they had anticipated. We hoped they would hate every minute.

As in the case of our SACU, every Western country had a friendship-with-China society. The rare arrival of a tour group from one of these organisations was something we longed for. Composed of more or less misguided seekers of some Oriental wisdom in Mao's kingdom, at least these were types with whom we could empathise and engage. Much of their fascination with China was ours too, though as time went by and our frustrations grew, we found ourselves coming from an increasingly obtuse angle. Sometimes this did not go down at all well – I recall a fractious evening in the company of some ardent German Maoists who doubtless put us down as counter-revolutionaries.

The two Australian friendship groups which passed through Nanjing in our first winter in the city were something else. Cheerily undogmatic about the great Chinese project, we drank the night away together. While Jo was more of a listener, basking in my status as one of those extremely rare creatures – a Western resident of Mao's China – I am afraid my audience was often wider-eyed than it should have been.

Unimagined by us, it would not be long before our impromptu salon was regarded by the powers-that-be as not merely a breach of etiquette, but a palpable threat to security too. I believe that what they hated most was the thought that we might be passing on information on the local power struggle, not that we knew much about it. A deeper isolation in Nanjing was just over the horizon.

V
'WE LEARN ENGLISH FOR THE REVOLUTION'

IT WAS DAY ONE of teaching. Lessons started at the unearthly hour of seven-thirty, and rolling out from our heavy cotton-padded quilts with their fancy satin covers, we stumbled to the cavernous dining hall to be served French toast and bitter coffee. The coffee must have been bartered for bicycles with some friendly African country having little else to offer the coffee-disdaining Chinese. How the French toast, a concoction of honey and eggs fried into white bread, had survived the Cultural Revolution I have no idea. With this hurried breakfast inside us, Driver Zhou sashayed us through the parting seas of rush hour bicycles towards the campus gates.

All too conscious of my inexperience as a language teacher, on that freezing Jiangsu winter day I walked nervously through the campus paths to a grey-brick two-storey house. This was the English building, and in the spirit of deliberately contrived proletarian shabbiness, it had obviously had no loving care since 1949. Guttering hung loose, shrubs sprouted from the cracks in the walls, and floorboards were gnarled and fissured. Worst of all, when I found my classroom, half the window panes were missing and frost was on the ground, the north wind hurtling down from Siberia.

The class rose as one, fifteen serious faces in unison declaring, 'Good morning teacher!'

I thought I had walked into a high school by mistake. They

looked like high school children but, no, these were my charges and I was soon to discover that most were not even teenagers any more, but like me were in their twenties. The 'girls' had pigtails, and wore short padded jackets in bright peasant colours, modestly concealed by drab loose covers. Their puffed-out trousers were plain blue or grey. The smooth-faced 'boys' sported peaked caps, and from under their blue cotton Zhongshan jackets – Mao jackets to us foreigners - peeped off-white homespun shirts. Rather than some proletarian revolutionary garb, the Mao jacket was merely a direct descendant of the mid-19th century European officer's tunic, passed onto the Chinese by the Bolsheviks. In China, it was known by the name of the leader of the 1911 revolution, Sun Zhongshan – aka Sun Yat-sen.

The homespun shirts impressed me greatly. To an outsider they might have had charm, but artificial fibres were already fast taking over in China, and even to Cultural Revolution youth homespun was something of an embarrassment. Later, one of the boys shyly told me that they felt obliged to wear the shirts because they were the parting gifts of mothers and grandmothers back in the village. For others who, as I was later to discover never had mothers and grandmothers anywhere near a village, the wearing of homespun was nothing more than dressing down, a political cover.

It was the same with footwear. Despite the sub-zero conditions, most of the class sported thin black cloth shoes, also homemade. Like factory-made shirts, leather footwear of any kind was to be avoided as un-proletarian. Those not shod in their grandmas' parting gifts of cotton-soled shoes sported worn PLA plimsolls, faded and often lace-less. This was army worship, and a wise affectation after 1968 when the PLA stepped in to sort out China's unruly youth.

The juvenile appearance of both boys and girls was reinforced by their thick winter underwear which revealed itself at cuffs and trouser bottoms, their padded jackets inflating them clown-like. In contrast to the extreme covering of trunk and limbs, I could never fathom why my students - indeed, everyone - excluded their feet from cosy wrappings. All they wore in the depth of winter were transparently thin nylon ankle socks.

The students were evidently unused to straying from the script, and introductions were muted. Judging from the number of young 'leaders' in this and every class, it was obvious that the new batch of young people in the only recently re-opened universities were on a tight rein. A group such as my fifteen was ruled by the Monitor (generally in charge of everything mundane), the Study Superintendent, the Physical Education chief, and most important of all the Communist Party Youth League Secretary.

Emblazoning the crumbling plaster was a colourful frieze on which foot-high red letters proclaimed WE LEARN ENGLISH FOR THE REVOLUTION. This robust and not unpleasing message (were it remotely true) was the protective shield of every classroom where China's youth were newly engaged in the risqué business of English study. Such displays, along with the 'wall newspaper' made up of pasted handwritten sheets with their arching slogans, were the business of each group's propaganda team.

Classes lasted a standard two hours with a ten-minute break in the middle. Like many other vital points in the daily timetable, the intermission was announced by a deafening blast from the huge horn-shaped loudspeakers which hung from lampposts or the boughs of trees, coughing and spluttering into every cranny of the campus. Initially I was astonished that the moment the break was signalled, the females pulled skipping ropes from their pockets and began hopping around the steps of the building. Other students crowded around me, giggling and wide-eyed, bravely hoping that my strange lips would move and they would actually understand something.

Suddenly the loudspeakers struck up a march, brass band and unmistakably martial. A lad who turned out to be the class physical education supremo quickly had his flock spread out in two lines, from where they started to throw their arms and legs around in a well-practiced routine of callisthenics. I soon understood that this patriotic dance was a good way of unfreezing, and to collective amusement I clumsily joined the end of the line. Such was to be our unchanging routine throughout the winter.

I certainly needed to keep my circulation going. Anchored to my spot at the front of the class during the long two hours, winter draughts wafting through the broken panes, there was a certain fascination in watching the floor between me and the first row of students. Both girls and boys would hawk and gob without shame, the favoured target for their expectorations being a spot in front of my brown plywood rostrum. Those first few icy weeks I developed a little private distraction from the humdrum of the classroom - a game of guessing how long it would take the unwholesome deposits to freeze into pretty nodules, glassy emerald and brown.

With a further splutter of the loudspeakers, morning lessons would be over. It was 11:30, and clutching their enamel bowls my students would join the stream heading towards the canteen, over Hankou Road on the south campus. Every one of them had their accommodation and tuition fees paid by the state, while their families bore the cost of their meals. For very basic rations the University charged them 15 *yuan* a month, this at a time when an average urban wage was perhaps 55 *yuan*.

Once, I followed my group to the south campus, where I thought to take a peep inside their canteen. My snooping revealed a dark chamber of a dining hall, its damp concrete floors matched by long benches and tables of the same greasy concrete conglomerate. Served through small wooden windows where they held their enamel bowls, the student throng was too intent on wolfing down their rations to take much notice of my presence. My male students liked to boast how many *liang* (ounces) of rice they could get through at a sitting. I could see that they were not exaggerating. Bowls were piled with mountainous quantities of the greyish grain, quantities unimaginable to a Westerner. Along with this vital food staple, or its less appealing alternative of *mantou* (ovoids of steamed wheat flour) what the students got for their money were a few vegetable stalks and some chips of bone with a little flesh adhering to it. The whole thing was finished off with a watery soup, which certainly saved on the washing up.

Delving where I was not meant to was always profitable, and this intrusion was something of a lesson for me. I realised for the first time that what the ordinary people ate was a very far cry from the average Westerner's idea of Chinese cuisine. My visit to the students' canteen had also put our own daily fare of pork, chicken and duck into some sort of perspective. I was mildly shocked, but then like most outsiders interested in China, I had only had foreigners' hotels and the glossy propaganda magazines like *China Reconstructs* as a source. What was more, I had never experienced life in any other so-called Third World country and my standards of comparison were sadly lacking.

The students rarely had classes in the afternoon. Apart from Wednesdays when they had compulsory sports, they would spend most of their time 'reviewing lessons', in what they amusingly (to an English English speaker) called 'self-study'. I could never myself bring this unfamiliar term to my own lips, for it smacked of navel gazing, or worse. 'Reviewing lessons' meant memorising words, whole passages indeed, from the classroom primers. I would watch them at it - frosty winter nights and sultry cicada evenings alike, all over the campus, lone figures would be mumbling to themselves under the dim light of a chosen lamppost or shady tree.

In the accustomed manner, it seemed appropriate for me, too, to call the students 'little' (*xiao*) along with their family names, even though I was hardly older than them. Before every class, Xiao Wang, Xiao Zhou, Xiao Wu and all the rest would bounce up to me and proudly announce their achievements:

'Teacher, at self study I learn fifty new words.'

'Teacher, und the wise leadship of Party and Chairm Mao China make great progresses.'

'Teacher, I review all lessons and knowed one hundred new words.'

I would be tempted to mutter 'So what?', and sometimes I almost swore under my breath with frustration. Xiao Wang, Zhou and Wu were still incapable of the simplest daily repartee, in the manner of 'What time is it?' or 'Where are you going?' Any mental map into which their torrent of 'new words' could be fitted was conspicuous by its absence. But it was not their fault. Such was the influence of the age-old Chinese habit of rote-learning.

'We must criticise Lin Biao and Confucius,' was a useful everyday phrase which my students were working on when I was first introduced to them. I soon found that old and young alike could 'firmly repudiate' Lin Biao and Confucius until the cows came home. We heard a lot about Lin Biao, whom Mao had chosen to take on his mantle but who had now flipped into being the most dastardly of traitors. Shortly before we arrived, a great campaign had been whipped up, mysteriously lumping together the Communist Marshall and the ancient philosopher. I greatly regretted that we just managed to miss the unusual opportunity offered by the Foreign Experts Bureau to 'study' the Lin Biao plot. This involved China's foreigners being locked in a room with an hour to get through the bizarre testimony which was supposed to prove how Mao's 'closest comrade-in-arms', the sole vice-chairman of the Communist Party, the very man who penned the hagiographic introduction to his Little Red Book, was in fact none other than the devil incarnate. Apparently he had been born in this unclean state, but had managed to conceal his true nature from Mao and everyone else for decades.

According to the official line, evil Lin Biao had hatched a plot to blow Mao's train off the rails as it passed through Jiangsu province. The plot failed and the plotters fled towards Moscow in a British-made Trident jetliner, which crashed in Mongolia, killing all on board.

Historians still dispute the most basic details of this tale; in China itself the subject remains taboo. As for poor old Confucius, he had expired some two and-a-half thousand years earlier than Lin Biao. Mao's latest campaign, apparently against any recidivism in the Cultural Revolution, and to promote the purging of thousands of high-ranking military officers, did have some gruesomely amusing moments. Some years later I was allowed to visit the Confucius ancestral seat at Qufu in Shandong. Here I wandered amongst the ancient trees of the clan graveyard where not long before, the sage's descendants had been dug up from their resting place, and 'punished'. This took the interesting form of hanging bits of skeletons from the branches.

To bind Confucius to the modern day Communist leader Lin Biao was something of a long shot, and amongst our colleagues I detected a raised eyebrow here and there, a little scepticism. The more competent of them were ordered to prepare suitable commentaries in English on the Lin Biao/Confucius campaign and these they struggled through in an embarrassed monotone during our Friday political study. Meanwhile the students did all they could to mention Lin Biao and Confucius every time we asked them about the weather.

More penetrable and almost good fun was a new political campaign sprung upon a weary Chinese public in early 1975. Suddenly everyone had to study an ancient epic of banditry, the *Shuihu zhuan*, a set of stories known in English as *Water Margin*.

'Song Jiang drinks much wine and kills tigers with his hands,' the students joyfully informed me.

'Why does the *People's Daily* tell us we have to read this book?' I innocently asked.

'I do not know,' the students replied in unison. They seemed genuinely mystified at Chairman Mao's latest idea.

After a few happy weeks of directionless but undemanding political study sessions, during which we simply enjoyed the next chunk of the outlaws' adventures, the *People's Daily* started to hint darkly at the real purpose. There was a traitor in the house! The hero of many of the tales, the tiger-slaying Song Jiang, was not all he appeared to be. 'Song Jiang is a traitor,' chanted my students, Song Jiang is a traitor!' It was as though they had cracked the last clue in a troublesome crossword.

'We must dig tunnels deep and store grain everywhere,' one of the PLA boys in my third-year group declared, to general nods of approval, for it was an important Mao quotation. But what could this strange slogan be all about? The underbellies of every town and city resembled Gruyere cheese, and these were Mao's tunnels. With his oft-repeated exhortation 'Dig tunnels deep and store grain everywhere', the Chairman had ordered the masses to burrow everywhere so that the population could be protected from the expected nuclear attack from Moscow. The shelters could be seen all over the city, and there were half a dozen barely disguised entrances on our campus.

On May 1st 1975, the last of the defeated American forces in Vietnam retreated from Saigon. At class that day, I was not sure if I should refer to this historic denouement of the seemingly endless

Vietnam War. The students seemed unsure, too, on how they should react, for everyone knew that the powers-that-be in Beijing much preferred the American presence to the south rather than a potential ally of the great evil one, the Soviet Union. Anyway, I made some reference to the happy day, and the class seemed fairly relaxed.

'Our two peoples are closer that the lips and the teeth,' piped up one of the brighter boys.

'What did you say?' I puzzled.

'The Chinese people and the Vietnam people are close like the tooth and the lip,' the poor boy stuttered.

I remembered seeing this unusual simile in recent issues of *Peking Review*, but I felt that this was taking a liberty too far with the language of Shakespeare. Lips and teeth might sound all right in Chinese, but surely there was a better way in English?

'If your Foreign Minister talks like this at the United Nations in New York, perhaps China will lose face,' I suggested. National Loss of Face was the worst sin.

But once again, I had strayed into forbidden territory – this time high politics - and it was not long before Commissar Xu came along waving a copy of the *Peking Review* and its Immutable Word. 'Lips and teeth' had to stay.

VI
FREEDOM OF THE CITY?

A REGULAR PRIVILEGE OF those appointed to chaperone China's tribe of foreigners was to ride around in one of those mysterious lace-curtained conveyances which yelled 'power' at Nanjing's streets. On our second day, the car which had met us at the airport turned up for the standard Nanjing tour – the Yangtze River Bridge, the dramatic Sun Yat-sen Mausoleum on the slopes of Purple Mountain, Xuanwu Lake.

'This is for you,' proudly declared Minder Wang as he pointed to the sleek lime-green Shanghai Mark I saloon, its oversize chrome bumpers being buffed to a mirror finish by driver Lao Zhou. People unfamiliar with the Chinese political lexicon used to ask me what was meant by the word 'cadre', pronounced something like the French way. I usually fell back on a weak but apposite pun:

'It's simple: a car...dre is anyone in China having the right to travel in a car.'

We noticed that when the University leaders graced us with their company – a frequent occurrence – even they did not dare to ride in our splendid vehicle. In a political climate where dressing down had become second nature, it was just too riskily bourgeois. The Zil limousine which had met us at the airport had disappeared – it had merely been borrowed for face. Our leaders made do with one of the car pool's old Russian Volgas, or sometimes even a Willis jeep, one of many which buzzed around the city a quarter of a century after they had been liberated from the defeated Nationalist army.

In those days, there was plenty of lorry traffic on China's streets, and even more enormous rubber-tyred handcarts hauled by ragged teams. These, I discovered to my surprise, were privately owned: they touted for work with the local factories. There were very few automobiles. The puritanism of the Cultural Revolution notwithstanding, we found to our surprise that in the eyes of the masses the motor car was a magnetic, a glamorous beast. Often when we were taken downtown to the post office or the No. 1 Department Store, we would return to our Shanghai saloon to find Driver Zhou fending off the crowds, his comic duster of hen feathers on a stout bamboo stick raised ready to strike. Usually someone would be pointing a camera at a family grouping draped over the bonnet of our gleaming symbol of modernity, an exploit which Zhou tolerated provided he could pose proprietarily by the driver's door.

At first, I had been astonished to find that ordinary urban mortals such as our teacher colleagues had never before seen the inside of a car. I hasten to add that my surprise was merely a measure of my Western insularity. On the rare occasions when one of them was allowed to accompany us on some official outing, they would gaze in wonder at the dashboard and struggle embarrassingly with the unfamiliar door handles. Then they would settle back with self-satisfied expressions, knowing that heads would be turned as they coursed through the milling crowds.

Those were the days when driving in China was considered a craft skill, when to be a driver was to be part of an elite brotherhood. You could bet on it that every one of them had learned their trade in the People's Liberation Army, China's only college of driving. Its graduates held to certain habits, most of them highly disconcerting, at least for anyone schooled in the British highway code. Night-time driving was without exception conducted on the lights-on, lights-off principle. Lights-on meant having a glance at the road ahead, and then switching off again - was it just in case a marauding aircraft might be circling overhead, or perhaps an artful reactionary was planning an ambush? This was after all the endlessly repeated theme of the Chinese cinema industry. Many a time when the lights were flicked back on, a cart or cyclist would loom into the windscreen and another miraculous near-miss would be notched up.

The ex-PLA truck drivers who served as China's chauffeur brigade adhered to another alarming custom, always reminding me of my father's parsimony in his old Ford Consul. On any good stretch of road they would zip up to a hair-raising velocity, and then switch off the ignition. Breakneck careering in neutral was soon exchanged for an absurd walking pace. On long downward inclines, our free-wheeling progress took on a distinctly fairground descent, fettered only by the overheating brakes rather than by the gears. I supposed that during the dark years before China had the benefit of its Daqing and Shengli oilfields, the army had ruled that this was the way to conserve precious fuel.

For ourselves, we just learned to keep our eyes tightly shut. But new to motoring, our front seat minders were happily oblivious to any danger. In any case, no lily-livered 'intellectual' would have dared to advise a proletarian stalwart how to mind his business. It was an unchallengeable truth of Mao's China that the driver was king. Not for nothing were drivers universally addressed as *shifu*, literally 'master tradesman', but when used by one of our cringing colleagues it was intended to puff up the *shifu* in question into 'lord and master'. Indispensable to the comfort of the leaders, they knew just a little too much about their charges' various comings and goings. Even high officials would be most careful not to cross their drivers; I was astonished that given the strict, almost feudal social order of the People's Republic under Mao, at the banquets and receptions laid on for us by all levels of the bureaucracy, a place would always be reserved for the driver.

Apart from the inherent dangers of living in a country where all aliens were automatically taken for spies, our greatest daily worry was being slaughtered in a pile-up. Chinese drivers drove recklessly as a matter of course, but if they had important cargo on board (a high official, a foreigner) it quite went to their heads. Never mind that no other road user had a clue who their passengers were and why they had the right to overtake on blind bends or sail through traffic lights on red.

A good few amongst our scattering of 'foreign experts' saw no reason to reject any of the creature comforts on offer, including their chauffeur-driven transports. For ourselves, though, we certainly had not come to this supposedly egalitarian land to ride around in curtained limousines. Like the ordinary folk of Nanjing, our humble aspiration was the freedom of the roads promised by two wheels. But this was a scenario far from the minds of our hosts.

'Outside the State's Plan, there are no bicycles in the shops for our foreign friends,' Minder Wang explained, an embarrassed twitch to his left cheek. 'And,' he added triumphantly, 'you do not have the correct ration tickets.'

It was true. Light industrial goods such as bicycles, sewing machines and watches all required special coupons, and this rebuff kept us quiet for a short time. Until, that is, we stumbled across the Nanjing Friendship Store, just behind Drum Tower Square. Its upper floor was restricted to non-existent foreign customers, but downstairs some Chinese at least seemed to be welcome. Here was a showcase for the premier brands of bicycle – the ones with 'Flying Pigeon' and 'Eternal' inscribed in English in gold letters on their crossbars, and the staff seemed eager to sell us whatever took our fancy. The other purchasers were in fact Overseas Chinese with wallets of foreign currency who were buying restricted goodies for their sheepish-looking and plainly-dressed Nanjing relatives.

Changing tack, Minder Wang claimed that the Revolutionary Committee was unwilling to let us buy bikes because of their solicitude for us. We well knew that this was mere self-protection, for the cadres would be in all kinds of trouble were we to sustain injury – or worse. Chinese officialdom was neurotic about that kind of thing. A story, surely apocryphal, did the rounds amongst us foreigners concerning a group of political tourists from somewhere in Europe who lost a member due to the strain of all those model factories and communes. The hosts arranged for the dead delegate to be carried around for the remainder of the tour, the coffin adorning meeting rooms, even having its own lidded mug of tea served up to it, not to mention its own hotel room. 'Fifteen people came from your country on a group visa and fifteen must leave the People's Republic together,' declared the comrades of the omnipresent travel service. They were in denial: dead foreigners were not a good advertisement for New China.

To try to convey the absurdity of worries for our safety, we pointed Minder Wang towards the danger which we were forced to confront because of Driver Zhou's antics in our seatbelt-free Shanghai car. This argument quite failed to chime, for Wang had not the slightest inkling of the deathly hazards of Chinese motoring.

Needless to say, our determination to own bicycles had motives other than humility. We had seen enough of the officials to know it was essential to carve out a little area of autonomy. Daily forays into the occluded byways of Nanjing might give the cadres apoplexy, but for us they promised exhilaration. We were determined to have our way.

It was our bicycle agitations which triggered the first of many missives fired off to the supreme Foreign Experts Bureau in faraway Beijing. This was a rare occasion when the Bureau ruled for us: since the Beijing and Shanghai foreigners were allowed bikes, Nanjing had no choice but to concede. One afternoon, our car delivered us to the Friendship Store where we were introduced to two black, coach-painted sit-up-and-beg Yongjiu ('Eternal') roadsters. Gearless like every Chinese bike, the Eternal was the Rolls Royce amongst Chinese bicycles, the best that Shanghai had to offer and, we were to find, quietly coveted by our colleagues.

Soon we were indefatigable peddlers, familiar invaders of every nook and cranny of the city. Our determination to cycle to work, however, soon evaporated. Rather than leave for our office before seven in the morning, come rain or shine, we exchanged our consciences for that extra half-hour in bed and the services of a victorious Driver Zhou. At least at such an early hour, we were still too dozy to worry about the ever-present dangers.

Our drivers and minders relished it when we were the least bit indisposed. We were considered a precious but delicate species, and at the drop of a hat we would be whisked off to the Nanjing Workers' Hospital. This lay in a gated compound on a hillside a few minutes from the University's south entrance. We were always driven up to a wing behind the main buildings, far from the crowded wards which catered to the masses. For in Mao's egalitarian world there was one sick bed for the poor and another for the powerful. Minder Wang had no hesitation in explaining.

'We are in the period of socialism, not communism. So different people get different treatment.'

'You mean Karl Marx's dictum 'from each according to his abilities, to each according to his needs' isn't for now?' I cheekily retorted. 'It's more like to each according to his rank?'

Wang grimaced and thought for a while. But he stuck to his guns.

'All the *ganbu* - cadres - of Grade 13 and under are welcome in the special place,' he helpfully volunteered.

The Chinese Communists had devised a ranking of the bureaucracy which ran to an amazing twenty-six tiers. This far outclassed the imperial Mandarinate which for hundreds of years had made do with only one third the number. Naturally, Chairman Mao himself was the sole occupant of Grade 1, while Grades 2 and 3 were kept vacant, preserving a respectful distance. With its private rooms and plentiful specialists – not to mention the best turned-out nurses – our oft-frequented wing of the Workers Hospital was nothing more than the habitual retreat of the province's mysterious leadership. Hard information was scarce and rumours rife. But a hospital visit, just like one to our hotel compound, was regarded as an opportunity to glean some valuable information about the struggles amongst the leaders. The higher-ups had established a routine of convenience illnesses which tended to come on just as the political heat heralded a *yundong*, a 'movement'. We had noticed a happy, mutual conspiracy in the work-place which meant that no questions were asked if a colleague reported in sick. Even in Mao's China there were ways and means of getting a bit of slack. In the same way, it was accepted as an unwritten rule that the high cadres could regularly succumb to mysterious but strategic illnesses, allowing them time out from the relentless political struggles.

While we were being attended to by solicitous specialists, our guardians would make it their business to chat up a nurse here, an orderly there, to discover which of their leaders might be hiding in the wards. Sometimes, even the mighty untouchables themselves might step out in their pyjamas and slippers, smoking furiously and spitting melon seeds, their curiosity at the foreigners in their midst getting the better of them.

'What's wrong with him, do you think?' I asked provocatively as a harmless-looking old fellow shuffled by, puffing furiously on an expensive Zhonghua cigarette. Our minders would invariably whisper, 'High blood pressure!'

It was usually some undefined flu-like bug or unruly bowels which took us to the Workers' Hospital. Whatever ailed us, our consultations with the finest physicians Jiangsu could offer usually concluded with the same painful injection in the rear, administered with a giant syringe. To demonstrate that they were pulling out all the stops, I was regularly directed to the special wing's radiology room, where ancient machines whirred and clicked whilst the operator hid behind a thick lead wall. At the time I knew no better, but I have often wondered when those Nanjing X-rays will come home to roost.

Hospital visits held out further attractions to our chaperones. China's health service, though a far cry from that of the early 21st century when outright bribery had become the order of the day, was certainly a ripe arena for use of the *houmen* – the 'back door'. We could not help noticing that our minders and drivers took every opportunity to chat up the top medics who were required to minister to our usually pathetic symptoms. As bourgeois elements, university and hospital people shared a common ignominy and thus a mutual sympathy – translatable into some advantage should one's family come upon a medical emergency. At the height of the Cultural Revolution, senior medical staff were likely to be targeted as the most feckless of the intellectual classes, and sent off to have their thinking put straight with a stint of hard labour. But despite all those Cultural Revolution tales of professors of medicine being forced to clean the toilets whilst the toilet cleaners got on with the brain surgery, we soon discerned that top cadres would settle for nothing less than the real thing.

We often puzzled over China's celebrated acupuncture anaesthesia. It was routinely arranged that foreign political tourists should witness this supposed miracle of Mao Zedong

Thought. On one occasion at the Workers' Hospital, I was invited to peer through a glass observation roof at a patient porcupined with acupuncture needles, still wide awake as her neck was cut open and a thyroid removed. The hapless woman had been well-tutored: the moment she was sewn up she rose from the operating table and croaked out *Dongfang hong* – the 'East is Red', the de facto national anthem which heaped praise on the Chairman's luminosity. More than once, Jo and I quavered, robed and masked, a couple of feet away from a beating heart in the surgeon's hand, the patient chattering limply behind a neck screen. Again, needles were said to be the only anaesthetic. I thought I would give it a go myself, and had some polyps removed from inside my throat using the magic needles. It was distinctly painful, and I could not blame the high cadres for doubting the remedies they had devised for the masses. We were pointedly informed that if we had to go under the knife, we would get the real thing – full Western-style gas - just like the officials.

While our University leaders lost no opportunity in hanging around the hotel grounds, our teacher-colleagues were another matter. They were not actually forbidden from coming to see us, and at first a gaggle of them would turn up at weekends. Our polite and inconsequential interchanges over tea and cigarettes lasted only until some bureaucrat decided that such visits should be subject to greater scrutiny. Though none of our colleagues would ever have visited without the political cover of a Party member in the group, it seemed that permission was now required. The new arrangements made it not worth the effort, and the teachers stopped coming.

To mollify us in our protests about isolation from our colleagues, every now and again we were invited to the home of one of the more important members of the Department. These events were highly choreographed - tense set pieces on both sides - where the authorities were always the invisible guests. The University even took care to supply the fancy ingredients for these banquets, pretending all the while that the fare was everyday family stuff. These occasions were nonetheless appreciated, and they enlightened us as to the cramped conditions and very basic cooking and lavatorial facilities which our colleagues had to put up with – a far cry from our cosseted hotel experience.

From one point of view, and one only, we were glad to be within the confines of a guarded compound. It was here that we could be free of the attentions of the staring masses who mobbed us on the city's streets. But despite a strong desire to hide away in our comfortable prison, we felt impelled towards the highways and byways of the city. The problem was that as the capital of a province with a population the size of Britain's, a goodly proportion of those thronging its streets were always bound to be out-of-towners who had never so much as dreamt of seeing a foreigner. Consequently, though buzzing through the neighbourhoods on our bikes was pleasant and almost normal (people would merely stare and point at one's retreating back, crash their bikes in the effort, fall off ladders), any foray on foot would invite an audience of rustics who could always be counted in tens and sometimes in hundreds. On one occasion I lingered too long outside a department store's display window. I must have been in some kind of daydream. I turned around to find an arc of starers several layers deep. There were hundreds of them, transfixed by the red-haired apparition, not one daring to cross an invisible line some three body lengths from me. It was the complete absence of communication that was the most disconcerting. I might have been from Mars.

In theory, Nanjing was a great place, with many fascinating old corners and much to see. But the back end of the Cultural Revolution was the wrong time to try and explore in any normal manner. While we got used to the place through our almost daily cycle rides - the familiar corners, the women on this lane re-combing the cotton-wool in old mattresses, the ancient tinsmiths on that stretch of street hammering worn-out pots and pans, the poster display at the Shaanxi Road junction, the place could never, ever get used to us. Even a simple walk down to the nearest collectively-owned corner shop to buy a packet of my favourite Great Front Gate cigarettes invited an ordeal of mobbing.

In certain quarters of the town we took on rather odd identities, a matter which reflected the general state of knowledge of the world beyond China. Comradely references to foreigners in the newspapers were reserved for Albanians, North Koreans, and of course the oppressed of the Third World. At a time when the Jiangsu provincial newspaper was carrying stories of the province's aid to its twin in Africa we found the whisper on the street had changed to *'Tan sang ni ren'*. We were happy to be Nanjing's honorary Africans - Tanzanians.

For variation and just to enjoy the reaction, I would sometimes claim to be a *shaoshu minzu* – a member of China's numerous ethnic minorities from the western reaches of the empire. When the street was really getting to me I would mouth the word *Sulian* - China's deadly enemy, the Soviet Union. This never evinced hostility, but was passed around the crowd in a matter-of-fact way. Later, my experiences alongside ordinary factory workers seemed to confirm that the propaganda-weary Chinese had learned to disconnect 'politics' from their day-to-day existence.

Still, one should keep a perspective on the way that foreigners were understood. Starved of real information about the world, the locals could be excused their ignorance. And it was a wonder that outright hostility was absent. Over the previous century and more, China had suffered horribly from foreign aggressors. And anyone over forty years had most likely witnessed the horrific atrocities which the merciless Japanese visited on our home of Nanjing, then the Chinese capital. And a generation before the Japanese, it was the eight foreign armies sent to relieve the Boxers' siege of the Beijing legations which had exacted a brutal revenge on a large past of northern China. It is hardly surprising, then, that in her early years in 1920s Sichuan, my mother had to brave the cries which followed her down every street; 'Big nose, big feet, foreign devil'.

By the 1970s, 'foreign devil' was heard only as a self-parody spoken exclusively by the few foreign residents of the country. In all my time in China only once have I been called a *yangguizi*, a foreign devil, and that was by a drunk. All one heard on the street, and endlessly, was *waiguoren* – a neutral term which just means 'outside country person'. This at least was a Chinese word which I early on learned to pronounce with panache. And of course, as more and more foreigners appeared, most urban folk fell into referring to *laowai*, a rather companionable term which translates as 'venerable outsider'. I still find it remarkable that the Communist Party could re-programme its citizenry so thoroughly into forgetting the well-deserved opprobrium heaped on Westerners for their arrogant use of China in the century following the First Opium War (1839-42). One thing is certain – this remoulding does not extend to the Japanese, who, within the living memory of many, destroyed Chinese lives in their millions.

The hermetic seal around China was a challenge to every foreign espionage service devoted to the anti-communist – or in the case of the Soviet Union – anti-China crusade. Professional China watchers of various political hues lapped up titbits of news from China without discrimination. The snakes-and-ladders of Party organisation, the collapse of a railway bridge, the price of vegetables in Beijing – all were of equal fascination to the hungry tribe of intelligence operatives and journalists who infested Hong Kong. Maybe there was a smattering of hostile agents actually on the ground in China, but most intelligence was certainly garnered remotely. Even in those days, it was reckoned that the U.S. spy satellites circling China had no difficulty reading something as small as a car's number-plate as it crossed the Nanjing Bridge. We were merely amused at the unspoken assumption that we were in China on behalf of the spooks. Since our every move was monitored, the idea that we could get stuck into any effective spying should have been dismissed as absurd. On one occasion when Minder Wang had said something which I took to mean we were not to be trusted, I rather foolishly defended myself.

'Look, whenever I go out my strangely coloured hair and big nose mean that I'm immediately surrounded by dozens, who comment on my every gesture. If I pick my nose, they pick their noses. If I move to the right, as one they move to the right too. I couldn't do much spying even if I wanted to.'

Poor Wang could only give back his tortured silence.

Oddly, while leaving the hotel compound was discouraged, certainly on our bikes, in theory we were free to go anywhere we wanted within the city limits. In our first week in Nanjing, we were taken to the Public Security headquarters to get our aliens' resident passes. In the yard, I spotted a pile of large metal signboards inscribed in Chinese and Russian. The newly appointed Officer in Charge of Aliens – that is, the two of us - thought it his duty to give us a lecture.

'You are our foreign friends and you are welcome to our country. But these notices will be put up at the side of the road on the edge of the city and if you see them you must stop and turn back.'

That Russian was chosen for the signboards was nothing short of bizarre. OK, a couple of decades earlier a few dozen Russian engineers had been in Nanjing to help build factories, and the notices had been cooked up for their benefit. But it was now fifteen years since the Sino-Soviet relationship had turned hostile and the Russians were daily vilified in the Chinese media. I could not help smirking at the irony. If by some miracle a Russian spy might be stalking the streets of Nanjing, the message of those signs would have been rather helpful: 'You're getting warm: secrets just ahead!'

Educated though he was, Minder Wang saw nothing funny in the Cyrillic signs. Others with even less exposure to the foreign world sometimes expressed surprise that we could read neither Chinese nor Russian. Gradually we became aware of a *yin-yang* perception of the world. There was Chinese language - *Zhongguohua* - on the one hand and *waiguohua* - 'foreign language'- on the other. On more than one occasion I had to disappoint officials who placed in front of me documents in strange scripts, once apparently Hindi and another time what I took to be Croatian. A Chinese could read Chinese and surely an educated foreigner could handle anything 'foreign'?

Apart from the need to move at some speed to escape being mobbed like owls in the daylight, our freedom to leave the confines of the hotel was not quite all that it promised. For a start, tradition meant that every factory, office block or housing area was shielded behind high walls and obligatory gatehouses. This meant that on most main roads you could see little of intimate life. Gatehouse designs were pretty standard - pillared and roofed constructions in concrete, echoing the *pailou*, the ceremonial arches, which once had dotted the traditional Chinese townscape. On the main roads you could ride for miles and all you would see would be walls, endless walls. The most you could hope for was to peer past an entrance until some busybody became a little too interested in your alien presence. Not by chance does the Chinese term for feudalism – *fengjianzhuyi* - have the literal sense of being enclosed, walled in. Those puzzling miles of barriers always made me think how remarkably urban life might be improved if the vast resources put into them had gone instead to useful things. To prove that the Soviet Union held no fear for them, our hosts made a point of showing us the entrances on the campus to labyrinths underground. These were everywhere in the cities, for Mao believed they could adequately protect his people from a Soviet nuclear attack. We had a chance to glimpse the rabbit warren of tunnels under our own University campus, and it seemed unlikely they would withstand even a few conventional bombs.

All this was going on when so few resources were being put into much-needed public infrastructure. Urban housing provision – not counting shared kitchens and toilets – was less than five square metres for each citizen. 'No room to swing a cat!' as the saying goes. Measure this out in your own commodious living room and you can see that even if the keeping of cats had been allowed in 1970s China, there would not have been enough room to swing one.

Another limiting factor of our two-wheeled lives in the streets of Nanjing was more insidious. Less visible than any wall or bomb shelter was the network of mini-spies whose job was to report anything amiss on their patch. The lookouts were usually retirees engaged for 'patriotic duty' by the Public Security; they were not to be confused with the old folk with red armbands who squatted on their stools at most street intersections, whose main concern was jay-walking and other minor infringements of public morality. Between them, the street vigilantes made it their business to closely track our movement across the cityscape.

We quickly learned not to engage in a public place with anyone who spoke English, especially our colleagues from the University. The strange sounds coming from our lips would ripple through the instant crowd, and whoever our interlocutor might be, they would end up flustered and embarrassed. Far worse, in the crowd there could well be some clever English speaker seeking merit with the police who would contrive hidden meanings in innocuous remarks about the weather or the price of cabbages. This might well lead to one of those feared 'little reports', a *xiao baogao* - a sneaky and unanswerable accusation sent to the authorities which was a sad feature of the times. After we found out what trouble any engagement caused, if we spotted someone we knew on the streets, we gave no hint of recognition, and neither did they. We would simply cross over and walk on by.

Like all foreigners, friendly or hostile, we were intent on trawling beneath the surface propaganda. China watchers were obsessed with finding cracks in the Cultural Revolution façade, and in this we were no exception. Take for instance 'class struggle', a phenomenon which Chairman Mao and every issue of *Peking Review* assured us was endemic and universal. So our hosts could hardly deny that 'class struggle' was raging out there. But there was an oddity, a paradox, which we would gleefully throw back at them. Class struggle was everywhere, but it was never of our particular time or place. Here, in Nanjing, to paraphrase a a much-heard phrase of Mao's, 'the situation was excellent', the people united and utterly devoted to the Party leadership and its latest edicts. So it had been yesterday, so it was today, and so it would be tomorrow. Yet when much of the power struggle was played out in the street *dazibao*, the 'big character posters', it was impossible to conceal the existence of raging strife in the city. The officials were necessarily in denial, for any admission to a foreigner that all was not peaceful in the land would have been a serious offence.

We would often cycle down Zhongshan Avenue to the Shaanxi Road intersection a few blocks south of our compound, and without getting too close, we would watch how the *dazibao* would mushroom, be ripped down by an opposing faction to be replaced by new diatribes. Further towards the city centre was Drum Tower Square with a rostrum complete with neoclassical columns and friezes. It was here that the big leaders would preside over political rallies and ceremonial marches-past. Beneath the rostrum was the city's prime site for *dazibao*, and often a milling crowd. To a foreigner hungry for some truth about what was going on in China, this was real meat. As we coursed through the square on a reconnaissance, we would cast only fleeting glances towards the seething crowd and the latest posters. The actual business would wait until Lao Zhou next whisked us by on our way to work. Now I could put those lace-curtained car windows to good use: they offered perfect cover for my Olympus OM1 with its cunning pre-set shutter speed priority, a refinement which meant all I had to do was point and press, however rapidly we were careering by. But the ruse was not as clever as I had imagined. Our camera manoeuvres at Drum Tower Square would come back to bite us.

VII
BANISHMENT

IT SEEMED THAT IN the main, only those foreigners who knew little or nothing of the language were invited to work in the China of the early 1970s. But even the exceptions, such as our friend Susan who was assigned to Shanghai fresh from a Chinese degree, could scarcely unravel more than the general drift when it came to the abstruse literary and political allusions of the street poster, the *dazibao*.

China's spy paranoia apart, as far as the officials were concerned it was preferable to deal with the foreigners at arms' length, through interpreters and translators. The buffer of mutually incomprehensible language provided every opportunity for delay, misunderstanding and the obfuscation beloved of bureaucrats everywhere. China's long tradition of linguistic exclusion was aimed at both the common herd and the foreigner. An imperial decree of the 1850s even promised execution to any native caught teaching Chinese to the Western invaders, and the present political climate was bound to be a spur to xenophobic impulses. But we knew too that unless we learned Chinese, our appreciation of what was going on around us would be even more constrained. More important, in coming to China I had a very specific mission – to uncover the mysteries of China's strange urbanisation process. Though serious investigation was impossible now, some time in the future there surely would be important things to read.

From the moment of our arrival, therefore, we badgered the cadres to arrange Chinese tuition. Again, we had not yet cracked the Chinese custom of saying 'yes' when they meant 'no'. Our requests to study Chinese were invariably met with smiling approval, but nothing, or almost nothing, was offered in the way of language classes. I say 'almost nothing' because of an illuminating episode in our relationship with Minder Wang.

We came to realise that our letters were not exactly *our* letters when Minder Wang suddenly announced that he was going to give us our first Chinese lesson. This he did, but it was delivered in such a way that we knew we would learn little. As the Chinese tend to do amongst themselves, poor Wang's explanations involved frantic tracing of characters on his palm. Confusion was compounded upon confusion.

By no coincidence, Wang's eagerness to assist came on the very day he delivered a badly sealed envelope from an acquaintance back in London. This was the person who had started us off with some basic Mandarin, or to be politically correct, *putonghua* ('common language'). Our correspondent was a fiery Maoist gentleman of Singaporean pedigree who kept guard at the London premises of SACU. Here he enjoyed terrorising with Maoist fire the bourgeois English clientele of retired school teachers, missionaries and social workers who were habitués of China's UK 'friendship' group. To Chinese officialdom, the irascible San was an important cadre in a vital diplomatic organ, and his whims were to be respected.

'I am travelling to China on SACU business and have asked the London embassy if I can make a detour to see you in Nanjing,' San's letter informed us. 'I am certain that the University will have been teaching you more Chinese, and that we'll be able to have a chat in the language.'

Little wonder, then, that Minder Wang had thought it wise to arrange that first Chinese lesson. He might just as well not have bothered, for in the event San never materialised and I never found out why. It seems likely that as with others who tried to look us up in Nanjing, he was told by the *Luxingshe* – the Travel Service -

that there were no such foreigners in the city. The determination of our hosts to keep us isolated was such that even Jo's mother was finally refused a visa, having first been promised one and having bought her wildly expensive tickets which was then unusable.

We left Minder Wang to practice his English on our as yet-to-be-delivered mail, and in the end, I learnt my Chinese by sheer bloody-mindedness and in semi-secret, grudgingly assisted by some books filched from the Beijing Languages Institute by the good Comrade Yang. Full of Cultural Revolution jargon, the Language Institute books hardly prepared the learner for everyday conversations about the weather, shopping or restaurant menus. Yet these were the only language primers on offer, and they must have done something for me – perhaps kicking off a process of unconscious osmosis, Four years later, when I returned to China to work in Shandong, I was browsing an illicitly acquired local newspaper (only the *People's Daily* and the *Guangming Daily* were allowed to foreigners) when an eureka moment overwhelmed me. Granted that Chinese journalists were probably ordered to produce copy for a reading age of twelve years, peppered with the political slogans of the day. Yet I could actually get the drift of some of the main articles.

After the incident with San's letter and language lessons, it became clear that little attempt was made to disguise the Big Brotherly oversight of our private mails. We discovered that when our letters arrived at Nanjing Hotel they were first placed in some mysterious quarantine upon a shelf at the back of an office annex. If we squinted through a side window of the locked room we could usually spy our foreign-looking envelopes and packages. Yet sometimes a week went by before Comrade Wang decided we were ready to receive them.

On one celebrated occasion, we had two letters handed to us on the same day from relatives on different sides of the family, people who were complete strangers to each other. Behind page one of Aunt Irene's letter was page two of Uncle Henry's. And vice versa, in the usual imperfectly re-sealed envelopes, still grubby with overuse of the glue pot. Someone should have told Wang that foreign envelopes had their own inbuilt adhesive.

Though we guffawed with abandon at this blunder, matters had really gone beyond a joke. Out came the Seagull typewriter, and soon another missive was on its way. As usual, we were forced to rely on our minder for translation, and on this occasion he did not bother to soften our barbarian tones, which resulted in something along these lines:

> To the Leading Comrades, Jiangsu Postal Bureau.
> You have the perfect right to read our mail – after all we
> might just be spies. But
> (a) could you read them more quickly, and (b) if you can't,
> we know a couple of
> local English natives who could assist your efforts.

We hoped they would appreciate the attempt at irony. Three months on, we were amazed to get a formal response, nicely produced on a Chinese printer-typewriter. This was a rare thing - never before had any official ever deigned to answer our complaints in writing. The Postal Bureau's reply was a sternly worded denial of any mail tampering:

> It is against Articles x, y and z of the Constitution of the
> People's Republic of China to interfere with the privacy of
> citizens' communications.
> Your accusation injures the undying friendship between
> the Chinese and British peoples.

While these remarks caused us a little wry mirth, there was also a hint of a threat. Unbeknown to me my file in the Security Section of the Foreign Experts Bureau was already swelling.

Six months after our arrival in Nanjing, when we had become totally fed up with Minder Wang's deadening hand, we realised there might be a simple way of removing him.

'We've got a rather annoying man looking after us called Wang,' I wrote to my parents in clear unjoined-up writing. This direct way of communicating with the authorities had immediate effect: the very day after I delivered my letter to the hotel post office, Wang announced he was handing us over to someone else.

Our new minder was - relatively speaking - a breath of fresh air. Comrade Liu was a cuddly, soft-spoken fellow who always put me in mind of a panda. When he smiled it was from pleasure and unlike his predecessor, only rarely from embarrassment. It quickly became clear that Liu's view of his job was to make all the petty constraints which were thrown at us as digestible as he was able. Occasionally he was resilient in the face of authority, and though he could never openly admit it, we got the sense that our own disappointments with officialdom were also his. Naturally he was a Party member, though unlike Minder Wang, he saw no reason to hide this from us.

It was not merely our relations with passing foreigners – real or imagined – which made the officials determined to quarantine us. A silly dispute with one of the provincial leaders sealed our fate. Some time after our arrival in Nanjing, we became aware that people were speaking of a new provincial Party supremo, one Xu Jiatun. We first met Xu at a banquet which he laid on in our honour to mark May Day in 1975. Down the line, Xu was to be both celebrated and vilified. But in the Nanjing of 1975, it was impossible to imagine this diminutive and unassuming military figure gaining prominence anywhere. Promoted in 1983 to the position of chief of the Xinhua News Agency in Hong Kong, in effect Beijing's de facto representative in the still-British colony, Xu Jiatun demonstrated sympathy for the June 1989 mass protests, and shortly after simply evaporated. He surprised everyone, probably himself included, by surfacing in California.

At our May Day event, we seemed to get on well with Xu and his entourage. Amongst those at the table was a regular guest, an elderly fellow with a jovial manner whose role was apparently to get the foreigner pie-eyed. In contrast to his fellow cadres in their carefully tailored and creaseless military tunics, he looked every bit the factory worker. He had a habit which I thought a bit strange at the well-mannered banqueting table: with a cigarette dangling from his lower lip between mouthfuls, he would push back his peaked Lenin cap and wipe his brow, as if on some hot shop floor. Every now and again this strange, nameless person would rise and edge around the table to clink my glass.

'Ganbei!' he would proclaim while looking deep into my eyes, as if to discern some hidden and untoward intent on my part.

'Ganbei!' I would return to general mirth. Whereupon we would both down yet another thimbleful of the deadly baijiu, the white lightning, the stuff that finally gets a little better after the fifth glass.

Little did I imagine that the man's friendly demeanour belied a thorough dislike for me, a dislike which was to translate into much trouble. The turning point came not long after the May Day event, when I came across our banqueting companion in the hotel lobby. As usual we nodded in greeting, but for once he became stern-faced and addressed me in rapid-fire Chinese. Mr Ding, our urbane acquaintance from the Luxingshe interpreter pool happened to be passing and the cadre beckoned him over.

'This comrade wants to know what you think about the Soviet

Social Imperialists and their plans to invade their neighbour France,' said Ding.

The comrade looked on, scowling.

'But France and the Soviet Union don't have a common border - they're not neighbours at all,' I blurted out without remembering the small issue of face.

This brought on a torrent in Chinese, which Ding failed to inject with quite the same vitriolic tones in translation.

'He says you are wrong. Sulian and Faguo are next to each other. He says that he should know about these matters better than you because he's the Director of Foreign Affairs of Jiangsu Province.'

Read Foreign Minister of a territory the size of Britain.

I was flabbergasted. For a start, the man with the Lenin cap was not at all the lowly factotum that I had imagined. And his elevated position had clearly not been won by an elevated command of European geography. For a moment, presence of mind eluded me. Not that I was ever a Moscow sympathiser, but I was heartily sick of the unceasing anti-Soviet diatribes which contrasted so obviously with the gentle treatment reserved for the United States.

'But I come from that part of Europe and I've often been to France,' I spluttered. At that, the Comrade Director marched off in an un-Chinese huff. Just a day after this unsettling encounter, Comrade Liu, Minder Wang's successor, breezily announced our removal to new quarters. We were still unused to such arbitrary diktats and protested loudly but uselessly to anyone who would listen.

On biking trips towards the north of the city, we had come across an incongruous scene. Enclosed by a high wall, on the brow of a hillock rising 150 feet above the sweltering city stood two mock-Tudor villas, each topped by characteristic tall brick chimneys.

Along a rutted lane around the perimeter, a shortcut which we sometimes took when cycling to the Double Gate Hotel, was a matching gatehouse, half overgrown and falling away where the locals had prised out the hard red bricks. It could have been the English Home Counties, except that in the foreground were neat Chinese vegetable fields where patched-trousered Chinese peasants ladled human manure from wheeled wooden barrels. This we learned was the Dingshan *Bingguan*, the Dingshan Guesthouse, and unbeknown to us it was shortly to be our home.

I reckoned that the older buildings must have dated from the late 19th century – the creation of some nostalgic jobbing architect from the old country. Later, consulting a 1930s map, I surmised that perhaps the Dingshan was an annex of the British Embassy once it had moved from Beijing to Nanjing in the mid-1930s. Whatever, the buildings were unmistakably British in origin, and three decades after the revolution, the British were going to back at the Dingshan.

On the appointed day of our removal, Driver Zhou drove us up to the Dingshan's gatehouse where the AK47-wielding PLA lads raised the heavy pine trunk that served as a barrier. We wound up a long drive and on the crest to our right we passed the two derelict mock-Tudor red brick houses. A hundred yards further on, we halted at a new administration block. Numbers of white-coated staff could be seen walking purposefully this way and that, some heading towards the kitchen with their enamel rice bowls held before them. To my surprise, amongst them I recognised two students who a few weeks ago had been in my class, and were now part of our array of 'servants'. It would not be the first time that the meagre English we had drilled into our students was put to use in watching over their teachers, although I could not quite work out why one of the two had been assigned to us. Little Zhang was the most obtuse learner in the whole year.

'You will see your new dining room,' chimed Xiao Jin, a spotty pigtailed young woman whom I had always liked as a student. I followed her into the block opposite the offices and found myself in a dining hall as cavernous as the one we had left behind. It also had the same weird mix of wall lights and chandeliers as the Nanjing Hotel. A whole book could be written on the strangeness of Cultural Revolution lighting fixtures.

Minder Liu retrieved us and we were ushered towards a courtyard and onto a canopied terrace. Well aware of our opposition to the Dingshan move, he was nervous.

'These are your rooms,' he ventured as he pulled back the wire netting mosquito screens. The French windows led into a lounge dominated by the usual array of deep armchairs and sofas. Our new quarters comprised half the ground floor of a 1920s European-style villa, fringed by a useful rain-proof stoop where we could sit out and park our bikes. Up a couple of steps from the sitting room was the bedroom, neatly arranged with two beds hung with mosquito nets, giving the appearance of four-posters. Off the bedroom was a bathroom of generous proportions, with a bath bearing the insignia of the Shanks Co. of Staffordshire.

For weeks we were in mourning for our former home on Zhongshan Road. The Dingshan was going to be even more prison-like than Nanjing Hotel. At least there we had been able to hear the buzz of the nearby street, giving some sense of connection to life outside. Even worse, we shared our new compound with a detail of PLA guards, forever coming and going with their rice bowls, occasionally waking us at dawn with practice fusillades of automatic fire in the sloping field to our rear.

The sense of incarceration was, as it happens, embedded in the very walls of the Dingshan, though at the time we did not know it. Two years later, in the brief 'Beijing Spring' of 1978, we were back in China on a special mission, a kind of Chinese truth-and-reconciliation week when our former colleagues could at long last open up to us. One of them, the outspoken Comrade Shen, had been amongst the many unfortunates caught up in a supposed plot against Mao Zedong's rule, the May 16th conspiracy which had been rumbling on since 1967, and raised its head in Nanjing in the early 1970s. Now Shen told us that he had been imprisoned in the very room which was now our lounge, and he and fellow prisoners were evacuated to make room for us. Shen was highly unusual: his slating of the Party was always from the democratic left-wing rather than the customary right. I was looking forward to meeting him in better times, but like quite a few of my ex-colleagues who only got through by incessant smoking, his life was cut short.

Initially, the Dingshan seemed like total isolation. In a pathetic effort to remedy our sense of loss, from time to time we would return to Nanjing Hotel in the hope of finding company. Any foreigner would have sufficed, like-minded or not. We were not actually stopped at the gate like the ordinary inhabitants of Nanjing, but Minder Liu put it unambiguously:

'It is not convenient for you to go to the Nanjing Hotel any more.'

'Oh yes, it bloody well is,' I thought. But we took the heavy hint and resigned ourselves to our own company and a relationship which was becoming ever more claustrophobic.

The authorities liked to keep us in the dark about developments, and we never had the slightest hint that newcomers were imminent. Nanjing University was expanding its language horizons, and after several months of complete isolation, the Dingshan was suddenly abuzz with new faces. First came a French couple, Renée and François, with their three charming young daughters. They arrived through their relationship with a member of the French literati who had some connection with the Chinese embassy in

Paris, and typical of Beijing's recruitment policy, they were in the usual state of ignorance about Chinese realities. As time went on and we sat together through many a factory revolutionary committee's 'brief introduction', our new neighbours ever more in tune with events, our political briefings with the officials became enlivened by his freshness and Gallic irrepressibility.

A different case was the Ecuadorean family who just as unexpectedly turned up to teach Spanish. Juan was a well-known poet of Maoist persuasion, steeped in the Cultural Revolution propaganda image of China, but apparently content to remain ignorant of the realities once he arrived at his Mecca. His wife Rosanna was too preoccupied with an autistic daughter and a lively son to take much notice of life outside the compound. Still, our little ghetto had grown several-fold and become multinational. We had not come to China to hob-nob with assorted foreigners, but since we could not do so with the Chinese, we were grateful for whatever company came our way. Our vast dining room now rang to the cries of five children, while the lovely Shanghai saloon was exchanged for a locally produced 'bread bus' - the Chinese name for a minibus -with cracked shards of glass for windows. Worse, the placid Driver Zhou was replaced by Lao Xia, a reckless rogue who terrorised us twice daily with his casual near-misses.

From their early years, Chinese children learn not to stand out in a crowd, and few of my students breached this conditioning. One individual alone in my first class of third years cut a distinctive profile. Further, I had no doubt that the young woman was actually what she said she was – the child of poor workers from a small north Jiangsu town. Even more exceptional, she had had a genuine spell of labour following school and there was no need for her to be despatched to a factory with the rest of her graduating class. As a school leaver of sixteen years, Iron Girl Wang, as she was universally known, had been sent off to the Siberian wastes of the Daqing oilfield, the industrial icon of the Cultural Revolution. Now, as everyone in China knew, Daqing was the stomping ground of China's most celebrated model worker, a Chinese Stakhanovite called Wang Tieren – Iron Man Wang. Along with China's hundreds of millions, I had read cartoon strips about Iron Man, watched stirring news reports about his exploits, and at the little Xinhua bookshop at the Shaanxi Road junction I had even purchased the poster depicting him as a supreme proletarian spirit.

Who knows? The Iron Man may have been no more than a figment of the propagandists' imagination. But with her striking presence, Iron Girl Wang was certainly very real. I discovered that when the University sports day came round and I found myself pitched against her in the long jump. She won by a leg-length. From that moment on, I have to admit, I was attracted to her, though any sexual thoughts were so outlandish in those repressive days in China that I do not think they ever came to the front of my brain.

What I did admire of the Iron Girl with her strong visage, her habit of looking you in the eye, and the fact that she seemed to embody all the advertised qualities of model youth. Perhaps I was unduly influenced by her demeanour, for unlike most of her peers, with her rich, alto tones, Iron Girl did not go all giggly-giggly girly-girly in the company of her foreign teacher. I was beginning to get a reading for Chinese taste in beauty, and for sure, Iron Girl's robust frame and coarse auburn hair bunched in an oversize pony tail hardly conformed. She might well have struggled with the beauty test for college entrance of which a colleague was later to inform me. But to me, Iron Girl's straightforward ways with the world were a breath of fresh air and I could not get enough of her.

I did not expect to see Iron Girl again after the students disappeared in July. But a few months later she popped up at the

Dingshan, with the mysterious excuse of some liaison role which seemed to involve a lot of following me around the compound. I was foolishly delighted, for as I have admitted, I found her a breath of fresh air. As we conducted our vigorous rounds of table tennis in which she effortlessly prevailed, I often got the feeling that Iron Girl Wang was at the Dingshan to keep a close watch on her former teacher. I cared not. It was just a relief that at least one of my worker-peasant-soldiers, despite the all-encompassing political pressures, could relate to the world, and to me, with all the naivety, curiosity and straightforwardness of youth.

VIII
TEACHER-STUDENTS &
BOURGEOIS PROFESSORS

OUR COLLEAGUES SURPRISED us by loftily referring to themselves in English as 'intellectuals.' I soon discovered that this was another of those impermeable mismatches between the Chinese and English languages, and one which had long been carved in stone. Charmingly, four characters formed the Chinese original: *zhi shi fen zi*, literally 'knowledge elements'. Chinese aesthetes might assure the world that their lexicon had as many as 30,000 characters. But in the same way that Britain's tabloid red-top newspapers are contrived for a reading age of twelve, there was nothing printed in Mao's China that demanded more than a couple of thousand characters. With them under one's belt, one was (almost) a 'knowledge element'.

By the early 1970s, China's ranks of the educated had long since lost the respect which society traditionally accorded them. The *zhishifenzi* had become the natural targets of the nation's unremitting *yundong* – the national or sometimes local political campaigns which were never sated until they had squashed some enemies. The Great Helmsman Mao had long before 1949 proclaimed that eight categories of class enemy had to be eliminated, but never comfortable with competing thinkers, he later decided to add a ninth category – the poor old intelligentsia.

'We are the *chou lao jiu* - the Stinking Ninth category of class enemy,' proclaimed the eccentric Chen Mingbai with a hysterical cackle.

'Does that make a foreign 'intellectual' like myself a member of the Stinking Ninth too?' I enquired, tongue in cheek.

'No – you're even worse,' he replied with another cackle. 'You're a *chou lao shi* – a stinking foreign intellectual of the tenth category of class enemy!'

If it brought us closer to our colleagues I was more than happy to wear this badge of ignominy.

Jesting apart, the victimisation of our poor colleagues as a class went all the way in explaining their downtrodden demeanour. They had had the stuffing knocked out of them and few would say boo to a goose. Our grown-up flock would jauntily call themselves 'Teacher Liu' or 'Teacher Wu', for it was vital to match the new batch of students, the 'worker-peasant-soldier studiers' with sufficient political humility. Actually, we soon unkindly concluded that in truth it would be foolhardy to call them anything but teachers. The Cultural Revolution meant that no graduates had emerged from the universities for almost a decade, so most of our teacher-students were products of the late 1950s and early 1960s; in their forties and fifties, they were by far our seniors. We had to remind ourselves that most had been shaped by the very different 'old society' - the era before the Communists took power. Whenever frustration was getting the better of me, it did well to remind myself that our teacher-students were survivors of a brutal civil war, not to mention the terrible Japanese invasion in which at least twenty millions lost their lives. And then, after 1949, they had been obliged to endure repeated waves of 'anti-Rightist' terror, the most recent of which was still resounding.

Alongside the Spanish, French German and Japanese sections in Foreign Languages, English was by far the largest. There were rumours, too, that some Russian was still being taught. Though that Russian had survived the bitter enmity with Moscow was not something to be admitted to outsiders. Despite the wildly hostile official rhetoric against the erstwhile Elder Brother, trade evidently continued across the Siberian wastes, and trade needed mutual comprehension in the form of languages. Textiles and industrial raw materials went north, bartered for cars, trucks and spare parts for the Soviet plant laid down in the 1950s - still the industrial backbone of China. Apart from the occasional newly-produced Shanghai car like ours, the only other recent models on the streets were the lumpish Volgas, with their overbearing chrome bumpers, which seemed to be the favoured transport of the PLA officer class in our Nanjing neighbourhood.

Of most immediate concern to we foreigners, occasionally privileged as we were to take to the Chinese skies, was the safety of the Soviet-made aircraft. We hoped and prayed that the much-maligned Elder Brother had not decided to send any dud spare parts to the Chinese. The Antonov-24 turbo-prop, a country bus with wings and forty-four worn canvas seats resting on lacerated tyres was our main means of conveyance whenever we had the chance to get out of Nanjing. As I later found when en route to Lhasa in the very first large jetliner to do the route - a huge Ilyushin - Russian language would still be necessary for a good time yet. Ignoring the 20,000 foot snow-capped Himalayan peaks seemingly only yards below us, the plane was left to its autopilot as the entire flight crew wandered down the aisle clutching tea mugs and smoking superior Zhonghua cigarettes. Spotting their strange passenger, for I was the sole foreigner on board, they plonked themselves down beside me and casually showed me a technical manual. This, of course, was in Russian, a language alien to me.

'There's Chinese language and foreign language,' the captain exclaimed. 'And aren't you a foreigner?'

The problem seemed to be something to do with the Ilyushin's wings. I demurred and shooed them back to the cockpit.

Our mature students fell into three groups. Nanjing University itself offered up the Special English teachers who taught the prime crop of English majors. There was a second, mixed group of 'General English' teachers from our Department. Alongside them, there arrived a number of individuals sent in from neighbouring work units. The University was no doubt trading well on our rarity value, and notching up many a return favour by allowing these extras to be exposed to the English natives. The first batch included a doctor from the Workers' Hospital, a lecturer from the Meteorology Institute, a chemist from the Nanjing Teachers College, and a couple of middle school teachers.

The General English teachers were responsible for teaching students in every other department of the University. Already at this primeval age of China's 'open door' era, most University students were obliged to learn some English alongside their science. My record book for August 1975 tells me that Wang Chengang taught in Politics, Feng Chao in Maths, Wu Xiuxia in Geology, and the gentle Fu Yuhua in the Astronomy Department. And so it went on through physics, meteorology, biology and chemistry. Every department seemed to be covered, though I often felt that the General English staff should never really have been let loose on students at all. We were never allowed to observe how they got on as they conveyed the beauties of the English language to their respective flocks. The usual paranoia – or could it just have been feudal-minded unit-itis? - meant that we were banned from setting foot in any department but our own.

One or two of the products of the General English teachers' handiwork did, however, seek me out, for like all the students they had a huge appetite for self-improvement. Every morning we were set down by our driver at the University gatehouse – more a ceremonial arch upon which, in huge applied red letters, Mao Zedong's ill-disciplined calligraphy proclaimed the University's name. We then marched up a broad walkway which after a hundred yards was interrupted by the *Wenge Lou*, the Cultural Revolution Building. This was a four-storey teaching block, already looking a bit dilapidated, which was the recent and proud creation of a mass mobilisation of all the University community.

For a while, whenever I stepped into this concrete monster I would be mobbed by the same small group of students, each hoping to hear some pearl of wisdom drop from my lips. I did my best for them, though there were limits. Once, I was hotly pursued into the second floor urinals by a member of this group, who perhaps thought he knew me as well as he did my voice, tape recordings of which had proliferated on the campus.

'My dear teacher,' he annoyingly addressed me, inching ever closer on the slimy concrete while I did my best to concentrate on the business in hand.

'One two four, *hao buhao?*' ('is that OK?'). 'Six, eleven, thirteen, *hao buhao?*'

I am afraid my uncharitable answer to these questionable triumphs of learning how to count in English was '*Bu hao, bu hao,*' ('Not good!'). But my verdict failed to deter this lavatorial acquaintance from hanging around the corridors on the off-chance that I might want to pee while providing him with a private lesson. Such was English mania, Nanjing style, 1975.

A social divide was evident between the Special and General English teachers. The former were definitely smarter, both in the subtle refinements of their dress and in the standard of their English. Not a few turned out to be Shanghainese exiles, a superior breed of intellectual which the First Five Year Plan had scattered throughout the land in a deliberate effort to seed skills widely.

There was an obvious set of equations at work here: my subtle enquiries showed that those chosen for the elite English students – taking the subject as a major – tended to be of minor rural landlord or urban petit-bourgeois backgrounds. They had attended the best schools, such as they were in the chaotic late 1930s and 1940s, and this had given them a head start with English, even though it had since been overlaid with Russian. Of course, most of them were still better at talking about the language rather than actually using it.

The General English teachers could do neither commendably. A lot of this went back to their more humble origins. Most were living witnesses to Mao's *fanshen* idea, his revolutionary precept that everything had to be turned on its head. Often they might be the first from their village or former urban slum, their region even, to go on to higher education. Lacking middle school English, quite a few of the General teachers had graduated with Russian as a main or second subject. Now, in their middle age they had been obliged to exchange the forked tongue of the Soviet revisionists for English. Poor things – from their attentive but anxious faces, it seemed they harboured the vain hope that from our very alien presence a kind of osmosis would suddenly transform them from ugly Russian ducklings to handsome English swans.

At the bottom of the academic heap, the General English team was inflicted on the eager worker-peasant-soldiers of the science and humanities departments. But perhaps they had some compensations, for doubtless their stronger proletarian antecedents meant they had suffered less political flak in the regular campaigns against 'bourgeois intellectuals'. And it was from amongst the General English teachers that the small number of Party leaders of the English Section seemed to be mostly drawn.

Coaxing the final year students towards some comprehensible utterances was only a part of our portfolio. In our eyes, though not in those of the powers that be, our most vital role was as improvers of the linguistic and pedagogic skills of their teachers. But we soon found that we had to start from basics. In a perfect example of 'first language interference,' the Sino-centric Chinese wanted to approach English in the way they had learned their mother tongue. With the Chinese language, progress is more or less measured by the number of new words and phrases committed to memory. Unfortunately, Western languages do not work like that. With Chinese, discrete characters and phrases can be imbibed in long abstract lists. But from the inability to string a simple sentence together, it was obvious to us that this reductionist technique was unproductive when it came to English learning.

If my teacher-students could appreciate the intellectual distinctions between a basically phonetic language such as English and largely non-phonetic, tonal Chinese then we might have been halfway there. For those unfamiliar with these ideas - say a new word to a learner of English and the approximate spelling springs to mind. With Chinese you would be pretty much at sea on hearing a new word.

'Individual words in English aren't the problem - you can always refer to a dictionary,' I pontificated. 'What counts is sentence structure, and this makes English quite different from Chinese.'

My teacher-students would nod knowledgably at such pearly insights. On I went:

'Imagine you're building a brick wall. In Chinese you have to concentrate on each individual brick and the wall takes care of itself. In English, you can forget each brick, but focus instead on the overall shape.'

Unfortunately, my clever metaphors were so much wasted breath. At the end of the session, the little group's monitor-spokesperson would pipe up:

'It is very interesting. But we think that English and Chinese are the same. You have your ABC and we have ours.'

Chinese has many things, but one attribute it clearly lacks is anything remotely resembling an ABC. This was the lovely but hopeless Zhu Dongji, of genuine poor peasant background and the nearest we got to a warm motherly figure in our Nanjing lives. A pre-Cultural Revolution graduate of the Department, she had obviously got where she was because of positive political discrimination. This was an admirable fruit of the revolution. But it was hardly designed to produce an intelligentsia as we would know it.

In the approved spirit of combining theory with practice (another of the daily slogans), we were forever asking our teacher-students to cut loose from their beloved rote learning and grammatical analysis and do something practical with their English. The trouble was face: if they were to abandon their custom of translating grammatical parallels when none existed between Chinese and English, they thought they would be diminished in front of their students. We were even willing to live with the absurd political content, if only there could be a radical change in methodology.

It was not as though, like my Quaker grandparents, I had arrived in China with any sense of mission. But to make some headway against a deeply reactionary pedagogy in this land of the revolution became something of a challenge. Little by little, we somehow got most of our teacher-students to experiment with the new-fangled foreign ways, but the problem of the content remained. With the Emperor still ruling over the Forbidden City, casting any slight doubt on 'Chairman Mao is the Sun' as the first lesson in the English textbooks was going to be a step too far. Somehow we had to learn to work around this uncomfortable given and leaven the national curriculum of political phraseology with practical everyday dialogues.

We realised it was going to be tricky, but were particularly keen to get the teacher-students reading some real, contemporary newspaper English. This was of course a time when official and commoner alike had unshakeable views of Western life which in some aspects pre-dated Dickens. London was a place of unceasing fog (or 'frog' as it usually seemed to come out); Western foreigners lived almost exclusively on bread ('we Chinese eat rice and *mantou* and you eat bread'); everyone in England was either a 'Christian' or 'Catholic' (many a time I was informed that there are two groups of Western foreigners – 'Christians', and *Tianzhujiao*-adherents, that is to say Catholics). And yes – bizarrely - all Westerners were accomplished at the then-forbidden waltz and quickstep.

My quest for contemporary material started just along the corridor from our office, at a usually-locked door which led into the English Section's periodicals room. I only ever saw one of our colleagues, Tang Dongru, enter its portals on a browsing mission. Tang was a likeable figure with a tobacco-stained long-toothed smile - a six-foot beanstalk topped by a full head of slicked back oiled locks. In a land where righteous cyclists were happy with Shanghai 'Eternal' and Tianjin 'Flying Pigeon' bikes, Tang chose to ride a fading green English Raleigh. A small but telling statement. In his deep and gentlemanly tones of almost perfect English, Tang eventually found a way of letting me know that he was in indeed a soul apart. He was an Overseas Chinese from Burma who, like so many of the Chinese diaspora's youth, had been sent 'home' to get a solid education prior to the Cultural Revolution. There was also an element of political calculation on the part of the many Chinese families in Southeast Asia and beyond who had sent their offspring back to the Great Motherland after the 1949 communist victory. The trouble was, things had not turned out as hoped. Just as for the *Yinni Huaqiao* – the Indonesian Overseas

Chinese despatched to China in their hundreds of thousands in the early 1960s - Tang was now stuck in a country which rarely offered exit visas. The returned Overseas Chinese were considered to be irretrievably tainted by the outside world, a condition which ironically permitted them a little privileged access to it. It was this that explained why Tang alone was able to enter the forbidden reading room.

Apart from the Xinhua Daily News bulletins, there were, amazingly, stacks of mostly unmolested newspapers imported from England and the U.S. Somewhere in the University, apparently, was a clutch of pen-pushers whose job it was to get the necessary foreign exchange for such dubious imports. *The Guardian*, published in New York and not to be confused with the *Guardian* back home, was an ecumenical leftist fortnightly with much coverage of U.S. strikes and struggles. Not an issue went by without some fierce condemnation of U.S. imperialism. In China, where all opprobrium had to be reserved for the wicked Soviet Social Imperialists, this could hardly have gone down well, but no one seemed too concerned. Indeed, I was even given permission to use selected extracts from *The Guardian* for the purpose of what was called 'extensive reading' (I assumed that this was reading which was only vaguely to be understood). Nonetheless some of what I chose was obviously too close to the bone: from time to time political commissar Comrade Xu would admonish me in his pleasant way for an incorrect emphasis.

The *Morning Star* was quite another matter. As the daily organ of the Soviet enemy's fraternal Communist Party in the U.K., how it managed to pass the Chinese censors I could never understand. I concluded that the *Star's* presence was not a sign of some lurking heterodox thought. It was far more likely to be the sheer inertia of bureaucrats who had not yet caught up with the Sino-Soviet split of fifteen years earlier. Whether or not the Department's cadres had noticed the *Morning Star's* Soviet sympathies, and its antipathy to American policy, I was certainly the only person ever to take it off that huge pile replenished daily by an unseen hand. I resisted introducing its renegade content to my classes.

It goes without saying that all the great classics of English literature were also taboo. It was, though, strongly enough rumoured for even my ears to resonate with the information that Mao's despised wife Jiang Qing had a taste for translated foreign books. It was even whispered that her favourite bedtime reading was a Chinese version of Jane Eyre. Perhaps the eponymous heroine chimed with Jiang Qing's hoped-for image as a person misunderstood, betrayed, but with determination of steel. It came to my ears that for political allegory Madame Mao was said to favour *The Count of Monte Christo*. I wondered why, and thought I might just know where a copy could be found.

There was a tale I heard about a placard hung above one of Beijing's great city gates to greet the new rulers, the Manchu invaders who took control of China in the mid-seventeenth century. When the Chinese Republic dawned in the early twentieth century, workmen were despatched to remove this odious reminder of the imperial past. Underneath it they discovered another identical placard, except this one dated from the fourteenth century and saluted the new Ming rulers of China. The Chinese obviously knew a thing or two about hedging their political bets. So it was with all the English language books at Nanda which had fallen out of favour in the many political campaigns since 1949.

Underneath one of the great 1920s teaching buildings, with its traditional Chinese tiled roof and pointed eaves, was a dank cavern with row upon row of mildewed volumes. By and large, the Cultural Revolution enthusiasts did not go in for mass book burnings. In Nanda's case, offending texts were hidden from sight, preserved for posterity, and perhaps too for the day when they were once again re-sanctified. And as aliens hopelessly beyond rescue, we were the only members of the University community allowed into the outlawed library.

In a pile of mouldy volumes, I found what I was looking for - *The Count of Monte Christo*. As I devoured Dumas' book in a night's sitting, it dawned on me why Jiang Qing – Madame Mao – was said to favour it above all the other foreign literature at her disposal. The book is all about revenge, the *sine qua non* of Chinese political life. Unfortunately, what was good for Mme. Mao - including the foreign films to which she was rumoured to be addicted - was not good enough for the masses. Yet I was still determined to push the boundaries and give my teacher-students something a bit more challenging and contemporary.

In this, I was greatly encouraged by a surreal event. I happened to be waiting for someone at the University gate one day, under the four giant red characters in Mao's unruly hand – *Nan jing da xue* – Nanjing University. Grinding slowly up Hankou Road I spied a strongman-coolie with shaven temples, a ragged, patched grey singlet and cotton trousers rolled to the knees - the summer uniform of pedicab drivers and handcart heavers. On the last hilly stretch he inched forward, standing on the pedals of his heavily-loaded flatbed bicycle truck. As usual, the throng of pedestrians gawped, no one lifting a finger to help. As the strongman strained past me through the gate and turned in the direction of the University's new library, I was staggered to see a huge pile of newly-bound volumes with *Daily Mirror* keyed in gold letters on their spines. This was the Cultural Revolution, for goodness sake.

Quite a few years had yet to pass before the now late and unlamented Robert Maxwell, the *Mirror's* proprietor, put his publishing house at the hagiographic service of Deng Xiaoping. Perhaps this was indeed high politics – intended as flattery of a crafty tycoon, well known as a visitor to the Kremlin and to sundry dictators elsewhere.

Whatever the case, I took my cue from the *Daily Mirror's* intrusion into the closed Chinese world, and renewed my request for permission to import into China multiple copies of one day's edition of *The Times*. I thought this would be a better bet, with its hard-line anti-Soviet position, than my own natural preference of the *Guardian*. No one was more surprised than me when the request was granted. Even more surprising, weeks later, fifteen copies of *The Times* dated 10 June 1975 and acquired by my mother from a bemused Barnard Castle newsagent, arrived at the Dingshan. By good fortune, that edition of the newspaper carried no stories about China.

In the weeks that followed, we exhausted every possibility in the use of those countless columns of newsprint, stopping only at the notorious crossword. My teacher-students lapped it all up. This was something of a triumph and our perorations were only brought to an end when an article was discovered which referred to the liberation of Saigon by North Vietnamese forces. The official Chinese line was that the northern forces had never come to the south and that it was an entirely indigenous victory over the Americans. Yet again, Comrade Xu was prevailed upon to give me a little talking to, and our fun with *The Times* abruptly ceased.

The third group of very mature 'students' we were let loose on were the professors. Yes, even during the Cultural Revolution, while lecturers were demoted to teachers, the Chinese regard for learning meant that the title of professor survived. Even more surprising, whilst the ordinary teachers earned perhaps 50-70 *yuan* monthly, the professors were rewarded with a princely 400 *yuan*. Their salaries even continued to be notched up when the professorial elite were sent to labour in the countryside, or to clean toilet blocks.

With the British and Americans as the all-pervasive powers in late Qing and Republican China, the English section of what was to become Nanjing University had long acquired an aura of elitism. Before 1949, it had taken in the sons and particularly the daughters of the new urban elite, the richer rural landlords, not to mention the offspring of Guomindang officialdom who, like the first Ming emperors, chose Nanjing as their national capital. Despite the endless levelling of the Mao system, an undercurrent of Nanda superiority could still be detected, kept alive by the presence of a clutch of elderly professors who had been well established long before the Communists arrived.

The most entertaining was 'Hubert' Liang, now well into his seventies. Hubert spoke fast and ceaselessly and had a penchant for Americanisms of the 1930s. He was distinguished by a most unusual soft pink complexion and a beak nose; I never saw him without a fine woollen peaked cap. I guessed that Hubert had survived the Red Guards because of his reputation as a tough journalist who had stuck his neck out against the old order long before the Communist takeover. He told us more than once of his role in exposing the brutality of U.S. soldiers in Beijing in the mid-1930s, a cause of a great wave of nationalist protests amongst China's youth, and one which the ruling Guomindang did its best to suppress.

Venerated by both Communists and Nationalists alike, the first historic impulse for a modern, free China was the famous May 4th movement of 1919. The Versailles Treaty had, outrageously, rewarded Japan with the defeated German possessions in China's Shandong Province, and Hubert had joined the angry rallies which swept Beijing. After the Second World War he had ascended to the lofty heights of editorship of the *China Times*, and was steeped in the political ferment of Nanjing, then the nation's capital, in the period leading up to the final battles leading to communist victory. So this good-humoured old ranter had been witness to all the great moments of China's twentieth century. I wish I had known to ask Hubert more.

'Of course, the Red Guards tried to frame me up a few years ago. I was King Lear, after all,' chuckled Hubert.

The young fanatics had tried to nail him as a bourgeois element – if not a U.S. agent. Hard though it was to imagine in straight-laced 1970s China, a decade earlier the English section had put on a production of Shakespeare's King Lear, with Hubert in the title role. Between productions, he had cheekily posed fully-gowned and crowned in front of one of the University's imposing ivy-clad towers, the one which now bore a large red star. Years later, the Red Guards found the incriminating photo, and claimed it as definite proof that Hubert was a bad lot, a 'feudal remnant' who harboured desires to lord it over the masses.

'It was a joke and I didn't give a damn,' drawled Hubert, pulling a crumpled photo from a drawer. 'I'd had my life and seen and done things these little thugs could never even dream of. As far as I was concerned they could do what they wanted with me, as long as they left my wife alone.'

As it happened they did little, though Hubert, like all his peers, was sent off for a bit of unproductive re-education. He even managed to hang onto his dilapidated Western-style cottage a hundred yards from the campus back gate. I could not fail to notice the gaping holes in the floorboards and the cracked windows, not to mention the scrubby distempered walls lacking any decoration.

'Oh', explained Hubert breezily, 'we keep the place like that to demonstrate our proletarian virtues.'

Heaven knows how, but Hubert and his wife got permission for us to visit for lunch. This venture would have been risky for the most proletarian of our colleagues, let alone a confirmed bourgeois professor.

'Do you how we can afford all these dishes we're offering you?' asked Hubert with a naughty smile. 'So that China wouldn't lose face in front of its foreign friends we were told by the Revolutionary Committee what to feed you, and even given a hand-out so we could go and buy the ingredients.' Our wry looks met.

Professor Mei had also managed to survive the Red Guards despite being educated at an American evangelical college. Yet hers was a far more precarious position as her husband was one of the rare Christian prelates who had escaped the worse attentions of the post-1949 regime. Most senior Christians, especially Catholics whose very existence depended on the now outlawed loyalty to Rome, had been jailed for years. Or worse.

Bishop Ding Guangxun and his family had obviously reconciled themselves to toeing a certain line and now their worries were set to diminish. As China opened up in the 1980s, Bishop Ding of Nanjing, head of the Communist Party-approved Protestant 'Three Self' movement and rumoured to be a high-ranking Party official too, became a mandatory stopover on the tour of any Christian group from the West, a living proof of the liberal credentials of the post-Mao regime. And the good Bishop had learnt great discretion, steadfastly defending the Party's restrictions on Christian activities. By 1984 when I and my fellow travellers from the Campaign for Nuclear Disarmament were granted an audience, it seemed from the size of the Bishop's meetings suite and the black limos arriving and leaving that it had become a full-blown tourist attraction. We found Bishop Ding the consummate diplomat.

We were sometimes informed that meetings were cancelled as the people we were to meet were 'not well'. We realised after a time that their ailments were political rather than medical. Happily, this was not the case with the Bishop's wife. Though Professor Mei was suffering badly from some sort of arthritic condition, and only struggled to the department on special occasions, she was obviously tolerated. The first time we came across her was at the end of our first semester, when in a fit of politically-inspired false humility, we asked for and were given an evaluation of our work to date. A kind of Star Chamber was hastily assembled. Excited at the attention, our janitor Lao Fan had stoked up the pot-bellied stove in honour of the gathering and we entered our normally vacant office to find the air thick with the evaporations from many layers of winter cotton padding. Seated in a circle were the three straight-laced student class monitors, and teachers from each of our English groups. Alongside our own political commissar, the bear-like and Comrade Xu with his crew cut and amiable bad teeth, hunched a frail old woman who piped up in perfect formal English:

'I am Professor Mei and I am glad to make your acquaintance. I am sorry I haven't been to see you before, but as you can see I am not too sprightly.'

It is a curious fact--more of an impression, perhaps--that Chinese long associated with the Western foreigners, especially the Christian ones, somehow take on European facial features. So it was with Professor Mei, who sat before us like an elderly English aunt, there unfathomably to pour the tea.

This melding of physiognomies, this chameleon effect, seems to work both ways. It turned out that we were not entirely alone as foreigners at Nanjing University. Flitting by to the next entrance in the Foreign Languages building, I occasionally spotted an elderly birdlike figure who someone had whispered was Chinese of German extraction. One day I saw her coming up rapidly behind me. I stopped and 'Guten Morgen-ed her and she Guten Morgen-ed me back. Full face on, I could have sworn she was Chinese. This ghost from the past, in China all her life and married to a local, was entirely Sinicised. A curious osmotic effect is at work on many of those who stay in China a long time. Much later, in the deserts of Xinjiang, I engaged a weather-beaten Han farmer in conversation. For once, I got the leading question in first.

'Where do you come from?' I enquired.

'I'm from Zhejiang province and the government moved us all here in the 1950s,' he replied with a loud sigh and an expert expulsion of spittle. Zhejiang is a thousand miles to the east and its lush rural environment is diametrically different to that of the arid Northwest.

'Ni laojia nali?' ('Your ancestral home is where?') he then countered. In those days when foreigners were so few on the ground, most Chinese in the sticks assumed that any weird stranger was one of their own country's fifty-five ethnic minorities. Inured to the way the conversation was going, I am afraid I gave him my usual tongue-in-cheek spiel: I was irrefutably a member of the Ying (England) national minority.

'It's been a very, very bitter life here, but I've gradually got used to it,' he volunteered. 'If you stay long enough you will too, and I can tell you your hair will turn black like we Han,' he added in sympathy to my curly ginger locks.

Perhaps he was right, but I had no intention of finding out.

But back to our little criticism meeting. Our factotum Lao Fan had put on his best black corduroy jacket and was busily bowing and scraping, gold teeth flashing as he delivered our lidded mugs of *molihua* tea. We soon regretted our invitation to our critics, for they turned out to be more sharp-toothed than we had ever expected. The monitors of each of the student groups had mugged up their scripts and gave us a pretty rough ride. I was fairly confident that this was no more than a political necessity. Professor Mei's summing up was rather gentler and we went away with our tails only half-drooping between our legs. One opaque comment which stuck in the craw, and indeed was never to be forgotten between us, was thus: 'You have both made great efforts, but one of you should learn from the other.' While I, as the amateur, was prepared to be a failure in the business of English teaching, and naturally claimed the downside of this enigmatic comment, Jo forever suspected that innate Chinese male chauvinism had aimed this little dagger at *her* heart.

Compared with Hubert Liang and the gentle Professor Mei, Professor Chen Jia with his East Coast American accent was quite a different kettle of fish, for as we have seen, he had somehow crossed the line and become a Party cadre. Modesty or political expediency meant that Chen Jia generally managed to conceal his erudition, but we guessed that he was no slouch when it came to the great literature of the English language. It was easy to imagine that he resented our intrusion into a realm which was rightly his own, one which the political straitjacket now denied him. In a long life of which the present Communist Party-ruled era still covered far less than half, Chen Jia had doubtless had sufficient experience of foreigners to judge us for what we were – two half-trained and semi-literate interlopers who did not know their Marlowe from their Melville. Yet there we were, being accorded all the privileges – car and driver, special office all to ourselves, not to mention salaries equal to his own. Just as in the 'old society' which the Communists had overthrown, and – as we to later find – in colonial Hong Kong, our chief qualifications were, ironically, our foreign big noses.

The bourgeois professor had transformed himself into The Good People's Teacher. Had he not done so, perhaps our instinctive dislike of him would have been tempered by a certain respect. Only now, all these years on, have I made the uncomfortable discovery - from a chance Internet hit - that Chen Jia was actually one of

China's most eminent scholar of early English and Shakespeare. How galling, then, to be forced to put aside his beloved classics and reconcile himself to the childish sloganising of the Cultural Revolution English curriculum.

The few mass meetings which we were allowed to attend took place on the dusty sports field. Here we lined up in perfect military formation in our thousands, to be regaled from the rostrum's forest of loudspeakers with strident denunciations and loud exhortations. In early 1976, it was here that we were assembled in the wailing hysteria of commemoration following the deaths of two big names in the revolutionary vanguard, Zhou Enlai and Zhu De.

Behind one of the teaching blocks was an ivy-strewn hangar-like building with huge red stars adorning each gable. This was the University's largest meeting hall, or 'auditorium' as Chen Jia insisted on Americanising it. Since in political terms we counted for nothing, it was a surprise when we were once invited there for a mass rally of the Party loyal. We were there, apparently, to enthusiastically greet Chairman Mao's 'Two Wise Decisions.' It was April 1976 and the Qingming festival of the Dead which the Communist Party had transmuted into an annual memorial for the revolutionary martyrs. The Qingming processions were used as the cover for vast demonstrations in our city of Nanjing, and later in Beijing. These took on a distinct anti-regime flavour, and the Mao mafia held the recently-rehabilitated Deng Xiaoping responsible. Deng was once more publicly shamed and removed from office. In his place, Mao – supposedly it was he – put Hua Guofeng, an unknown grey apparatchik from his own province of Hunan. Within two years, Hua Guofeng was ousted from power himself, and with Deng becoming China's supremo for more than a decade, the 'wise decisions' we were celebrating that day, like much in Chinese historiography, were later shown to be unwise.

We agitated to attend the Party rally, for we had no idea what direction such events took. Amazingly, for once we were allowed to join in. It was like a revivalist Church meeting, from the pulpit emerged a scatter-gun of fire and brimstone, the congregation belting out their responses. With these came the mandatory shaking of clenched fists, only the right ones. Across the aisle and a couple of rows in front sat Professor Chen Jia, mouthing the responses and wielding his fist with the best of them. Suddenly he turned and spied me observing him. From then on in the meeting, his fist wavered uncertainly at shoulder level. Unlike his younger colleagues, who had known little else, our presence had reminded the elderly, erudite professor of another world, one where Westerners and Chinese academics mingled without much thought of 'politics'. Our insistence at being at the rally had in fact shamed him. We had to understand – hard though it was – that the pompous, politically correct Chen Jia had taken on the Maoist liturgy for reasons of sheer survival.

Shortly after, we joined him at a very different meeting, and we still felt like rubbing his face in it for all the political pomposity and hypocrisy he had shown us since we had arrived in Nanjing.

'Good morning! And do you know whose birth anniversary it is today?' Chen Jia greeted us as we seated ourselves in the deep armchairs of the Revolutionary Committee's meeting room. It was one of our regular audiences with the local Mandarins. As it happened, Jo must have been reading her Xinhua News Bulletin the night before.

'Birthday? Yes, it's Lenin's,' she proclaimed triumphantly.

Poor Chen Jia had temporarily forgotten himself. 'Shakespeare's...I meant Shakespeare's,' he stuttered.

So oppressed were we by all Chinese authority, I am afraid we rather enjoyed his discomfort. But all these years on, I am chastened. My casual coursing through cyberspace reveals that in the years after Mao, Chen Jia revelled in a renaissance of his beloved Shakespeare. In his mid-eighties he had even managed to put together some major literary editions about the bard, ready for a new and very different audience amongst China's tens of millions of English language devotees.

Perhaps our time with our teacher-students was not entirely wasted. With the reign of Mao Zedong a receding memory, political orthodoxy in language teaching methods was gradually thrown to the winds. At the time, I think I can claim that Jo and I were the true pioneers in China of the 'direct method' of language acquisition, and the practical routines which we painfully pioneered were gradually accepted. Seeds planted so laboriously in Nanjing in the mid-1970s eventually blossomed, to become standard practice throughout the land.

IX
FOREIGN EXPERTS?

IT APPARENTLY WAS not quite friendly enough – that 'friends of China' group which first took me to the country back in 1973. At the last minute, Beijing was struck off the itinerary, a rap over the knuckles which the 'Whateverists' of the Society for Anglo-Chinese Understanding had never before experienced. 'Whateverism' was the creed of those who swallowed whatever Chairman Mao and the Party said, regardless of whether it was the complete opposite of an equally strident Party line the day before. There was a lot of it about at SACU's London headquarters of the 1970s. Our being kept out of Beijing, the highlight of any trip to China, was SACU's punishment for smuggling John Gittings, then a *Guardian* journalist and academic, onto a recent 'friendship' tour. He had naturally reported what he saw, and what he saw up in China's Northeast were manifestations of struggle and strife which the Chinese authorities were always desperate to conceal. Yet did not the Chairman himself teach us that 'class struggle is everywhere'?

A couple of years had gone by and it was now May 1975, almost six months into our stint in Nanjing, and high time that we made good that unhappy omission of Beijing. Surprisingly, our Jiangsu officials seemed to agree and we got the prized passes to the capital with little delay. In those days, it was unheard of for any foreign traveller to simply arrive in a city and find their way to their final destination. Just as you were sent off at the beginning of your journey, you would invariably be greeted at the station or airport by a minion from a 'responsible unit' who would shake your hand and usher you into a curtained Shanghai saloon and make unintelligible remarks of local significance as you were funnelled towards your residence. From then on, there would be no escaping the presence of one's hosts, and fat chance of deciding yourself how best to spend the time, other than in a thoroughly politically correct manner.

On this occasion, things were going to be deliciously different. After a thirty-six hour haul from Nanjing, our steam engine emitted a final great sigh in Beijing station. We gathered our bags and stepped down onto the platform. Normally the foreigners' cadres assembled where they calculated the soft-class coach would draw to a halt. This time, no one, just no one was there to stumble over our strange names and shake our hands. Little point hanging around – we thrust ourselves into the jostle of soldiers with their padded cotton bedrolls and cadres with their blue Dacron Zhongshan jackets, each clutching that universal badge of small officialdom, a small black plastic twin-handled bag. The throng carried us through scrubby underpasses and up spittle-strewn concrete steps towards a narrow metal-barred cattle run. Squeezing through the steel barriers, on the outside a red-cheeked woman in the blue cotton uniform of the railways scrutinised our tickets and our strange faces. Then the crush from behind more or less ejected us onto the station concourse.

Within a minute, our fellow travellers had melted away, and the square was all-but deserted. There were none of the hustlers, the trinket sellers, the hotel and taxi touts which mob new arrivals outside stations in today's China. Just a few pea-green taxis parked on the side of the square, and beyond them a cluster of ancient two-seater pedicabs. From where we were standing, all we could glimpse of their owners were bronzed, wiry legs and loosened sandals emerging from under the pedicabs' faded hoods. Ragged masters of one of the few occupations still in private hands, the pedicab drivers had long ago thought it wise to cast aside the customary yells and gestures towards likely punters. But unlike some of the other 'friends of China' we knew, we never allowed our foreign selves to be conveyed across Beijing, imperialist style, by the straining muscles of these shrunken old timers.

We headed instead towards the small taxi park and tapped on the window of one of the vehicles, rousing the somnambulant figure curled on the front bench seat. Unaccompanied foreigners hailing their own taxi was an unknown event in China's capital. The driver looked terrified and waved his hand rapidly in front of his face in the Chinese gesture meaning 'no'. Fortunately, I had our destination written down in Chinese, leaving him little choice. Soon we were settling back on his lace-trimmed rear seat, and speeding along the twenty-mile-long Chang'an Boulevard, through Tiananmen Square and on towards the west. Our goal was the Friendship Hotel – the *Youyi Bingguan*, ghetto to Beijing's non-diplomatic foreigners. Lying in the northwest of the city in the university quarter, the Youyi (as it was universally known) was a vast compound put up in the early 1950s to accommodate the thousands of Soviet specialists who came to the aid of China's first Five Year Plan. Now, its grey brick four-storey blocks, its theatre, shop, tennis courts, swimming with diving pool, and leafy paths were home to a rag-tag united nations, the 'foreign experts' for the new era of purged and pure Maoism.

As we drew to a halt by the first block of the Youyi, my eyes became fixed on a knot of non-Chinese people entering the building. Along the worn paths wandered Caucasian couples with children in tow. From somewhere nearby came the pock-pock of tennis. In Nanjing we had been immersed in never ending sea of Chinese faces. Here we were suddenly back on a familiar planet.

I was jolted from my reverie by a thin slip of paper being thrust towards us. Of course – the fare - the first time we had ever been asked to pay for transport in a land where all was mysteriously taken care of. The taxi swung round and past the two bayonet-wielding sentries. A passing European pointed us towards a corridor at the end of which was a typical Chinese office - sheaves of official forms in red and black ink falling from chairs, a shiny lacquered desk with a glass cover, almost bare except for a large blotter pad and a cluster of ink and paste bottles. As ever, the familiar portrait of Mao in his grey jacket presided over the room. A woman in pink plastic glasses addressed us in correct English:

'What is your work-unit and which unit is receiving you?'

'We're from Nanjing University and they've made the arrangements for our trip.'

The cadre pored over a hand-written list on a lined pad. 'No one coming from Nanjing,'she declared. 'Names and travel passes?'

After more examination of her list, the woman turned towards an anteroom and yelled something. A burly man appeared in a too-tight cadre jacket, and a rapid conversation ensued. After a minute or two, the woman wrote a few words on an official slip.

'Take this to the room desk, please,' she said dismissing us.

Down another dingy corridor of the administration building, we found ourselves in the company of two affable young men in starched white jackets. With no hesitation, one of them handed us a door key and explained in faltering English where we were meant to go.

We plodded towards the most distant block of the compound and entered the stairwell. A man in a smart peaked cap and immaculate dark blue uniform coming passed us on the stairs and turning, asked if he could direct us. He pointed up another flight of stairs.

'Just up there on the right – not a bad billet,' he informed us. 'Oh – I can see you're wondering what a flying man is doing in this neck of the woods,' he went on in the clipped and undulating English of the subcontinent.

'I'm a captain in Pakistan Airways and occasionally when we fly VIPs in from Islamabad we're put up here,' he explained. 'All the odds and sods of the Youyi end up in this block,' he helpfully added, casting his eyes over our bedraggled figures.

We soon found a door that opened to our key, and entered a little one-bedroomed flat, adequately furnished and smelling of tung oil polish. We had realised from our visits to the modern housing blocks that timber in China was at a premium. Here, the wooden flooring, lacquered dark red, gave an added sense of luxury.

Settling to a refreshing mug of jasmine tea, we reflected on our odd reception, or lack of one. There must have been an unheard of mix-up between the Foreign Experts Bureau and the dreaded *Luxingshe*, the China Travel Service, each of which thought the other was looking after us. As it dawned on us what must have happened, we were overcome by the novelty of the situation. Even in China, where nothing was left to chance, it seemed that human error sometimes prevailed. Could we get away with it for the duration? The prospect of a few days in Beijing, for the first time in months deciding ourselves what to do and when, seemed gloriously appealing.

Our short-lived spell of freedom and convivial company at the Youyi also provided the opportunity to reflect on that strange animal, the foreigner in China – or 'foreign expert' as the officials insisted we must be called.

We set out in celebratory mood to find the only Youyi resident whose name was familiar. Everyone else around the Youyi seemed to know Ken Craig too, and we were soon being waved into his second floor flat in a block near the dining hall. Ken and his many intrigues are the subject of a later chapter; it is enough to say that the man was remarkable in many ways, not least in his sheer scale, for China was still a land of universal slimness. Ken's florid features suggested a devotion to the bottle, and over the next few days we were to spend many an hour helping him in this cause.

It was obvious as he regaled us with tart observations on their foibles and shortcomings that Ken was obsessed by his fellow inmates. And having acquainted myself with a good few of the Youyi crowd in the dining block, I myself had some serious questions on the same subject.

'Ken, you and I seem to burn with curiosity about what's going on in China, but I get the feeling that most of the foreigners here are just passing the time in rather comfortable surroundings.'

'Look, just because you're a starry-eyed politico it doesn't mean most people are. And China's embassies have been told to recruit people who won't cause trouble. Surely you've heard of David Crook and his mates, not to mention Rittenberg?'

Ken was referring to some of the old lags who had been around since the beginnings of the People's Republic, and who had got a little too carried away by the Red Guard fervour of the 1960s. Probably because he had risen to a considerable height in the Communist Party, Sidney Rittenberg was, as far as anyone knew, still in a gaol somewhere, while Crook and the others had been let out on condition that they kept their mouths shut about what they had been through in the notorious Beijing gaol. A couple of years later, one of Crook's sons told me he despaired of his father and his policy of sweet-talking the regime, for he had witnessed the most barbaric of tortures.

'I've decided that there are a few simple qualifications for recruitment to Chairman Mao's cause,' Ken went on, waving imperiously at the line of Westerners heading towards the canteen. 'First and foremost you shouldn't have much of an interest in politics, at home or in China. Second, you definitely shouldn't know Chinese, or you'd be likely to get up to all kinds of mischief, what with the street posters everywhere. Next, the Chinese are paranoid about photos, so you shouldn't really know one end of a camera from another.'

I could appreciate the last point, as I'd already had a few run-ins with the cadres about pointing my Olympus OM1 in the wrong direction.

'I've not finished yet,' Ken went on, an ironic grin broadening his broad cheeks. 'The ideal recruits also have a few young kids to keep them busy, and they should relish all creature comforts – cleaners for their rooms, cooks preparing their meals, special shops full of goodies, chauffeur-driven cars, trips out to scenic spots – the lot. If they head into town, the only places they go are the Friendship Store, Beijing Hotel or the so-called International Club. Did you know that the Club is so international that no Chinese is allowed to set foot in it? Same goes for the other places.'

In Nanjing we were on our own and so could not test Ken's sharp assertions about China's foreign expert community. But anyone who spent a few days here in the Youyi could be in little doubt that he was right. We hoped that the same could not be said of the nearest foreign residents to Nanjing, Shanghai's dozen or more foreigners cocooned in the magnificent King Kong Art Deco monster formerly known as Broadway Mansions.

There were, of course, honourable exceptions to Ken's rules of thumb, amongst whom, naturally, we numbered ourselves. Yet ironically, in some ways Ken himself met many of the Chinese criteria. Childless and not even possessing a camera, he also shamelessly revelled in the colonial lifestyle of flunkey-dom that was the Youyi. And in a number of vital respects, Ken should have been anathema to his hosts. I could not help being impressed by his easy repartee with the room boys, who ever seemed to be at his door for some reason or another. Ken spoke Chinese with an unexplained fluency. Even more unexplained were his casual boasts of intimacy with this or that august member of the Central

Committee. It seemed that old Ken was up to his florid ears in politicking.

'How come you slipped through the net?' I archly enquired once his Chinese fluency and his high connections were out. Ken's response, eased from him little by little, was as astonishing as everything else about him.

If we had wanted to teach English to make money and indulge in a life of luxury, like plenty of our compatriots, we would have headed for the Gulf States. Yet the Chinese insisted on showering us with privileges and thrusting luxury upon our unwilling shoulders. Foreign invitees came under the unyielding authority of the grandly titled *Waiguozhuanjia Ju*, the Foreign Experts Bureau, or FEB, as we referred to it. This was an office of the highest body of China's governance – the State Council. When more foreigners were needed, it was the FEB which sent the signals to the Foreign Ministry and thence to the embassies abroad. Surprisingly in a country where most arrangements were left to word-of-mouth, the FEB had managed to cobble together a formal contract which said all that was needed on a single page and was worth most of the paper it was written on, too.

In its eyes, couples - preferably with children to keep them occupied – were considered the least troublesome candidates. Normally, only one in the couple was accorded the 'foreign expert' status, while the partner had to make do with the much more lowly *jiashu* – 'family dependent' position. Chinese male chauvinism was alive and well, and regardless of who was best qualified in the native language, the male in the couple invariably bagged expert status. In most interactions with officials and colleagues, it was the foreign male who would be deferred to. This rightly infuriated Jo, whose professional background as a highly-skilled EFL teacher seemed to count for nothing, while my own meagre experience of EFL was often lauded to the skies. I was a mere hanger-on, but somehow we were both rewarded with foreign expert status. Maybe it was because I had been to China earlier, with an esteemed friendship delegation, and someone on high felt I had to be recognised as a minor Old Friend of China, a *lao pengyou*.

The foreign expert label did have material advantages, none of which we sought but some of which later unexpectedly showed their worth. Experts got higher salaries than non-experts, as well as other privileges such as several weeks' summer trip at government expense. At a ratio of around eight-to-one, our salaries stood in shocking contrast to the 'young' teachers (mostly our seniors by up to a couple of decades) who were our students. But it was our perks which catapulted our lives into the realms of real luxury. At a time when the average housing area for an urban Chinese was a mere 4.5 square metres (and try measuring out that in your spacious lounge), our accommodation was both capacious and luxurious. Hot water on tap, floors swathed in thick Tianjin rugs, starched bed sheets – it was these things which really set us apart. What was more, we did not have to pay a cent for our homes.

Then there was our food. Our colleagues, as for every urban family, faced a daily struggle to put food on their tables. While the rationing system meant that no one was on the rice-line, it was the complicated and time-consuming process of lining up coupons and doing the actual shopping which was so troublesome. Especially as no one had refrigerators, and so it was necessary for a family member to rise at five daily armed with the correct coupons to join the queues for meat and vegetables. For the latter, there was no private selling allowed, and the only source for all was a district covered vegetable market run by the municipality. To the average Chinese family of the time food purchases represented around two-thirds of income, but the monthly bills our beaming chefs delivered to us were a mere 120 *yuan* – around one seventh of our combined 840 *yuan* salaries. To add insult to injury, our employers made a point of supplying us with copious quantities of ration tickets for grain and cotton cloth which we could never use, apparently just to show their munificence.

A sheaf of other privileges attached to foreign expert status. While we suffered the enforced indignity of our chauffeured transport to work, our Chinese colleagues had to struggle in by bike, or squeeze into the ancient trolley buses which at rush-hours were so crushed that breathing could be a difficulty. In those days, no tickets were available for sale at the film theatres, the Chinese opera houses, or for the tediously routine song-and-dance shows, choreographed to press home the latest political message. Rather, tickets were allocated to local work-units, and their leaders were supposed to distribute them on the basis of merit. Even though most shows had little artistic appeal, China's citizenry was so deprived of amusements that there was always steep demand for mass entertainment. As foreigners, we had the dubious honour of getting as many as we desired. Even for us, any puncturing of the monotony was welcome relief, and we never refused an evening outing.

Our fat salaries proved to be an interesting point of dispute with our University bosses. Along with our perennial petitions to the Revolutionary Committee on matters relating to our work and our hoped-for travel plans, there was one which returned to kick us in the pants. Even if we could not live on the campus, ride to work on our bikes or otherwise commune with the masses, at least we were at liberty – or so we thought – to reject some of our outlandish remuneration. For a good few months, we pressed half our monthly wad of cash back onto our protesting minder, instructing him to return it to the University. Far from praising our self-abnegation, we met incomprehension, even anger. Finally the

Committee called us to their lair, the Yellow House.

'You are not satisfied with your treatment,' Comrade Zhou told us sternly. 'Giving back your salary is a bad thing and it is ultra-leftist.'

Next to pro-Soviet tendencies, at this stage of the Cultural Revolution ultra-leftism had become a feared political label, with plenty of its perceived adherents being locked up, persecuted, and in the case of a supposed conspiracy known as the 'May 16th', even executed. In truth, our selfless gesture for the revolution was a threat to the natural order – or at least to the perquisites expected by those of higher station – including no doubt the very leaders who wished to criticise us. But we stuck to our guns.

For some unknown and infuriating reason our first New Year trip, February 1975, never came about, and we had to await the summer holiday before we got the chance to properly leave Nanjing. The summer holiday trips were paid for by the Foreign Experts Bureau, whereas the Spring Festival tour we had to manage ourselves. It was this, in 1976, which put an end to our misguided proletarian gesture. The dreaded *Luxingshe* made no distinction between foreign employees of the Chinese government, foreign diplomats or the odd overseas business person who had permits to visit some of the only thirty or so 'open' places in the country. Each of these had a designated foreigners' hotel, always cavernous and usually almost empty, but charging practically international-scale room rates. A day's stay in these halls of luxury, plus the unwanted but mandatory attention of guides and chauffeurs, could easily set one back a couple of monthly workers' salaries. Before our 1976 Spring Festival trip to Beijing, our minder cleverly foresaw the difficulties we would encounter, and insisted on restoring to us all the thousands of *yuan* we had earlier returned. From that point, we rather quickly ate humble pie and hung onto our foreign expert stipends.

Beijing's Youyi residents were for the most part Western Europeans – French, Italians, a few from Spain. If you met a Latin American, he or she was almost certainly with a Maoist group, maybe even a member of a guerrilla band. The full spectrum of ages could be observed – from elderly Canadian Sinophiles living out a lifetime's dream of China, to a sprinkling of singles in their twenties who had washed up on China's shores almost by chance.

While there were rumours of solitary Romanian or even Polish students arriving in the country, Eastern bloc people were glaringly absent from foreign expert circles. This was, remember, an era of intense anti-Sovietism and the official enmity extended to all of Eastern Europe, barring the Albanians (staunch friends), the Yugoslavs (tolerated) and the Romanians (appreciated for Ceaucescu's ambivalent relationship with Moscow). If there were any foreign experts in town of these latter nationalities, they certainly were not housed in the Youyi.

Unsurprisingly, the most strongly represented group at the Youyi were the English speakers, though more by Australians and New Zealanders than by the British. Few of the latter were sufficiently self-aware to realise that to the Chinese Communist Party, the matter of Hong Kong was an ever-smouldering issue. Despite the routine remarks about American imperialism, I am sure that in the pantheon of wicked foreigners, from the first Opium War onwards, the British were still quietly regarded as the chief tormentors of China. They were, of course, now somewhat challenged in this position by the Russians.

It was not unexpected to find Canadians at the Youyi, for in contrast to the British, they basked in the light of that most heroic and beloved of foreigners – Dr Norman Bethune. Bethune had come to China to aid the Communists against the Japanese, and he had 'sacrificed himself for the revolution'. Mao's famous essay on 'Bai Qiuen' as the Chinese knew him was meant to demonstrate socialist internationalism. The small Canadian contingent had a lot to live up to.

Among the foreigners in the Youyi were a few citizens of the United States, a country which had yet to solidify formal relations with the People's Republic. One or two were even serious China scholars masquerading as ordinary English teachers. If they thought they were going to burnish their academic credentials from within China, they were to be sorely disappointed. No proper research on Chinese society was permitted to foreign academics until 1979, and then only to a tiny, select band.

When it came to the political credentials of at least some of the Youyi foreigners, Ken was not far wrong. In the way that right-wingers back home simplistically used to lump all 'commies' together, whether they were Maoists, Soviet-inspired Stalinists, or adherents of Trotsky, amongst the Youyi crowd there quite a few who had made the extraordinary effort to get themselves into China but remained in seeming ignorance of the chasms which beset the 'communists' of the world. For at least a decade, Beijing and Moscow had been at each other's throats, with communist groupings in Europe and elsewhere rent in two, yet it was still possible to sit next to someone in the Youyi canteen who had never heard of the Sino-Soviet split. I suppose these innocents, having done the rounds of language teaching in tamer lands, merely saw China as the last frontier, and it was the challenge of a lifetime to cross it.

There was, however, a small number of the Youyi band who were certainly in China because of their political disposition. These were the out-and-out Maoists, who divided mainly between Latin Americans and Southeast Asians. Amongst the former, the leftists from Peru and Ecuador seemed to be prominent. There was also a group of rather more mysterious characters who to my unschooled eye might have been from any of the small countries to the southwest of China. Unbeknown to me at the time, the diminutive intellectual-looking man who shared our Youyi staircase was none other than a reputedly firebrand leader of the stalled Malaysian revolution. A few years later, I came across his photo in an article in the *Far Eastern Economic Review* which described how China had turned its back on the armed struggle in the wider world and abandoned erstwhile comrades-in-arms to their fates. All part of the deal between Beijing and Washington.

The foreign Maoists kept themselves to themselves. Though they had come to China either out of necessity as political exiles, or to commune with their Chinese comrades-in-arms, with the exception of a Party reception here or an extra banquet there, the Comrades were treated much the same as other foreigners. Obsessed by anti-Sovietism, Beijing was even then soft-peddling on any support it might have been giving to their movements back home, a matter which they occasionally muttered about.

The Maoists apart, so apolitical were most of the Youyi crowd that in my darker moments I used to wonder how on earth the beleaguered Chinese diplomats locked away in their London embassy went about selecting and vetting the few of us sent to China. The idea which I earlier mooted of the Chinese relying on MI5 was so outlandish that it might have been true. But Beijing's selection criteria for foreigners were probably far simpler. One thing was certain: linguistic or pedagogic expertise seemed of little concern. China's outposts in London, Sydney, Bonn, Paris and Rome knew little and cared less of the exigencies of teaching or editing. Our credentials rested merely on our narrow ability to speak and, in most cases, write our respective native tongues. Regardless of our skills as teacher, 'polisher' of propaganda tracts (that is, 'editor', the task being to render the incomprehensible just comprehensible) for China's myriad foreign language publications or short-wave transmissions, to our Chinese hosts we were all equally valid material. Having said that, it was vital that those chosen should not be boat-rockers, for Chinese officialdom was terrified of anyone who demonstrated too great an interest in the country's 'internal affairs'. Unlike their own population – locked as they were within the Middle Kingdom – in due course foreign experts would go home, and perhaps broadcast their strange experiences to a world which was almost entirely devoid of first-hand information about life in China. In my own case (a boat-rocker to the core), out of respect for the safety of my many interlocutors, I have left a healthy interval of four decades before penning the present memoir.

No one in China in those days, and that included the foreigners, had the luxury of nominating their place of employment. You were simply 'assigned' to your post. Ken, for example, had ended up in the No.2 Foreign Languages Institute, rather than the prestigious No.1, which he claimed had been promised him in Hong Kong. The plummest of the plum postings in Beijing was undoubtedly Beijing University, which hosted a handful of foreign language teachers, amongst them the son of stalwarts of the Society for Anglo-Chinese Understanding. And later, Ken too. The No.1 Foreign Languages Institute had the ageing but 'reliable' Crook couple on its staff as well as a few younger European newcomers.

Then there were the foreign language propaganda media of the Chinese government: *China Reconstructs*, *China Pictorial*, and *Peking Review*, each published in English, French, and Spanish. Not to forget Esperanto, the translation of which was left to the mysterious coterie of Chinese Esperantists. None of the above publications, and especially the weekly *Peking Review* which served as the foreigners' *People's Daily* in a slightly less dowdy frock, allowed much scope for their foreign recruits. Beyond the merest polishing of the Chinese translators' often tortured political prose, the foreign presence seemed to be for trophy purposes only. This was even more true for the sacrosanct tier of official propaganda, China's official wire service, the New China News Agency, which we all knew by its simple Chinese moniker of Xinhua. Also on this level was China's international broadcasting operation which foreigner's called simply 'Radio', housed on Chang'an Boulevard in a Stalinesque tower which showered the world with non-stop shortwave accounts of the glorious victories of Chairman Mao's revolutionary line.

Later in the decade, Jo and I passed some weeks in Beijing while awaiting the arrival of our son Yongshan. Mao had by then 'gone to see Marx' while his ultra-left coterie had gone to gaol. But in the realm of propaganda, little had changed. One of the people I perversely enjoyed as dinner companion in the Youyi canteen had drawn the short straw: he was a 'polisher' at Xinhua. Robin, who had been sent to Beijing by the Chinese embassy in Ottawa, could be guaranteed to entertain me by his rants on his daily struggle with Xinhua English. Perhaps poor Robin's experience was the reason why the serious, mainly Third World, adherents of Maoism were over-represented in China's propaganda media. They were generally types who were not inclined to kick up a fuss. A number of unwritten commandments circumscribed the life of the foreign expert. In their work, just as for the Chinese, the foreign employee was expected to fulfil whatever duties were requested and without demur. The idea of employee consultation had not yet reached China. Unsurprisingly, we never quite got used to having our duties altered at the drop of a hat.

Other than Beijing, the Foreign Experts Bureau channelled its flock to just a handful of places of learning around the country, almost all of which were in the elite club of 'key-point' universities. After Beijing, with its several dozen foreign experts, came Shanghai with around fifteen assorted foreigners - spread between Tongji and Fudan Universities and the Shanghai Foreign Languages Institute. Tianjin, with its famed Nankai University, managed to grab a few foreigners, amongst whom were Maurice and Helen – to whom I shall return soon. That our Nanjing University merited a quota of 'experts' was unsurprising. Nanda considered itself, on the quiet, second only to Beijing University. If appearances were anything to go by, with its fine buildings spread around a leafy campus, it certainly was.

Apart from these four traditional centres of learning, there was a mere handful of other cities where foreign intruders were allowed. Xi'an's Foreign Languages Institute had a single Australian, Hangzhou University a couple of English people, and in Suzhou, the ancient Jiangsu city of canals and formal gardens, resided another lone Australian female, assigned to the Textile Institute. This was an odd case: perhaps it was because of China's growing textile exports and the need to supply correct English on those little silky labels, as well as on the garments themselves. With T-shirts, this was always a bit of a problem in the early days. I found that in Hong Kong, where almost everyone relied on cheap Mainland clothes, you could find the locals wandering the streets with 'I love labour', or even 'Squeeze Here', emblazoned across their chests.

The alluring foreign devil community at Shanghai was a mere five hours to the east of Nanjing by slow train, though in view of the elusiveness of Shanghai Travel Passes it often seemed five light-years distant. The great metropolis, we were informed in hushed tones, was not a suitable place. 'Class struggle is fierce in Shanghai,' our Nanjing hosts would inform us, as if to suggest we would somehow be swallowed up in an evil ideological pit full of sharp bamboo spikes. After a time, we realised that Nanjing officials lived in fear and awe of their Shanghai counterparts, and simply did not want to get involved with them. And sending foreigners to their patch meant getting involved. At the best of times, Shanghai people were known to give non-Shanghainese a hard time; now, in the poisoned, final phase of the Cultural Revolution, all Mao's movers and shakers had coalesced in the city, and it was a place to be avoided.

Not that we were intimidated – far from it. More than once on a Saturday morning we had our bags packed and waited vainly for Driver Zhou to whisk us to Nanjing station for the Shanghai express. Had not Li An, the department's Party boss, agreed so smilingly to our weekend in Shanghai? Not a bit of it – he was only being polite and giving us the desired answer. So during over two years in Nanjing, we managed to get to the great city just twice. The train journey was an experience in itself, the steam locomotive and its smut-filled draught adding to the charm of our brief escape. Normally we had no choice but to travel in an enclosed first-class sleeper, away from the common herd. But the Nanjing to Shanghai stretch was considered too short to confine us to 'the usual 'soft-bed' compartment.' We were allowed instead to occupy 'soft seats', admittedly still highly superior, as demonstrated by our travelling companions - PLA grandees and smartly-dressed cadres. But in an open carriage for once, there was at least some aura of normality.

The route eastwards followed the ever-widening Great River, the Yangtze. We rattled along past thatched peasant huts, beside the neatest of wheat or rice fields, and through the old world townscapes of Changzhou, Wuxi and Suzhou. Once in Shanghai's nineteenth century station, now long demolished, our unattended hours ended. There was no question of finding our own way to Shanghai Mansions, the *Dasha*, where the resident foreigners lived, and where a spare apartment awaited us. Thankfully our meeters and greeters from the Shanghai *Luxingshe* were a little more worldly-wise than elsewhere, and made only half-hearted efforts to fill our precious two days with factory tours and the like. When I was in the city back in 1973, I informed them to their evident relief, I had already done the standard round, including a visit to the Children's Palace. This showpiece run for the offspring of the politically favoured was located in one of the Kadoorie family's confiscated villas; the children were always ready to give passing foreigners a thrashing at table tennis.

The *Dasha* was excitement in itself. Its rooms and apartments were sheer 1930s Art Deco luxury – maple panelling, chromium plated fittings everywhere – today all sadly swept away in a slew of modernisation. Towering King Kong-like over the confluence of the Suzhou Creek and the great Huangpu River, far below our fourteenth floor room, coastal sailing junks with patched rust-hued sales tacked to-and-fro against the powerful flow. Heavily-laden coal barges, awash to the gunnels, inched out into the main stream in strings hundreds of yards long. Next to the famous steel bailey bridge over the Suzhou Creek –the Garden Bridge - lurked a grey Baroque building half shrouded in trees and surrounded by a high, spiked fence. Before the Bolsheviks, this colonial-style structure had been the Russian consulate, and had later been taken over by the Soviet Union. By the late 1960s, there were no consulates left in Shanghai, let alone that of the Soviet enemy. Nonetheless, a Soviet presence of sorts still existed and the building was now home to a Soviet shipping company. Trade had to go on, even with the hated former 'Elder Brother'. I was told that the Russian staff never ventured onto the streets, but left that to a complement of Chinese staff supplied by the central government. No doubt they were well trained in matters other than the buying of cabbages in the market.

Just over the Suzhou Creek we could look into the red-tiled roofs of a building in European style, set in a large garden, the former British Consulate, only seized by the Chinese a few years earlier.

If the surroundings were exhilarating, the company at the *Dasha* was even more so. Starved of companionship for months, we revelled in the company of Shanghai's foreign community – the fiery Italian Maoists, the staid young Germans and the ever-wickedly amusing Susan, one of the few graduates of Chinese to get into China. In contrast to most of the *Youyi* crowd up in Beijing, the dozen or so Shanghai foreign experts seemed interested in Chinese affairs, in particular in the ever-present power struggle at the top of the Party. Shanghai was, after all, the epicentre of the Cultural Revolution ideological battle. Fuelled by Chinese booze from the red-tiled building in the old British Consulate grounds – now the Friendship Store – we indulged in a fiesta of debate with our Shanghai colleagues.

While it was this simple circumstance of interchange with like-minded friends which really made Shanghai, there was also the buzz of the great commercial thoroughfares like Nanjing Road. Here, in the giant Xinhua bookshop, I might even find a newly-published children's atlas of China or some political ephemera of more than passing interest. And then there was the ships'chandlers down near the docks. This was a dark treasure cavern where hard cheddar-like cheese and brown-skinned lemons could be found in enough quantity to last us several weeks, sometimes months. It was here that I bumped into a middle-aged Westerner in a smart suit, looking entirely out of place amongst the dusty piles of rope and sacks of pulses. The stranger surprised us by introducing himself as a resident banker. Despite the ban on Western businesses since the mid-1950s, and despite the Red Guards of the 1960s, two of the old imperialist *hongs* had been able to maintain a quiet presence in the city. Both the Standard Chartered and the Hong Kong & Shanghai banks had for a century operated out of prominent premises in downtown Shanghai. To the passer-by in the 1970s, their buildings appeared locked and barred, the window panes unwashed for years. Outside, wandering up and down the pavement, you could usually see an armed militia man.

From the early 1950s, through to the late 1970s, a single representative from each bank stayed in the city, living in their offices. They were not allowed to leave until a foreign colleague arrived to replace them. Difficult as it is to believe in the teeming and cosmopolitan metropolis which is 21st century Shanghai, in the 1970s the lonesome duo were the only resident Western capitalists across the vast territory of China.

Beijing's accommodation with select members of the foreign capitalist class was evident wherever a pragmatic advantage was to be had. In early 1975 we shared a table at the Nanjing Hotel with two rare visitors – should I describe them as exotic? Maggie Keswick, whom I had known when we were both students at London's Architectural Association, was on a tour authorised personally by Premier Zhou Enlai. The Keswicks were, and remain to this day, the principal family associated with the 19th century opium-running of the firm Jardine Matheson. In the twentieth century, the company developed into a dominating Shanghai, and latterly Hong Kong-based trading conglomerate. Interestingly it is now Bermuda-registered: rumour has it that Deng Xiaoping refused to proceed to the 1997 'Chinese takeaway' of Hong Kong until the old sinners removed themselves. But back in 1975, neither Jardine Matheson's nefarious history, nor the radical Maoist supremacy of the time seemed to disturb either side of the bargain. Maggie and her aristocratic mother seemed quite at home in Cultural Revolution China, while the Chinese Communist Party seemed quite comfortable to use the old opium smugglers in their overseas trading through their Hong Kong base.

As has been endlessly remarked, social contacts between the

foreigner and Chinese colleagues were confined to the abstrusely formal. It goes without saying that sexual liaisons were absolutely taboo: any slight hint of a Chinese-foreign relationship was firmly stamped upon, usually with the Chinese partner being sent into distant exile. Yet despite the risks, I knew one ardent Chinese lover, a gangly man in his thirties, who risked being shot night after night. Incredible though it may seem, he managed to slip past the armed patrols and scale the high perimeter wall of the Youyi to spend nights with a lovesick Australian expert called Pat. I asked Pat straight out how it worked. She was philosophical, explaining as Mao once might have done in terms of 'contradictions', the 'unity of opposites'. On the one hand, Pat speculated, an evident national trait was submission to authority, a fear of standing out in the crowd. On the other, some Chinese might engage in breathtaking acts of individual daring with no thought to the consequences. In a different context entirely, one thinks today of the lone figure nonchalantly challenging a tank during the 1989 Tiananmen uprising.

There were, however, rumours of an officially connived-at exception to the prohibition on inter-racial sex. Just about the only proletarian visitors to China were seafarers arriving on the occasional foreign vessel docking at Shanghai, Qingdao or Tianjin. The authorities laid on every welcoming luxury for their surprised guests – the best food, the most interesting evening entertainment, and so on. But there was a problem: if the foreign seafarers were sent away from China's shores unsatisfied in all their appetites, it would be bad for the country's image. A powerful traditional belief in China is that unlike the natives, all foreigners are sexually incontinent. Thus, the International Seamen's Clubs in each port were told to procure women for the foreign sailors. Prostitutes were available, but only for those with a drop of Chinese blood in their veins. In this way, the Southeast Asians at least could not complain that the Chinese revolution was deficient in proletarian internationalism.

I shall relate the tale of the very first foreigner permitted to marry a Chinese citizen for well over a decade. Australian Susan D was a lone foreign expert at one of Xi'an's top universities. Back in the eighth century when the city, then Chang'an, was capital of the Tang dynasty and terminus to the Silk Route, it was home to tens of thousands of foreign souls. But in the early 1970s the place was an isolated backwater, for it was not yet famed for the Qin emperor's terracotta army, only discovered in 1974. Like us, Susan D was the only non-Chinese in a province of tens of millions.

It might be thought that Easterners 'running amok' is nothing more than a colonialist's patronising fantasy, worthy only of a Somerset Maugham tale. That is not the case – in many countries of the East it is a rare but recognised social phenomenon. Often the perpetrator may well be regarded as not truly responsible for his actions, and thus escape serious punishment for his (usually his) horrific acts of violence. In China at the time, foreigners were so few that they were perhaps natural targets, though we never heard of any other such case. Anyway, Susan D was strolling in one of Xi'an's parks when a man attacked her with a meat cleaver. Somewhat half-heartedly, it has to be surmised, for she survived and eventually recovered from her injuries, minus part of her scalp.

The thing about Susan was that she had fallen for one of her students, a cheeky soldier of her own age, who apparently reciprocated her feelings. In China, nothing can be hidden. What made it worse was that the young man's father was a very senior People's Liberation Army officer, so those ubiquitous state secrets came into the equation. Predictably, the lad was swiftly exiled to an unknown location.

'But how about Susan's assailant?' you might ask. Unlike in the

Soviet Union, where the perfectly sane were often locked away in mental institutions, the official line in China was that in a society steeped in cleansing Mao Zedong Thought, mental illness did not - indeed *could* not - exist. Amongst the foreigners who got to hear of it, the Susan incident quite blew this cover. And it did not help that the runner-amok suffered the ultimate punishment of a bullet in the back of his neck – or so it was said.

The affair took on an unexpected twist. The Susan D incident in Xi'an could not be hidden from the Australian Embassy, and when Gough Whitlam, Australia's recently deposed premier and an 'old friend' of China, visited Beijing in 1977, he decided to mention Susan's plight to the up-and-coming supreme leader, Deng Xiaoping. Now, Deng and Whitlam had a thing going: Whitlam had first brought tribute to the court of Beijing back in 1971, a year before Kissinger and Nixon and their ice breaking 'ping-pong diplomacy', and one of Whitlam's first acts as premier had been to establish full diplomatic relations between Australia and China, in 1972.

'It would be most damaging to our two countries' relations if my people knew of the terrible attack on one of our citizens,' Whitlam ventured. 'Perhaps everything would be forgotten if Susan D were allowed to marry the man she loves.'

Deng must have blanched at this, but decided to take the medicine. Within months, Susan and her would-be lover were married, and out of China. On their way to Australia in the summer of 1978, they stayed with us a few days on the island of Cheung Chau. Susan's new husband, Chen, was certainly a character. He claimed to have evaded the police for some time by slipping into the well-guarded Beijing Hotel and making himself comfortable in vacant suites. We chortled together as Susan and he regaled us with their story - how a blow to a foreigner's head could force the authorities to abandon one of their sacred principles. Years later, in

1989, Whitlam returned the compliment to Deng by urging foreign powers not to boycott China following the Tiananmen debacle.

My Trotskyist leanings notwithstanding, I had gone to China half-believing in the anti-bureaucracy egalitarian propaganda of the Cultural Revolution. And any foreigner who thought they were in China to participate in the local political process was badly mistaken. Granted, under pressure from their flock, the FEB had conceded that those who wished it could have some kind of regular 'political study'. This took place in parallel with whatever the population had been told to 'study' – always relating to whatever was the latest *yundong* launched by the chief ideologues. As such, it was hidebound sloganeering, boring, and often the purpose was entirely opaque.

Despite the ubiquitous slogan 'politics in command', our hosts were not the least moved by the political passions which a minority of their foreign workforce brought to China. In our case, these passions came from our own heady experiences in the anti-Vietnam War movement, in all the struggles we had engaged in against corporate capital's transgressions in our native land. So living in China was like inhabiting a political vacuum: we could neither properly engage in the country's political processes (even had we wished to, which would have been perverse), nor could we relate to what was happening back home and in the wider world.

Precious few foreign experts ever dared to challenge their political straitjackets. Stars amongst these were Maurice and Helen, Londoners attached to Tianjin's Nankai University. Along with Ken Craig, a mutual friend, these two were our closest kindred spirits in China. Not that we actually met them more than two or three times. But we wrote, though the Chinese post office seemed to take 'special care' of our letters (perhaps walking them between

Tianjin and Nanjing, so long did they usually take to arrive).

We first came across the Tianjin couple on Nanjing's North Zhongshan Road, the artery beyond our hotel's walls. It was astonishing enough to see foreigners out strolling on our streets, but Maurice and Helen were making a real performance of it. Waltzing along the pavement, they would whirl round and then rush forward in tango mode. Naturally a large number of cyclists were halted in their tracks by the outlandish show, spilling over from the cycle lane onto the main carriageway and causing the olive Liberation trucks to swerve and honk their impressive horns. Suddenly Maurice, the spitting image of Groucho Marx, moustache and all, broke away and proceeded to chase up the street in a Monty Pythonesque funny walk. Helen, diminutive and busty, caught up with him and took to beating him on the backside in admonition. The crowd, now gathered around them in a large circle, gawped in amazement at the bizarre street theatre, and only parted when another weird being – this time myself – pushed through them to hale the delightful strangers. After bowing to their audience the couple backed themselves in past our sentry post and into the privileged serenity of the Nanjing Hotel compound.

M & H, it turned out, were on holiday from Nankai. Or more accurately, they had been despatched to Nanjing for a spell of political tourism, to see with their own eyes that First Wonder of the Cultural Revolution, the Nanjing Yangtze River Bridge. We made the most of their boisterous presence, and it was definitely an occasion to uncork a couple of bottles of *xiangbin* which laid up from the Friendship Store. This *xiangbin* beverage came in a heavy-duty bottle with a wired cork. In defiance of common marketing sense, let alone political rectitude, right through the Cultural Revolution some winery in North China continued to produce a Chinese 'champagne' which no local could possibly either desire or if foolish enough, purchase.

Though their greatest act of defiance was yet to come, Maurice and Helen described how they had gone about establishing something of a dissident reputation in Tianjin.

'Ever seen owls in the daylight being mobbed by other birds? Well that's how it is in Tianjin,' Helen said bitterly.

'It's the same wherever foreigners are in short supply,' I replied. 'Look at that crowd you've just been entertaining.'

More forthright than us, the couple had decided to kick up a fuss about this staring and street mobbing. Routinely, when China's National Day came round, municipal Revolutionary Committees got orders from Beijing to invite any foreigner in town to a banquet. M and H had used the occasion in 1974 to fire a broadside against the Tianjin leaders on the matter of the staring masses. Etiquette had been seriously breached, yet the leaders nonetheless responded by launching a 'be polite to our foreign friends' campaign: notices were sent out to work-units and neighbourhood committees, meetings were held. But as in Nanjing, there were so many out-of-towners on the streets that just as with the periodic anti-spitting campaigns, nothing changed. Having witnessed M & H's shameless attention-seeking on the streets of Nanjing, I could not help thinking that no one could blame the Tianjin masses for gawping at these particular foreign devils.

M & H had stuck their necks out, and in turbulent Cultural Revolution China that was an invitation to trouble. And trouble arrived with a vengeance, for our friends strayed well into forbidden territory. On the childish basis of 'my enemy's enemy is my friend', Beijing had developed a loathsome habit of issuing gushing invitations to the most anti-Soviet personalities of Europe and the America. No line was drawn between still-serving politicians and those whom their citizens reviled and had rejected. Of the former Special Friends to be wined and dined by the Chinese Communist leaders were the likes of Henry Kissinger (architect of the rapprochement with China of the early 1970s, while bombing the people of Indochina back towards the Stone Age), and from Europe the much-hated fascist-leaning Franz-Josef Strauss of Bavaria.

It was not the invitation to the deposed Prime Minister of Britain, Edward Heath, that was to seal the fate of Maurice and Helen, but Heath's visit to China allowed us all a practice run. With the hindsight of decades of British governments since, far, far to the right of Heath's administration, it is hard to credit that the avuncular and bumbling Heath was so hated at the time by us leftists. But the Chinese loved Heath almost as much as they loved Richard Nixon, for it was during his government's tenure that China and the U.K. moved to full diplomatic relations. Why did this matter? Beijing was obsessed with the idea of Soviet encirclement. Their hysterical calculation was that if the Americans were thrown out of Vietnam, as they were about to be, the Russians would move in. Heath and his like murmured their agreement. To our utter disgust, the Chinese government sent a special plane to fetch Heath to Beijing, along with his beloved grand piano. Heath then spent a pleasant week or two being banqueted and soireed by the ex-guerrilla fighters who now led China – all copiously reported in the official press. In Nanjing, we became heartily sick of our students' starry eyed questions about our 'great leader' and his piano.

We agreed in advance with Maurice and Helen that when this Heath outrage came to pass, we would mount some sort of protest. But in the event, the most all four of us dared to do was a stay-at-home, hardly a courageous stand. On the day Edward Heath was feted in the Great Hall of the People in Beijing, we claimed to be too ill to go to work.

Troubled by their own cowardice, M & H were determined

to pull out all the stops when the Chinese leaders invited the disgraced ex-President Nixon to town. This time their protest was loud and magnificent. Not only did they refuse to teach, but from their upstairs window they hung a bed-sheet emblazoned with the words 'Nixon go home'.

For their pains, they were harangued for hours by the local political commissars, a frightening experience even to our bold comrades. Nixon carried on being the toast of Beijing and it was Maurice and Helen who went home. The pair were put on the next plane to Guangzhou and escorted to the border, where they took a one-way walk over the Lowu Bridge into Hong Kong.

I admired M & H and always wondered what happened to them. Some years later while attending an anti-Cruise missile demonstration in London, I was delighted to bump into Helen, now single. Apparently Maurice had managed to go native in a more welcoming land than China. He had last been spotted somewhere down the Nile, living out his fantasies in full Arab robes and headgear.

I knew of several foreign experts who could not hack it in China and left long before the end of their contracts. But I was aware of only one other expulsion, and this was somewhat closer to home. Well into our second year in Nanjing, the Spanish section of our department was allowed to recruit a couple of experts from overseas. One of these was a short, wiry Peruvian called Antonio, a convinced Maoist who up until the Chairman's death in September 1976 could be relied upon to faithfully parrot the Party line. The Party machine then started to heavily promote new Chairman on the grounds that he was Mao's 'chosen successor'. 'Ni ban shi wo fangxin' -'With you in charge, I am at ease' - Mao was supposed to have told Hua Guofeng and for a few weeks this phrase became the leitmotif of a strident propaganda campaign. One day I was busy teaching my third-year students when a couple of University workers strode into the classroom and without a by-your-leave made themselves busy behind me. They were moving the Great Leader Mao's portrait a little to the left and matching it with an identically-sized portrait of the new Wise Leader Hua. The newly crowned Chairman had contrived a slicked-back hairstyle identicial to Mao's.

To my great surprise (for I had thought him to be just another opportunist) this kind of thing was too much for Antonio, who went round the place loudly denouncing China as no better than a hereditary monarchy. The erstwhile Comrade was summarily expelled, and the last time I heard of him he had apparently gone off to join the Shining Path guerrillas, probably to be gunned down on some dusty Andean hillside.

Above all it was power politics rather than the inconveniences thrown in our path by the bureaucrats, or for that matter by the staring masses, which for me made China such a trial. In the mid-1970s, China was becoming ever more aligned with all the global forces which repelled me – the ultra-right who had come to power after the Allende government's overthrow in Chile, the ghastly Mobutu in Zaire/Congo, the brutal U.S.-supported guerrilla forces in Portuguese Africa, the right-wing Tories in my own country. In 1979, when the Americans were kicked out of Iran, the Pentagon struck a still-secret deal with Beijing. Their listening stations against the Soviet Union which had been overrun by Iran's revolutionary guard were replaced by ones in China's far western province of Xinjiang. Even worse, as part of the deal with Washington, Beijing launched a ground war against Vietnam, whose long-suffering people were only just recovering from over two decades of invasion and terror.

I was always cynical about China's official 'friendship' policy, but I went along with it ultimately for the sake of my research into China's urbanisation process in its peculiar centrally planned economy. I had, after all, committed years of my life to this project. I will always be in awe of the Communist Party's record during its long struggle for power; against overwhelming odds, the Communists saw off the imperialist forces of both West and East, and at the same time rid the country of the corrupt amalgam of comprador capital and landlordism that was the Guomindang. Despite the distortions and often cruelty of the Party, my view is that the verdict of history on the pre-1949 period is positive. But if I had any socialistic illusions about the Chinese Communist Party's policies, especially those towards the outside world after, say, 1970, they died long before the great uprising of 1989 - known to the world simply as 'Tiananmen'.

X
AT THE RICE ROOTS

EXHAUSTED AFTER A DAY'S labour under a burning sun, I had just enough energy to slurp up some of the rice and vegetables offered by our chain-smoking cooks. Our bowls were filled from a huge vessel balanced over the mud-brick straw-burning stove which we had built under a bamboo awning by our cottage. Before falling insensible under my thick cotton quilt – for despite the heat, the cottage was always damp - I would head outside to satisfy a call of nature. More pressingly, my hope was to gain a few minutes on my own. Westerners are not easily attuned to *renao* – the comfort of a crush of other human beings, their 'noise and warmth' as the untranslatable term is perhaps best rendered.

My hoped-for place of solace was nearby our billet in the house of the three rosy-cheeked lasses. Opposite their single-storey cottage and a short walk over the threshing ground, lay the village privy. Like all such facilities in the countryside, it was constructed of mud-bricks and thatch. The males on one side, the females on the other. Inside, the 'plumbing' was like this: the back wall, constructed a few feet over the emerald rows of the rice seedling beds was perforated at ground level by three brick-less apertures. One did one's business against this wall, and gravity did the rest, or so it was hoped. Cleaning of the latrines was a popular theme in the 'Serve the People' sermons with which the Party regaled stubborn Chinese individualism. But just as in the shops, where most assistants only served the people with the greatest reluctance, when it came to the latrines no one sought the laurel crown.

The stench and then the sight was never enough to discourage me from my evening sortie. I would even wield the wooden paddle and helped the stinking, variegated little heaps of human waste, crawling with enormous white maggots, on their way down to nurture the seedlings. Even when I was observed at this task on consecutive days I was never proclaimed a selfless hero of the people.

That did not bother me so much as did two persistent students. I still wonder whether it was Minder Wang who sent them after me to see what nefarious activity the foreigner could get up to in a privy. Or was it, more innocently, just to stop me from feeling lonely?

More likely it was my students' interest in the corporeal realities of a strange red-haired apparition with his trousers below his knees. A lad called Chen, the ex-barefoot doctor, would thrust down his own pants and squat beside me, while another of my third years did the same on my other side. Chen would then withdraw an un-tipped acrid cigarette from his jacket's top flap, light it and thrust it into my mouth. A few awkward minutes passed, punctuated perhaps by a question or two about English grammar. Abandoning any further effort to find peace and quiet, I would be escorted back to the *renao* of our cottage.

It was not as though we had never before had a chance to make sorties into the villages and workshops of China. But being *in situ* for days, weeks, on end was another thing altogether. As any political tourist well knew, the Chinese hosts were all too eager to arrange tours of not-quite-Potemkin villages, or opportunities to scribble down the innumerable production figures offered up by factory chieftains. And in truth, I was never reluctant to enter the portals of yet another revolutionary committee's reception room, with its armchairs and low-slung tables protected by sheets of glass, its black-lacquered trays piled with Zhonghua cigarettes, rarely-seen fruit, and wrappered 'White Rabbit' bon-bons. Our thirst would be quenched with tea in fine porcelain lidded mugs, watchfully recharged by smiling young attendants, and all overseen by a centrally placed framed portrait of the Great Helmsman, Chairman Mao.

At least these forays broke the monotony of cloistered lives, and they sometimes meant the bonus of cancelled classes too. And yes – you could often glean some little sense of what was going on in the country at large from these visits. Doubtless, for most of China's miniscule foreign community the novelty of such outings was clouded by the weary repetition of the latest slogans. As for myself, I was always up for the game, always prepared to fire suitably couched questions at the 'responsible comrades'. And just occasionally we would be rewarded with a heterodox straying from the script. We China-watchers-from-within were always intent on divining the runes, and when the chairman of this or that revolutionary committee slipped in an unexpected remark about the latest political campaign, I felt the tedium had been worth it. This was a period when *yundong* rolled in like ocean breakers, and you were never quite sure when the last had ended and the next was upon us.

This chapter is no treatise on the nature of China's countryside under Mao; rather, it offers a glimpse of rural life in the mid-1970s in a tiny slice of the vast nation; in particular, the observations of a sometime naive foreigner parachuted into a village to work alongside their his worker-peasant-soldier students.

It was 1975, and a few weeks after the February holiday; in our ignorance we had been cheated of that Spring Festival break, literally ordered to stay in Nanjing Hotel and map out yet more teaching plans. Now, out of the blue, we were informed that our students would be disappearing from early May onwards. Announced Minder Wang in perfect *Peking Review*-ese:

'The third-year students must go to labour in the countryside to learn the spirit of hard struggle and plain living from the poor-and-lower middle peasants. And you will stay in Nanjing and prepare more lesson plans.'

We had heard, wrongly as it turned out, that Michael S, the sole imported member of the English faculty at Beijing University, had been allowed to join his students when they went off-site to 'learn from' the workers and peasants. To our growing pile of appeals to the distant Foreign Experts Bureau, typed laboriously on our lumbering Seagull typewriter, was added a new missive. If the students needed a dose of hard labour alongside the masses to keep them on the straight and narrow, surely their bourgeois foreign teachers did too? The *Yingguoren* (Englishman) at Beida had been included, we loudly pointed out, and in China where rules were thin there was nothing like a precedent, especially when the name of Beida, our Nanda's arch-rival, was invoked.

The Nanda cadres ummed and ahhed for a time and then came their surprise decision, delivered to us by the Party Secretary of Foreign Languages, Li An. If I call Li An inscrutable then maybe I am in danger of stereotyping. This was the man who had been first in the greeting line at the airport when we arrived, and since then he had assumed the role of University mouthpiece. On one occasion when we asked to visit a particular place outside city limits, Li An responded that, sadly, the road was under repair. When we insisted, he claimed that in fact there was no road to the place. Further insistence brought the classic: 'Even if there were a road it would be under repair.' This was Li An at his worst.

Decades later, I was delighted to have a visitor to our Lake District home, my favourite Nanda acquaintance, Professor Yang. Back then, in Nanjing University days, he had been one of my mature students, and after the passing of the Mao era he had risen to erudition as a senior academic with a national reputation. His visit was the first chance I had really ever had to reminisce with someone closely involved with our Nanjing lives, in that strange final phase of the Cultural Revolution. Yang assured me that the long-departed Li An wa not such a bad fellow, he was simply neurotic about making an error with regard to the foreigners. He had earlier been accused of being one of the University's 'bourgeois authorities' and savagely treated, and now with our arrival on the scene the poor man had drawn the short straw. Li An had the infuriating habit of addressing us in riddles: on several occasions he confounded our foreign minds by promising 'x' when he did not even mean 'y'. In part this was the Chinese way with words (never refuse a request, at least verbally) but mostly it was his terror of making a wrong decision.

During a ritual audience in the Yellow House, however, the man's message was straightforward: 'You will go out of the campus with the students to witness the poor-and-lower-middle peasants' struggle against nature and feudal remnants to build the glorious socialist countryside.'

He went on: 'Your new home will be the 15th Team of the Dongwang Brigade of Moling *renmin gongshe* (people's commune).'

There was no mention of how long we would be in our new home, and I guess Li An had no idea either. It all depended on the direction of the constantly evolving political campaigns, the *yundong*. We had heard that in some universities the worker-peasant-soldier students had been rusticated indefinitely.

But we were astonished. Whoopee! A chance at last to get down to the rice roots, to get beyond the reception hall and sanitised *kanyikan* ('look see') on yet another revolutionary committee's patch. Our students were to embark on a stint of *kaimen banxue* - 'open door schooling', a key feature of Mao's much heralded 'revolution in education'. Since the founding of the People's Republic, urban folk had routinely been sent to the nearby countryside to assist with the harvest. This represented a rather more serious Chinese version, with solid political cover, of the traditional potato picking holiday I was just old enough to have enjoyed in the rural Yorkshire of my childhood. Here, on the far side of the world and in the Yangtze valley, May was always the most frenetic of the farming seasons, for the winter wheat had to be brought in and in the same fields, the first crop of paddy rice had to be quickly planted. We were soon to discover what heroic effort this entailed.

Apart from the excitement of a whole new world of experience, I had solid personal reasons for wanting to get deeper into real rural conditions. After all, my overriding purpose of being in China was to investigate, as best I could under the uncomfortable circumstances, the weird urbanisation process undertaken by the Communist Party since it took nationwide power in 1949. Yet proper academic research was impossible at that point for a foreigner. Indeed, it was impossible for any Chinese too when it came to 'social science': Marxism-Leninism-Mao Zedong Thought (yes – that mouthful was the officially sanctified term) was meant to answer all the mysteries of the universe.

In fact, it would be three years after Mao Zedong's death before the powers-that-be started reporting serious, relatively real information about their country. Following a severe data drought of two decades, in 1979 the floodgates opened with the re-publication of a thick tome entitled the *Statistical Yearbook of China*. Reams of novel figures on every aspect of the country's economy and population were offered, although they were an effort to interpret, given the sparse footnotes and explanations. But for China watchers such as myself this was still an enormous leap forward. When eventually I published my book *Urbanisation in China*, I think, I hope, that all the weave and weft of my experiences described here supplied enriching ingredients. I wanted my analysis to be a little more than the average academic's screed. After all, almost none of the contemporary China experts in Western universities had ever set foot in the country.

I was well acquainted with the history of rural collectivisation under the Communist Party, its ups and downs and the disastrous years after the establishment of the people's communes in 1958. The fiercest, most persistent ideological struggles pinioned on the tension between the private versus the 'collective'; in rural China, it centered on the question of the peasants' household gardens, their 'private plots', and the disposal of any surplus which might derive from them. Private peasant markets made something of an unofficial comeback in 1975, but in Nanjing's streets I from time to time witnessed truck-loads of stern-faced militia arresting petty peasant traders and carting them off. Even a teenage girl trying to sell three forlorn carrots to passers-by suffered this treatment.

The collective economy had many advantages, for it provided the scale required for agricultural modernisation. And during the Cultural Revolution, Mao's Red Guard shock troops were cast out in their millions from the cities with many becoming rural teachers or 'barefoot doctors' – paramedics with a little training in Western and Chinese medicine. This was all possible because the rural communes could tax and spend on local services. But the tension between collective production and distribution on the one hand, and the interests and priorities of the individual farmer on the other, was palpable. When the Maoist radicals had the upper hand, policies pushed for 100 percent collective and nil private. Given the immovable mass of the peasantry on the one hand, and the demands of the non-agricultural population for produce which the state was often incapable of supplying on the other, periods of radical extreme were always followed by interludes of softening, of policy retreat. In the stark absence of other sources of capital, the government depended on the countryside for what the

Soviet economist Preobrazhensky had called 'primitive socialist accumulation', which because of the Chinese Party's historical relationship to the peasantry could never be as brutal as Stalin's. In the recovery years of the early 1960s, after the disasters of the Great Leap Forward, came a marked relaxation of political directives on the farming population. Then came the extremes of the first years of the Cultural Revolution.

In 1973, with Deng Xiaoping back on the scene following his dismissal and long rural exile, came another slight loosening of political controls on agriculture. Indeed, in every staged visit we made to people's communes, private plots were presented as a natural part of the scenery. But the diehard ideologues had no intention of letting matters rest. Whenever in our political study sessions I turned the conversation towards the collective vs. private issue, my interlocutors felt obligated to repeat the leftist mantra that the 'tail might start to wag the dog'. That is, the latter-day Maoists maintained implausibly, that to permit the 'capitalist tail' (*zibenzhuyi weiba*) to grow even an inch would eventually bring down the whole system and thus guarantee a nationwide 'restoration of capitalism'.

Their ideological foes, the moderates, would justify themselves by resort to the classics: 'right' (in the sense of 'Recht') as Marx and Engels defined it, could never be higher than the level of material development of society. In other words, you cannot push a revolution too fast and the people's consciousness cannot be expected to soar above their everyday realities. And though there were pockets of advancement (no doubt our destination of Moling People's Commune was going to prove one of them, located as it was in a three-crop-per-year region), China's vast rural population was still in an age-old primitive state as far as agricultural development was concerned.

A large part of the peasantry had supported the Communist

Party and its objectives because of a century of immiseration and hopelessness. The overthrow of the last imperial dynasty in 1911 was followed by chaotic warlordism, civil war, and the attack on China by the Japanese which killed upwards of fifteen million and displaced almost one hundred million. During the decades of war and strife, the Party had largely played down social reform in the countryside, but the majority of the rural population doubtless hoped that once peace came, their reward should be a thoroughgoing land distribution. And in the land reform of the early 1950s, that is exactly what the long-suffering peasantry got. Yet within a few years, their hard-won land holdings were subsumed into Mao's dream of a rural collective system, the unwieldy and distant people's communes spread uniformly throughout the land.

Mindful of the controversies which continued to surround the rural collectives, before arriving at the Moling People's Commune, I contrived an array of searching questions. My carefully preserved. 1975 Moling notebooks record that these questions ranged over a wide canvas:

> *History of the collectivisation process, how many landlords and what happened to them in the land reform, the reclaiming of land/enlargement of fields 'Dazhai style', the private plot situation, irrigation control, housing – how built, owned etc, variety of crops, how they calculate wages, how men's work-points compare with women's, how is the value of a work-point figured, family incomes, mechanisation, health, snail fever, Party membership and role, the commune militia, payment of cadres, state grain tax, fertilisers – what types and where from, the Commune Revolutionary Committee – who appoints members? And Team Leaders?* Etcetera, exhaustively.

By the time our stay in the countryside had ended, many questions had been put, and many remained enigmatic. But this was a real place, with real, practical tasks to do, and I came to realise that for the peasants, while 'politics' certainly intruded, their preoccupation was always how best to farm and how best to survive.

Our sparkling new Shanghai saloon was, we guessed, deemed politically unsuitable for the countryside, so in its place we rode out of Nanjing in the University's splendid black Mercedes 180 Ponton, mid-1950s vintage. This was, by coincidence, the very vehicle on which our new Shanghai Mark I saloon had been modelled. A few years earlier, Cultural Revolution or no Cultural Revolution, the government must have imported the redundant Mercedes plant from Germany.

The students meanwhile, greying *pugai* (cotton-stuffed bedrolls) strung across their backs, had climbed into a couple of olive-green Liberation trucks from the University's transport pool and were cheerily waving us on our way. We set off down to the Xinjiekou junction and continued travelling south until the last plane tree-clad streets of Nanjing were behind us. Plane trees imported from France were one of the legacies of the Chiang Kai-shek government's capital in the late 1920s for which one could be grateful, for they moderated the stifling Nanjing summer heat.

I realised from the map the urban planners had once shown me (maps, of course generally being 'secret') that we must be heading into Jiangning County - one of the two large rural areas under Nanjing's jurisdiction. The Mercedes, under Lao Zhou's confident and only occasionally hair-raising control, was now dodging handcarts and stray farming folk as it coursed along one of those wide tree-lined rural highways found all over the North China Plain. The lower tree trunks were, as ever, whitewashed, I suppose to provide some guidance to night-time traffic - for Chinese drivers were inexplicably reluctant to use their headlights. And as everywhere where there were 'public' trees, below perhaps twenty feet, all small branches had been systematically removed. China was already a country of severe fuel shortage; from time to time we passed foragers shamelessly at work on the roadside, their saw blades lashed to long bamboo poles.

Next to our faithful driver sat Minder Wang. For practical reasons, and certainly for political ones, Wang had divested himself of his royal-blue Dacron tunic and his unblemished cotton trousers, not to mention his leather shoes. Now he was attired in a faded buff jacket and well-patched pants, finished off by ancient plimsolls. As ever, the back of Wang's head with its curious tufts of black hair, was all he had to offer us: he remained silent and impassive, with apparently not the least interest in the world beyond the windscreen. He had not been instructed that we could be told anything, and he certainly was not going to volunteer a word about our countryside assignment.

An hour or so later, the road coursed by a settlement with some largish buildings, one even two-storeyed, which we later visited. It housed, we guessed, the headquarters of Moling People's Commune. The car squealed to a halt and Lao Zhou interrogated a startled, ragged passer-by. We cruised along for a mile or two and onto a narrow grassy track. Soon we arrived at a clearing, a kind of village square, a large pond to one side with a line of huge jars beside it, a privy to the other, and several brick-and-tile single storey dwellings to the two sides. On the far side of the pond, a classic scene - a water buffalo being led along a narrow path by a ring through its nostrils attached to a rope. From time to time, the animal dipped its huge head for a mouthful of weeds in the drainage ditch below the path, pulling on its rope and almost flooring the shaven-headed infant who led it.

From one of the houses came an elderly woman in faded padded jacket and trousers, her face distorted by a lopsided goitre. Behind her, from the darkened inner recesses of the cottage stepped a lithe and good-looking man, his smooth face of an almost golden hue, his trouser legs rolled to the knee, his feet bare and deeply mud-ingrained. While his wife gaped open-mouthed, the man too was unsmiling and hardly batted an eyelid over the two foreign apparitions. Though Wang could not or would not tell us, he turned out to be the village head, aka (in commune style) the team leader of the 15th Team.

Meanwhile Lao Zhou had dumped our bags and was turning the Mercedes on the square, half of which was in actuality the newly-tamped and still-fragile earth of the village's threshing floor. Angry-faced, the team leader leapt at the car, but Lao Zhou was away down the narrow lane as fast as he dared. It did not do for an urban proletarian, let alone a respected chauffeur, to linger too long with backward village folk.

We hung around as Minder Wang engaged the team leader in a lengthy discussion about something, and by and by the man's wife appeared with some rough bowls of the beverage which rural people call *bai cha* – 'white tea'. Warm boiled water. Even in the poorest of villages - and this turned out to be hardly one of them - people stuck to their age-old, hygienic practice of boiling all drinking water. Soon a ragged song could be heard, and in military formation into the village marched our students, each of them equipped with carrying pole and baskets, as well as those dusty bedrolls. Xu Xin, the class's stocky shock-haired and good-natured Communist Youth League monitor, had been assigned the task of foreigners' minder in the village. From the luggage disgorged from the Mercedes, he grabbed a sack and told us to follow him into one of the low houses fronting the square. We entered through the neat brickwork of the threshold and found ourselves stepping down into a dark interior, its low roof raised on concrete rafters from which hung a sickle, a mattock, some dried plants and a white cotton sack which looked as though it held grain. Why stepping down, I wondered? The floor was of clay but even now squishy in places. Later, after a few hours rain, we had to navigate our way onto our bedstead through sticky mud.

'If we make our floors higher than the outside,' I was earnestly informed by one of the villagers, 'then all our gold and silver will flow out.' Metaphorical gold and silver, to be sure, and about as convincing as our colleague and first-generation-in-the-city Yu F's reply when I asked if her family had mosquito nets. 'Yes, of course we do!' she replied.

'Then why are your daughter's legs covered in bites?' I asked in all innocence.

'It is not yet the time to use them,' was Yu's answer.

And later I was to observe in Hong Kong, with the popular mind supposedly clarified by a century and more of Western dominance, everyone put on their *meen laap*, their padded jackets, at exactly the same time - New Year's Day - regardless of actual weather conditions. What such instances illustrate, I came to understand, was that China's millennial agrarian past weighed heavily on its present, the lunar calendar and protective superstition still the subconscious guiding forces. But this was a lesson which took a long time to penetrate, for we had been over-enthused by the notion that all was new, all was revolutionary in Mao's China. In our darker moments, whilst the *People's Daily* railed against the 'Soviet Social Imperialists', such paradoxes – not to mention the overweening bureaucracy which controlled our lives - found us muttering 'Bloody Chinese Social Feudalists'.

Inside our new home, Xu Xin steered us to the left of the door and through a thin partition to find a double bedstead. A similar division was on the right, and through the door we glimpsed three narrow cots of thick bamboo shoved together. Beyond that there was a corner with a typical country cooking range, hung around with a few blackened utensils as well as bamboo steamers, large and small. With his characteristic broad smile, Xu Xin pointed at the bed and emptied a folded mosquito net onto it. Around the bed-ends were vertical bamboo poles, and in a few moments our helper had strung the net into an enclosure. We were provided with a new kapok-filled mattress, hard but serviceable and not dissimilar to the ones in Nanjing Hotel. Perhaps, indeed, it had been lent out by Hotel, for there was also a heavy cotton quilt with a fancy cover; the pillow cases with embroidered flowers and artistic Qi Baishi shrimps were just like the ones we had become used to. Except these pillows were rock-hard and seemed to be filled with some kind of straw. At least we were not going to be too cold, only damp. The month of May in the Lower Yangtze region is a mostly balmy but humid time, the lush growth all around a testament to the onset of a fine growing season.

'But whose house is this?' we enquired. The usual rule with foreigners was to only tell them things on an absolute need-to-know basis. Instead of answering, our student smiled and mouthed 'Xiuxi yixia', the routine instruction to rest after a journey - and probably a signal that we should keep out of the way for a while. So we nodded off until mid-afternoon, when woken by female voices and what turned out to be the clattering of tools as they were set against the wall outside. Three ruddy-cheeked and pigtailed young women in their best flowery over-jackets poked their way through the partition and stood to attention by our bedstead. We crawled through the gap in the net as decorously as we could and received their muted greetings. For them, no doubt, it was as if we were creatures from another planet and they were the chosen ones, our earthly reception committee. Once they had recovered from their shock, two of the threesome opened up, telling us they had been in the village for a year. All three were from the same graduating class of one of Nanjing's junior middle schools.

I was inquisitive about how the villagers felt about the girls, as rumours abounded of much trouble with the sending-down policy and sometimes of much abuse of the urban youth. By now, five years into the programme, the cities had sweetened the pill somewhat, and communes prepared to receive their youngsters were provided with cash grants. These were intended to support the cost of providing accommodation, though there was something left over too towards a stipend to help the youngsters supplement their incomes. As everywhere, the rural collectives based their remuneration to each member on 'work-points', which accumulated until the annual accounting when there would be a share-out of the profits (or in poorer areas or after disasters, of the debts). Strapping can-do males got higher work-points than all females (whatever their physical prowess in the fields), whilst the elderly and these young inexperienced and unhardened urbanites could expect very meagre points. Whether the grants received in this village for our *zhiqing* (educated youth) trio were enough for the construction of this brick and tile home of three 'rooms' (or *jian* – a rural standard) I doubted. My questioning later turned up that the girls' home had cost 1,500 *yuan*, a figure way beyond the dreams of most rural communities, with household income distributed at the annual accounting at most a few tens of *yuan* – if anything at all. It was already becoming clear that, despite Li An's protestations, Moling People's Commune was not an average place.

The students were busy sorting out their own sleeping arrangements. One of the team's sheds had been turned over to them, boys at one end, girls at the other, with woven mat-screens between. They seemed to have plenty of bamboo frame beds, though how they had arrived we could only guess. Maybe, I thought, this village was a regular destination for urban youth brigades? I wandered into the shed and found the boys erecting mosquito nets stamped in red with the four characters of the University's name. Not a bad idea, as at least a couple of my first group of fifteen admitted to be suffering from regular bouts of malaria. On their stout bamboo frames there were no mattresses, but in the corner was a pile of straw which apparently had to serve. At least the students had each brought stripy sheets to shield them from the prickles. Party Secretary Li An had arrived in one of the student' trucks and, lo and behold, was billeted alongside Wang at the far end of the student quarters. Despite my antipathy towards him, I was glad to see that the elderly Party Secretary had a bed with rather more straw padding than the students. Though he looked sickly and, like most Chinese bureaucrats, was a chain-smoker, I was soon to discover that I had no need to fear for Li An's physical prowess with the carrying pole. He had obviously had some years of practice during earlier *yundong*, when people like him were sent off to the May 7th Cadre Schools for months - sometimes years - of hard labour to correct their attitude.

Eating times back in Nanjing were strictly regulated: eleven-thirty for lunch, and five o'clock for the evening meal. So it was here in the village, though not when a mountain of wheat sheaves was waiting to be put through the threshing machine. To the side of our cottage was a space where an open-sided canteen was being erected with stout bamboos and large woven mats for the roof. Taking shape were two traditional country stoves – ranges, really – of whitewashed yellow bricks with large round holes on the top surface for the oversized steel *guo* – the concave cooking pot the Cantonese (and we too) call a wok. At ground level at the front were square holes, a bit like in a steam locomotives footplate, where you shoved in the fuel, fast and furious. The fuel was exclusively straw and dried grass, which made me realise for the first time, while observing the cooks, why Chinese cuisine has evolved the way it has. Straw burns with intense heat but only for a minute or two, and that is the essence of Chinese stir-frying. Later when the non-stop cycle of work began we outsiders appreciated how ready calories cooked with speed and downed with speed were an indispensable part of the countryside routine.

While we were getting our bearings, I noticed that, despite all their rhetoric about being at one with the masses, our 'revolutionary' students seemed to be maintaining a distance from their rustic hosts. A group of villagers was hard at it, tamping down the threshing floor while shifting from it a large heap of hardened mud dredged from the nearby pond. The stuff, I correctly surmised, was to be used as fertiliser on the yet-to-be created paddy fields. The job took several hours of hacking with mattocks and carrying by shoulder pole, but strangely it never seemed to cross the minds of the newcomers that they should help. In the village we were very much under orders, and Jo and I felt unable to pitch in ourselves.

It gradually became clear that like many political sideshows of the time, *kaimen banxue* (open-door schooling) had its ritualistic element: the students were there to help the peasants at set times and in prescribed ways only. But did their initial stand-offishness with these Moling peasants reflect mere ritual or was there something more at play? Did these young people, now on a conveyor belt to privilege, actually *believe* (as they endlessly professed) in the need to keep themselves close to the labouring masses? This was a question which endlessly puzzled me, and which I never resolved.

Our cooks meanwhile had been preparing the evening meal.

Remarkably, apart from a few banquets with high officials, this was the very first time we had actually been allowed to eat in the company of ordinary citizens since our arrival in China six months earlier. There was nothing decorous about our repast, but it served its purpose. As was going to be the rule, the students stood around, their bowls raised to mouth level, their chopsticks whirring in a circular fashion, and it was all over in two minutes. These young people seemed to regard the act of eating as mere re-fuelling: it was astonishing how quickly bowls were being licked and put away. What was on offer for the whole Nanjing team may have been embellished for our sakes, but like every subsequent lunch and supper it was still basic: a mountain of dirty-looking but tasty rice (tiny stones included) upon which was ladled green vegetables and a few fragments of animal flesh, usually with tiny bones attached. Every meal was polished off with a watery soup, unappetising but at least it saved washing one's bowl.

After our first supper we were called to a work meeting. Squatting in a rough circle on the threshing floor, Li An began the proceedings with a few stern remarks delivered with his usual nervous smile, his puffed-out cheeks almost obscuring his eyes. Then, team leader Zhang took over. They were all Zhangs here - like so many villages, almost everyone had the same family name and in the past, the place had been known simply as Zhang village. I liked this leader's style. No nonsense, certainly no attempt at humour, but with a hectoring voice he laid out the pattern for the coming campaign. We were to rise at six and work would begin at six-thirty, through until eleven. Then lunch, and on with labour until five, when we would have an hour's break to eat and rest. Thereafter we could be called to further efforts if the battle demanded it. Until the job was done.

And what was the job? The team's small fields were now all down to winter wheat, ripe and golden and ruffling in the breeze around the village. To me, brought up with English wheat, this looked like be-whiskered barley. But a type of wheat indeed it was. Those who imagine that the traditional grain of all the Chinese has to be rice are under a misapprehension. From the Yangtze valley northwards, the staple has long been wheat, steamed into unleavened blobs called *mantou* – supplemented in hilly areas by the sticky steamed maize *wotou*, by creations from millet and other grains which the southern Chinese regard as primitive and even loathsome. Wheat was likely to become more universal, for I knew that on the quiet in this land where 'self-reliance' (the much-mentioned *zili gengsheng*) was supposed to be the watchword, China was secretly exporting high-priced rice and importing much cheaper-by-weight Australian and Canadian wheat.

Not all had to be explained by the team leader. The processes were just too involved, and in any case not a few of the students already had years of farm work under their belts. Our task was to magically replace the ripe wheat in the fields with jade green rice shoots, planted ankle-deep in muddy water. The village was, I already suspected, an 'advanced unit', though when I put this to Li An he insisted – as he had to - that it was merely average for the region. One telling sign could be seen along the track from the highway: on crudely hewn poles was strung a power line. It turned out that the village's electricity was strictly to meet the demands of production rather than to light up the cottages. Indeed, since outside the busy seasons the inhabitants went to bed and rose with the light, electric lighting was still considered an unnecessary luxury for rural folk. In this village, it powered a medium-sized field pump, a small threshing machine with perhaps double the dimensions of, say, an old fashioned treadle sewing machine, and most vitally, in the corner of an outhouse the equipment for a public address system which relayed uplifting broadcasts from the Jiangsu People's Radio station.

Lashed to a wobbly post on the far edge of the threshing ground was one of those standard Chinese *laba* – an oversized loudspeaker horn (our imported bell-bottomed trousers, high fashion in the early 1970s, were amusingly dubbed *laba kuzi* by the locals for their horn-like leg bottoms). No doubt, of the three uses to which precious electricity was put in Zhang village, the Party chieftains back at Moling HQ regarded the loudspeaker system as the most vital. In the fields where we were to harvest the wheat and plant the paddy – and some hundreds of yards distant from the village centre - I was amazed to find another, a mobile loudspeaker. Whilst painfully delivering rice seedlings one day, I was even more amazed to hear it blaring out familiar sentences in English along the lines: 'Lesson 1: Chairman Mao is the Sun.' It was the province's broadcast of English lessons. I wondered what the villagers could possibly make of it.

Beyond electricity, the village, our team, possessed one of those phut-phut two-stroke petrol-driven hand tractors to which a small rotating plough blade could be attached. With its two long handles and their control levers it could be hitched to a steel cart for road use - very handy for transport of humans and cargoes. I suspected that only in affluent regions could this innovation be found. Then there was that water buffalo, huge and lumbering, wet-nosed, with large and wise brown eyes, its flanks with mud-coated wispy hairs. I was fascinated by the creature, and got one of the students to ask its young minder all about it.

'How old is your buffalo?' I enquired.

'Fifty-seven,' came the incredible answer. My interpreter was never one of the most proficient of the students, it has to be said. In fact, the animal was a mere seven years, and would go on for a few more, I was told.

After that, it came down to the human beasts of burden. The most useful and universal of Chinese farming equipment is the bamboo carrying pole. Unlike its European equivalent, the wooden shoulder yoke, the Chinese *danzi* makes no concessions to the human form. Anyone who was a regular user, as I was to observe, had a groove and crab apple-sized hump worn into their right shoulder where the unyielding bamboo sat. I was to find that lacking such a groove and the gnarled skin that went with it, the carrying pole would be the bane of my countryside life. Beyond the dreadful carrying pole were a few more wieldable hand tools, the most vital being the sickle.

Our first work morning had arrived. We had spent a night fighting off the huge mosquitoes which clung to the outside of the net only millimetres from our flesh. At least one worked out how to penetrate through the entrance gap – closed with a wooden peg but not closed carefully enough – and we had our inflamed bumps to show for it. At five, we were awakened by a loud, strident soliloquy which seemed to be just feet from our tiny unglazed but heavily-barred window. It was the voice of the team leader, a different, a black voice, and from his cadences and unyielding vocal assault he was a very angry man indeed. At whom, and why we naturally had no clue. But through the aperture we could just see his audience - the entire working team of around three dozen - seated around him and soaking up his ire. *Laurence Olivier has nothing on him!* my notebook records. The team sit around in the dawn light, looking more than subdued, not daring to speak. Or so it appeared. Clearly some big struggle going on – I never found out what.

The eerie blast went on for a full three-quarters of an hour, then all was silent and it was time to rise and face our first day at work. As I eased on my oldest cotton trousers and an old olive cotton U.S. ex-military jacket I had rather perversely brought to China, we could already smell hot cooking oil. The scraping noise which had been going on just outside our door since the team leader's hectoring had ended was a couple of wiry men sharpening sickles on a large circular smooth weapons on a huge granite boulder. This rock was to serve later as my makeshift typewriter table, as I had brought along my much soldered-together East German portable. It surprised me that the men could sharpen the steel so well using just a rock with water as a lubricant rather than scarce oil.

So it was a-harvesting that we were going.

'How Tolstoyan a prospect!' I bethought myself as I recalled that romantic image of Levin in *Anna Karenina*.

At that point, of course, I had no notion of the back-breaking reality. Meanwhile, the students were emerging from their long hut, and a few were vigorously wielding their toothbrushes and rinsing from tin mugs, and, inevitably, spitting wherever they fancied. While all water to be consumed was by custom boiled, my notebook registered yet another crusty remark:

> *Washing is in the pond, from which drinking and cooking*
> *water is drawn. Basic hygiene is lacking – I even caught*
> *one of the girl students rinsing out a filthy reed loo brush*
> *in the pond the other day! Still, no one seems to get ill,*
> *the least us, and I've even had constipation (needing*
> *medication) here...*

In the cook-house, one of the pair of giant woks was already spitting with *youtiao*, golden fried dough sticks, while the other was steaming wheat *mantou*. Breakfast was done in a flash, and then, hi-ho, it was off to work we went in a two-by-two line, each dangling a sickle.

We marched to a field of some two acres located a couple hundred yards from the village. Once there, the team leader halted us to issue curt instructions. Our student guide Xu Xin indicated to Jo and me to join the end of a line of a dozen sickle-wielders, and the task then began. Like scything, cutting a stand of grain requires a steady action, and it is not one achieved without practice. Our inexperience was soon showing, for the rest of the line were advancing pretty much in unison, very Tolstoy's Levin-like. The felled stalks with their precious ears of grain had to be grasped by the bunch in the left hand, and then dropped in a sort of semi-ordered pile as the line advanced.

This back-bending labour went on, ever more painfully in my case, for a full four hours. After a time, our end of the line was a miserable curve: we had been achieving only about half the pace of the others. We were exhausted, yet our students, and even Li An and Minder Wang, seemed as fresh as daisies. The villagers looked as though they had not even started the day's work.

But it was re-fuelling time, and back to the square we marched for our lunch. The other sickle team was just that minute returning from the wheat field on the opposite side of the village. My notebook again:

> Eating is a gobbling affair, meals often over before my chopsticks had clicked together twice. The team leader's pigs get the slops (if there are any) which shows that some pigs are more equal than others....

Returning to our labours, and wondering how we would get through the five hours after lunch, we passed a line of village women with their faded floral blouses and straw hats with the four characters 'Serve the People' around their brims, each bearing the fruits of our morning's sickle work. Wielding long bamboo poles with spiked ends, they had speared up great bundles of wheat sheaves which they were taking back to the village. By the evening these had become a high stack on the fringe of the threshing ground. Meanwhile, our cooks had decided on a treat of pork dumplings, *jiaozi*, that evening; we guessed that this was to strengthen us for the coming battle, the flavour of which I tried to capture at the time:

> *Threshing is a frantic war of annihilation, generally at night, by dim floodlight. The thresher, or 'little tiger' as it's known, is clamped to bolts on the threshing ground. Power is by a large 7000kw electric motor. Electricity supply looks makeshift, with poorly insulated wires. The heart of the thresher is just a simple toothed roller, and the straw and grain is forced in at one end, the chaff, dust, straw and grain coming out at the other. A frantic team of masked pitchforkers then remove the straw, pile it up, and shove it through again (twice is the rule). The machine's quite efficient, though two things go wrong: the (drive) belt falls off or the machine is blocked and it fails. For this, the Team's electrician (so-called) is on hand. The belt is unprotected, and the peasants work furiously shoving in straw only inches from it. The chaff and grain were swept aside with wooden 'pushers' and rough besoms, then carried in large woven baskets on the end of carrying poles to the new barn.*

On a tiny hill farm in North Yorkshire years before, I had stood and watched men work at a very different kind of thresher – a giant Edwardian painted monster of steel and brightly painted coachwork, whirring blades for its guts and powered through an undulating, frayed belt by a smoking traction engine. The men from the surrounding farms had gathered, each with their heaped cartloads of sheaves for a joint effort of threshing. A traditional, primitive collectivism, as was the harvesting itself. All the host farmer was expected to do when his neighbours were helping on his land was to supply them with bread, cheese and a jug of beer. I was six, a big boy, and my memory is clear of the day I was allowed to deliver the baskets of 'snap' to the harvest team.

My father had let me come to the next door farm to watch the threshing; his meagre cartload of barley was coming up soon. As the men used their pitchforks to toss the grain-bearing straw into the monster, one of them got in too close to its business end and had his arm sliced. Someone removed me to the farmhouse, away from the awful scene.

Now, in Zhang Village, 15th production team of the Dongwang Brigade, I was being kept well away from this very different machine and its madly screeching innards. The team leader, always in the thick of things and always a skilled operator, waved me towards the group of village women, well clear of the little tiger. With pitchforks not so different from those Yorkshire ones, we shifted the stripped straw to an ever-growing circular stack.

That first and the following nights we went on until late, almost midnight. Despite a poor start with the locals, the students threw themselves into the task, often taking the lead at the growling and shrieking thresher. Every evening the stripped straw was quickly removed by the villagers. With the steel-spiked carrying poles, each household carted off their bundle.

'This will be enough for everyone's cooking until the rice harvest in late July,' explained Xu Xin.

The second crop of rice would go in early August and be harvested in early November. Then back to the beginning of the three crop cycle, the paddy fields transformed through much application of dung and pond weed, and much harnessing to harrow and crude plough by that faithful buffalo so that the winter wheat could be sown once again.

Our precious threshing floor was bearing up well. One of our house-mates explained that its grey hue came from the straw ash added to the clay soil so that it formed a hardened crust. Before we arrived, the villagers had spent days rolling the floor by hauling across it a massive cylinder of stone, perhaps a quarter of a tonne in weight, which was now parked near our cottage's door. I recorded:

> *Primitive, effective – wonder if they'll ever get a cement threshing floor? Centre part only, for machine, is concrete. Stands up to hard wear – even in bad rain it stays quite firm, though a bit shiny. There are drainage channels... Only disadvantage – dusty, and when the surface cracks in the sun, there's a grain loss which must add up to several hundred-weight in a year.*

Provided the weather stayed fine (and except for a day or two it did) and there was a breeze in the air, the baskets of chaff and grain were brought back each morning to the threshing floor. Here the winnowing and re-winnowing began. Two straw-hatted women, each wearing a strip of cloth as masks, tossed the contents of their woven circular baskets in a ten-foot high arc, the grain falling to the threshing floor and the chaff drifting to the side. The grain would then be swept up for a second toss in the air in this effective but arduous exercise. Then it was carefully spread across the threshing ground in the hope that the warm May sun would dry the vital staple sufficiently for storage. Finally, shovelled into clean woven baskets and then fifty kilogramme burlap sacks, it was ready for de-husking at the mill run by the commune, at Moling HQ. With a part set aside for reserves and the next planting, I was told that the grain would be apportioned to households according to the work points they had accrued. This was China's rural collective economy at its shining best. In the great interior, however, where slopes were the norm, rainfall sporadic and soils poor, it had to be a very different story.

This tough work schedule was repeated for another four days, and little by little our sickle skills improved and sometimes we could almost keep pace with the rest of the team. Our end of the advancing line into the golden wheat was becoming less of a curve. At long last, the No.15 team's harvest was done.

A complete change of pace was now the order of the day, but would it promise welcome respite from the bending to a sickle for hours on end, and fighting the little tiger until midnight? The clue to our next assignment lay below that outside privy and its stinking slurry. Because rice seedlings can be nurtured in their first weeks in great density, and as cultivable land in China has always been at a premium, the rice seedlings are started off in closely planted beds which in most villages in those days would be adjacent to the village privy. Holding onto the crumbling adobe wall of the toilet, I peered down at the beds some six feet beneath. And there the fine emerald shoots were, nine inches high with their roots sucking up the rich, stinking mess of mud and human waste. Before digging them up and transporting them to the rice paddy to be re-planted, the rich soup in which they had spent their first weeks of life had to be extracted. From the brick-built barn at the far side of the square, a team of six barefooted villagers carried a strange contraption some fifteen feet in length, at one end a kind of platform and hand-rail. Invaluable to Chinese wetland agriculture for a millennium as a water-lifting device, entirely made of bamboo and without any iron fasteners, this was the famous 'dragon's back'. The bottom of the machine with its continuous belt of bamboo slats as paddles, was thrust down into the goo of the seedling beds.

'Climb on and peddle, like a bicycle going up hill!' ordered Xu Xin with his usual broad smile. So I joined a couple of strapping peasants at the top of the machine and began treadling furiously alongside them. This calf-stretching labour turned the crude belt and little by little the black gold was lifted by the bamboo slats, the 'scales' of the dragon, where it poured and trickled into a pit by the side of the privy. A women's team lined up with pairs of wooden pails dangling from their carrying poles, each scooping up the liquid and heading off in that rapid wobble of the Chinese rice farmer in the direction of the paddy field-to-be. Naturally this and all else that moved in our village I recorded on Ektachrome, but I was not expecting the severe rap across the knuckles I received from gauleiter Li An:

'Why did you take photographs of the old machine for water?' he demanded that evening as I was preparing for a good night's rest. 'It is a backward legacy of the bitter past in the countryside. You should only photograph the hand tractor and the pump in the paddy field.'

Once again, what was quaint and interesting to an outsider was a matter of shame, of political face, to our hosts. I had no satisfactory answer for my interrogator. On my part, I could understand his ire, while on his part he would never be able to fathom the fascination such wonderful 'primitive' machines had for this alien from another world.

Much effort, meantime, had to be applied to the erstwhile wheat field. The field divisions in this part of China consisted of narrow elevated walkways, perhaps a foot wide and usually treacherously slippery. These banks had to be checked and any breaches sealed and made watertight. Foreigners, ourselves not excluded, always revel in the incongruities of China, and here was one which I just had to record with my trusty Olympus OM1. In the renovated field, the patient buffalo was rolling along with a wooden-bladed plough and its mud-splashed 'driver' skating on a board behind, while chugging along in parallel in its own furrow was the team's rotavating hand tractor. Not long to go now before the wheat field became a rice paddy. And Li An could hardly complain of a shot which included both the pump and the hand tractor, even if the old-fashioned, shameful buffalo was caught in it too.

Next, our urban team was marshalled to load up the mud which had been shifted to the edge of the threshing floor, and it was my first go at a carrying pole. It all looked so easy, though watching my students take off towards the distant field I could see the method involved a certain wobbling rhythm. And bare feet.

One of the girls shovelled the fertiliser mud into the split bamboo panniers which hung from my pole, and off I went. Even the first few steps were agonising. She was doing the rhythmical walk behind me and when I stumbled and came to a stop, she took pity on me and off-loaded some of the mud onto her own panniers.

'How much can you carry?' I asked this diminutive young woman with tiny wrists and ankles.

'Seventy *jin*,' she replied. 'But you should carry only forty, I think.'

A *jin* is half a kilogramme. From then on, when one of the students loaded my panniers it was with great care not to overburden their pathetic foreign teacher. I had only one advantage over my fellow workers: my foreigner's size nine wide (and somewhat prehensile) feet became something of an asset, for I found I could grip the treacherous surface of the field boundary with my toes, through which I squeezed the rich brown mud as I inched my way along.

After we had taken all the pond mud and chucked it from the narrow walkways into the field it was the turn of the green fertiliser from the pond, which had to be captured with wooden scoops and carried to the still-incomplete paddy. Meanwhile, the ploughing had finished and the earth was being smoothed out by a primitive wooden harrow drawn by the faithful buffalo. All this field preparation was going on while the last of the wheat was being dealt with back on the threshing floor.

Finally the moment arrived to make a dry field into a wet rice paddy. Balanced on a chunk of concrete next to a borehole in the centre of the field was a pump to which the engine of the tractor was belt-linked, and thus began the two-day task of filling the paddy with water to a depth of a foot or so.

With the transplanting about to start, I was assigned to the team which, with special narrow spades, carefully cut away just below the roots of each clump of rice seedlings and ejected them onto the panniers of the carrying poles. Once up and ready, a line of us, mainly students, waddled in formation out of the square towards the paddy field. Once there, it was a matter of tossing each clump to the line of women who made up the planting team. If my task was painful, so much more was Jo's, as planting required constant bending for hours on end. Each clump had to be broken into individual shoots and pressed into the mud under a foot of muddy water, and to just the right depth. The planters' work was not only back-breaking but hazardous too: I watched with mild horror as small snakes slithered off the banks and to use the flooded paddy as a swimming pool. Snake-bite is an enduring hazard of rice planting, though the improbable story has it that when a snake is swimming it is incapable of sinking its fangs into anything.

Interspersed with the realities of real village life - the harvesting and planting - were the inevitable 'politics' which suffused all life in Mao's People's Republic. Even here in Zhang Village, the cadres had to be mindful of the reports of our rustic progress, to be scrutinised by the higher-ups including ultimately the dreaded provincial education revolutionary committee. University affairs were always firmly on the political agenda, and nothing was left to chance when it came to the deportment of the worker-peasant-soldier students. Memories were still fresh of rampaging youth and the campus battlefields.

The 'model worker', 'model work-unit', 'model mother' (in the 1950s, that meant a baby machine) was, and remains an enduring feature of post-1949 China. All this is an unconscious fusion of the Confucian and the Soviet Stakhonivite traditions. And in the pantheon of Cultural Revolution heroics, model individuals were very often dead individuals. The most tediously cited was a semi-mythical young soldier called Lei Feng, who led a life of 'selfless devotion to the Party and the people' and had the honour of dying a hero's death in 1963 when struck by a falling telegraph pole. No one brought up in China after the early 1960s could possibly be ignorant of the Lei Feng story. What was more, every locality had to have its own Lei Fengs – jumping into raging torrents to save a matchstick for the state, as we used to sourly lampoon these heroic individuals.

Unfortunately our village sojourn coincided with Jiangsu province's Party newspaper, the *Xinhua Daily*, promoting a local lad called Wang Anming, an 'educated youth' like our three house-mates, who had made the supreme sacrifice. My Moling journal again:

> *Had a sickeningly boring session the other day to 'learn from Wang Anming'. The province authorities, in the Hsinhua Ribao (Xinhua Daily)- Jiangsu province's Party daily - have recently been pushing the example of this young Ed. Youth who died in the countryside. In every*

way, Wang was a model young person – Party member, practical yet intellectual, rebellious, etc. It is clear that his example is being pushed to persuade those remaining (few?) unpersuaded parents that going to the countryside is a virtuous thing. Maybe, as hinted before, this is a particular problem in the province. But the application of the lesson seems tedious and mechanical. All the students repeated one after another (in a session lasting the statutory two hours) 'I am deeply moved'. 'I have made up my mind to learn from him (Wang Anming) and follow his example for the rest of my life.' These heartrending avowals had a rather hollow ring to them – maybe their over-zealousness has something to do with the fact that the time for decision-making about their futures is drawing nigh.

'After all,' I said to Comrade Duan, who I knew had a sense of humour under his buttoned-up Zhongshan jacket, 'how can they follow this Wang Anming's example for their rest of their lives if it means dying for the revolution before they've had their lives?' Duan looked discomfited, gave me a wry smile, and said nothing.

Such episodes aroused my fascination with the students and their complex psychological state. Not so long ago, they had been pretty well free as Red Guards to indulge in all sorts of adventures and horrors, but here they now were as students under the iron hand of rectitude and discipline:

The students act like sixth form kids – that's how it appears. Girls and boys go about separately, and there's a certain amount of juvenile banter and flirtatious exchanges between them. The question of sexual repression is still one to be investigated.

I wrote this long before the publication of Cultural Revolution memoirs such as Anchee Min's *Red Azalea*. Sent to a people's commune, Min relates how two of her classmates who had an amorous attraction (that was all) were put to death by the local cadres. Other such accounts of the 'down to the countryside' movement speak of rape and torture by the local rural chiefs. So flirtatiousness, such as I was now observing, could be a dangerous thing in China, 1975. No wonder that many of my students exhibited a nervous tick, usually in the legs, whenever they were involved in any kind of untoward social interaction.

When it came to *laodong*, labour, I did admire the willingness and ability of the students, especially the several slightly-built girls, but my feelings towards them were always ambivalent. What got to me most was an inability (or unwillingness?) to use their initiative in unscripted situations. For instance, as already mentioned, several of the students had suffered from malaria and a couple continued to have bouts of fever. Yet on the margins of the square and by our cottage too were stagnant pools where you could watch the detested mosquito larvae rise and, breaking the surface tension, fly off to find their first victims.

'I must pluck up courage to criticise all this' I wrote in my journal. 'Even the student barefoot doctor is quite unconcerned by all these things, which would horrify the average boy scout at home.'

In fact it was Chen, a medical auxiliary 'barefoot doctor' during his period in the countryside , who got to me most. A jaunty lad in his early twenties, he was called upon when the team leader's wife needed an abscess in her cheek attending to. From a filthy cloth Chen extracted his acupuncture needles which he applied to the woman's face. Over the next days her cheek became ever more swollen - she was in great pain. Watching him at work, I was not surprised; the lad never once sterilised his needles, and indeed

I caught him shoving them straight into another student's knee after he had used them on the poor woman.

Matters really came to a head one evening after we returned from the paddy. Someone had trapped a rat, and Chen decided on an amusing performance. Holding the animal by its tail, he took a brand from the stove and tortured it to a slow death. The students around him, meanwhile, cheered and clapped like infants at a pantomime. At our next afternoon's political study session I became more than the interested observer: I let fire at the students, both for the mosquitoes and the poor rat. 'Mosquitoes and village vermin – these are politics too' was my angry point. The students looked sulky and subdued, but was it because I had strayed from the usual script of political study sessions, or was it because they were genuinely ashamed?

Jo did not stay the course in Zhang village – a recurring sickness saw her carted back to the comforts of Nanjing. But I stayed on only a little while longer until the University had deemed that our little charges had 'learned from the 'poor-and-lower-middle peasants' sufficiently. Whether the villagers had learned anything from our semi-educated throng is doubtful, but they had certainly benefited from their sincere and strident labours. The wheat harvest was in, and our three girls were loading their grain onto a handcart and heading off towards the commune's mill; the rice shoots were already waving in the breeze, and as the sun crept ever higher in the sky we packed our bags and prepared to leave. Our 'open door schooling' was exchanged for confinement to the campus and that dreary English building. But I was ever grateful for the chance to absorb so much more than during those routine set-piece visits to the people's communes, the usual lot of the political tourist in China's vast countryside.

XI

1976

OF THE TWELVE ANIMALS signs of the Zodiac under which every Chinese is born, it is the Dragon which is most cautiously anticipated. This is the sign presaging threatening events, the time when it is inauspicious to launch new projects or plan long journeys. But as the lunar New Year of 1976 approached, and our first twelve months in China were coming to an end, we remained oblivious to such omens, for no one could speak of them. Even 'New Year' had been wiped from the official lexicon – you could only refer to it as *chunjie* – the Spring Festival. All this no-speak and new-speak dated from the first weeks of the Cultural Revolution in 1966, when Mao and his zealots had ordered the masses to rid themselves of the 'Four Olds' – Old Customs, Old Culture, Old Habits, Old Ideas. Anything smacking remotely of *mixin* – superstition – was dangerously taboo; if our colleagues were aware of the Dragon Year's baleful promise, they certainly could not share their heterodox fears.

In the event, 1976 turned out to be everything the Dragon promised. The year was ushered in by the death of Zhou Enlai, a stalwart of the Chinese Communist Party and one of the founding fathers of the People's Republic. Even in those politically-charged days, people would speak of *women zongli* - 'our premier' - with undisguised affection. Perhaps, we thought, it was a demonstration not so much as a cherishing of Zhou, as signalling a coldness to Mao. It would soon become clear that Zhou Enlai's death on 8th January was going to be a milestone in the life of the People's Republic, then only in its third decade. 'It's a national disaster,' whispered a colleague portentously.

Ex-military commander, premier and in the 1950s the handsome face of the young People's Republic's new diplomacy, Zhou Enlai seemed to be regarded by an exhausted Chinese nation as the only buffer against the irascible, dangerous impulses of the Supreme Leader. After Mao had also died, this idea gained almost mythical status: without fail when we were taken to a historic site – a temple, an ancient monument of some kind - it was Premier Zhou who had supposedly personally protected it from the ravages of the Red Guards. In February 1976, in the fading days of the old lunar year, my colleagues at Nanjing University were inwardly shuddering. Since 1968, the high tide of the Red Guards, the environment had become ever-more dangerous for our University colleagues, for the ultras who clustered around the ailing Chairman were unleashed and on the warpath. Hundreds of thousands of members of the urban elite, including Party members, had already fallen foul of the repeated political campaigns launched by the radicals, and now their symbolic protector, Zhou Enlai, was no more.

Most things were kept secret from the handful of foreigners in China in the mid-1970s, and woe betide any Chinese who forgot this unwritten rule. But much as our officials wished otherwise, it was impossible to shield us totally from the struggles of ideology and personality which erupted regularly in our city of Nanjing. The Shaanxi Road intersection just down Zhongshan North Road from our residence was always interesting - on one side were the old tinsmiths who squatted in their wooden stalls mending pots and pans. Beyond them were the kapok combers who took old quilts and mattresses apart and reconstituted them. At the junction itself was a small department store where it was always a struggle to get served - the shop assistants seemed to hate the customers. Alongside it was the Worker-Peasant-Soldier Photographic Shop where we had our official photos taken.

On the opposite side of the intersection stood the Xinhua bookshop, which I visited regularly to pick up the latest brightly coloured propaganda posters (my collection, incidentally, can now be seen in the Ashmolean Museum, Oxford). Once in early spring 1975, I happened to be visiting the bookshop when a Liberation truck pulled up. Out leapt half a dozen strapping militia men who roughly grabbed a pair of down-at-heel peasants standing over a few bunches of spinach and offering them to passers-by. Any money-making by the rural dwellers was frowned upon by the ultras, and it was the militia - the *minbing* - who did their bidding in Nanjing. I was upset, and later raised the issue with Minder Wang. He informed me gleefully that the miscreants would be punished by dumping them out into the countryside far from their people's commune.

'If we don't deal with them,' he explained, 'the capitalist tail will end up wagging the socialist dog.'

Then there were the ruddy-cheeked teenage girls in their floral padded jackets - peasant lasses from the nearby countryside - who stood forlornly mid-pavement at the Shaanxi Road roundabout darning socks for a few *fen*, while their barefoot customers crouched sheepishly nearby. Once again, I witnessed the militia rolling up in their open truck and carting them off. They accepted their fate without protest.

I was particularly upset when Wang applied his strident 'capitalist tail' formula to our popcorn man. Pushing his home-made tricycle up the drive of the Dingshan as far as the PLA guard post, the ancient popcorn man, with straggly beard, clothed in a holy black apron, would always have a gaggle of happy children in tow. A youngster would offer a handful of maize which the popcorn man would clamp into a pressure vessel with the appearance of an old bomb casing. He would then set to work with his bellows on the charcoal under the bomb, and after a few minutes, with a fearsome bang, he would release the cover, the popcorn flying everywhere, to the delight of the crowd. In a landscape of monochrome, it was a colourful performance. But it was not one which the politically correct could tolerate. As 1976 wore on, the popcorn man no longer made his appearance and I asked Minder Wang where he had gone. Again, he started mumbling about capitalist tails, and I felt like punching him.

'How on earth can China's massive planned economy be affected by a little trading at the margins?' I pleaded. Wang had no answer.

Far more dramatic in Nanjing's ideological maelstrom was the ongoing struggle down at Gulou Square where the earnest - and sometime vicious - wall-poster campaigns burst periodically into life. Knots of jostling onlookers would be clustered around the latest postings on the wall of the great rostrum; sometimes you could even witness, from a safe distance, an untidy scuffle in the crowd, posters ripped down and fists raised.

With Beijing today spreading its 'soft diplomacy' throughout the world through its Confucius Institutes - in the manner of the British Council or Alliance Francaise - the ancient philosopher is now seamlessly, shamelessly even, restored as the apparent lodestone of China's harmony. It was very different back in those days. I have before me a booklet issued for bed-time reading in 1974 - the title screaming 'Confucius - 'Sage' of the Reactionary Classes'. In the mid-1970s, Confucius had fallen from his pedestal and was officially a dangerous pest. We arrived in China just in time to catch the tail-end of the 'Criticise Lin Biao and Confucius' campaign, and the booklet was handed to us in order that we might catch up.

There was more 'education of the masses' with which we had to get up-to-speed. The ordained account of the turncoat Lin Biao and his apparent attempt to flee the country in 1971 must have stretched the credulity of even the most faithful servants of the new orthodoxy. Unfortunately we had arrived just too late to be allowed to see the documents which 'proved' that Marshall Lin Biao, previously Chairman Mao's anointed successor, was from the moment he emerged from his mother's womb a confirmed counter-revolutionary. The Politburo had sanctioned senior Party members a glimpse of the lengthy screed on the Lin Biao affair; for some unfathomable reason, and for a short period of time, Beijing's foreign employees were included. The materials had to be read under close supervision, no writing instruments allowed. Lin Biao was accused, improbably, of trying to blow up Mao's train as it passed through Jiangsu, after which he met an ignominious end on the grasslands of Mongolia. Further allegations concerning the supposed plot finally emerged during the trial of the 'Gang of Four' in 1981).

'You know that the traitor Lin Biao fled towards the Soviet enemy in a British-made Trident airliner,' our Party interlocutors took delight in reminding us.

As for Confucius, while no one around us would comment directly, we had our trusted radio: the foreign broadcasts picked up on our crackly forty-seven yuan Panda valve set were telling us that the campaign's target was none other than Zhou Enlai. It was an inexplicable paradox that most radios in the shops included the short-wave bands, yet severe punishment would be meted out to anyone caught listening to foreign broadcasts. When night came, we could always be found surreptitiously tuning into any foreign broadcast which could be picked up in eastern China.

Every work unit had to devote ample time to *zhengzhi xuexi* - political study. Just as in the factory to which we were later sent to have our bourgeois foreign consciousnesses 'remoulded' by the workers, in our English Section's sessions the women got through the tedium by knitting whilst the men chain-smoked. Foreign residents of China were not permitted access to local papers, but they were allowed the Party's official newspapers, *People's Daily* and *Guangming Daily*. Since we were for a long time forbidden Chinese lessons, and I only got the language surreptitiously and very gradually, this was little help. Our minders, however, would ensure regular delivery of Xinhua News Agency bulletins which regurgitated in unspeakable English the official messages. It was these Xinhua bulletins which were our focus at political study sessions; the Party members among our colleagues would sit around us reading the original version and we would read the same in English. Then a 'discussion' would ensue, each participant proclaiming how much they had benefitted from the experience.

In mid-1975, our twice-weekly political study had suddenly bucked up when we were mysteriously delivered copies of *Water Margin*, popular tales of ancient derring-do and one of China's most-renowned classic works in the vernacular. Set in the Song dynasty, it tells of the exploits of the outlaw Song Jiang and his merry gang of outlaws - boozers and womanisers to a man (actually there were also three women, to the one hundred and five 'brothers'). Our fellow political-studiers pored over the classic in its rich original while we enjoyed Pearl Buck's 1933 translation which she had entitled *All Men are Brothers*. The book was dug up from heaven-knows-where by our political commissars (in this they were actually guilty of political heresy, for the American writer's entire body of work on China was banned). The tale I most enjoyed – for it was so far from the omnipresent 'class struggle' of the current Chinese reality - was that of Wu Song, who in his cups fought and defeated a tiger (poor tiger). As for Song Jiang, apart from his obvious bad habits, he seemed a chivalrous and likeable character.

We tried hard to fathom the *Water Margin* business and its relevance to current circumstances. We were aware that the

Cultural Revolution had kicked off back in 1966 with a supposed literary debate: Wu Han, a prominent Party leader, had written a play about a Ming official who was unfairly deposed by the emperor. *Hai Rui Dismissed from Office (Hai Rui ba guan)* was not unreasonably read by Mao's circle as an attack on him, and thus the Cultural Revolution was launched. So when an incautious colleague hinted that perhaps not all was as it appeared in the *Water Margin* stories, we were not a bit surprised.

Some weeks into the campaign, our study group suddenly turned on Song Jiang. The brave and hearty outlaw was none other than a scoundrel. Worse, he was a traitor to his band of men, a 'capitulationists'. If the Party's 'theoretical' journal *Red Flag*, and the *People's Daily* said so, who were the benighted intelligentsia to argue? Once again, though the accusation remained ambiguous, the ultras were apparently trying to frame both Deng Xiaoping and Zhou Enlai as 'modern Song Jiangs'. Perhaps this was a step too far for China's long-suffering people. Anyway, the *Water Margin* campaign suddenly died away and our regular political study sessions returned to the hectoring *People's Daily* editorials.

Thinking back, it was hardly surprising that the Cultural Revolution enthusiasts led by the cabal around Mao's wife Jiang Qing were gunning for 'the moderates'. Already by mid-1975, even foreign commentators had started calling the radicals the 'Shanghai Mafia'. But the public display of harmony at the top of the Party remained, and we were inclined to dismiss the often-lurid tales of assorted foreign-based China-watchers. But they were dead right, and we did not have to wait too long before the Shanghai Mafia would be universally reviled as the 'Gang of Four'. I shall go on to describe our experiences leading up to the coup of autumn 1976, shortly after Mao's death, the ousting of those who had instigated the Criticise Lin Biao and Confucius and *Water Margin* campaigns - and the triumphant rehabilitation of the dead Zhou Enlai.

The ultras had a severe problem in keeping their Cultural Revolution on track. In the early 1970s, it was Mao himself who decided to step back from the chaos of his Cultural Revolution. Whether the Chairman had relented somewhat and now wanted whole layers of disgraced officials to be restored - not least of them Zhou's supposed protégé, the often publicly-vilified Deng Xiaoping - is another matter. But it is said that Mao had personally ordered Deng's return to high office. Almost on the quiet, in 1973 the diminutive survivor emerged from his rural exile, to be immediately elevated to vice-premiership, and chief of staff of the Central Military Commission to boot. Quite a comeback and a devastating reversal for the Cultural Revolution's true believers. The move infuriated the radical faction around Mao's wife, Jiang Qing. But the population-at-large remained under the spell of a mood which was later labelled 'whateverism' – whatever Mao had said or done was to be upheld. If Deng had made a comeback, *ipso facto* it was because Chairman Mao had authorised it, and anything that Chairman Mao saw fit to endorse had to be unanimously supported by all the top leaders. Or at least, that's what we mistakenly believed at the time.

By January 1976, with Zhou Enlai dead and gone, the man whom the Red Guards had castigated as 'China's Second Khrushchev' was well-entrenched. But for the diehards it was never too late to return the Chinese nation to the pressing tasks of ceaseless revolution. The Dragon Year cast its baleful shadow, and Deng Xiaoping was in for yet another reversal of fortunes and dismissal from office.

What in truth did we resident but isolated foreigners understand of these twists and turns of Chinese high politics? As I have suggested, being immersed within this vast land rather than amongst the China-watchers of Hong Kong or Washington meant that we often failed to see the wood for the trees. Yet now, with Zhou Enlai's death, it was only those within the Bamboo Curtain who could truly sense the atmosphere of neurotic uncertainty. Nanjing felt suddenly tense and exciting, the familiar norms of public ritual no longer seeming to prevail. We were in a heady, anthropological mood, ready to witness the unfolding of unscripted events which no one outside China could share. At our teacher training classes, our colleagues were strained and monosyllabic. What was next for China, for them, the intelligentsia, the Stinking Ninth category of class enemy, and indeed for 'foreign intellectuals' too, if the normal rules were to be suspended and the Cultural Revolution extremists were again in the driving seat?

By January 1976, we had a 14-inch black-and-white TV in one of the Dingshan's many empty public rooms. We were encouraged to go and watch the comings and goings of doddery Politburo elders at Zhou's lying-in-state, always a guide to who was up and who down at the Party's slippery apex. We also observed his funeral cortège as it coursed through the frozen boulevards of Beijing towards Babaoshan, the revolutionaries' burial ground. The fuzzy screen showed dense rows of onlookers braving the cold, though whether they were 'official' crowds or there spontaneously and freely wasn't yet evident. All that was clear was their number.

In our city of Nanjing, the commanding march-by rostrum at Gulou Square was overnight bedecked with huge, circular white and black wreaths from Party organisations and work units. On campus, teams of female students were hard at work sewing armbands and soon everyone, including ourselves, had a black silk wrapper on their upper left sleeve. On the second morning after Zhou's death was announced, I watched from the bottom of the University drive as Nanjing's citizens in their tens of thousands left their homes and workplaces, formed up into discipline columns in Zhongshan Road and headed off towards Changjiang Road.

This was where Zhou had been stationed in the late 1940s, before China's second period of civil war which brought the defeat of the American-backed Nationalists and the eventual victory of the Communist Party. We were not well-pleased that of the University community, only we seemed to have been excluded. However, the following day Minder Zhao disclosed that the rally had taken a dangerous turn when the crush had brought down walls and left many injured.

Meanwhile, the loudspeakers in work units and on the street blared out an unending funereal dirge, one which I can replay, note-perfect, all these years on. By the next day all the female students had replaced their coloured ribbons in the plaits with white ones, and were formed up in sobbing knots around the campus mass as they crocheted piles of white rosettes.

The day after the big rally, we were told to turn up at the University. On the scrubby winter lawns of our quadrangle, several dozen members of the Foreign Languages department had gathered, exchanging nods and stern glances. Minder Liu beckoned us over to the ranks of the English Section.

'Today is the University's ceremony to remember our beloved premier,' he said chokingly, 'and we thought our foreign friends should join us because we know they too loved our premier.'

This might have been gilding the lily rather, but anyway we appreciated the fact that for once we had been included. A person whom Minder Liu identified as the Party secretary of the Russian Section was giving soft orders. Until that moment, we had been unaware that Foreign Languages still taught Russian, the language of China's sworn enemy. Another secret to be kept from the foreigner. Maybe China was just hedging its bets. It was obvious to us that trade was still going on between the two arch-enemies – we rode sometimes in new Volga cars and flew in ageing Ilyushin and Andronov aircraft, which presumably had to have imported spares. And where there was trade there had to be linguists. Another case of Chinese pragmatism trumping politics.

Lining up with our colleagues, soon we were marching with a ragged military gait down to the nearby sports field. Little was left to chance - the frozen fringe of grass was divided by a matrix of small white crosses, perfectly symmetrical, upon which we had to position ourselves. We arrived to a half-empty field, but from different sides came phalanxes of staff and students, and within a few minutes the entire six-thousand-strong University community was assembled. On the far side of the field and to our right, a stage, a rostrum, had been erected from stout bamboos, and draped with two great lengths of blue cloth, enclosing a huge portrait of Zhou.

'One of the foreign language students painted that overnight,' whispered Liu proudly.

With the thousands now standing silently to attention, members of each department brought forward their wreath, huge things carefully fashioned around two metre-wide hoops bordered by evergreen sprigs and covered with paper flowers of all hues, not just the mourning white. In the centre of each, in gold letters, was the bold character *bei* – 'sorrow'. As the wreaths moved forward from different corners of the sports field, carried from behind by unseen bearers they appeared as weird automata, redolent of the Daleks. If it were not for the occasion and the tear-streaked cheeks all around us, it would have been a hilarious sight. Equally incongruous was the scene on the margins of the heaving and sobbing sports field. From the corner of my eye, I could see a gaggle of ten-year-olds gambolling around quite noisily. No one tried to restrain them, and it reminded me of an observation by a social psychologist who had remarked that in China, children were treated like adults, and adults like children. Never more true than in the Cultural Revolution.

The master of ceremonies took centre stage and blew down his microphone. It was an unnecessary precaution - you could always rely on Chinese public address systems to work infallibly.

'He's a young man from the Revolutionary Committee,' relayed Liu in that odd way he had of hissing straight into my ear. Then started the speeches, at which all the males - myself included - doffed their blue-peaked caps. As in Europe a century ago, in 1970s China a man was naked without his head covering. The elusive Party Secretary of Nanjing University was then announced. Whatever he intended, Gu Ping was unable to convey a single sentence. His sobs were magnified around the field by a dozen oversized loudspeakers and must have been heard a couple of miles away. Everyone around us now started to weep uncontrollably, the younger women wailing their grief. Such mass emotion is infectious and there was no way that Jo and I could have resisted our own tears.

Further incoherent speeches followed, the final one by a girl student from whom not a word could be unravelled through the sobs. Someone decided to abandon further speechifying and the loudspeakers started to play a loop of the eight mournful bars of the funeral dirge. Thinking later about the mass emotion out there on the Nanjing University sports field, I recalled reading of the domestic reaction to Stalin's death in 1953. Monster though he must have been to a significant part of the Soviet people, it was the defeat of the horrendous German invasion with which he had already become identified by the 'broad masses'. And just as for Stalin, Zhou's death was now marked by much wailing and gnashing of the teeth. With hindsight, however, I estimate that for most urban dwellers this was not fond sentiment, but rather a fear of what the future held, now that the supposed people's shield against the great and terrible leader had passed from the scene.

The ceremony ending, the entire assembly was marshalled to

leave the sports field via the rostrum. We watched as first students and then staff filed by, bowing three times according to a timeless Chinese tradition which the ultras had banned as a 'feudal remnant'. Soon it was the turn of our line to move forward. Reaching the rostrum, I found myself presented with a book of condolence. I looked at Minder Liu in surprise, and he nodded conspiratorially. Overcome by the moment, I quickly filled the blank sheet before me with words which in more sober times would have appeared extravagant, hagiographic even. Flash bulbs popped and without realising it, I became part of the nascent anti-Gang of Four alliance. Much later with Mao and his cohorts gone, this photograph was circulated in China as proof that the foreigners too were against the Gang of Four.

Edgar Snow and Agnes Smedley wrote extraordinary profiles of the Long Marchers whom they met in Yan'an in the late 1930s, though there is now much insinuation of hagiography. Nonetheless, I was genuine in my admiration for Zhou Enlai as a revolutionary leader and fighter. For me, Mao too was technically on the right side of history when he declared in a 1957 essay 'Only socialism can save China'. For most Chinese, myself included, that was actually the year when he should have stood down had he wished to preserve his reputation across a spectrum of the population. The disastrous Great Leap Forward of 1958 and its aftermath of mass starvation, let alone Mao's Great Proletarian Cultural Revolution, might have been avoided under a more pragmatic leadership.

My own broad view of the China I experienced under Mao was, and indeed remains, as follows: with a huge population, an impoverished economic base ravaged by a century of war and invasion, with external enemies anxious to reverse the revolution, with a people weighed down by feudal tradition, the Communist Party in power was bound to bring forth a polity of much distorted collectivism and over-weaning bureaucracy. Beijing's propaganda ranted endlessly about the Soviet Union being a 'social imperialist' country - a characterisation far from any scientific validity as far as the Marxist method is concerned. Frustrated by our everyday experiences of the system, we used to take secret delight in our own label for China in the throes of its eternal Cultural Revolution: if the Soviet Union was 'social imperialist', this country was incorrigibly 'social feudalist'.

Actually, seeing both the achievements of a basically non-market economy and yet all of its shortcomings, our confidence in the future of our own society back home in the U.K. was hugely boosted. Though much remains in European society of feudal ways of thinking - the worship of royalty being a glaring example – on the whole, post-Enlightenment European society had made progress in excising pre-rational thought processes. And this has happened gradually within the interstices of a capitalist system. Our own task of creating a new order – in our youthful yearning one for which Jo and I felt a heavy responsibility - might, therefore, be all the less arduous. Admittedly by the second decade of the 21st century, state deregulation, privatisation, super-concentration of capital, and all the ills of the global market system have done much to erode the country that we left behind in 1974. But in the mid-1970s, the experience of China created in us a powerful belief in a bright, egalitarian, social-collectivist future for Europe.

With Zhou Enlai's death, the Central Committee apparently decided to try and head off any untoward currents which might sweep the grieving nation to the 'wrong' conclusions. We were deluged at every turn with the official slogan of the moment: 'Turn grief into strength' (*hua beitong wei liliang*). Endless repetition being the best route to language learning, this obscure phrase is one which I shall never fail to call up. But it was clear that the constant harping on 'strength' had a mundane purpose, the intended message being this: the only fitting tribute to the deceased leader was to work even harder and to consume even less. Yet both foreign and Chinese students of recent history conclude that the Cultural Revolution caused production in town and country to slump drastically. That might have been the case between 1966 and 1968, but by the turn of the 1970s the shrill tenor of propaganda was production, production, production. On an hourly, daily basis the Chinese people were exhorted to pursue the exemplary models of the Daqing oilfield in industry, and the supposedly superhuman efforts of the Dazhai villagers in agriculture. The respective leaders of these places, two national Stakhonivites, Wang Jinxi and Chen Yonggui, were extolled at every turn. Wherever the Chinese lived and worked, they were never more than a few yards from red-painted wall slogans advertising the Daqing and Dazhai production models. And you could never escape either from the universally daubed slogan 'Grasp revolution, promote production'.

Our own experiences of weeks of redeeming *laodong* in a village, and later in a large chemical plant, was that labour discipline in China was absolute. And when it came to Zhou's funeral in Beijing, which we were encouraged to watch on the little TV in the capacious dining room of Nanjing Hotel, the opportunity was not missed. The oration, performed by one of those over-the-top voices of the Jiang Qing model opera school, was shockingly blatant. The Chinese David Dimbleby began on a low tone, clear, respectful. When he came towards the end and started to exhort the Chinese nation towards greater efforts in production, his voice rose and quickened to a mad crescendo.

From the day of Zhou Enlai's funeral the struggle intensified, the outwards signs being unremitting poster campaigns on the streets and on campus. With the Spring Festival arriving a month after Zhou's death, we somehow persuaded the University to let us visit Beijing. Their reluctant agreement was in part due to the lambasting we had given them about the previous year's New Year holiday, when they had cunningly confined us to Nanjing on the grounds that foreign staff were not entitled to a break. Our trip to Beijing in February 1976 - the first for both of us - turned out to be one of those rare and wonderful occasions when one arm of the bureaucracy was unaware of what its other arm was doing. The outcome was that for the first time in over a year, we were free of minders, interpreters, drivers, flunkies. It was the most potent interlude of freedom.

Before we left for the capital, we heard on the BBC World Service that some important, mould-shattering posters had appeared at Beijing University, always known as 'Beida'. Arriving by train, we got ourselves into the Friendship Hotel, and then took a short bus ride up to Beida's illustrious campus. Now we had to get ourselves through the heavily-patrolled archway inscribed with the huge red characters *Beijing daxue* in Mao's unmistakeable, unruly hand. We had made prior contact with Michael S, then the one-and-only foreign teacher of English at Beida, who helpfully supplied us with little red enamel badges which made us out to be staff. Our aim was to get into the enclosure on the campus where bamboo matting had been erected in a long avenue for the poster campaign. Tough-looking young men with red armbands were patrolling the entrance and we were on edge, for this was the radicals' lion's den.

By chance - or perhaps not - wandering the campus with its fine pagoda water tower and landscaped lake, we had been approached by a young man who introduced himself as a cadre in the University's foreign affairs department. Someone had apparently instructed him to take these out-of-towners in hand, to let them witness the Beida message. In those days, transmission of unprintable news was often done through individuals moving around the country, and maybe our new acquaintance had that in mind. And the message at Beida was angrily anti-Zhou Enlai, and his protégé Deng Xiaoping too. We followed our guide to a corner of the campus where hundreds, thousand were milling around an avenue flanked by the specially constructed hoardings plastered in *dazibao*, 'big character' posters. At the top end of the avenue several guards were checking people in and out. The cadre pulled rank, and we were in. I wandered down the bamboo stalls and recorded each and every unfathomable poster for posterity.

Back once again in Nanjing, people seemed to aware of what was going on at the Beida campus, and it was clearly very unwelcome. The bolder of our teacher colleagues came to us one by one and in a dark mood to ask what we had seen. We were at a loss. Our Ektachrome slide film had been packed off to the Worker-Peasant-Soldier Photo Studio in Shanghai's Nanjing Road, and we had nothing to show. But it did not take long for the essence of the Beijing campaign to flow into every corner of the land. A couple of weeks later, the Nanjing posters, too, were shouting the old Cultural Revolution epithets - capitalist roaders in the Party had to be sought out and pulled down. Usually in such campaigns there was a riposte, a counter-current, new posters being slapped up over the offending ones. On this occasion, it seemed it was just too dangerous to put forth any contrary view. The radicals were unchallenged in their ascendancy. *A stifling type of lily-liveredness*, my diary records.

In the midst of all this, a diplomatic interlude took our attention for a few days. While the poster campaign shrieked of capitalist roaders, the disgraced and deposed Nixon was invited to China and feted by the so-called leftist as an 'old friend'. My diary entry is again angry:

Tuesday 24th Feb – the campaign spreads. Rather a contradiction that the biggest cap. roader in the world's history, hoodlum and fascist opportunist, is now conferring with China's heads of Party and State. Nixon got yesterday 1 +. hours with CM, only a few mins less than (President) Ford last autumn. Clearly the Chinese are trying to push the US admin. further right, and even hope for a Reagan nomination. Nixon, who 'met the people' today – clearly sees himself as the future US ambassador in Peking.

Our exasperation at Nixon's fine treatment was quite pointless and all we could do was vent our displeasure on our poor minder.

'How would you like it if the U.S. invited Lin Biao or Liu Shaoqi (recent Chinese 'traitors') and sent a special plane for them too?' I taunted Liu. Embarrassed smiles were his only possible response.

No one could have known that the last week of March and first days of April of the year 1976 were to be so remarkable in the history of the People's Republic. The previous year at this time, the traditional Qingming festival for the dead, our minder had turned up late one evening to tell us that all lessons were cancelled the next day, and perhaps the day after too. We were to stay firmly at home. No explanation. When we were allowed back on campus, our students informed us that we had missed the annual procession to the martyrs' fields of Nanjing – the Yuhuatai (Rain Flower Terrace) park to the south of the city. In their two phases of national power both before and after the Japanese invasion, the Nationalists executed vast numbers of their opponents, perhaps one hundred thousand people at Yuhuatai. In the 1950s, a huge socialist-realist statue of nine figures was erected in the new public park there to represent the Party members and the members of the different classes executed. A stele commemorating the revolutionary martyrs in Mao's handwriting was also erected at the execution site.

Since coming to power, the Communist Party had transmuted the traditional Qingming to a revolutionary purpose. It was no longer a time for families to visit family graves, do a general clean-up, and leave offerings of food. In post-1949 Nanjing, the custom had long been that all the school and university students were marched off to Yuhuatai for speeches and mass obeisance. We were furious to be left out of this innocuous celebration, and in no uncertain terms petitioned the University revolutionary committee. For once they seemed embarrassed by our righteous complaints, and sincere promises were extracted that at the following Qingming, this year of 1976, we would definitely be included in the Yuhuatai memorial event.

What we, and no one else could foresee was that in 1976, the Qingming festival would take on an entirely different, indeed a seditious, character. As with much of the action in those days, it all began in the cockpit of the radicals - Shanghai. There, on 25 March, the nationally-distributed Shanghai newspaper *Wenhui bao* published an article which attacked the dead Zhou Enlai by name, calling him a capitalist roader. On 30th March I was surreptitiously tuning into the Moscow station, Radio Peace and Progress, which to my amazement was reporting things happening in our very own Nanjing. Perhaps there was some truth to the paranoia about Soviet spies! Moscow claimed that the angry citizens of Shanghai had plastered the sides of trains leaving for the north with slogans and posters denouncing the Shanghai radicals' attack on Zhou Enlai. The first major stop on the railway to Beijing was Nanjing.

March 31st was the chosen day for the students' annual Qingming pilgrimage to Yuhuatai. True to their word, the University let us know that we were welcome to join our students in the march to the memorial park. As it happened, I had developed a rare bout of flu, and was unable to rise from my sick-bed. But off Jo marched with the student lines. It was quite a way to Yuhuatai; as the column wound its way south, it was joined at every road junction by solemn columns of workers, each with a large portrait of Zhou Enlai held high. Jo realised that this was clearly now a demonstration rather than a pilgrimage, and as the massed ranks inched along, groups broke away to paint slogans wherever there was an inviting surface - walls, stalled buses, even the cabs of trucks. By the time Jo reached Yuhuatai, she was surrounded by a sea of silent demonstrators perhaps a million strong. Though her Chinese language was at a primitive level, the anti-radical, anti-establishment tenor of the massive Yuhuatai demonstration was unmistakeable. Our trusty Olympus camera did the rest. I listened later with heightened jealousy as Jo recounted the strange events; we sealed her two exposed films in their grey plastic canisters and readied them for despatch to Shanghai for processing.

On the same day, on the last day of March, slogans and posters had gone up on every wall of central Nanjing, and our colleagues were uncharacteristically prepared to let in on the fact that these were virulent denunciations of certain people in Shanghai. A focus of the poster campaign, as ever, was the high concrete wall which supported the march-by rostrum at Gulou Square. The upper part of the rostrum was decorated with a huge portrait of Mao Zedong. As we were driven through the square on the way to the university, I poked my camera through the lace curtains and took snapshot after snapshot of the large crowd milling round the *dazibao*. On the way home, we witnessed something of a fracas - people were clearly trying to rip some of the posters down. The Olympus OM1 was the first commercial camera with automatic shutter speed priority, and in the bright Nanjing daylight it was a simple matter of pointing and shooting.

By now, northbound poster-bedecked trains had reached

Beijing, where they aroused the same angry reaction as they had met in Nanjing. More or less spontaneously, the citizens of the capital in their hundreds of thousands started to head for Tiananmen Square, the symbolic centre of the city. Once there, they surrounded the great Monument to the Martyrs with great white wreaths, while anti-radical agitators glued their poems and posters to the walls of the edifice. The mass occupation of Tiananmen Square, the fiery speeches, impromptu poetry readings and declamations around the monument continued until 5th April. At one point the crowd surged towards the security outpost on the south side of the Great Hall of the People where a building was set afire as well as police cars (we learned this from our shortwave radio, and were surprised when China's official media quickly confirmed the bare facts).

Now almost paralysed by Parkinson's disease, Mao Zedong was consulted by his nephew Mao Yuanxin, who acted as liaison with the radical Shanghai faction. Mao was informed that a counter-revolutionary coup was underway. On the night of the 5th, when demonstrators were fewer, Mao Yuanxin and Mao's wife Jiang Qing ordered the security forces to move in: hundreds were dragged away, many injured, and untold numbers put to death out of sight of the crowd.

To what extent was Mao personally culpable? In the months leading up to April 1976, his collapsed state of health had been an open secret. His entourage insisted on a photo-shoot every time a foreign dignitary came to pay homage, and all the doctoring in the world of his front-page *People's Daily* portrait could not conceal the truth. Mao was propped up in his armchair, his body askew and his features contorted. We could see that the end was nigh, and perhaps that was the idea. Yet Mao was such a demigod, so much a part of the architecture of the new China, that many amongst the great masses considered him immortal. But the Qingming affair dealt a huge blow to Mao Zedong's reputation within the urban classes.

Like the much greater Tiananmen struggle thirteen years on, the one the world knows about, the 1976 Qingming uprising was immediately condemned as counter-revolutionary. In the regime's terms, there was no label more severe. It was clear that the government needed a prominent scapegoat, and it was, naturally, Deng Xiaoping who was presented as the 'black hand' behind the nationwide protests. Anyone who had taken a leading part in the events in Nanjing, Beijing and in countless other places throughout the country was now to be a target. By the 8th April, whoever was holding the reins of power in Beijing had stripped Deng Xiaoping of all his posts for the second time since the beginning of the Cultural Revolution.

That morning at the usual hour of 7:30 am we were driven to the University through streets plastered with slogans denouncing the moderates, now vilified as counter-revolutionaries.

Emblazoned on every wall were new slogans in huge letters: 'Down with Deng Xiaoping', 'Carry the Class Struggle Through to the End'.

Passing at speed through Gulou Square, we could see that a major event was going to be staged. The metal railings had been removed around the huge oval, and painters had overnight criss-crossed the tarmac with white lines. Our tough new chain-smoking driver Lao Xia dropped us off at the University gates, where our foreign languages colleagues were lined up alongside the massed ranks of the University community. It certainly was not going to be a routine day in the classroom.

For once, our colleagues were talkative and nervy and clearly mystified about events in faraway Beijing. The *People's Daily* on 7th April had spoken of a 'handful' of counter-revolutionaries causing trouble in Beijing, yet at the same time acknowledged that over one hundred thousand citizens of the capital had been at the Tiananmen protest. A glaring and probably deliberately revealing contradiction slipped in by ambivalent players. A few of our more daring friends sidled up to ask what we knew from foreign broadcasts. It seemed wise to say nothing.

As we awaited the signal to march off down Hankou Road, a colleague whispered to us that the night before there had been a kind of loyalty parade on campus for the victors of Tiananmen Square, the radicals. This we were not surprised to hear, as the final outcome of the disturbances remained in question and in China it was always advisable to be on both sides of the fence. Similar manifestations had apparently taken place in every work unit in Nanjing. According to one colleague, the campus loudspeakers had only stopped blaring out their loyalty to the radical line at an unprecedented one o'clock in the morning.

We were lined up four abreast at the University gates, girl students with girls, boys with boys, and the teaching staff in similarly puritanically correct formation. At last, at eight-thirty we set off for the nearby square, merging at Zhongshan Road with a great phalanx of factory workers in their blue overalls and bamboo safety helmets. As we reached Gulou (Drum Tower) Square, from the north came hundreds, thousands of soldiers and sailors from the Nanjing garrisons, all heavily armed, many wielding little triangular flags with the now easily-recognisable slogans - 'Down with Deng Xiaoping', 'Long live Chairman Mao'.

Our English section colleagues seemed familiar with the drill, for soon enough each of us was positioned on one of the little white markers painted on the ground. I gazed towards the wall under the high rostrum which only hours before had been defaced by slogans and half-ripped down posters. It had been scrubbed completely clean and now displayed a huge banner. One of our colleagues whispered its meaning: 'Firmly grasp the Central Committee's 9th and 10th Directives'.

In my hand was the latest issue of the *Xinhua* Daily News bulletin. Minder Zhao had thrust it at me back at the University gate. While awaiting the action - and it was a long wait - I glanced at the bulletin's front page. In bold red letters, those usually reserved for pronouncements by the Chairman himself, the bulletin recounted word for word the current *People's Daily* front page. The 'Two Directives' proclaimed the dismissal of Deng Xiaoping and the appointment as premier of an unfamiliar name - Hua Guofeng.

We stood on the spot for well over an hour as the square filled up. Then at ten o'clock the rally was kicked off by an unenthusiastic ritual of slogan shouting, fists just about raised in the air. The province's leaders, high above on the rostrum, many of them in the green uniforms of the military, began their mechanical speechifying, which seemed confined to reading out the official verdicts on the dastardly counter-revolutionary affair. Their dirge-like efforts were punctuated by choreographed slogan chanting from the square. After each statement blared out, those on the rostrum clapped. The massed ranks below didn't follow suit, which I thought was unusual. Suddenly it was over, and the assembly started peeling off in the direction of the city centre.

One of our colleagues managed to shuffle over beside us:

'Who is this Hua Guofeng?' he asked.

Like him, we were clueless about the man who would soon become the new Chairman of the Chinese Communist Party, comically adjusting his hairstyle to mimic Mao's own swept back style.

In spite of all this, life went on much as before, though contact such as it was with our colleagues dwindled to almost nil. From time to time, we were told not to appear at the campus. In the middle of May, though, the events of Qingming came back to bite us, and bite us hard. It just happened that Party Secretary Duan was visiting us at the Dingshan - for the first time in months - when a white-uniformed hotel attendant knocked on our door and brought in a parcel. I recognised immediately the seal of the Worker-Peasant-Soldier Photographic Studio in Shanghai, the only laboratory outside of Beijing where Kodak films could be processed. Whenever we had a large enough batch of exposed cartridges we encased them in a cotton package as the post office decreed and despatch them to the gloriously named studios on Shanghai's Nanjing Road. When they came back, we would be always be notified by the post office downtown, where we had to present ourselves to receive our property. This time, oddly, the parcel came straight to our door, just when one of our political overseers happened to be present. What a coincidence.

We had long decided that Comrade Duan was one of the few in the leadership who seemed genuinely sympathetic to us on a human level. It was he who accompanied us on our trip to Shaanxi and Henan the previous summer, and though he inexplicably dropped us in the shit when we returned to Nanjing, under the circumstances Duan had been a fine travelling companion. If we could think of anyone as a friend – to the extent that China in that era allowed friendships with foreigners, Duan would have come closest. A portly figure with glasses, he had a great domed, bald forehead which made him look like the fat Buddha – Budai – so beloved of the Cantonese. Duan's face usually shone with a suppressed pleasantness, for it did not do to appear too openly friendly. And yes, Comrade Duan was also the only person who had ever told us a joke, weak but risqué in buttoned-down China.

'I'm thirty and my wife's thirty-two,' he said, with the 'th' said as 'd'.

But now Duan was unsmiling.

'You have taken some photographs which are sensitive,' he began as he picked up the parcel from the seat where I had left it. 'You must attend a meeting tomorrow at the University.'

That was all. He departed with the offending parcel under his arm.

The following day, no car came at 7:00 am. Obviously our classes had been suspended. Eventually late morning, an unfamiliar Volga rolled up outside the Dingshan office. A stern-faced Duan delivered us straight to the Yellow House, the stuccoed villa a hundred yards from the University gates where we would routinely be called to some meeting or other by the Revolutionary Committee. In the main meeting room, a pleasant room with polished wooden floor and the usual array of loose-covered sofas, a posse of cadres awaited us. Some were familiar faces and others we didn't recognise.

It was the tall and handsome Zhou Songshan - the University Foreign Affairs main liaison with any foreigner who turned up at Nanda - who rose to address us:

'You have offended the Chinese people,' he informed us. 'The masses are very angry with you. You took some photographs which are not revolutionary.'

I was grateful that he had not yet used the phrase *fan geming* - counter-revolutionary.

One of the strangers then rose, a man in an ordinary blue cadre suit, and Minder Zhao interpreted.

'I am Officer Li from the Nanjing Public Security Bureau. You have taken some reactionary photographs. If a Chinese had done this, then the revolutionary masses would punish them severely. But you are our foreign friends and do not know our rules. Therefore we ask you to confess your wrong actions and apologise to the Chinese people.'

So this was the infamous criticism meeting of the Chinese Communist Party. It did not seem wise to argue.

'If we've made some mistakes, we do apologise,' I stuttered.

Where the proceedings were meant to go next, no one seemed to know. After a short pause Comrade Zhou rose and we were shown the door. Without, of course, our treasured photos, all twenty-six rolls of them, including those recording the Qingming events. As we drove back to the Dingshan, Comrade Duan turned to us, looking relieved and speaking softly:

'You must understand, that if a *Zhongguoren*, a Chinese person, had done what you have done, he might be executed.'

We had our suspicions, but without the photographs it was to be two years before we discovered the true depths of our crimes. There were the shots of the radical-inspired Beijing University posters - at that juncture all innocuously 'revolutionary'. But when Jo had joined the April Qingming commemoration, which turned out to be an angry demonstration against the foremost power mongers, the Shanghai radicals, she had been the only person amongst hundreds of thousands who had dared to use a camera; of course, at the time, her act was unwitting. The Qingming events in Nanjing, which sparked off the Tiananmen demonstrations, in April 1976 stood condemned as counter-revolutionary. Our photos of the Yuhuatai demonstration were the only record on celluloid of that massive upheaval, that first mass rebellion against the leadership since 1949. Heaven knows what anti-regime slogans Jo in her innocence had captured.

In February 1977, we were to leave Nanjing, and passing through Hong Kong on the way home, we somehow got stuck to the odd British colony and found a comfortable perch on one of its outer islands, Cheung Chau – Long Island.

As the Chinese New year of 1978 approached, we received a

telegram from Nanjing University mysteriously inviting us back to the city, all expenses paid. Tickets could be picked up immediately from the Kowloon China Travel Office.

It was only when we arrived in Nanjing that we were told the purpose. Once again, we were called to the Yellow House, but this time to a smiling reception, the low tables laden with buns and sticky sweets.

'The Nanjing Counter-Revolutionary Incident of Qingming two years ago has now become the Nanjing Revolutionary Incident. You two played an important part in the activities against the Gang of Four and you are now named as foreign revolutionary heroes,' a beaming Zhou Songshan announced.

'The Public Security department apologises for their criticism of you and wants to return your property,' he went on. At this, our impromptu welcoming committee rose to their feet with round of applause. We were stunned. It just showed how clueless foreigners could get mixed up in Chinese affairs without even trying.

Apparently all those condemned as counter-revolutionaries, including some of the teaching staff who had been jailed for their part in the protest, were now lauded as brave saviours of the people.

So the provincial Public Security had had to eat humble pie over our photographs. Even worse, they had been obliged to return them to the troublesome foreigners and even make a public apology. This was an astonishing turnaround. We had our precious rolls of film again. That night Comrade Duan came to the hotel.

'I have bought you several books of poems and stories about the Revolutionary Incident,' he said, handing us a brown paper package. 'These include many of your photographs of the demonstration to Yuhuatai.'

Later, back in Hong Kong, we were astonished to discover when we compared the photos in the books with our long lost slides, that extra elements had been introduced into the published versions. These consisted in the main of additional and more explicit slogans against Mao's widow Jiang Qing and the 'Shanghai Mafia'. The official discourse in China has a habit of rubbishing the overthrown dynasty, so the doctoring of our photos was par for the course.

'It was not only the Yuhuatai photographs that the police wanted,' continued Duan. 'You did something much worse in the eyes of the authorities, though at your criticism meeting they couldn't even say the words.'

What had happened was that as we sped past the Gulou rostrum in the days before the Qingming affair, we had managed to commit a monstrous act of *lèse majesté*. Adorning the top half of the Gulou rostrum was a portrait of Chairman Mao, some twenty feet high. Underneath, at street level, was a crowd agitating against the *Wenhui bao* newspaper's criticism of the deceased Zhou Enlai. As we photographed the melee from our fast-moving car, we had focussed on the crowds and contrived to cut off Mao's head at nose level. Symbolism in China is powerful. We had decapitated the Chairman and 'celebrated' the bunch of then-counter-revolutionaries milling around by the rostrum.

In Jiangsu province that seemed to be the end of the matter. But it did not actually go away, and came back to haunt me when I moved to Shandong University in 1978. I was of course unaware that Shandong in 1978 was the last bastion of the Maoist diehards. Hearing of our return to China, the Jiangsu security police, still bristling at being forced into an apology, had – I was told years later - called a meeting with their counterparts in Shandong.

'Li Caide (my Chinese name) is a *huaidan*, a bad element, who has been sent to China by those who wish our revolution ill,' was their message. 'You must place him under maximum surveillance.'

The consequence was that for the next eighteen months, unbeknown to myself, I was to keep a team of undercover security officers well occupied. Much later, Li Hua was to tell me how four of them even shadowed me right to the top of Mount Tai. Indeed, I have quite a few photos of this group of well-dressed Mr Plods, resting on their haunches for an energising smoke, and smiling directly at camera.

Even more surprising was a discovery I made years on from that 1977 trip back to Nanjing from Hong Kong. Duan, who had been responsible for confiscating our photos, had folded a thin sheet of notepaper within one of the poetry volumes he had given us. I only noticed it on the occasion of our old Nanjing friend Yang's visit to our Cumbrian home in 2015. We were reminiscing and I was showing him the poetry books. The fading characters moved me as we deciphered them:

> *Dear Jo and Richard*
> *These two booklets contain a collection of revolutionary poems composed with tears and blood by Chinese people in those darkest days. What the Chinese people want is scientific socialism and not feudal socialism or fascist dictatorship. The poems collected here are the work of countless anonymous heroes, and some of the photos in them are your contributions. At the time these photos were labelled 'criminal evidence' [zui jun] and were confiscated. But today they turn out to be historical evidence of the heroic struggles of the people of Nanjing. As you have witnessed the process of the whole affair, I would like to present these two books to you a token of remembrance.*
> *Duan Zibing*

As things turned, that Dragon was to cast its baleful eyes far beyond its year of 1976. My interesting status as 'foreign spy' was to haunt my remaining time in China, and three years on, to culminate in an uncomfortable retreat from Shandong back to Hong Kong.

XII
SWIMMING FOR THE CHAIRMAN

OUR GUARDIANS NEVER ceased to impress upon us their absolute horror of any accidental damage to our fragile and valuable foreign selves, even insisting that we walked our bikes down the steep Dingshan driveway. With the furnace-like Nanjing summer looming, the new bone of contention was whether or not we would be allowed to swim.

All my adult life, swimming had been a passion, an addiction almost. Added to the frustrations of our Dingshan confinement, its absence was making me inordinately irritable. So I was overjoyed to discover that they had been hiding an Olympic-sized swimming pool at the back of the sports field. This was another legacy of the foreigners who had once ruled the campus. I could hardly wait for my first swim in a year, and as the days started to become uncomfortably hot, word came down the line that permission was granted.

As every Chinese will instantly tell you, Nanjing has the distinction of being one of the country's 'Three Furnaces'. With summer temperatures in the mid-to-high thirties Celsius, the humidity levels caused bacteria to proliferate almost in front of your eyes. Place a jacket or a pair of sweaty shoes in the cupboard overnight and they would come out streaked with mould. Leave them there for a summer and they would have to be thrown away.

Now to the swimming pool. On the appointed day I was escorted there by a small posse. and practically lowered into the water by my concerned companions. If the pool had ever boasted a filtration system, I doubt whether there was one now. Everywhere were thrashing bodies and more than a couple of strokes of crawl was impossible. I wallowed uncomfortably for a few minutes in the tepid stew whilst my minder team, definitely non-swimmers, moithered by the poolside. They need not have worried. When some naked youngsters conducted a who-can-piss-higher competition onto their immobile targets below, I thought it time to seek fresher waters.

One Sunday, we slipped out of the Dingshan on our bikes and headed for the city's great park. Xuanwu Lake in the shadow of the Ming walls even had an area which was a swimming enclosure. The water was warm and muddy, and slightly alarming too as little snakes occasionally whizzed by one's head - though I had read somewhere that when swimming, snakes are incapable of biting. Whatever the drawbacks, at least here we were in open water. Families frolicked on the banks and children – and a few adults – floundered alongside us in the turgid soup. But it was naive of us to imagine we could escape the vigilance of the local busybodies, for that very evening the cadres arrived from the University.

'Swimming in Xuanwu Lake is strictly forbidden, and the masses observe this rule,' announced the tall and suave Comrade Zhou, who had become our main point of contact in the University's revolutionary committee. Zhou's kindly face and gentle manner made him impossible to confront with anger when he reprimanded us or was guilty of naked untruthfulness.

'But there's a swimming area in the lake, clearly marked out, with whole families enjoying themselves, and it's much safer than the University pool,' I protested.

Zhou settled back into our deep sofa and pulled on a Peony cigarette. 'There is no swimming area at the lake and the masses never swim there,' he responded with quiet assurance.

We well knew that the chief motive behind this was fear that we might drown. Even educated Chinese were impervious to the germ theory of disease, putting illness down to the weather. It was no good mentioning the far greater dangers lurking in the pool, where every known water-borne disease was undoubtedly clammering for new hosts.

Summer vacation trips arranged by the University - always political tourism to the key sites of the revolution - at least offered some promising opportunities of open water. In the summer of 1975 we were sent off to northwest Henan province to inspect that revolutionary icon, the Red Flag canal. It was a sweltering North China summer, and our programme of model villages and factories was gruelling. One morning we slipped our swimming gear under our clothes. As the minibus swept by a delicious-looking mountain reservoir, we suggested a quick photo-stop to record this fine achievement of the working masses. Quick as a flash we stripped off, dived in and free-styled out a few dozen yards. From the minibus came loud hooting. On the shore, Comrade Duan and the local accompaniers were on their knees, imploring us with wails and imprecations to return. For an all-too-brief few minutes, we were out of official reach, autonomous.

When we eventually decided to come to shore, we found ourselves a few yards from a stinking privy of rotting mud bricks - a common sight on any country road. This would have to do as a changing room. As I raised my patch of a towel over my head, it flicked against a hornets' nest lodged in a low roof beam. Two screaming and semi-naked figures tumbled out onto the road. Driver and minders fell to the ground again, this time doubled up in mirth. Perfectly safe swimming was considered a mortal danger, yet the real prospect of our being stung to death merely caused hilarity. Another unfathomable cultural paradox.

I had not learned my lesson from this episode, and was actually determined to participate in China's ultimate swim. Every year, a mass event was staged to commemorate Mao's political dip in the Yangtze of July 1966, at the outset of the Cultural Revolution. The Chairman had taken to the swirling waters as a cunning, elliptical way of proving he was still up to the job. With dozens of non-swimmer bodyguards in the water desperately clinging to floats (not shown in the heroic photographs which were published in next day's *People's Daily*), the old man lazed down the Yangtze at Wuhan to give to the nation a typically Mao-ish signal that despite rumours to the contrary he was very much alive and kicking.

Thereafter, on the anniversary of this event, all over the country millions of China's best and bravest took to any nearby stretch of water. Unfortunately, thousands of them also drowned each year, the revolutionary zeal of China's youth far outstripping their swimming skills. It was the city's own stretch of the Great River, a mile wide, which was the customary venue for Nanjing's heroes. My written petitions to participate in the anniversary event were fired off to the Revolutionary Committee almost the moment I arrived. The University, however, was determined that I should forget all about it. And for once, when the anniversary came round, Jiangsu province decreed that no one should take to the muddy waters of the Yangtze. All public displays would take place elsewhere, and in any case would be confined to the People's Liberation Army. I felt cheated and even pondered whether the change was on my account. Whatever, denied a chance to take part, I at least wanted to witness the event.

'This is a military affair of our country,' was Minder Wang's rebuff.

Someone on high, however, decided it would not be a bad idea after all to demonstrate the PLA's military prowess to the foreigner. The venue turned out to be our very own Xuanwu Lake, where thousands of soldiers had been marshalled for a revolutionary swimathon across the widest stretch of the lake, towards the new railway station to the north. Like the other spectators we squatted cross-kneed on the grass, spat a few melon seeds, and awaited the starting signal. A cannon fired, loudspeakers strung from every tree blared out martial songs. I watched enviously as the massed ranks of the People's Liberation Army waded into water, and swam boldly off in formation, pushing ahead of them floats bearing huge portraits of Mao.

Near us on a worn knoll in the shade of some struggling saplings sat an elderly man in the green fatigues of the PLA, sipping tea from a porcelain mug, the inevitable cigarette between his fingers, closely attended by two fierce PLA giants. Rather than observing the swimmers, he was taking an unusual interest in me. Presently, Minder Wang was beckoned over for an interrogation. Unexpectedly the man was soon smiling in my direction. He waved to one of his bodyguards, who dutifully trundled over to deliver a paper bag of sweeties. I suddenly recognised him as one of the habitués of our hotel.

'Comrade Wang, can you tell me who that is?' I asked with little confidence of a straight answer and without mentioning that I had seen the man around the hotel and had a shrewd idea of his identity.

'He is a high commander of this military region,' Minder Wang flustered with uncharacteristic candour. Both of us knew that the man's daughter was my student. We knew, too, that it would be indelicate to acknowledge the fact. The young lady in question was still presenting herself to me as being from an ordinary worker's family.

Not long after, despite the cadres, I thought to try a surreptitious dip in the same part of Xuanwu Lake as the heroic soldiers. It had all been smoke and mirrors: in that part of the lake the water was so shallow that you could stride across with ease. The revolutionary heroes of the PLA were village lads - poor swimmers but good actors.

Of my choice of Xuanwu Lake over the University swimming pool, there is an ironic afterword. Four years later, with China's news media nervously starting to report 'bad' things as well as good, I was idly leafing through a copy of the magazine *China Reconstructs* when an article caught my eye: 'China's most polluted urban lake'. Nanjing's environmental bureau had decided to announce that four hundred backyard factories were pouring every imaginable pollutant into the city's lake. Among them was a workshop which daily washed out its cyanide sacks. For once, the University bureaucrats had been right about the dangers of the great outdoors. But for quite the wrong reasons.

XIII
CHOOSING THE CHAIRMAN'S
SUCCESSOR

To VENTURE OUTSIDE THE BOUNDS of the city was a big deal, demanding sheaves of paperwork from our many unseen minders. Before every rare escape from Nanjing we would be summoned to the Yellow House for an audience with the Revolutionary Committee. The Yellow House was an incongruous stuccoed European villa close to the main campus gates; in the distant pre-Communist Party past it must have served as the residence of some expatriate University chancellor. We were ushered into the pleasant reception room on the ground floor, with sofas deep, set around a long low table laid out with doilies and lidded tea mugs – not to mention the cigarette dish.

Of the four or five bureaucrats present on this occasion it was Li An, Party Secretary of the Foreign Languages Department, who had been chosen to deliver the sermon. He was the champion of the political cliché:

'You will go to Yan'an, the cradle of the Chinese revolution,' he intoned. 'You will learn how our wise leader Chairman Mao defeated the Japanese imperialists despite the blockade of the reactionary Guomindang. You will visit the headquarters of the glorious Eighth Route Army in Xi'an. You will witness the hard work and self-reliance of the working people in the factories and people's communes, and their determination to repudiate the revisionist line of Lin Biao and Confucius. And you will also go to Lin County and see for yourself how the poor and lower-middle peasants have defeated nature by building the Red Flag Canal.'

Much as the parish priest blesses a bevy of pilgrims before they set off for Lourdes, Li An's duty was to get us in the right frame of mind for our mission, to speak out the correct catechism for each sacred revolutionary shrine we were to visit, and generally to impress upon us that this trip was a serious business. Beyond the good of our souls, the cadres had their own reasons for this: in the eyes of the provincial authorities, and ultimately of the high-ups in Beijing, any transgressions on our part would count as their own. In China everything concerning foreigners was tightly choreographed and any cadre who was found to have allowed the mask to slip was in deep trouble. But the University bureaucrats could scarcely have imagined just how far from the script our politically irreproachable itinerary would stray. Li An had gone on about the peasants defeating nature, and it was precisely the raging of raw nature nature which was to dominate our political tourism in that summer of 1975.

We only had ourselves to blame for the heavy briefing session. The Revolutionary Committee's initial idea for our summer was to dump us in a lakeside hotel in the nearby city of Yangzhou. We had petitioned furiously for something more adventurous, at least for a trip beyond Jiangsu province.

'It is impossible to make contact with the neighbouring provinces,' came the reply. But at the eleventh hour, the bureaucrats relented, Li An comical in his face-saving:

'We are unfortunately not able to meet your request to holiday in Yangzhou. It has been decided that you must learn something of our revolutionary history. You must go to the *Xibei* - the Northwest.'

We bit our lips and inwardly smiled.

Fortunately, Comrade Li An was considered too vital to the University to release for our trips, but a political chaperone was nonetheless demanded. On this occasion, we were relieved that the task would fall to the quietly spoken and kindly Party secretary of the English Section, Comrade Duan.

Cabin fever! Confined to Nanjing for six months, we were in a state of glorious release as Driver Zhou steered us through the crowded streets towards the airport. It was a day of windless blue skies, but no planes were flying until the late afternoon because of bad weather up north. Chinese air traffic controllers always took the ultra-precautionary approach, not unwise given the state of their old Russian fleet, and long airport delays were almost the rule. After a mere half-day wait at Nanjing aerodrome, the first day of August saw us humming through low cloud towards China's Northwest.

In those days, China's masses were earthbound, and the old Russian turbo-prop was as ever laden with high-up bureaucrats, each nursing that badge of rank - the black plastic zip-up handbag. By this point in the Cultural Revolution, the PLA stewardesses in their baggy green fatigues were no longer expected to provide in-flight entertainment by pirouetting in the aisles to an aria from one of Madame Mao's revolutionary operas. It was whispered that the elderly commanders of the PLA had an unwritten rule - female army recruits should always be the willowy creatures of a Chinese painting. So it was on this flight. The four pretty young females wafted up and down the aisle, laconically dispensing hot water onto the swollen leaves in our lidded mugs. One girl was in charge of little gifts - a floral paper fan on a black tin frame, the airline lapel badge – and that rare thing, a red pack of high-class Zhonghua cigarettes. These I could save to offer honoured guests who hated my cheap *Da Qianmen* brand in its grey pack decorated with a risqué 'feudal' picture of one of the gates in old Beijing's walls.

A couple of hours of low cruising in our little Antonov AN-12 turboprop and we exchanged the lush, water-strewn patchwork of the Yangtze plain for the desiccated brown of the Yellow River basin. We refuelled at the tiny airport of Zhengzhou, Henan Province's capital, lunching in a low canteen practically on the runway, and were impressed by our companion-minder Duan's flouting of the rules. Those with the rare duty of travelling with foreigners were meant to dine separately somewhere round the back, where they were served up the standard canteen fare of a few *liang* of rice, vegetable stalks and slivers of meat amongst the bone and gristle. But Duan's good manners overcame his fear of criticism, and apart from our hurried standing meals in May in the commune, for the first time ever, we had the pleasure of companionably sharing a non-banquet meal in the company of a Chinese person – in China! It was a promising start to our trip.

Back into our sagging bucket seats, through the portholes we watched as the refuelling truck drew away and the starter motor was plugged into the battery cart. Soon came the first uneven swishing of the propellers, and we lurched towards the grassy runway. Once at its 3,000 metres cruising height, the little plane religiously circled a hillside emblazoned with giant characters, 'Learn from Dazhai in moving rivers and mountains.' Dazhai was the model village in Shanxi which Mao had sanctified as the byword of self-reliant struggle. Unlikely though it seemed as we coursed towards the Northwest over a placid and well-arranged countryside, the hubris of placing man over nature, especially when it came to the Yellow River, was soon going to be all too apparent.

The ancient city of Xi'an, over a millennium earlier the great capital of the Tang dynasty, was the first stop on our pilgrimage. We were conveyed straight to a vast and empty edifice, the main hotel in town built, like our first Nanjing home, by the Soviet experts of the early 1950s.

There was always a fixed form to our welcome by the locals. With hardly time to wash the grit from our faces, a knock would come at our door and in would stride two or three well-dressed representatives of the China Travel Service, the dreaded *Luxingshe*. The senior amongst them would then launch into his well-rehearsed 'brief introduction'. This would invariably commence with a litany of the brave revolutionary credentials of the place. But this was merely cover: the main course was how they would be filling our time for us on their splendid patch. There would scarcely be a moment left to rest our weary feet, let alone wander un-chaperoned on city streets. We were to be tightly corralled and then sped to the next destination before there was a chance of any trouble. A little sideshow of democracy always came at the conclusion of the itinerary speech. But 'please give us your valuable comments and criticisms' was an invitation as routinely passed over as it was issued. After I had become something of a veteran at this game, I usually managed to wheedle in an hour or two with a clutch of local cadres who presented themselves as city planners. This required an excess of oily flattery of whatever locality we happened to be visiting before putting the knife in.

On this occasion in Xi'an, we were happy enough to go along with the *Luxingshe* menu of the revolutionary army headquarters during the Anti-Japanese War, a Street Committee and a People's Commune on the outskirts. Again, there was a standard routine: the chieftains would always be awaiting our arrival, hovering on the threshold in timeless Chinese courtesy. We would then be ushered into a meeting room, and seated on low, loose-covered sofas under Chairman Mao's enigmatic gaze, spittoons strategically arrayed to the side. Tea would be served in lidded mugs, cigarettes and sweets thrust at us. We would then take the full force of yet another 'brief introduction', illustrated by the latest political references mixed up with sheaves of statistics. Everything was dutifully inscribed in my lined notebook. Only then would we be thought ready to actually *qu kankan* – have a look round.

This was Xi'an long before the magnet of the Terracotta Army, though the ancient city's tourist highlight in 1975 was nonetheless a destination attesting – in the cliché of the day - to 'the genius of the Chinese masses'. At the Shaanxi Provincial Museum, it was proudly announced, Jiang Qing herself had rearranged the exhibits. Mao's cultural supremo wife had decided that China's Neolithic period was a matriarchal society: we were led open-mouthed along row after row of glassed-in diorama, depicting fierce-looking Amazons hunting and fighting, their cowering men-folk tilling the fields or quietly getting on with domestic chores. Well, at least the museum was open. Back in Nanjing, we had never been allowed near one, for the Cultural Revolution was all about overturning the wicked past. Moreover, the constant political *yundong* demanded (usually with menaces) an ever-changing interpretation of China's history. The safest policy was to keep all museum doors barred, and the same went for the country's civic libraries. In almost four years' residence, the only one in Nanjing open to us – and us alone – was the University dungeon where all forbidden literature was mouldering.

Xi'an continued to surprise. Not only were museums normally out-of-bounds, but other than the Forbidden City, it was unusual for foreign visitors to be permitted anywhere near ancient buildings or areas of celebrated natural beauty. Normally, all reminders of China's feudal past were to be shunned.

'If the masses touch black, their hearts will become black, but if they touch red then they will become revolutionary', was how Minder Wang had once tried to explain it. But perhaps foreigners were simply beyond the Pale. Our Xi'an minders allowed a few places of historical interest to creep into the itinerary: the magnificent Ming walls, and the two Wild Goose pagodas, landmarks for over a millennium. No Chinese could risk the contagion of such places, and they were ours to wander in solitude.

Both politics and rare hedonism were to be served by a trip out to the Huaqing Hot Springs. Arriving at the pleasant park, planted with willows around pretty walkways, first came the mandatory politics: a half-hour lecture on the 1936 Xi'an Incident. At this vital point in the first Civil War (1927-36), Chiang Kai-shek was detained by the former warlord Zhang Xueliang who wanted him to resist the invading Japanese more strenuously rather than concentrating on fighting Mao and his Red Army. We were taken, as millions before us, to the cleft in the cliffs where the fleeing President had been detained in his underpants. Then came our playtime: we were shown to an obviously modern building which we were assured was the very place where more than a thousand years before, the Emperor Tai Zong and his alluring concubine had taken the hot spa waters. We were left to wallow for over an hour in the almost boiling soup, our reverie ending only by a row of sniggering faces pressed against the elevated windows. This was obviously the locals' free entertainment, now unexpectedly enriched by our gross barbarian forms.

We moved on for a few pleasant days in the revolutionary shrines of Ya'nan, the town nestling in the dry loess hills which had played such a crucial role in the Communist Party's struggle with first the Nationalist forces, then the Japanese occupiers in North China, and finally in the second civil war against the Nationaliss. From Ya'nan, back to Xi'an, and from there into the neighbouring province of Henan, via the ancient settlement of Anyang with its storehouse of mysterious oracle bones bearing the precursor Chinese script.

We were approaching the climax of our summer trip, for Henan was meant to demonstrate some vital contemporary lessons.

In the political advertising which surrounded every aspect of our existence, Lin County, ultra-poor by tradition, had grasped Chairman Mao's revolutionary line and was now marching towards a bright future. The key to all this was the water brought across the mountain barriers to this arid area by the heroically constructed Red Flag Canal.

Entering Lin County involved a hair-raising day's journey by minibus along one of those dead straight rural highways which could be found all over the North China Plain. We crossed the county border and were in lowland territory latticed by canals and culverts, all fed by the famed Red Flag Canal. Yet even to the untutored eye, the irrigation network told an odd story. Many of the waterways were gushing in flood, their sides eroded. Others were strangely dry. And as we travelled deeper into the county, everywhere we saw roads and bridges were half washed away. For the moment, we accepted the explanation of our *Luxingshe* guides: it was just some kind of regular annual flooding, a little like the inundations of a monsoon. Yet where was the rain? Oddly, we did not think to question their explanation. In the event, Lin County provided us with a pleasant few days of farm visits, the highlight being an illicit swim in an ice-cold mountain reservoir.

There was a subtext to our Lin County itinerary. Madame Mao – Jiang Qing – had taken the extraordinary decision to allow a foreigner to record for the world the wonders of Lin County, and the *avante-garde* film-maker Antonioni had been her choice. We now realised that our route was precisely that of the great man. Unfortunately, Antonioni had not quite followed the Chinese script, and once the film was released in the West, a huge campaign of 'repudiation' of the impudent Italian hit China. We walked right into the back end of this *yundong* when we first arrived in China the year before.

An irrefutable point in the official denunciation is worth recording:

> *When visiting a rural production team, the deceitful Antonioni filmed a pig pen and a washing line with its fluttering clothes. In his film he portrayed these scenes to the background music of a great revolutionary piano concerto. Comrades who accompanied Antonioni attest that no music was being played at the time.*

That is to say, in socialist realism, pigs do not root to the strains of a revolutionary piano.

As 'true foreign friends' we would be setting the record straight on the wonders of Lin County, or so the local *Luxingshe* obviously hoped. Something of a tall order. We had heard rumours of the mobbing which camera-laden foreigners had recently received from the 'angered masses'. We always took an excessive number of photos wherever we went, an awkward pastime as so much could be read into an innocent shot. The Antonioni effect meant that now we were under closer camera scrutiny than ever. On one trip out, a landscape was so captivating that I did not notice the peasant road builder in the foreground, stripped to the waist. As it was, the Comrade Zhang of the *Luxingshe* saved the day by obtusely shifting right into my line of fire, saving me from insulting the Chinese nation.

Our final destination was the ancient capital of Luoyang, reborn in the famous First Five Year Plan as a thrusting centre of heavy industry, safely distant from the militarily vulnerable coast. As in Nanjing, and in Xi'an – indeed in every place open to foreigners (and there were few enough of them) there was often just one hotel designated for our use. Only groups of very senior Chinese on official business could hope to enter the gates of such places, so they were normally guest-less. In Luoyang, there had been a heavy team of Soviet technicians in town during the Five Year Plan, and so we expected and got one of those familiar grey-stuccoed symmetrical structures thrown up with all mod-cons (baths and flush toilets) for the Soviet Elder Brothers. The Luoyang Hotel, though, was minute compared with the cavernous place in Xi'an.

Off we obediently trooped to massive sheds of industry - the Red Flag Tractor Plant, the glass works, and the ball-bearing factory. Ideologically immunised by this political tourism, Comrade Duan felt we could hazard an unscheduled visit to the great Buddhist grottoes of Longmen – Dragon Gate. This quest for 'feudal remnants' was a problem for the Luoyang *Luxingshe* cadres, but after a day of arm twisting, we were offered a car and driver and off we went without them.

We headed towards Longmen through a landscape like that of Lin County - fallen culverts, gullied banks, and damaged bridges. We knew from our *Nagel's Encyclopedia- Guide* that the massive Longmen Buddhist statues rise above the river and are approached by a valley road. But there was no road, only brown waters gushing through the gorge. This presented a challenge and after a little persuasion, Duan agreed to our plan. We would roll up our trousers and wade barefoot along the fringe of the torrent. After half a mile we were there, and the amazing Longmen cliff side proved well worth a soaking.

Our summer trip was drawing to a close, and the following morning we were to head south by road and plane to Nanjing. But over breakfast, Duan came to us wearing an odd expression. The local comrades would welcome us to stay a few days longer in Luoyang. There were more fine factories to be seen. Great! This was Friday and who wanted to face a new class of bright young faces the following Monday morning at the unholy hour of half-past-seven? We lugged our bags upstairs again and were shown into a much smaller room than we had just vacated by smiling white-jacketed attendants. No call came that morning, none after lunch, and we were experiencing that rare thing on a China trip, a day with no compulsory sightseeing when we could catch up on our sleep and our diaries.

That evening we went down for dinner to an ever-louder babble of voices. The lobby, normally deserted, had been invaded by a regiment of newcomers. Cadre-types to a man, and far too senior to take any interest in a couple of Westerners. In the terse heat of the North China summer, you could tell 'at ease' had been called, for trouser bottoms were rolled up and uniform off-white silk shirts unbuttoned over uniform cotton singlets. The elderly cadres, all male, milled in and out of the main entrance or sat fanning themselves in the portico. My anthropological antennae were up and I decided to watch their goings-on.

By the hotel entrance was the usual little shop selling nail clippers, wooden combs, grainy toilet paper, carton-towers of Fenghuang and Zhonghua cigarettes, fancy cellophane-wrapped and ribboned bottles of sorghum liquor as well as Shanghai's premium Maxam toothpaste – all unavailable on the street. I watched in fascination as the unruly knots of ganbu shamelessly stripped the place bare.

At a signal from a couple of pretty ushers, the old men buttoned their shirts, rolled down their trousers and jostled into the main corridor. After a while, I could not resist snooping down the roped-off passage. A dozen huge round tables were awash with rich banqueting food. Demure waitresses scuttled back and forth filling dishes and glasses. In those austere days, foreigners were always warned that normally a Chinese banquet comes to an abrupt stop: the chief host simply rises, and whether or not their appetites are sated, the company must depart in his wake.

But on this occasion, the happy gaggle of officials saw no need to bring their pleasure to an early end. White lightning-fuelled speechifying and drinking games could be heard echoing down the corridors long after ordinary citizens were tucked up in bed.

The following morning there was still no word from our guides. No exhortation to visit yet another factory or commune. Nothing. Comrade Duan finally made an appearance, ashen faced and quietly spoken.

'I want to tell you what's happening,' he said 'You must have guessed that the situation in Lin County was far from normal. There's been too much rain. It's very serious. A disaster.'

'But why can't we just go to the airport and fly out?' I asked, much puzzled.

'There are no planes for you,' Duan enigmatically replied.

'Then we can change our plans and go south by train – we don't mind,' I generously suggested.

'There are no railway lines available,' was all Duan would say. 'You will enjoy your stay in Luoyang for a few more days. But can I ask you not to go outside the hotel or speak to any of the other guests,' he added.

In those paranoid Cultural Revolution days, seamless organisation and routine were demanded whenever foreigners were on the loose. Unscripted events always carried danger. As we were to learn the following year in the wake of the terrible Tangshan earthquake, in Chairman Mao's China no one dared admit that nature might just be more powerful than the emperor. Duan had not said much, but even his comment about the rain was risky and we appreciated this man all the more for his candour.

Idling away the next couple of days in that Luoyang hotel, our main amusement was to observe the several dozen fellow guests. They seemed set on non-stop junketing, interspersed with haranguing meetings in the hotel's conference room. We tried asking Duan what it was all about, but he had a way of looking at us blankly as though his English had deserted him.

But then next day, out of the blue, came a terse remark: 'Some people are enjoying themselves while other people are having a hard time,' was all Duan said, a rare frown creasing his brow.

Early the following week, we were told we could head south towards Nanjing on a branch line which was now passable. We said a final goodbye to the Luoyang Hotel and headed for a strangely deserted railway station. One minute we were rattling by the ever-crowded level crossings, the engine klaxon evocatively sounding, and the next we were traversing a watery world of immersed villages, floating debris and drowned oxen. The scene put me immediately in mind of those pictures of the disastrous Yellow River floods of the 1920s, when millions had perished. Flood water cleared roofs in many of the villages, and where it did not, peasant dwellings of mud and straw had crumbled into the swirling brown soup. Encamped on the railway embankment were the survivors of the deluge, the lucky ones with their sodden bed quilts, sticks of furniture, a gaggle of geese, feet bound together. In a fleeting vignette, a half-naked man spun hopelessly in a tiny coracle as he tried to head off a piece of bobbing driftwood, the perch for three bedraggled chickens.

With all other man-made things under water, one's eyes were drawn to the soft, wispy grave mounds which dotted every un-ploughable hillock. The government had long been trying to force the peasants to stop burying their dead in their ancestral fields, but with little success here in remote Henan. Now there were plenty more to bury, for the railway embankment was the temporary resting place of many a crumpled, lifeless muddy form. All three of us stood transfixed in the corridor as mile after endless mile of the same pitiful sights trundled past our window. Occasionally we slowed to a walking pace as the train negotiated a flooded cutting, and ragged figures sprang to the couplings in their urge to escape the deathly new world of water.

We knew almost instinctively that we had the heavy responsibility of being the only outside witnesses to a tragedy on a national scale. Lesser people than Duan would have drawn down the blinds and ordered us back to our seats. We returned his compliment by refraining from any comment which might prove a hostage to his fortune. We certainly did not wield our dangerous camera. But after an hour watching the untouchable misery outside our sealed world, I stretched out on the top bunk and set about making some kind of diary record of what we had seen.

It was at dead of night that the train lurched to a halt, with a clanking of couplings and then the silence broken only by the steam blowing off from the engine up ahead. After a considerable time, in which my thoughts awoke fully to the scenes of the day before, there came the sound of another train approaching. It too came to a stop, and the night was filled with muffled shouts and the dull pounding of feet. I stole from my bunk and into the half-lit corridor. Padding along below was an endless line of jogging soldiers, each with quilt backpack, bandoleer, and automatic rifle. A touch to my shoulder, and Duan urged me away from this mysterious spectacle. Soon after, the train coughed itself back to its soporific clickety-click and we awoke the next morning to unexceptional track-side vistas and the usual tasty bowl of shredded pork and noodles in which the Chinese railways always seemed to excel.

Safely back in our Nanjing *danwei*, our work-unit, we had the pleasure of our mandatory debriefing session back at the Yellow House. The same group from the Revolutionary Committee, the same deep sofa with its off-white cotton covers and antimacassars, the same portrait of a jaunty Chairman Mao in PLA uniform sanctifying the proceedings. And a virtually identical speech from

Comrade Li An except this time it was in the past tense – 'You went to Yan'an, you went to Xi'an,' etc. All places where none of our debriefers had ever been themselves. We understood that before this quasi-religious ritual could be allowed to finish, we had to stand up and make our own declarations. Like any Chinese in this situation, our job was to attest publicly to the great revolutionary lessons we had learned. We did so in as perfunctory a manner as we could get away with. As befitted his station, Duan remained silent throughout. But suddenly he piped up with a single, unprompted remark which astounded us for its sheer untruthfulness: 'I have to tell you that when our foreign friends were staying in the hotel in Luoyang, they severely criticised the other guests.'

'The bloody nerve,' I thought. 'You bastard.'

Roll the clock forward four years, to April 1979. We were back in China and Mao and his cronies were a fading memory. His chosen successor, the ungainly Hua Guofeng, was clearly soon to be a man of the past. This was a new China, a China of the 'Four Modernisations' and the 'Open Door', Deng Xiaoping once again at the helm. For the first time in a generation, normal human behaviour was beginning to reassert itself and no longer was everything refracted through the perverse prism of 'politics'. Little by little, the neighbourhoods were coming alive again with flowers on the balconies, old men paraded their songbirds, and children their tropical fish. All such things had been banished for years.

One of the missing elements during our earlier period in China was the experience of nature in the raw. I had always been a keen hiker and even heavily-peopled East China had a few wild wildernesses, especially in the adjacent province of Anhui. But there had been no way we could have got close to them. Like in every peasant land, the idea of enjoyment of nature for its own sake was simply incomprehensible. There was also the overlay of philistine patriotism. In Mao's China, physical exercise had one purpose and one purpose alone: to steel young bodies in defence of their country. Strident chants of *Duanlian shenti, baowei zuguo* – 'Strengthen ourselves to protect the Motherland' was often heard from our students.

Now, though, the contemplation of China's wilder places for their sheer exhilaration was once again possible. In the south of our new province of Shandong lay the massif of Mount Tai, the most revered of China's five sacred peaks. The idea of a weekend climbing trip was happily agreed to by the easy-going Li Hua, our guardian at Shandong University.

We were longing to see our old friend from our Nanjing days, Duan, with whom we had shared our 1975 adventure in Henan. So Li Hua was pestered until she agreed to invite him along. We all met up in the sleepy, dusty county town of Tai'an, at the foot of the great mountain where in the absence of a foreigners' hotel we enjoyed the hospitality of the county government's official guesthouse.

The ascent took a very long day, and there was ample opportunity to reminisce about the strange life we had been forced to lead in Cultural Revolution Nanjing. It was not Duan's fault that he had been one of our overseers, forcing him to tax our daily lives with foolish things. So I held off from broaching painful events. But after we had progressed past Mount Tai's half-way point, the Gate of Middle Heaven, perhaps the mountain air got to Duan. With little prompting he became ever-more expansive about our time in Nanjing. One incident in particular still stuck in my throat, and I was determined to raise it.

'Do you remember our meeting with the Revolutionary Committee after our Northwest trip in 1975? I'm still wondering why you told them that we'd criticised the cadres in the Luoyang

Hotel, when it was you who'd actually done so.'

'Ah,' Duan replied. 'You see, this was the only way to let Beijing know what was happening in that hotel, and it was too dangerous for me to appear to be saying such things.'

'You mean we big noses are known to be so stupid that we're forgiven for saying or doing things that would be a real danger to you Chinese?'

'That's it,' agreed Duan. 'It's an old trick to put our thoughts into the mouths of you foreigners.'

'Can I be your teacher again and just tell you an important new English expression,' I responded. 'To "drop someone in the shit"? Anyway, Comrade Duan, who were those cadres in the hotel you said we'd criticised? They must have been pretty big potatoes.' One of Duan's favourite English expressions.

'Yes, they were,' he replied. 'They were the Work Team sent from Beijing by Chairman Mao and the Party Central Committee to sort out the flood emergency in Henan. I knew immediately that they were top cadres from the Central Committee, and that leading them was a man called Ji Dengkui.'

I was aware of the name. Ji Dengkui was known as a powerful Central Committee member and a supporter of what would later be called the Gang of Four. He was known as one of the 'helicopters' – a man who had risen very fast from nowhere.

'I was disgusted at the way they behaved at the hotel, with their banquets and games. And unlike you, I knew how serious the flooding actually was just outside the city.'

As a confirmed Party moderate, Duan was determined to do his little bit against the ultra-leftists. The only way he could tell the outside world about the bad behaviour was by using we big-noses.

It was the State Council's Foreign Experts Bureau which was our ultimate employer, and it was they who demanded regular reports from the University about our 'political progress' and our many mainly unintentional slights on the People's Republic. Trip debriefing sessions were given special attention, and any negative remarks about officialdom of the type Duan cunningly inserted was bound to be a massively starred item. Duan had gambled that the Foreign Experts Bureau would read between the lines and know what to do with the Nanjing report.

'They did know – the report about your trip, and the criticism I made on your behalf about the leading cadres went to the office of the Foreign Minister.'

And according to Duan, the man found it too hot to handle, whereupon it was propelled ever upwards, finally into the hands of Chairman Mao himself. This was just the moment when Mao was trying to divine the imperial succession. In the spring of 1976, the Chairman was wavering between two candidates - the solid Hunanese bureaucrat Hua Guofeng, who had kept a certain distance from the Cultural Revolution group's scheming, and the Ji Dengkui of Luoyang Hotel fame. By now, the stench of the Henan affair was beginning to reach Beijing. What the terminally ill Mao heard from outside the cloistered Forbidden City was tightly controlled by his wife and her cronies. But he perhaps retained just enough political nowse to understand that he could hardly leave China in the hands of a discredited and corrupt official.

As it happened, Mao was already well disposed to Hua, who as a fellow Hunanese spoke the same language and had the same bluff ways as the Chairman. And had not Hua done a good job as Minister for Public Security! He had dealt decisively with quite a few counter-revolutionary rumblings, and had apparently been implicated just prior to his appointment in the crushing of a Hui Moslem rebellion in Yunnan province (in 1979 we were to meet some of the surviving victims when we visited Kunming). But according to Duan, what really swung it for Hua was that

Mao read the supposed observations by a couple of wide-eyed foreigners on the goings-on in that Luoyang Hotel.

In April 1976, following the mass demonstrations which ended in the Tiananmen brutality, we had stood to attention in Nanjing's Gulou Square along with thousands of other sullen state employees forced one morning to leave their workplaces for a rally in favour of the 'Two Directives' - the dismissal of Deng Xiaoping and his replacement as Premier by Hua Guofeng. After Mao's death, September 1976, Hua was declared supreme leader. Ironically he then participated in the coup against his mentor Mao's closest followers.

'So,' joked Duan, 'you and Jo played your part in Chairman Mao's choice of successor.'

Not something we wished any credit for. Hua seemed a mixture of buffoon and bully and there was much laughing behind hands when his first act on taking over was to adopt a hairstyle identical to Mao's own. Yet it all went to prove how far out of our depth we foreigners were in Cultural Revolution China.

To this tale of the great Henan floods of 1975 I can add a further postscript. It was an evening at Shandong University some four years after the Henan disaster. One of my students, Xiao Hou, came by our flat to apologise that she had been unable to keep an appointment earlier in the week. All Party members had been asked to attend a film show in the University auditorium. There were, she said, two related documentaries. The first was about the problems of disasters and their relief, in the context of a major flood of seven counties in Henan province in the summer of 1975. This film spared no sensibilities, and Xiao Hou was obviously finding it hard to get the horrific images from her mind - hundreds, thousands of piled-up bodies on patches of higher land -'like a human Great Wall', she said smiling (as the Chinese tend to do at great emotion), but obviously close to tears. I asked how this had happened.

'Because a *shuiku* was broken by too much water and a big wave killed forty thousand peasants,' she explained. Xiao Hou was referring to a reservoir, and presumably to a burst dam.

Was this the Yellow River?' I asked, recalling the many past floods of 'China's Sorrow'.

She fiddled with her little notebook: 'No, it was a river called Ru River,' Xiao Hou explained, 'and the *shuiku* is called 'Banqiao'. And the wave was wide fifty kilometres.'

The second film my student described that night concerned abuse of public funds by rural officials in the swathe of countryside affected by the floods. While the commentary hinted at a level of mismanagement by the central government, it concentrated its fire on the local officials who had used relief funds to build new villas and hold banquets.

'Many many peasants died afterwards because they had no food or got sick,' Xiao Hou added.

The film also demonstrated graphically the punishments meted out to the worst offenders. China's rulers are not shy in letting the masses know what a bullet in the back of the neck does.

I am amazed that for all its web of intelligence, including even in those days constant satellite spying on China, at the time neither the CIA nor the many other outside agencies with an overdeveloped interest in Beijing's affairs apparently picked up on the great Henan flood of 1975. Yet the Henan inundation had casualty figures in their hundreds of thousands, comparable to those of the great Asian *tsunami* forty years later.

At that uncertain moment in China's history, with Mao entering his final days and factional fighting intensifying around him, who knows what would have happened if China's quiescent but always potentially volatile masses had learned of the Henan disaster? The

Mandate of Heaven was supposed to bring omnipotence over nature; in the dying days of the regime, the great flood was the deadliest of state secrets. Along with the Tangshan earthquake a year later, the superstitious rural dwellers were said to have taken these disasters as auguries of dynastic change.

Twenty years on, and there appeared the first Western media report of the Henan tragedy which I had come across. In 1996, a brief story appeared in the *Guardian* newspaper concerning the forces of nature, and the difficulty in predicting the consequences of China's controversial mega-project to dam the Yangtze gorges. The article based its doubts on newly discovered events of 1975 in Henan Province, where several hundred thousand farmers lost their lives because engineers had underestimated the raging power of 'China's Sorrow', the Yellow River and its tributaries.

But the manner in which the Henan disaster steered Mao Zedong to anoint his unworthy successor Hua Guofeng is a tale only now told.

XIV
CAMPUS SHENANIGANS

THE NANDA ENGLISH SECTION cadres who organised our twice-weekly political study were at pains to emphasise that our students were, from their peaked caps to their cotton soles, the stalwart sons and daughters of the labouring masses. Later, we found that they were protesting too much, and as the year drew on, different realities were revealed.

With entrance examinations abolished, the main criterion for college entry was meant to be advanced political consciousness. As we had been endlessly informed, this could only be gained through labour alongside the 'revolutionary masses', and only they could recommend someone for the privilege of college entry. My charges were, after all, 'worker-peasant-soldier studiers', the *gongnongbing xueyuan* of Mao's revolution. Not 'students', which sounded too bourgeois, but 'studiers'.

The three Chinese characters *gong* (industry), *nong* (agriculture), and *bing* (soldier) were to become tediously familiar. We bought our tea in the Gongnongbing Teashop, rattan furniture at the Gongnongbing Furniture Store at the end of Hankou Road, and most important of all, had our precious Kodak slide films processed by Gongnongbing Photographic Shop on Shanghai's famous Nanjing Road. This was one of only two places in China which could handle Kodak processing, and our regular packages of films were always given special care. And as I have related in an earlier chapter, they received some extra political care from the shop's workers which we had not bargained for.

After just a few weeks with my third year group, I began to

suspect that the new university recruitment policy was not quite all it was cracked up to be. Two of the provincial dignitaries who sometimes feted and banqueted us were General Chen and General Yang. General Chen Bingde was not just any PLA chief: he ran the entire Nanjing Military Region, which extended over most of East China. The General was a chirpy birdlike figure; in his crumpled fatigues I found it hard to imagine him commander of all he surveyed.

As for General Yang, he was among other things the de facto head of the Jiangsu Revolutionary Committee – in plain words, provincial governor of one of China's most advanced industrial and agricultural regions with a population about the size of the United Kingdom's. General Yang was tall, urbane and patrician, slightly podgy but carrying his weight well. He was always turned out in the finest grey worsted Zhongshan suit, finished off with brilliantly polished brown brogues. I was surprised that many of the high-up officials who wandered smugly around the hotel compound were so brazen in their finery. Their immaculately cut tunics, their charcoal cashmere overcoats often slung jauntily over the shoulders and their highly polished footwear were a far cry from the proletarian image.

General Yang seemed to enjoy the novelty of foreign company, and sometimes he would send for us from his private pavilion on an island on Nanjing's Xuanwu Lake. Memorably, we were invited there to toast the liberation of Saigon from the Americans on 1st May 1975. I had not yet realised that the Chinese were celebrating the defeat of the Americans rather than the victory of the Vietnamese, their future foe.

Each of the generals had a favourite daughter, and guess what? Both just happened to be in my first class of fifteen students. I rumbled Ms Yang and Ms Chen when I found them inside the hallowed ground of our hotel compound, wandering amongst the bonsai trees in the little nursery behind the huge concrete screen of the Yangtze River Bridge. From time to time I would spot them tearing past us in the backs of their fathers' official limousines. The less-than-humble antecedents of Ms Chen and Ms Yang were without doubt another State Secret. But in the end, the fact that the daughters of the province's most powerful were our charges could hardly be concealed from us. Far from it – amongst the top leaders there seemed to be an inbred tendency to flout their power and to hell with the consequences.

Ms Yang was a well-rounded beauty who in another time and place would definitely have qualified as a kind of Chinese debutante. Ms Chen was pale, starved-looking and inclined to spottiness. Like their august fathers, both were in the PLA and in my lessons they self-consciously modelled their well-tailored olive green army fatigues. It was an open secret even in those puritan days that females were in the army mainly for the delectation of their male commanders.

'What did you do in the PLA?' I innocently enquired, not wishing to breach any military secrets.

'I was dancer,' was Ms Yang's surprising answer.

'And I was telephone people and singer,' was Ms Chen's coy revelation of her telephonist status. Most of the PLA females seemed to be in communications.

Ms Chen once stayed behind in the classroom long after the rest of them had rushed off to get their lunch. I wondered what she was up to. I knew enough to be uncomfortable being left alone with a single female.

'My uniform much better now,' she coyly announced, as she ripped off her red PLA collar flashes. I suddenly realised that Ms Chen wanted to demonstrate her privileged modernity. The flashes were secured by Velcro. Where she got such cutting edge stuff in the sealed realm of China was a mystery.

Not to be outdone, a few days later Ms Yang put on a little demonstration of her own. Producing a new Japanese camera – the only such import I had ever seen in China – she made a good pretence of needing help with the English instructions. Needless to say, such flagrant indulgences in less protected species would have invited accusations of corruption by that Maoism, the 'sugar-coated [foreign] bullet'.

This is not to say that the ordinary people were immune from a little self-embellishment. I often came across Westerners' accounts claiming that the Chinese were all clothed in identical 'blue boiler suits'. Even professional China watchers, who should have known better, wrote such nonsense. From the ground up, I saw things rather differently: though the ordinary folk, the 'old hundred names' could not flout their taste in the way their leaders sometimes did, their desire for individual self-adornment readily survived the straitjacketed years. You only had to visit the drapery section of any department store to realise that Cultural Revolution or no, the appetite for bright hues was far from extinguished. If you knew how to look, there was finesse in the attire of most people around you, and there were definitely this year's buttons and last year's buttons. But it was true that from day to day, it was thought more modest to conceal the bright hues under nondescript covers. When we did *laodong* – improving labour – on the campus alongside our colleagues, jackets would come off, and it was surprising what brightness was under them.

As my suspicions about the realities of China 'revolution in education' deepened, I thought to better acquaint myself with all members of my class of '75. To this end, I organised a sort of confessional. Here was a great opportunity to pry into my students' alarming Red Guard pasts and thus get a sense of what the nation had gone through in recent years.

The group was provided with clear instructions on the squeaky blackboard, and a week in which to rehearse. Allowing only the use of simple English sentence patterns, each had to describe briefly who they were and where they came from. I also asked them to talk about their compulsory work assignments after leaving high school, for it was these which qualified them to become *gong-nong-bing* students at Nanda.

I dutifully scribbled down the profiles of each worker-peasant-soldier in my little lined notebook, the one illustrated with colourful scenes from Madame Mao's favourite revolutionary opera, *The White Haired Girl*.

'Before coming to the University I was worker in Nanjing Watch Factory. I learn much about the hard struggle and plain living from the great work class,' said one.

'I was new peasant in production brigade in commune in Jiangning County. I also learn much from the revolutionary spirit of moving mountains from the poor and low-mid-peasants,' stumbled another.

'I was soldier with People's Lib-elation Army defend our Great Motherland against Soviet Social Impee-lists,' avowed a stocky fellow in crumpled green uniform and red-starred cap, his eyes lighting up like a hero in a propaganda film.

And so it went on, each protesting his or her sterling revolutionary credentials, every word innocently noted down by myself.

I was both delighted with these little life vignettes and at the same time taxed by a nagging thought, for they chimed rather too closely with the model lessons of textbook orthodoxy:

> *Li Wei is 21 years old and from a worker's family. His family was very poor before Liberation. Thanks to the wise leader Chairman Mao and the Party, his family is*

*now enjoying a happy life. After graduating from middle
school, Li Wei went to Nanfang County of Anhui province
where he learned from the poor-and-lower middle peasants.
He loves labour and vows to serve the Party and people
forever.*

As it happened too, not a few of my charges had the given name
'Wei'. As Red Guards they had abandoned their original, often
flowery names in favour of simple Wei, which means 'protect'.
And what did every Red Guard vow to protect? It was, naturally,
the life and reputation of Chairman Mao.

Ms Yang and Ms Chen had already been revealed as more than
normal mortals and now the credentials claimed by the rest of
my students started to look suspect too. Eventually I was pretty
sure that at least half were not exactly sons and daughters of the
toiling masses. So these charming innocents had boldly sat there
in front of me and blatantly fibbed. If the 'revolution in education'
was meant to prevent the inheritance of privilege it was hardly
working here. In any country you care to name, you will find
that college language schools, and their English departments in
particular, are populated by children of the local elite. Particularly
their daughters. Astonishingly, so it was too in Mao's China, even
after years of supposedly anti-elitist struggle. And the Cultural
Revolution's new class had managed to colonise our English
section the moment it re-opened for business. I was angry at being
deceived, but then I could hardly blame the young people, for
much was at stake.

If a student did have a genuine rural background it was likely
that he or she was from the family of a county or commune official.
Children of genuine poor farming folk were certainly there, but in
small numbers - indeed, a smattering of true sons and daughters
of toil was present in each of my groups. I think of the round-

faced boy, hair already streaked with grey, from the dusty and impoverished region of Subei, that is, the part of Jiangsu north of the Yangtze. The sad tale he related, and his gratitude to the Party were both genuine (father dying when he was tiny, an upbringing amongst numerous siblings in semi-starvation). Two decades on, I came across this former student in a vastly different incarnation. He had transmuted into a multi-millionaire with a penthouse office in the most expensive skyscraper in Hong Kong, not to mention a vast mansion in London. Huang Junban had somehow cornered the market for China's import of non-ferrous metals such as aluminium and copper – the bedrock materials of modern industry.

I was not quite prepared for my next discovery about the students. It was true that there was no more chance of a former rich landlord's son, or the daughter of a former Guomindang officer of getting into the reopened and revolutionary universities than of the proverbial camel getting through the eye of a needle. Never mind that the offspring of such former class enemies might have forsworn their birth and proved a true dedication to the regime. The Maoists justified this discrimination on crude grounds of heredity and blood.

Commissars like our Comrade Xu, who kept an ideological eye on us, convinced me that he truly did believe a person's behaviour stemmed directly from his or her *chusheng* – 'birth background'. One's *chusheng* was prominently recorded in all personnel files and was as common knowledge in Mao's China as hair colour is in ours. Discrimination against the former possessors, in favour of the formerly dispossessed, would, it was believed, guarantee that China would never be overtaken by a new elite.

So well into the second half of the twentieth century, the Chinese were still bound up by the dubious code of eugenics, the pseudo-science which had been so discredited in our own world by the Nazi experience. Given our own backgrounds, we found the Chinese stance genuinely shocking.

While the children of the new class - Mao's trusted lieutenants - now dominated the universities, not all could be expected to gain entry. Among our teacher-students there was one, Chen Mingbai, who occasionally exhibited unusual signs of eccentricity in his dress and in his forward comments. We had been talking in my class in conventional clichés about the 'revolution in education', and no one had strayed beyond the official script. At the end of the session, however, Chen lingered in the office and then came over and drew up a chair to the front of my desk.

'Do you know that the most important thing is to be good looking?' he said in a loud and matter-of-fact voice.

'Most important for what?' I enquired, genuinely puzzled.

'For getting into this University. And every university in China.'

Chen was telling me that a candidate irreproachable by all other measures would not be admitted unless they passed an informal beauty test.

'And the people deciding who is good-looking enough to get into the University are themselves ugly old cadres,' he laughed behind his hand.

When local cadres took Mao's 'self-reliance' slogan too literally, there were often bizarre outcomes. We discovered that during our time in Nanjing, two English dictionary compiling groups - one in an army college and one at Nanda itself - were beavering away in complete and parallel ignorance of each other. Their respective compiling HQs were a mere hop-and-a-skip away from each other. This kind of thing went on all over the place: plenty of towns set up parallel factories making the same product with no reference to each other. It was all a result of the vertical lines of authority by which China was being run.

In a similar spirit, every college seemed to possess a recording studio - quite a sophisticated facility for China at the time - producing their own version of language tapes exclusively for their own students. Little did it matter that what we were given to record were usually just translated tracts from the classroom texts, which in turn were identical to primary school texts in Chinese. These were stuffed full of revolutionary orthodoxy and heroics, modified by the latest twists in the political stratosphere.

Our recording careers began just as soon as we had settled into the campus routine. We had never been near a recording studio before and I approached this new duty with trepidation. But once I got used to modulating my voice in the exaggerated manner which the Chinese seemed to expect of their broadcasts, I started to rather enjoy our sessions in the glass box. The tape recorders were perfect Chinese copies of the Ferrograph, the industry standard in the West. Our minder would snooze in the adjoining cabin, visible through the thick glass wall; if we needed his attention to sort out a hitch or top up our tea mugs we could arouse him via a handy intercom button.

Our master tapes were serially copied, every classroom having its own small reel-to-reel tape recorder around which groups of eager students did their best to reproduce our stilted sentences. It was an odd experience to traipse over the campus in the dusk with one's voice emanating dissonantly from many quarters. Sometimes it cackled forth from the huge loudspeakers nesting in the eaves of every building.

A few months before, the name 'Norman Bethune' had meant nothing, but since our arrival in China he seemed to be everywhere. Like us, Bethune was a rare foreigner cast into the great Chinese sea. Unlike us, he was the glowing subject of one of Chairman

Mao's 'Three Frequently Read Articles', In Memory of Norman Bethune. 'Frequently read' was an understatement: Mao's moral stories had to be not only read, but learned by heart, backwards if necessary (yes, this really happened). Marx, Engels, Lenin and Stalin apart, praise for foreigners did not fit naturally within Mao's universe. So Norman Bethune had to be a very special person.

Bai Qiuen, as he was known in China, was a Canadian tuberculosis surgeon and member of the Canadian Communist Party who in 1938 gave up all to assist the Chinese communist forces in the struggle against the Japanese invaders.

Happily, for his later reputation, he managed to expire heroically by contracting blood poisoning as he was operating on a Chinese soldier. Generally, if you wanted to be a hero in Mao's China it was best to be dead.

'Just like Bai Qiuen,' our hosts at factories and communes would proclaim, 'you have come across oceans to assist the Chinese people in their arduous struggle for socialism.'

We hoped that this did not presage our own early demise.

Along with the mass of teaching materials we had brought into the country were a few more readable tracts. Among these was a biography of Norman Bethune authored by two Canadians, Sydney Gordon and Ted Allan. Though years later Allan's widow informed me that the tale was somewhat embroidered, there was little doubt about Bethune's heroism. I have to confess being truly moved to tears by his death scene ('moved to tears' was a favourite of my sentimental students, and an expression which usually made my hair curl). The powers-that-be seemed happy enough when we came up with the idea of using *The Scalpel, the Sword* for our extensive reading recordings, and week after week we intoned the Bethune story into our microphones.

At last the job was done, but strangely, the campus loudspeakers remained silent on Bethune, merely replaying our standard lessons

(*Lesson 1: Chairman Mao is the Sun*). Eventually, the man whose job it was to keep us on the straight and narrow, our Commissar Xu, appeared in the office with an embarrassed smile.

'You have recorded the stories about Bai Qiuen but the masses have pointed out some problems,' he said, his brow creasing.

'Where are the problems?' we asked. 'Chairman Mao himself has often praised Bai Qiuen.'

The poor man shuffled his feet and blushed, not because of the explanation he was about to give but because of our obvious irritation.

'Our government has warm relations with *Xibanya, Xide* and *Idali*, who all strongly oppose the Soviet Social Imperialists,' he declared.

We were flabbergasted. Spain, West Germany, Italy – what on earth could all this be about? Then the penny dropped. In the midst of his medical work in China Bethune had gone off to Europe on a speaking tour, to raise funds for his mobile operating theatres. Bethune was a communist, and in condemning Japan's acts against the Chinese he drew unavoidable comparisons with the European fascists – Italy's barbarous invasion of Abyssinia and Germany's intervention in the Spanish Civil War, where he himself had worked as a doctor for the losing Republican side, and where he had developed the concept of mobile field operating theatres.

So now, in mid-1970s China, it was taboo to criticise 1930s European fascism for fear of upsetting its present-day rulers! Admittedly, Franco was still in charge in Spain but so what? China's foreign policy had come to a sorry state if it had to please every regime in the anti-Soviet camp – for that was what it was all about.

'These things all happened fifty years ago and there's a problem for us Europeans if we're prevented from criticising the fascists,' I exclaimed, by now really angry.

'China follows the revolutionary internationalist line of non-interference in other countries' internal affairs and you must not criticise in your recording,' Xu answered as imperiously as he could manage. We were incandescent. But all references to the nations which were once fascist regimes were removed from our recordings.

As our time in Nanjing wore on, I became ever more conscious of the paradoxical psychological state of my young charges. On the one hand, they appeared and behaved like innocent children. On the other, I knew that not long before most had been the stern foot-soldiers of Mao, in one of those gangs calling themselves Red Guards. These adolescent ideologues had humiliated and victimised any and every authority figure within their reach. Teachers, Communist Party officials both high and low, their very parents even, had not long since been the targets of their cruelty. Most of my students must have at least witnessed terrible things – humiliations, beatings, and executions included.

But alongside the angry anarchy of the late 1960s, there were other aspects to the early years of the Cultural Revolution which were more creative for young minds. My teenage students had enjoyed a season of freedom, the like of which no youthful Chinese generation had ever before known. In 1967, when Mao's young shock troops had done their work for him, millions of youngsters who had never been outside their neighbourhoods were sent off on the 'great exchange of experience'. This was basically a free-for-all of political tourism. For the youngsters, the thing to do was to head for the famed sites of the revolution: Jiangxi province's Jinggangshan where Mao's Red Army had first gained strength, or Hunan's Shaoshan where the family home of Mao Zedong was artfully reproduced in duplicate to cope with the pilgrim hordes

(I myself had witnessed this subterfuge when I visited Shaoshan in 1973). They trekked in their thousands to Yan'an in Shaanxi province, ultimate destination of the epic Long March and crucible of the revolution. As they fanned out across the huge territory of China, the Red Guards were confident that they could live off the fat of the land, for no one would risk refusing to feed them or give them shelter. On the railways and country buses no one dared to ask for fares, and the youngsters went where they pleased. This, then, was the reward that Mao granted his young faithful. To the immense relief of their elders, it also got the troublesome tearaways far, far away.

All my students said they had taken part in this great adventure, and several claimed an added aura too: they had actually been able to get to Beijing to join one of the mass rallies in Tiananmen Square when Chairman Mao himself had saluted them. A million young people would gather in a frenzy of hero worship for each of Mao's audiences, their Little Red Books waving frantically above their heads. Even now, in 1975, with Mao only just hanging on to life behind the vermillion walls of the Imperial City, my students would speak in hushed tones about the chances of getting to Beijing again, in their tender minds a place imbued with mystical powers.

Apart from the Spring Festival, the Chinese New Year, when those separated from family could have a week's home leave, ordinary folk were not allowed to travel. That was why almost the only people you would see on the trains with their little black plastic zip bags, their miniature multi-coloured towels and their tannin-stained jam jars half-full of bloated green tea leaves to a man (and very occasional woman) were middle-ranking cadres. It was plain from many an overheard comment amongst our little leaders that they just loved their 'official business', their meetings and 'inspection of advanced experience' in faraway exotic places.

The rail system was reserved for essential goods, and yet across China's vastness, there were plenty of regional specialities awaiting the discerning traveller. They would return bags bulging with edible goodies, not to mention some prized sorghum spirit from whichever province they had travelled to.

China was just beginning to emerge from an anchored peasant culture, in which the village in the next valley was almost as alien as the distant capital. Educated people longed to see their country, yet when they had the rare chance to do so, 'abroad' was not always as good as they had hoped. In the Spring Festival holiday of 1975, two well-connected lads in my class somehow wangled a trip to the capital. Everyone knew that to get to the big cities such as Beijing or Shanghai was almost impossible, and their classmates seemed genuinely excited for them.

At the beginning of the new term, the first thing we did was interrogate the two about their adventure.

'It was all right,' these supposedly hardened ex-Red Guards explained without great enthusiasm. 'But we couldn't get used to the water or food and we were glad to get back in Jiangsu.'

Shui tu bufu, literally 'water and soil are discommodious', was a phrase often heard. It was a reminder that in spite of all the strident posturing of youth, even after a quarter of a century of Mao's New China the old peasant parochialism was never far beneath the surface. If the Chinese vilified the Soviet Union as 'social imperialist', in our frustration it often seemed that 'social feudalist' fitted the world we now inhabited.

One day, towards the summer and the graduation of my first class of ex-Red Guards, posters began to appear at the University gates condemning the 'bourgeois authorities' in the provincial Education Bureau.

'Chairman Mao's revolutionary line on college admission

procedures has been brazenly flouted,' shrieked the slogans scrawled on huge sheets of white paper. We had to walk past the poster hotspot twice daily and for once it was impossible to hide such ructions from us. A crowd pressed against the wall, and I sidled up to one of my bolder students, who unexpectedly offered me the gist of a densely-written *dazibao*. The message was clear enough: bureaucrats' heads should roll and the students involved should be punished.

The core of the accusation was that, in glaring breach of national policy, in Jiangsu province students had been enrolled without the mandatory few years amongst the toiling masses. Somehow the provincial authorities had contravened all the rules: apart from the minority from genuine farming families, there had been little grafting in field or factory, nor much tutelage by those poor-and-lower middle peasants and selfless industrial workers.

'My students all told me in great detail about their lives in the countryside and in the factory,' I assailed our minder that afternoon, for I felt betrayed.

'The Party will handle well this contradiction amongst the people,' was all he could say, looking shamefaced.

I was not used to naked lies, though as I came to better understand the political pressures people were under, I could understand why fibbing was often a necessity. And as already remarked, I was beginning to appreciate that in Chinese culture, telling untruths in itself was no great sin. The fierce struggles of the past years had brought this trait to a very sharp edge, for in Cultural Revolution China, mastering the art of dissembling could well be a matter of life and death. So the disjunction between what someone said with a straight face and what they actually meant was a problem for the listener rather than the speaker.

Anyway, the serious charges of this poster campaign propelled the students into a flat panic, and a meeting was hurriedly called by the Party monitor. Overnight, the walls of my classroom were plastered with single-sheet loyalty pledges, penned in neat English and Chinese writing. I copied down a typical one: 'To our Great Leader Chairman Mao and the Party; I promise to serve the people heart and soul and to go anywhere the wise Party sends me after graduating, even to the deepest countryside or to Tibet.'

It was worth their mentioning Tibet, that epitome of unpleasantness. To the romantic Westerner, an assignment to the forbidden Himalayan realm might be the dream ticket. To these young Han Chinese, though, the prospect of even a plum job on high pay in some far-flung Tibetan outpost was regarded with the utmost horror.

On this score at least, the pledgers did not need to alarm themselves, or were cunningly aware of how the system worked. The eventual outcome proved that a kind of inverse principle operated: the more a student appealed for a hardship posting the more likely it was that he or she would end up with a cushy number in the *Luxingshe*, the guardians of all guests from afar, or in the 'foreign affairs' bureaucracy of provincial government. The regime could hardly afford to expel its valuable new graduates to the back of beyond, as it had done just a few years earlier. It was all theatre. And in the event, in the graduating class of 1975, only one Nanda student was sent to Tibet. We only found out about this because he was killed in a road accident, and being dead, was naturally now a 'revolutionary hero'. The episode provided the meat for a couple of days of political study throughout our University community.

Once the hullabaloo had calmed, a compromise punishment was quietly announced for the errant intake of 1972. All those like my precious English students who were to graduate in 1975 and had skipped their spell with the masses were to be despatched to Nanjing's factories for an indoctrinating year of labour. Thereafter, the province's Education Bureau would assign them to their professional jobs, and reading between the lines, Tibet would definitely be off the list. At the very least the students had expected a few years of cleansing labour in the villages: they breathed a collective sigh of relief and the song and dance party at the end of the summer semester were touched by only the lightest of grey clouds.

XV
DINGSHAN DENOUEMENT

STRANGELY UNREMARKED BY the China watchers, in the early 1970s Beijing decided to import industrial plant from the West. Nothing like this had been seen since the revolution and the decision marked a watershed on the grand scale. And it was also, at heart, why we and other foreigners had recently been brought into the country, for the huge contracts had English as the official language, with the day-to-day work in a multitude of European tongues. Throughout the country, seventeen foreign-built naphtha cracking plants were to be constructed, each with an annual capacity of over a million tonnes. The Americans had yet to have full diplomatic relations with China, and though the technology was theirs, the work was to be done at arm's length by an Italian contractor and a multinational workforce. Mao had long been urging every one of the two thousand counties to build a low-tech fertiliser plant, each producing a few thousand tonnes. Now at a stroke, China's production of fertiliser would be doubled. And one of the foreign super-plants was to be located on the Yangtze River, within Nanjing's boundary at nearby Qixiashan.

With the arrival of the French and Ecuadorean teachers, the Dingshan was fast becoming the city's foreigner ghetto, and the Jiangsu authorities naturally decided to put the foreign engineers there too. The compound's mock-Tudor mansions were hastily refurbished to accommodate a dozen mainly French newcomers, led by a taciturn Englishman who inexplicably had brought along his bouffant-haired Yorkshire wife.

Once again, I was astonished to discover the engineers'

indifference to the country they happened to be in. At a time when countless outsiders would have killed to get into China, these newly-arrived Westerners knew nothing of their surroundings and cared even less. But as events were soon to prove, if the newcomers saw this as just another posting, China just one more country, then they were badly mistaken. Always eager for any exciting ruptures in our routine, I gleefully anticipated the misunderstandings and culture clashes which the situation promised.

By and large, the foreign engineers kept themselves to themselves, and our encounters were confined to a few nods across the dining hall where they seemed forever to be arguing with the staff about how many beers they had ordered and how many they should pay for. This was a little rich since apart from the huge salaries being banked back home, their *per diem* stipends exceeded the entire monthly wages of the locals. By conforming to the stereotype of brash imperialists, they were doing harm to our own reputations, tarring us with the same brush. Sadly, even to our well-educated Chinese colleagues, foreigners were foreigners were foreigners.

The unwelcome presence of the engineers did, though, create some of the anticipated diversions. It seemed that every couple of weeks they would be sent back from the worksite to hang around the Dingshan while their hundreds of Chinese co-workers simply evaporated. The 'struggle between two lines' was everywhere as an abstract propaganda slogan, but now we were all to have a rare glimpse of the supposedly titanic battle. Behind the scenes, the modernising faction had lifted China's Bamboo Curtain a fraction, but the ultras were far from being reconciled to China's opening up. To them, no doubt, the gigantic turnkey projects from the West were a direct affront to the much-lauded 'self-reliance' of the Chinese revolution.

On the regular occasions when the worksite was locked and

barred, the bemused engineers would idle away their days in the Dingshan compound, drinking and playing cards. From time to time, their guardians would try to distract them with an outing to some local tourist spot or to an evening's entertainment of an incomprehensible revolutionary opera. Most declined the opportunity, preferring to hang around the restaurant block morosely downing bottles of beer.

Just one of the bunch, Bernard, was of a different mould. Bernard was actually quite taken by the fact he had ended up in the forbidding fortress of Mao's China.

'I prefair your company to the uzzer peoples,' Bernard generously proclaimed, once he became a regular visitor to our overstuffed lounge and our cache of Cultural Revolution Vermouth. We, too, came to relish his unexpected companionship and his hilarious briefings from the Qixiashan worksite, not to mention his stories from Beijing.

We ourselves had never dared to make contact with the British embassy in Beijing, for any relations with diplomats would have been grist to the mill of our unseen enemies. Indeed, throughout our stay in China, to the best of my knowledge official Britain was ignorant of our presence in the country. The engineers had no need for such inhibitions and were kept well informed by French diplomatic staff eager for an excuse to leave the capital and go on a little relaxing tour to the provinces. Bernard had a personal friend in his embassy who delivered him *foie gras* and kept him up to date with all the latest news.

Over a sun-downer, Bernard would regale us with the latest happenings between his countrymen and the officials. As well as civil projects like the fertiliser plants, the Chinese military, too, had begun to feel out relations with Western arms companies. The supposedly hush-hush deal between Rolls Royce and a military aircraft factory in Shaanxi province was almost common knowledge. And now, apparently, the PLA wanted some modern helicopters to replace their ancient Soviet-pattern models. So on the quiet again, a French company was invited to tender, provided they could meet a certain condition. Of the four machines to be purchased initially, one had to be flown in stages all the way from Paris to Beijing. Failure in this would mean the whole deal was off, and the French made elaborate preparations for this eccentric odyssey. The crew turned out to be so keen that they arrived on Chinese southwest flank a day ahead of schedule. 'We'll show them what we can do!' they thought.

Up and over the Karakorum sailed the little aircraft before setting a course northeast towards Beijing. Before the helicopter penetrated far into Chinese airspace it was surrounded by Mig 19 fighters which forced it down onto a remote airstrip.

'The poor fellows are now in prison, one accuses them of illegal entry into Chine,' Bernard explained, scarcely able to stifle a guffaw.

'And 'e thought the Chinois would congratulate eem for arriving one day en avance.'

Life on the huge construction site seemed to settle down for a while, with only an occasional interruption as the Chinese workers attended a mass rally or denounced a minor infraction. But presently a longer lockout transpired, and this time there was a major *causus belli*. Bernard could hardly contain himself and was barely able to find his English.

'Everysing come up the Yangzee river in a beeg beeg sheep,' Bernard began. Apparently, when the long-awaited centrepiece of the plant was landed, a huge retort half the length of a football pitch, it was found wanting. The Chinese inspection team at the docks, charged with ascertaining that all was present and correct in the shipment, noticed an obstruction in the monster's bowels.

Refusing to sign off on the consignment, a labourer was sent crawling down the great tube to investigate.

'E came out wis a pair of culotte in ees 'and, waving like zeese!' Bernard cackled.

Some French fitter had, naturally, been using a pair of knickers as a cleaning rag and they had been dropped - accidentally, or perhaps not so accidentally.

Here was a huge gift to the anti-foreign faction, who lost no time in whipping up the workforce and organising a mass denunciation meeting which all the French were obliged to attend.

'You must humbly repudiate this great insult to the Chinese people,' the engineers were ordered. 'Or else you must take every last screw back to France,' the site commissar thundered.

The expatriate project chief demurred, whereupon the whole project was simply shut down and the gates locked. We wondered who would blink first. A couple of weeks later, the site quietly started up again, the foreign engineers went off from the Dingshan on their regular morning bus, and it was as though the incident had never happened.

As it happened, the great retort was to offer further mischief, and of a rather more dramatic nature. When the fertiliser plant was nearing completion, to mark the Everlasting Friendship between the Chinese and Foreign Friendly Peoples it was announced that there would be a ceremonial raising of the massive vessel. The grand occasion would be witnessed by potentates from Beijing, the provincial leadership and the PLA. Accordingly, at the worksite a rostrum was created with banks of seating laid out in front, for this would definitely be an occasion for the long and turgid speeches so beloved of Chinese officialdom.

To the trumpeting of an army band, the retort was raised to semi-vertical when suddenly one of the lugs attaching it to the crane's chains snapped off. The huge cylinder came crashing down, by a short margin missing ministers and vice-ministers, not to mention the entire Party leadership of Jiangsu province and Nanjing Military Region.

Far beyond the affair of the knickers, this was seized upon by all factions as an act of calculated foreign sabotage.

'But it wuz zee crane drivers who did it too quickly,' insisted a mirthful Bernard.

This time the site was sealed off and the engineer's chief held virtually hostage for weeks. Eventually we learned that while sabotage was no longer charged, the Chinese insisted that the French side take all the blame and pay for a new retort. Weeks later it arrived up the Yangtze, this time minus knickers, and in due course all was back to normal and a group of happy and relieved engineers departed for home. But not before Bernard and I had toasted another good story to dine out on.

It was in the deepest winter of 1976 that our schadenfreude was deflated by a depressing episode at the Dingshan. At seven o'clock one dark morning, we were gulping down our coffee in the dining hall when a gaggle of young soldiers rushed in, screaming their heads off about a fire. The cooks, all six of them, belted off in the direction of the building site on the brow of the hill where the new Dingshan Hotel was slowly rising. One of the tool stores was smouldering, and the PLA boys were panicking, darting hither and thither whilst the hut continued to burn. As we arrived on the scene, an ancient fire engine was making its way through the gates below, with a dozen helmeted soldiers clinging to its sides. They ran towards us in formation, but when they reached the burning hut they seemed to have no idea what to do next. Presently a couple of the firemen-soldiers made a feint to enter the conflagration, but were melodramatically held back by their comrades.

From our position a safe distance from the fire, we heard a

high-pitched moaning.

Someone was whimpering 'Jiu wo, jiu wo, jiu wo' 'Save me, save me'. On the frozen ground amongst clumps of rimed shrubs was a blackened form, barely recognisable as human, strips of smoking clothing glued to its melted flesh. We shouted for assistance but none came. The soldiers were too busy being heroes elsewhere. All I could think of was to race off to our rooms and grab one of the fancy satin-covered quilts from our bed. Meanwhile, Jo stood guard over the victim.

I noticed our minibus had arrived to take us to our 7:30 lesson.

'We must take this man to hospital,' I shouted at Lao Xia our reckless driver, as I beckoned him over to look at the burnt figure. The six-foot Xia, a natural thug, gave a nonchalant scowl and continued to drag deeply on his cigarette. We realised it was up to us, and with a couple of soldiers helping, we somehow rolled the man onto the quilt and lifted him onto the floor of the minibus. Gu Lou hospital was en route for the University; when we arrived at its gates, the watchman simply refused to open up to Lao Xia. It was only when I stuck my head out of the window and showed my barbarian features that he swung open the heavy metal gates of the hospital. The injured man was eventually manhandled onto a stretcher and removed from our sight.

Utterly shaken, we walked up to our classrooms and tried to get through our morning's teaching.

'How is the burns victim doing? 'I asked our good Party Secretary Duan the next day. Duan looked shamefaced and muttered something. The next day I repeated my enquiry and Duan remained silent. He had been got at – the order had come down to give nothing away, though we took Duan's grimaces to mean that the poor soul had not made it. To add insult to injury, when our monthly food bill came, the hotel had added on the cost of a new quilt.

I decided I had to let off steam by writing an account of the fire and sending it to the Nanjing Municipal Foreign Affairs Office. My righteous anger was, it seems, an added cause of later official vengeance.

I do not relate this event to demonstrate the cheapness of life in China, a notion so beloved of the missionaries. The post-1949 generation had been raised on endless tales of self-sacrifice. The way to become a 'revolutionary martyr' seemed to be to jump into the nearest raging torrent to rescue a matchstick for the state. There were no stories about saving people's lives.

Towards the end of our Dingshan confinement we managed to release some at least of our pent-up frustrations. Chinese New Year of 1977 was fast approaching, our time in China's ancient southern capital drawing to a close. So, as it happened, was the life of a venerable German shepherd. And in the final days of our long confinement in Nanjing's Dingshan compound, the animal in question had become our very own Scapehound.

Occasionally Jo and I could stand the thought of the Dingshan dining room no longer, and in a small act of defiance we would slip through the gates and get ourselves downtown for a fiery dinner at the Sichuan Restaurant. Only a very few public eateries had survived the austere raging of the Cultural Revolution. Even common noodle or dumpling shops were rare sights, though a renowned *baozi* establishment was said to still ply its dumplings down at the old Fuzimiao, the Confucius Temple district. But in the wake of the hysterical 'criticise Confucius' movement, Fuzimiao was off-limits to us. As for street food, the birthright of the Chinese, it was entirely missing from Nanjing's highways and byways. To the Maoists, street selling was the wicked 'tail of capitalism' which might end up wagging the Chinese dog into counter-revolution.

Of establishments to which you could attach the name 'restaurant' there were merely two left in Nanjing - a Cantonese dining room in the special hotel for Overseas Chinese near the central Xinjiekou Square, where we were not welcome on account of our big foreign noses. The other was the Sichuan Restaurant. Tucked away on the second floor of a 1920s Art Deco-ish terrace on Taiping Road, the Sichuan was not really meant to be visited by foreigners either. If honoured guests were to be banqueted by the local big-wigs it was always in secluded private chambers, either at the Nanjing Hotel where we first lived, or at the nearby Shuangmen Lou - the Double Gate Guesthouse. The Sichuan might have survived the Red Guards, but dining etiquette demonstrably had not. The proletarian customers hunched over bone-spattered tables, slurping and belching, with regular vigorous expectorations on the floor. Grimy dishes were gracelessly plonked down by scowling serving staff, their once-white food-splattered jackets. Much of this dressing down was deliberate but some had already become a bad habit.

The arrival of two outsiders always aroused a commotion, the diners gawking and pointing, the Sichuan's staff visibly wondering to how to manage such dangerous guests. We would remonstrate pointlessly before being locked away in a draughty room with red lacquered floor boards and lace curtains, the lonely diners at a vast disk of a table. Here, in a state of sunken misery we would work our way through the more digestible-looking bits of pork, laced with burning red chillies from my mother's birthplace in the far interior.

If our forays to the restaurant were never a pleasure, we pursued them from a sense of duty to ourselves, a token of our determination not to be corralled in our soft prison on the hill. Throughout our time in China, we laboured under a constant impulse to commune with the Great Chinese Masses, to slum it a

276

little for the sake of our consciences.

Ironically, if it was closeness to the citizenry we were after, every journey downtown to the Sichuan offered it with a vengeance, for Nanjing's battered blue and white buses were always packed to bone-breaking. This always brought another embarrassing stand-off with the unwritten rules. The conductor with her harshly bobbed hair and floral jacket would invariably order some poor souls to vacate seats in our honour. The word had gone out about how the rare foreigner must be welcomed in Nanjing. It was a point of honour to resist, and in this we always prevailed. Conductors were seated within a metal enclosure by the rear door: they were powerless to get through the crush of bodies to assert their authority. When the braver of our fellow passengers nodded their approval at our democratic defiance it was the best part of the whole evening.

We would squeeze off the bus at the dual carriageway and taking off down the dimly lit Chahaer Road, past the middle school with the broken glass on its wall-tops glistening in the moonlight, until we reached the vegetable field reeking warmly of human wastes which nestled under our hilltop retreat. So far so good, but it was past the hour when our squad of soldier-guards had barred the main entrance at the foot of the Dingshan to mount their nightly vigil. We would head for a point in the perimeter wall where it had been well-pilfered by the locals to become a shadow of its former self. Building materials were precious and could not be bought at any price: Chahaer Road was lined with private cottages plainly built of fine Dingshan 'great wall' bricks.

Though you could practically step through the wall without rousing the soldiers, what you really had to worry about was the lumbering German shepherd, our Scapehound. Unleashed after nightfall to savage the bad elements who we were always assured were lurking in the undergrowth, the animal was actually no longer in the bloom of youth. We always managed to outrun it, a breathless finale to an evening of frustration.

One day Xiao Zhang, an ex-student of mine who had been assigned to the Dingshan turned up with torn jacket-tails and a sheepish grin. Apparently he too had broken curfew and ended up tangling with the great beast. And he was not the only one amongst the numerous Dingshan personnel to duel with the four-legged terror. One frozen morning, we arrived in the dining room to a riot. Past us raced the animal, a line of yelling cooks in hot pursuit, their stained white caps flying, ropes and choppers at the ready. I chased after them, and was just in time to see their quarry dash into the ladies' room off the dining room lobby. A few gruesome yelps were followed by silence.

That lunchtime, the cooks jovially waved us over. On their huge enamel draining board lay a partly dismembered carcass, vaguely familiar.

'Which bit do you fancy?' they mimed, beaming. We looked at each other in astonishment and pointed gingerly at a meatier section of the creature's bloody trunk. We had heard about dogs on the menu and knew that it only happened in winter – in Chinese terms, dogs are 'hot' food which the weak-livered should never overdo. The season was right, true enough, but then you were only meant to sink your teeth into specially-bred, cuddly little creatures and certainly not ancient German shepherds.

Placed before us that evening was the usual mountain of rice, some green vegetables, and a dish of sweet and sour ribs of unusual size and impossible toughness. We sank our fangs into our erstwhile tormentor and a kind of revenge was ours, a catharsis for all the petty frustrations and indignities of our years in Nanjing's soft prisons.

XVI
COLONY TO EMPIRE

HONG KONG - FEBRUARY 1977 to December 1978 - turned out to be an interlude, a breathing space. And we were well in need of a little R & R. The last months of our apprenticeship to China were a strain on the nerves. As the lofty leaders of the revolution succumbed one by one to old age, societal tensions stretched to breaking point. The death of Zhou Enlai in January 1976, followed by that of the former warlord and redoubtable Red Army general Zhu De, fomented the most spectacular demonstrations seen in China since 1949. Our 'counter-revolutionary' activities with the camera got us into a tight spot.

It was three months later that Tangshan in north China was destroyed by a huge earthquake, the most destructive act of nature in the modern world until 2005 when the great Asian Tsunami struck. While the Chinese government tried to hide the severity of Tangshan and refused all help from abroad, rumours soon came to our ears that a quarter of a million people had died instantly. As many again succumbed to their injuries. On that fateful day, 28th July 1976, Jo and I were en route for Beidaihe via the Tangshan epicentre; our train was stopped a short distance from Tianjin and put into reverse while troop trains sped north to as near Tangshan as they could get. We had a lucky escape: all trains nearer Tangshan were wrecked on mangled lines.

The University did not want us back in Nanjing. Though hundreds of miles from the affected area, the government had ordered people to live outdoors for the coming months, and soon primitive shelters could be seen anywhere where there was a patch of land away from a building. We were taken instead to spend our summer on an inlet of the great Lake Tai in our province of Jiangsu, unwilling guests of a villa which was once the home of China's premier 'patriotic' capitalist clan headed by Rong Yiren, The Rong empire, based on textiles and flour-milling stretched from Shanghai up to Wuxi, where we now were. The family had a rough time in the Cultural Revolution, of course, but both before it and in its wake Rong Yiren was feted by the Communists, given lots of dosh and honorary state positions. By the early 1980s all had been forgiven, and by the 1990s son Rong Zhijian (restyling himself in Hong Kong as 'Larry Yung') was put in charge of China's premier investment fund– CITIC Asia. Larry was quickly a man of great wealth, and for a time chief steward of the Jockey Club. In colonial and post-colonial Hong Kong you do not get much higher than that. When I was once invited to the inner sanctum at the new race course at Shatin, Larry was amused to learn from me that I had stayed at his old family home on Lake Tai while he, then about thirty-five, was still exiled with his family in faraway Sichuan. I was in Hong Kong on one of my frequent fund-raising missions for my research institute at Liverpool University. Not a few members of Hong Kong's great and good were Liverpool graduates, including Dong Jianhua (Tung Chee-hwa), the first post-British chief of Hong Kong. To keep me entertained, the Hong Kong luminaries and Liverpool alumni such as Anson Chan and Chamson Chau (chairman of my committee) would invite me into the stewards' enclosure at Shatin. I found the Hong Kong elite at play more interesting than the horses.

To China's ever-superstitious people, the great 'quake was a portent of massive change in the land. Sure enough, only weeks later, Mao himself died. In time-honoured tradition, with the emperor gone, Mao's coterie was finished off in a palace coup. This, then, was the tense backcloth to our final year in Nanjing.

Six months into the post-Mao order, the University carpenters crated up our trophies - bolts of silk, rolls of Cultural Revolution propaganda posters, cheap silk paintings from the Friendship Store, bales of shirts and trousers assiduously copied from much-worn denim prototypes by the nervous tailor at Gulou Square. We had to accompany our precious cargo to Shanghai and be present for a customs inspection.

Shanghai's bureaucrats, normally arrogant in the face of peasants such as we from outside their fabled city, on this occasion were well-mannered. Everyone knew that Mao's Gang of Four were Shanghai political mafia, and the city's officials were now on their best behaviour. This was a stroke of luck, as the customs inspectors let the crates through on the nod, even though their cursory examination uncovered an illicit tape recording of the arrested Gang of Four member Wang Hongwen, as well as lots of other trivia which might normally be construed 'anti-China'. In the event, nothing was taken from us and we watched the residue of our Nanjing days as it was hoisted in a great coir net into the hold of one of China's few ocean-going general cargo vessels. It was some years before we were to see our Nanjing crates again.

The Beijing Foreign Experts Bureau provided us cash to buy London-bound tickets, and we were put on a plane for Guangzhou and then escorted to the Hong Kong border by one of the unavoidable guides from the *Luxingshe*. We had negotiated a paid stopover in one of the Communist-owned hotels in Kowloon. After our almost total isolation in Nanjing, Hong Kong at New Year 1977 was just too much. We lay abed and spied on the exotic world outside through Hong Kong's wild television stations. It was three days before we dared to venture out into the maelstrom of Kowloon's brimming streets to seek out the friends of friends who we hoped would help us with a place to stay. When we did eventually get out though, we were troubled by the lack of attention, by the fact that we longer gathered crowds around us.

Despite the unpromising start, Hong Kong gradually worked its magic on us, and like many Westerners who came for a couple of days and stayed for years, we never made it to Kai Tak airport and a plane to London. Instead, through Andrew D, an investigative journalist on the *Far Eastern Economic Review*, we installed ourselves on Cheung Chau, one of the myriad isles of the South China Sea belonging to the then-British colony. Cheung Chau was favoured by the more bohemian foreigners who lacked the lavish housing benefits of proper Hong Kong expatriates. In the main, our island companions were jobbing journalists and teachers, and we were happy to join their life of semi-indolence under a semi-tropical sun where food and booze were cheap and the locals indifferent to the few dozen invaders in their midst.

The hour-long ferry ride to Hong Kong Island belied the distance of the Cheung Chau crowd from the official colonial expatriates. These would-be nabobs with their live-in servants and roomy apartments at Mid-Levels (or even higher up on the Peak of Victoria Island) had no worries about the colony's outrageous rents. Most had never stepped on the slimy duckboards of a local street market to buy their fruit and vegetables.

We too found that minimal work routines were enough to buy the foreign devil - the *gweilo* – daily rice, a few bottles of San Miguel, and a decent roof over one's head. We fell into jobs at the British Council on the top floor of Star House at Kowloon's tip, from which we dreamily observed the fabled Star ferries weaving their way between rusty Chinese coasters and container-laden lighters. After China, the requirements of teaching eager young Cantonese was a well-paid dodge; I soon worked out that it was unnecessary to labour more than twelve hours a week. The rest of the time I hid myself away in the library of one of Hong Kong's more discreet corners of academe.

Cheung Chau was an exotic never-never land which was going to be hard to leave. Every Wednesday for a year, over tea and chicken feet, the boss of the not-so-secret Chinese Party apparatus in the British colony – known universally by its Chinese name of Xinhua - sent a minion to probe me. My long acquaintance with Huang Binyuan had begun at one of the speaker-lunches held at the research centre, which kept open house to the local China-watching pundits. Huang proposed that we should meet in surroundings more congenial than that unmarked Art Deco villa on Argyle Street, under the landing path of Kai Tak airport. An important consideration, as it often is in China, was doubtless the food. I could see that Xiao Huang was struggling with the Centre's lunch offering, and was not surprised that he proposed meeting in a more salubrious place downtown.

Perhaps I was singled out because of some articles commissioned by the local Communist press about Nanjing in Mao's twilight years. It was unusual for a foreigner to seek such a platform. Maybe the reason it happened was that the research centre where I had a niche was well known to be a nest of spooks. Whatever, at the appointed time, Xiao Huang would be waiting for me at a certain Wanchai street corner, from where he would guide me to an eatery worthy of a Beijing expense account.

Huang was born and brought up in a Hong Kong which we foreigners would simply not have recognized, a Hong Kong where the cradle-to-grave system of Mao's China was replicated in sealed capsules in the colonial landscape. This world knew itself as *aiguo* - 'patriotic', its offspring observing (though in watered-down form) all the political ritual of the Beijing regime. At Communist Party-run schools, the young *aiguo* learned a funny flat Cantonese-influenced Mandarin, in which they chanted their patriotic songs and recited Beijing's latest political message. School leavers were guaranteed a job in one of the many obscure *aiguo* Communist

283

Party-controlled trading outfits, various propaganda outlets and even the department stores like China Products in Queen's Road Central, run on strict capitalist lines by Communist Party placemen. In the Mainland manner, they were housed in company dormitories and expected to marry within their own community. In short, though it was a slightly watered-down version, their entire lives were bounded by the Maoist cosmos.

With the first warm eddies filtering into to his cloistered world from the post-Mao north, Xiao Huang must have sensed that a liberation was on its way. What a novelty that he was now being encouraged to cultivate supposedly useful *gweilos* and feast them in the hitherto gilded, forbidden walls of Wanchai's most decadent *dim sum* palaces.

I cannot imagine what Xiao Huang told his bosses. Having seen how things were done in Nanjing, I suspected that every encounter would require a lengthy and formulaic report from him. My inclination was not to hold back on any topic and certainly not to respect the sensibilities of the People's Republic. This presented Xiao Huang with a problem. His interlocutor was a foreigner who was not only well-read in his Marxism but was inclined to criticize Beijing from the left. Yet the Western foreigner was supposed to be synonymous with anti-communism. All very puzzling.

I knew that to attempt to explain the convoluted roots of this position (Bukharin, Stalin, Trotsky, not to mention Rosa Luxembourg, Gramsci, the Spanish Civil War) would be pointless. For the post-1949 Chinese, 'China = Socialism' was an irrefutable axiom. Huang had no more conceived of the average Hong Kong foreigner who believed in socialism than a self-proclaimed socialist who questioned China's revolutionary credentials. I could only hope that the poor lad had imbibed enough of Mao's earthy version of dialectical materialism to be able to simultaneously accommodate in his brain such contradictory messages.

RICHARD KIRKBY

After almost a year of the *dim sum* routine, Xiao Huang started on a new tack at our weekly tête-à-tête. We had witnessed China under the evil regime of the Gang of Four. Now with the brave new world of Deng Xiaoping's China, how could we even think of returning to Europe without witnessing its pleasures? And did not China now need the help of good foreigners? A return to the bosom of the motherland, as he put it, was becoming less of an option and more of a duty.

Xiao Huang was persuasive: if I refused to succumb to his wishes I would be spoiling the ship for a ha'porth of tar. Why put in all these years of effort if I was only going to have half the China experience? I had to have both the 'before' and the 'after'.

But I was tired of China, and of Hong Kong too where political life for the Chinese and humble expatriate alike was pretty well nil, and where the long years of colonial rule had naturally made the locals wary of any friendships with us intruders. My engagement with China had always had a central ambition – to unravel the country's quirkish urbanism. It was this fascination which had kept me going through the hard days in Nanjing, and which now anchored me to Hong Kong. Now, forays into official Sinology at the Universities Service Centre had already led to publication of a few articles; a good academic publisher had even proposed a book. As a 'barefoot academic' I was edging towards a scholarly career. But I quickly found that there were no jobs for me in Hong Kong. Even in the late 1970s, colonial myopia decreed that the colony's only ivory tower, Hong Kong University, had no more interest in studying China than did the average UK provincial polytechnic.

Many a foreign visitor during these times felt able to write a fat book after a slim visit to China. For myself, I was determined that my own writing should tap richer seams. In my two-and-a-half years in China, I had kept my ear to the ground. Prolonged spells of *kaimen banxue* ('open-door schooling') had transformed me first into a rice farmer, and later a skilled metal turner in a machine shop. This unique exposure to the realities of city and countryside was the best ever foundation for understanding China's odd urbanisation process. Now, it seemed, there was a political climate in which there was a chance to do research that was more systematic than the informed snooping which had been my Nanjing mode.

There were some big problems. The most obvious was that Jo and I had deliberately uncoupled ourselves, and we occupied separate houses up on Cheung Chau's Peak Road. The rigours of our long Nanjing confinement had brought out the worst in our relationship. We both understood that despite temptations to recreate a romantic Oriental retreat, a return to China together would likely result in the problems of our Nanjing days being repeated. 'Never step into the same river twice' rang through my mind.

A different obstacle, but one no less vital, was our fear of being thrust into an environment in which we were again kept at arm's length from the real China. So we insisted to Xinhua that any return had to be to a provincial posting where there was no foreigners' ghetto. Beijing was ruled out from the start: even during the early 1970s, the foreign population of its Friendship Hotel numbered well over a hundred. In Shanghai there was a smaller complement of 'foreign friends'. But they were still completely ghettoized, inhabiting the 14th floor of the Shanghai Mansions, the former Broadway Mansions.

Nor would we agree to a posting to one of those provincial capitals such as Xi'an, Guangzhou, or Hangzhou where foreign language teachers had been inducted in ones and twos during the last phase of the Cultural Revolution. Here the ghettoising habits had already seeped in with the new 'open door' policy. *Zhuanjialou* ('foreign experts' buildings') were suddenly de rigueur for any university wanting to get with the game. But this time, no isolated guest-house for us. It was cheek-by-jowl with our Chinese colleagues or nothing. We knew this was contentious. But we felt we were in a sellers' market.

I was also really anxious not to take on a teaching job in China which would simply leave me no time to do my own thing. In Nanjing we had at least had plenty of days off, as teaching programmes were often interrupted for days or occasionally weeks by the latest political campaign or the interludes of *kaimen banxue*. But there was no way I could put the time to useful use. Now, in 1978, the Chinese government had begun to reverse Mao's educational experiments: the pendulum seemed poised to swing in the opposite direction. Intensive cramming was on its way, and I could see myself being buried under it.

So when we were finally invited to the lair of Xinhua's Number 1 Boss in Happy Valley, I was determined not to fall too easily to his blandishments. I tried my usual tactic of arguing in ways which Chinese officialdom could easily relate to. Mao, famously, had a habit of taking it out on the educated classes, the *zhishifenzi*, and we were all familiar with the stories of their fate. If they were not banished to 'reform through labour' at a cadre school farm, hospital surgeons were demoted to ward cleaners, architects to hod carriers, professors of English to cabbage growers. Now with the 'reversal of verdicts' the Party newspapers were vigorously advertising their new policy of restoring the intellectuals to their rightful place. I, too, presented myself as something of a victim. The thought of more deadening days of English teaching might suit Jo, but it appalled me.

'Zhou Nanshan is a specialist teacher of English, but for years I had to serve the people by doing this job too,' I opportunistically ventured. 'Now I too want to be allowed to go back to my own profession if I have another posting in China.'

This was of course a very long shot, as for years no foreigners had been allowed to stray outside their native language, either as teachers, or as polishers in one of the foreign language publishing houses. But it was my pitch, and I meant to stay with it.

As the summer of 1978 turned to autumn, the change in China's political firmament was signalled by a new phenomenon, a widely reported 'Democracy Movement'. This news gladdened my heart and raised in me real hopes that China might move towards a better, a democratic socialist future. It was all very exciting and I wanted to be there, to witness the breath-taking changes which this new mass protest seemed to promise. The Democracy Movement's aims were novel: not so much the targeting of individual leaders as was the tradition, but changing the underlying political system itself. Nightly TV news in Hong Kong showed the crowds at Beijing's Xidan crossroads and its 'Democracy Wall', where hundreds of *dazibao*, 'big character posters', demanded every freedom imaginable. With Mao quite dead and safely in his crystal sarcophagus on Tiananmen Square, the pent-up desire for change was overwhelming. And amazingly, so far the forces of repression were nowhere to be seen.

Sitting in Hong Kong and avidly devouring each snippet of news from up north, I found it impossible to imagine that the genie could be returned to the bottle. Now, surely, the moment was near for China to take a new road, building on the revolution with new popular institutions? Mao's dictum was 'Only socialism can save China', yet he had ignored that essential ingredient – democracy. My recipe for the Chinese was more socialism, not less, but with a proper system of voting in leaders.

Watching China with such a perspective was lonesome. There were pitifully few amongst our hedonistic circle of foreigners who showed any interest in the political scene a few miles to the north. As for the professional China-watchers, born of the Cold War their aspirations for China were rather different than my own. Wondering what to do, what to think, I sought out some Quakers, Tony and Johanne Reynolds, friends of my maternal Sichuan family, who had known the country a generation before I got to it. Wise birds, they were inclined towards the longer view of the Democracy Wall movement.

As we sipped our coffees in the alien surroundings of the Mandarin Hotel lobby shop, Tony's scepticism shone through.

'Always remember that a single swallow doesn't make a summer, Richard,' was his parting shot.

It turned out he was right. My notion that the age of enlightenment was finally dawning for the Chinese was mostly, it turned out, wishful thinking, and by late 1979, the democracy movement was over, *dazibao* banned forever.

I had a worrying notion about the Chinese mass psyche, both hopeful and not so hopeful. Seeing all that anti-government agitation on my TV screen, I could not help wondering how the people I had known in the Nanjing years were able to flip so easily from an unedifying quiescence to such reckless anti-authoritarianism. China's rulers through history have perhaps recognised this national trait, and that is why they have always feared *luan* (chaos) amongst their huge population. Personally, after Nanjing and its numbing orthodoxy, I was very much up for a bit of cleansing *luan*.

My appetite for the heterodox was whetted by a short trip back to Nanjing. In the spring of 1978, we had been very surprised when a telegram arrived at Heights Villa, Cheung Chau. Out of the blue came an invitation to an all-expenses trip, courtesy of Nanjing University. The telegram hinted in official-ese that 'verdicts were to be reversed' and our rather flattering association with the *fan geming pai* ('counter-revolutionaries') was to be repudiated.

So we got ourselves once again to Nanjing and were astonished by the changes just one year after we had left the city. As related earlier, the face-losing apologies from the police were amazing in themselves, as was the restoration to us of confiscated films. But what really touched us were the outpourings of our ex-colleagues about events long-since forgotten.

'Do you remember me telling you that there were wolves on Purple Mountain when you said you were planning to climb it? I was lying, but I couldn't let you know that the whole hillside is a military area or I'd have been in big trouble for telling foreigners secrets.' In fact, Jo and I had made this foolhardy discovery ourselves, almost stumbling over a manned machine-gun nest near the summit. Fortunately, the soldiers did not spot us.

There were many such confessions, about things of so little consequence that we could not even recall them. Even Lao Wang, our first Party minder after we arrived, an ambitious straight-down-the-line cipher, shared memories with us of disarming openness. Yet he was the one who, so very recently, had been the most closely buttoned-up-to-the-brain in his Mao jacket. Ask Comrade Wang the time and you could almost trace the question as it went past his internal censor. But poor man. To 'make a mistake' with a foreigner in those days really could mean criticism, arrest and even worse.

On our first night we were taken to an informal dinner by a crowd of our old Nanjing colleagues. This had never happened to us before, for in the old regime, the one which we had got so used to, Chinese and foreigner could never sit down at table together except on very formal, cadre-infested occasions.

Even more astonishing to us, one of our ex-colleagues, a man with a reputation for outspokenness, launched into an impassioned speech of welcome. Shen Zhijing's long discourse was a broadside against the systemic failures of Party rule, both past and present. I was immediately put in mind of the still-outlawed document, the *Li-Yi-Zhe* manifesto dating from the early 1970s. *Li-Yi-Zhe* was the made-up name of a brotherhood of dissidents based in Guangzhou who had somehow published China's then-most celebrated and cogent critique of Party rule. This broke with the usual coordinates of Chinese political polemic – personality-focussed diatribe - and could almost have been contrived by European New Leftists. We had devoured the *Li-Yi-Zhe* manifesto back in London, as a samizdat version had reached Hong Kong and was relayed in translation to would-be revolutionists in Europe. Even back in the dark days of Nanjing, someone had once whispered news of the manifesto and asked us if we had a copy. We certainly did not - far too dangerous to bring it to China in our large library trunk.

I had always had a lot of time for this fellow Shen. We had come across him only occasionally, but he stood out as one incapable of concealing his true thoughts. There was always something about his little comments which was not quite *People's Daily*. Though we did not know it at the time, Shen was regularly hauled off for 're-education'. Now, over dinner, he was telling us that our rooms in the Dingshan guesthouse, to which we had been unceremoniously shifted after too much contact with visiting foreigners, were once his prison. Hard to imagine.

Shen went on to reveal that he had been caught up in the supposed anti-Party conspiracy known as the 'May 16th', the one relating somehow to Lin Biao's death plot against Mao Zedong. From what I now know, he was lucky to escape with his life, as thousands of suspects were tortured and killed in 1973 and 1974. I would have loved to have gone deeper with Shen, but when next in Nanjing - almost a decade on - I found that his chain-smoking had finally finished him off. I glanced around the circular table at our dozen companions, and there was only the faintest embarrassment that we should be witness to Shen's daring diatribe.

The difference between this China and the one we had left just a year before was startling. For the first time ever, our colleagues presented themselves en masse as actual human beings. Nevertheless, once back in Hong Kong we continued to weigh up the pros and cons of a return. Anyway, our hard-to-get stance with the boss of Xinhua was not exactly diplomatic, and so we did not really expect much of a response from Beijing. But after just a couple of months, an excited Xiao Huang announced that the Foreign Experts Bureau had come up with an offer. We were to go to Shandong University as their first-ever post-1949 foreign staff; we would live on the campus; we were wanted immediately.

'How about Richard's job in Shandong?' we enquired.

'There's nothing mentioned about that. It just says "He can do what he wants".'

Decision time was upon us. We hopped onto one of the phut-phut sampans, and a squatting Hakka grandma flashed her gold teeth as she steered us between the ocean-going fishing junks with their high Tudor-like sterns, out through the typhoon barrier of Cheung Chau's harbour. Soon we were over the straits and disembarking on the mountainous island known in English since opium smuggling days as Lantau. As a neutral third party, we called along our adoptive guard dog, Chairman, a dun-coated opportunist who for the odd bowl of rice kept the snakes from creeping through the grass straight into our hall. It was one of those walks when the discussion was so intense that we neither of us noticed how far we had gone – an un-rancorous retelling of a relationship which had already lasted over a decade. Should we succumb to temptation and go off to China together yet again, in the hope that this would bring us back together? Or was this the time to part? By the time we were chugging back towards

Cheung Chau, the matter seemed to have resolved itself: Jo would be taking on Shandong on her own, while I would break the Hong Kong daydream and head back to England. Once this painful move was decided, we got on with it, and within a fortnight my erstwhile partner – still my wife - was waving farewell to her friends at Kowloon's Hunghom station. I took the cheapest flight I could find back to London en route for the family home in County Durham.

It was now October of 1978. It was a shock to be back in the familiar but unfamiliar England, and I found it hard to get to grips with what I should be doing with the rest of my life. The answer was provided almost by default: it was a solution which half of me had all along hoped for, were I to admit it. Out of the blue, I received a crackly phone call from Jo in Jinan. Would I reconsider coming? The University president Wu Fuheng was about to invite me.

'How are things there?' I wanted to know. Jo responded that it was all a little weird in Shandong, though the person in charge of the University foreign affairs office was great. And there was this very strange foreign man, Lao Wen, who bugged her every move. She could not say more right now.

Shortly after, though it seems improbable in today's world of DHL and emails, up chugged a little red motorbike to my parents' Barnard Castle house with yet another Chinese telegram. In a flowery three paragraph message, Shandong University was inviting me to get myself to Jinan. I would be honoured as a full 'foreign expert' (I cared not a jot about that) and yet would have to teach a mere four hours a week. The rest of the time I could get on with whatever I wanted. My urbanisation research! I was to contact China's London embassy immediately, and arrangements were underway to get me without delay to Hong Kong and onward via Guangzhou to Jinan.

It was a slow return to the Middle Kingdom as my new employers had cunningly decided to make good on my unexpected late arrival. A shopping list awaited me in Hong Kong, and on it was every type of teaching hardware from tape recorders to overhead projectors. Within days of my arrival, the University printers managed to reproduce all the language teaching texts I brought with me, and embarked on a nationwide sales campaign with the pirated copies of Longman's famous *Kernel Lessons*. I was off to a good start at Shandong University, a 'foreign friend' with added dollar value.

It did not take many days in Shandong before I realised that by comparison to this strange place, our previous posting at Nanjing was a cosmopolitan haven. People in the south of China had often told us that Shandong was a *wenhua shuiping hen di* ('cultural level very low') kind of place. They looked on the natives as either bumpkins or atavistic schemers. Amused Shanghai sophisticates once told me that at the height of the Cultural Revolution, when ferocious hand-to-hand skirmishing was a regular occurrence, it was always the students from Shandong who were to the fore. The wily Shanghainese locals would allow their big-boned confrères the privilege of heading up the tougher rallies: they were the ones that came back with broken heads. At the same time, Shandong also maintained something of its reputation for feuding, intrigue and the secret cabal. Mao's widow Jiang Qing, now presented to the world as a she-devil manipulator, was a daughter of the province. With the frustrations and privations of the Cultural Revolution receding, these were certainly better times by far. It was just the place that was the problem and it would indeed be the darker side of Shandong which was to dominate my fifteen months there. Civilised Nanjing had been right place, wrong time. Shandong proved to be the opposite.

The august seat of learning of Shandong was an odd place to end up for a second stint in the country. Shandong University was plonked down some miles outside the capital city of Jinan, in the loamy yellow fields and along the grimy lanes of an outlying county town. In Hong Kong, I had met a Taiwan Chinese woman who claimed Jinan as her *laojia* – her family's place of origin – and she had confirmed all the best bits in my ancient edition of *The Nagel's Encyclopaedic-Guide*. Jinan was the City of Springs (seventy-two of them, no less), of exquisite Suzhou-style gardens, of the Thousand Buddha Mountain. But all we could find on our bike rides were dusty streets set out on a grid, lined with one and two-storey nondescript pre-1949 buildings, these punctuated by the usual concrete and brick four-storey structures of the 1960s and '70s. Apart from one or two which remained, the famed gardens and their springs had long been buried under new factories, and housing blocks with their unloved stairwells. In short, Mao's super-drive for 'productive cities' had sucked all the groundwater from under Jinan. As for the historical attractions, a decade before our arrival the Red Guards had systematically decapitated and vandalized the thousand Buddhas of the eponymous mountain. In contrast to the southern lushness and relative order, variety and indeed beauty of the ancient capital Nanjing, we found Jinan a thoroughly depressing place. And the very proletarian-looking population seemed beaten down and dispirited.

Our little town of Licheng, location of the University, was neither picturesque nor joyously and dirtily productive. It was merely filthy, heavily-polluted, and disarrayed. The civic pride of the commune era had evaporated and Licheng town had fallen into the desuetude common to thousands of North China settlements, which under the new dog-eat-dog profit economy were now places of crumbling facades, potholed roads, chaotic tractor and lorry traffic, piled up garbage, and squabbling peasants.

A distinguishing feature of Licheng was its surreal backcloth. Towering three hundred feet over its shabby huts was a huge dinosaur – a great cathedral church of the nineteenth century proselytising Catholics. The crosses of its spire and gables had been supplanted by large brick-red metal stars in three dimensions, their panels already loose and flapping in the relentless, dusty wind. Unlike other such unwelcome reminders of foreign intrusions,, rather than being razed, the cathedral had been re-sanctified. In its new incarnation as a sandpaper factory, the enormous structure remained an abrasive intruder on the flat Yellow River landscape. Internally, the lofty nave and side chapels had been stripped of all furnishings; in many a peasant hut of Licheng one could catch a glimpse of cathedral trophies. Later, in a campus cottage, I would be seated for dinner of noodles and pig guts on an amputated Gothic pew.

Once inside the University's campus, the eye was somewhat relieved from the chaos and filth of the streets. Yet the treeless, desiccated borders to the walkways, the expanse of swirling yellow dust which was the sports field, the two-storey buildings in grey brick, even the ersatz post-1949 copies of the 'big Chinese roof' buildings of Beijing and Nanjing Universities – all was neglected and sad-looking.

When a Chinese work unit reached a certain eminence it would establish a 'foreign affairs' department, really an office dealing with all external links. Now that we had arrived, the University could not do without one. Its boss was a fat and sleepy official whom we rarely saw. The de facto director was a bright-eyed and highly engaging woman in her forties, Li Hua, and for the first time ever we were allowed to get to know an ordinary family. Li Hua's two children. Weiwei, a thick-plaited teenage beauty, and son Qunqun, a live-wire of nine, soon became familiar faces. As did bald and bespectacled husband Lao Guo, a minor official in the University accounts office.

Li Hua was determined to make our second stay in China as normal and homely as possible. Eyebrows were raised all around but Li Hua cared not. Her home had an ever-open door. It was always a special treat to engage with her mother, a dignified peasant lady from the Shandong peninsula who, though she had never before set eyes on a foreign devil, let alone had one in her living room, took us in her stride and chatted away to us like long lost friends. The older Mrs Li would beckon us into her little cooking area, where she would regularly invite us to a celebratory rolling of those delicious steamed dumplings, *jiaozi*. She even created for me a traditional silk padded jacket which, decades on, remains a valued and serviceable member of my winter wardrobe.

Li Hua and her lovely family were housed in the University's No. 2 Residential Compound. Its appearance put one in mind of something between a village and the kind of Second World War hut encampment where the British put their German captives. Red-brick one-storey cottages rose in clumps of four along the packed earth pathways. Most had extended their front areas into informal gardens, fenced off from the common area by makeshift barriers of bamboo. Some had crude fences of steel waste filched from some neighbourhood metal stamping shop; all over China one saw window barriers and fencing made from this stuff, and I often thought it ironic that China's drive for steel production was undermined so overtly by such usage.

Within reason, the University had been as good as its promise about how we would be accommodated, and our new home comprised the whole ground floor of the first building inside the gatehouse of the No.1 Residential Compound, *Diyi sushe*. This was conveniently planted just a few yards from the main entry to the campus. At last we were to be allowed to live more or less cheek-by-jowl with our Chinese colleagues. Maybe 'colleagues' was not quite the word, as the No.1 Compound was really the home for all the University's superiors – the Party bosses plus a few well-placed professors. Still, this was a very different from anything that we had experienced until now in China. With the exception of a sprinkling of old timers who had stayed on in Beijing and Shanghai after the revolution, foreign employees of the government had always been confined within guarded compounds like our old Dingshan in Nanjing.

Our apartment in the cottagey grey brick and grey-tiled house with its own dusty, beaten earth yard. Apart from the spacious living room, it offered a large bedroom and an ante-room used as a store. As always in the China of that era, we had a running battle with the toilet cistern and its ill-designed innards, which would start hissing water into the bowl at any moment it chose. Walls were whitewashed, wooden door frames and windows painted in that reddish brown lacquer universal in China at the time, furniture was similarly surfaced and heavy chairs covered in off-white loose covers. Our bedroom had the usual solid frame cots with hard cotton mattresses, spread over with quilt covers of embroidered satin. The flat always lacked the warmth of a home, but that was not for lack of effort on Li Hua's part. It was the frigid composite concrete floors. Even the kitchen sink and the bath were made of the stuff. And yet we had that important symbol of independence, our own kitchen. In the small entrance lobby Li Hua had installed a blue-enamelled two-ring gas burner. While most of our colleagues still had to put up with the smoky 'economy' stove - an open-topped steel cylinder with an aperture half way down for removing ash – we were privileged to be one of the first households in town to cook on bottled gas.

To the economy stove's definite credit, it was no danger to life and limb. As the fashion for bottled gas spread, in the locality almost weekly a kitchen would explode and its occupants expire. I was not in the least surprised: the standard-sized steel bottles supplied to us invariably had valves which if shoved a little to the side would issue a freezing stream of vapour. But with all its problems, our Shandong home provided a generous enough living space – what a high-ranking official or respected professor might merit before the Cultural Revolution's levelling. The most important thing was that we were housed amongst Chinese colleagues rather in super-privileged hotel isolation. The University – or more accurately Li Hua – had done right by us.

The recruitment of foreign teaching staff to university languages departments was just becoming the fashion in the China of the later 1970s. Until now, such exotic flowers had been permitted only in a handful of the great national educational centres known as key-point (*zhongdian*) universities. But there was more than simply one-upmanship involved: now that our University could boast a couple of staff from England, one from Japan, and perhaps even some visiting professors from America in the offing, the leaders could claim princely bounties from the central government. I found out in a moment of Li Hua loose talk that a single expert merited a 25,000 *yuan* bounty from the Foreign Experts' Bureau in Beijing. Our three (including young Myumi, teaching Japanese) meant 75,000 *yuan* – equivalent in those days to the collective annual pay of over one hundred of our Chinese teaching colleagues. Intended mainly to save China's face where there were somewhat backward local conditions, this largesse could be deployed at the leaders' discretion.

In our case, it was soon decided to use the money prudently and with maximum local effect, especially upon some of the University's Party committee members who still doubted the wisdom of having foreigners around. Lest the bonanza was for some reason clawed back, within a week of our coming, a team of peasant builders had thrown up a new structure in our compound, a kind of private restaurant with a large take-away window. Expense was not spared and this was actually the first time I had ever seen wallpaper in China. But far from keeping the foreign devils in the manner to which they were accustomed, the new restaurant block was pretty well immediately taken over as the main venue for wining and dining by the University leaders. And the Chinese do know something about corporate entertaining.

An ante-room of the new installation housed an industrial scale coal-fired steam boiler, the pipes from which performed a variety of tasks. To my amazement, one was sunk into the concrete floor and issued upwards through a huge bamboo steamer over a metre wide. Here the specially-hired chefs from Qingdao (quaintly thought of as a 'foreign' place even though half a century had passed since the old Treaty Ports had been abolished) mass produced bread and garlic-filled *baozi* which the children of the compound, the gilded youth of the University bosses, would carry back to their apartments.

Another of the superheated steam pipes was slung from trees towards our building, and let in through a rough hole knocked in our wall. Within, it was linked up to ancient banks of radiators. Each evening, the appointed hour for heat was heralded by a frightful cranking of cast iron and a deadly sizzling of radiator valves. Bathing was a high-risk venture of scorching, exploding gases. First, the water was sluiced in, icy cold, to fill a passable concrete copy of a Western-style tub. Next, you had to introduce below water level a fearsome superheated steam nozzle. Within a minute or two, your bathwater was at boiling point. Leaving the door open in winter would speedily produce a foggy miasma in every room. When the whole system ran out of steam, as it frequently would, bath-time would be followed by shimmering condensation on the freezing walls which gathered in little pools on the concrete floors. But when the radiators were functioning as designed, the problem was one of furnace-like heat, which in the intensely dry north China climate produced an unpleasant sensation hardly softened by wide-open windows. Doubtless part of the attraction to our queues of visitors from their bleak winter dormitories was the apartment's luxuriating warmth.

Luckily, Li Hua was a Party member of some standing, and she was loudly unimpressed by the patriarchal authoritarians who saw the advent of foreigners on their patch as, at best, a necessary evil. Nonetheless, whether or not the considerable traffic to our door within the No.1 Compound should be detained at the gatehouse, or allowed in only when papers had been shown, remained a hot issue throughout our stay. It became clear from his deliberate snubs that our most powerful antagonist was the almighty Party Secretary of the University, a taciturn fellow unusually lacking in the Chinese polite face as he slunk grumpily past our door several times daily. This despite the fact that I demanded respect as his twin daughters' tutor. Both in their late twenties, one was sly, ugly and bitter like her father and the other comely and demure. But Li Hua had her own weapons of natural charm and obstinacy, and even more almighty reinforcements in the form of the Beijing Foreign Experts Bureau. This was the time when China was heavily advertising its new openness to the world, and Li Hua was in tune. By and large, she was the victor in the struggle for our personal 'open door'.

The weather-beaten, unsmiling peasant who commanded our gatehouse spent most of his days pulling on a huge tube of tobacco, while aimlessly flicking through one of those dog-eared cartoon books of worthy tales which the Party deemed suitable for the lower orders. While we noticed him reluctantly waving on our visitors, and challenging all others, there were exceptions to his vigilance which we applauded. Striding straight into the compound without a by-your-leave were the egg-peddling lady, the knife sharpener, and the bean-curd man with his cloth-covered basket of chalky dank stuff and his cries of *'Dofu, mai dofu!'* This was a huge novelty, as our China experience to date had been one in which the street peddlers of yore were sternly banished. After all, in 1976, Mao himself had declared them the 'capitalist tail' which might eventually wag the whole Chinese body-politic.

But now, in the brave new China of Deng Xiaoping, once again life was going on as it had for centuries, adding a little spice to the grey Shandong landscape.

We foreigners in Licheng were an exciting novelty, and as the weeks went on, the locals began to regard us as trophy figures. News of our arrival soon spread far and wide, and people started turning up both from the University and even further afield. The inconvenience of what became a stream of visitors was mostly outweighed by the sense of normalcy: for the first time we were able to have unfettered encounters with the great Chinese public. Quite a contrast with Nanjing in the fading years of the Cultural Revolution.

Now Li Hua, our Party minder, was actually encouraging us to hold open house, and not just to our lecturer colleagues and students. For a time, the stream of inquisitive locals was constant, and we got the feeling that for most of them the aim was simply to bask in the vapours breathed by an alien species.

Our most frequent visitor (he carted in our heavy gas bottles) was a man in his early thirties whose family had been cursed by the 'capitalist' label. His father had been a minor functionary in a pre-Liberation bank and under Mao's dictum the sins of the father were also those of the children. Xiao Zhang's post-Mao mission in life was to fathom the hitherto illicit delights of ballroom dancing. He would brook no resistance, hauling me to my feet and drag me around the living room as his rag-doll partner. Simultaneous musical accompaniment was provided by his vocal rendering of a Palm Court orchestra. Poor Xiao Zhang could never be persuaded that I, the great Western-country-person, was as much a stranger as he to the intricacies of the quick-step and the waltz. To cement our friendship, Xiao Zhang tried to give me some of the family treasures recently retrieved from their hiding place in a muddy ditch. I politely refused all his offerings. I was not in China to enrich myself, especially at the expense of someone so vulnerable.

A couple of years later, when back in Shandong, I enquired after Xiao Zhang. I was amazed to learn that he had cast off the persecution of his hated mining equipment factory and stepped out as a full-time dancing coach. The splendid Ming dynasty carved inkstone which he had once offered me as a gift he had managed to sell for 12,000 *yuan* – a Chairman's ransom, and his business capital. How times had changed.

Another memorable eccentric would cycle several miles from the city merely to consult us on the inner meaning of an abstruse entry in his mangled pre-1949 English dictionary. If we failed to answer his knocks, he would inoffensively parade up and down outside with the book balanced on his head. Meeting the Chinese in an undressed state, the novelty far outweighed the nuisance.

An equally comic but more sinister tone was introduced when we came to the attention of the town's nascent Mr Big, who appeared to us one dark night in a creakily-new black leather coat. This in itself was something of a revelation: in the China of Mao, such garb had only been worn by the arch-villain (normally a yellow-faced Nationalist agent) of the propagandist film studio. Mr Big's authority was also asserted by his absurdly undersized moped upon which he made every effort to roar up to our door. This was another first – the possession of a powered vehicle of any kind was unknown in the terrain of Mao's China. Mr Big demanded an inspection of our exotic foreign trappings, leaving us to 'think carefully' about his various hard-to-refuse business propositions. Mr Big's significant presence in 1979 Licheng prefigured a China in which wheeler-dealing was soon the norm. 'To get rich is glorious' was to become Deng Xiaoping's most famous – or notorious - catchphrase.

The only deal actually closed was rather to my advantage – a straight swap of a temperamental quartz alarm clock (never before seen in China) for a couple of worn but worthy rings. It was an exchange which for once had no political undertones, but I did it mainly to get the man off my back.

Anyway, for the first time in years of residence we were discovering that the Chinese are after all just human beings. That was something in which I revelled, and it also turned out to be a real problem in the making.

Our closest neighbour in No.1 Compound was the occupant of the upstairs flat. We hardly ever heard a squeak from the Widow Wang, a mousy and moustachioed woman whose passions were to surprise us. She was occasionally joined by her son, an ex-Red Guard in his twenties who had somehow wangled his way back from the farm and was now trying to make good his lack of schooling, and job, through devotion to study. When I first bumped into this shy lad he had mentioned the TV University – the *dianshe daxue*. A long time later, I realised that he sat upstairs and watched the television, rather than attending an exciting new course in electronics in some specialist establishment. This was China's informal version of Britain's Open University.

Widow Wang would disappear for weeks on end. She was seen as more than a little odd, as she liked travelling to other parts of the country. Until the late 1970s absolutely no one could get away from home base without the official excuse of 'going out on business'. A very small number with the right credentials might have been lucky enough to go on a rare political pilgrimage to some holy shrine of the revolution. But by-and-large, ordinary Chinese could not be travellers.

Now, it was suddenly both permissible and possible (travel passes abolished, food ration tickets becoming irrelevant, tickets there for the buying) to take to the road (actually the railroad) and just enjoy one of the myriad 'scenic spots' which each locality was keen to boast. But the idea of an elderly woman travelling unaccompanied was too much for the conservative Shandong mind. The poor lady was shunned. When we asked Widow Wang about her odysseys she would become gratefully animated.

By far the most disturbing of our neighbours seemed to lodge in the Party Secretary's flat, so perhaps he was not all that bad. A demented girl of perhaps seventeen would wander shrieking through the compound, tearing her hair as she threw herself from tree to tree, from wall to wall. Noting the aliens who had moved in the block by the gate, the young thing took to slipping into our flat unnoticed and seating herself quietly in our living room. We were agnostic about this, letting her help herself to whatever fruit or tit-bits that caught her gaze. But Li Hua decided it was not on, and encouraged us to bolt our door. The girl's story was emblematic of the madness and human toll of the Cultural Revolution, a period which was now rarely referred to just three years after Mao had gone. Her mother, a professor, had been persecuted and sent away for 'reform'. When she returned to her family, she was taken ill and died of a lingering disease. Father had been sent off to some distant province to one of the rural reform camps known as the May 7th Cadre Schools. In her distress, the girl became permanently crazed.

Because he was inconspicuous in standard local uniform, his face hidden under an overlarge cap, it was easy to forget that our No.1 Compound had another foreign resident, albeit one with solid Chinese citizenship. In one of the larger multiple occupation blocks at the Compound's rear lived Professor Jin Zebo - Professor Ginsburg, a Jewish 'White Russian' who had elected long before 1949 to throw in his lot with the Communists guerrilla forces in the Shandong liberated zone. Naturally, when the provincial University was rebuilding itself in the 1950s, this 'patriotic' fluent English speaker must have been considered a valued asset. Ginsburg kept himself to himself, knowing full well that association with the new foreigners on the block was fraught with danger. Married to a lecturer, and with a pretty non-Chinese looking daughter who happened to be one of the few students assigned to me, Ginsburg had doubtless suffered every persecution during the difficult years. All this was, however, pathetically glossed over in his 'all is rosy' life story, which as a veteran foreign resident he was more or less expected to offer the post-Mao world. The book, published by the Foreign Languages Press, contained contributions from most of the old-timer foreigners who had cast their lot with China after 1949.

When Ginsburg did on rare occasions look us up, we were pretty sure he was there at official prompting, to try to discern our thoughts on the hot issues of the moment. Since shortly after our arrival, China orchestrated a full scale military attack on Vietnam, Ginsburg and his minders had plenty of robust views to contemplate. I was not surprised when he turned up one evening with his characteristic over-affability and some irrelevant enquiry about new teaching materials. I guessed that his real purpose was to seed us with some misinformation about a supposed Soviet incursion into a town in the far northwest of Xinjiang. The idea, I guessed, was to see how we go about passing on this 'news', and to whom. Naturally it only got as far as my diary.

It was understood that my duties in the University's English department would be nominal: after all, I had arrived at Shandong

University on the condition that I should at last be able to prepare my long-delayed book on China's urban development. Teaching was to be an afterthought. I conceded just a couple of hours of tutoring final-year English students, along with irregular sessions in the departmental recording studio. Just as in Nanjing, Jo and I were required to produce mind-numbing imitation tapes which a few days later would echo eerily back at us from huge outdoor loudspeakers as we trudged through the fading light of the campus. On the cusp of old habits of national isolation and the new 'opening up', the China of 1979 was a very weird place.

That year started with a defining moment. After three decades of hatred, Beijing and Washington resumed a formal diplomatic relationship. The Chinese authorities achieved an Orwellian stroke when overnight they transformed the Voice of America propaganda broadcasts from 'counter-revolutionary' to ...well, at least 'non-political'. The VOA suddenly seemed to be wired into every public address system in the land. On campus, as they slurped their meagre rations in the canteen, marched across the ochre sports field sandblasted by the northern wind, the students were soon intoning as one the drawled VOA 'special English' non-sequitur of the day: 'Have you a pen? Yes, I have three sisters' (the previous day, it had been 'Are you going to the ball game tonight? Yes, my coat is blue').

Even the traditional revolutionary 5:30am wake-up blast, a robust PLA marching song, was now abandoned for exotic Disney. An endless reeling of 'Doe's a deer, a female deer, ray's a golden drop of light...' was for us a reveille too far. We made a written plea that the nearest loudspeaker be silenced. The next day, the University bosses had it removed – to a new position in the very tree that caressed our window panes.

Chinese youth brought up in Mao's China had notions of Western life which were essentially 19th century. One story we absolutely refused to put on tape for the students concerned a child who was sent out to sell matches on the streets of London, returning to his cold food-less garret where father was assiduously consuming the *Selected Works* of Mao. Yes, this was the London of the 1970s. On the other hand, and to my huge dismay, the image of the so-called developing countries projected by official propaganda was that, just like China, their brave peoples had 'stood up' and were striding towards a brilliant future.

I was once watching a China Central TV news clip lifted, it seemed, from the BBC. The scene was a huge textile mill somewhere in Pakistan and just behind the Chinese voice-over I could still detect the original soundtrack in English. This was describing a fiercely defended workers' strike. The theatrical Chinese newsreader's voice was regaling us with the selfless devotion of the Pakistani workers striding ever forward to new victories in production, etc, etc. I suppose that this false image-building about the so-called Third World relieved the Chinese bureaucracy of any possible responsibility for international solidarity. Beijing also pursued a childish policy of never criticising any nation's government that had recognised the People's Republic and cast off Taiwan. But the strategy was actually counterproductive: for the urban youth of the post-Mao dawn, it was further evidence that their relatively safe and stable lot, built as it was upon the lives of millions of their forebears, was sadly deficient compared with that of their brothers and sisters in the world out there. The stupidity of this approach was the subject of a lecture I gave to the whole Communist Youth League on their special day in 1979. I imagine my frank criticism won me no new friends in the University's leadership.

By the time we were both becoming settled in that Shandong township, the freedom of political expression which centred on Beijing's Democracy Wall was over and done with. I began to understand what had prompted my Hong Kong Quaker friends in their 'single swallow' caution. Back in 1956, the Party had committed its first great crime against its natural allies, the educated classes. This was the 'Hundred Flowers' campaign. The masses were first encouraged to speak out, to be critical of their leaders. Having identified themselves in this manner, millions then became targets of the 1957 'Anti-Rightist' crackdown. The legacy of that mass cruelty had come home, right to our campus. Bedraggled, displaced survivors of two decades of harsh confinement were at that very moment being released back into society: we noticed the newcomers at the University's reception centre where our meals were served. The new edict meant that all released prisoners should return to their original work units, and yet no one knew how the sorry souls were supposed to survive after years of harsh confinement.

The fate of the 1978-1979 Democracy Movement was apparently going to create a similar array of victims. This time round, Deng Xiaoping's purpose was to purge the Party of Maoists and install in their place his own coterie. The new brooms in the Party, the post-Mao authoritarians – were simply utilising popular grievances to whip up an atmosphere which would unseat the remnants of the Cultural Revolution regime. So ironically, just as in the dreadful 1957 'Anti-Rightist' campaign, it was the 'liberal' Deng Xiaoping who was once again pulling the strings.

On the 1st of October 1979, along with dozens of 'foreign friends', I was invited to a grand banquet at Beijing's Great Hall of the People to celebrate three decades of the People's Republic. Having listened to Chairman Hua Guofeng's rambling eulogy, we moved on to the vast main auditorium of the Hall where I was surprised to find myself seated right next to Deng Xiaoping. We were watching a programme of patriotic singing and dancing, of daring acrobatics more elaborate (and long-winded) than any I had ever experienced. I have often wondered since what would have happened if I had leaned over, looked Deng in the eye and asked him point-blank whether the now-stillborn 'Democracy Movement' had been a set-up, just like the 'Hundred Flowers' of the mid-1950s. Fortunately, I was deprived of martyrdom as Deng's bodyguards inexplicably decided to shift him to another row.

Since the Nixon-Kissinger visits to Beijing in 1971, the U.S. had been forced out of Indochina.. The Chinese Communist leadership decided that now was the time to seal the relationship with Washington, and thus strike a mortal blow at Moscow. There was some clear nervousness within the new leadership concerning popular reaction to the new pro-American stance. After all, up to only a few years back – and for nearly three decades in total – the Chinese nation had been taught to denounce U.S. imperialism at every turn. Deng Xiaoping was now planning the first state visit to America by a Chinese leader since the 1949 revolution. What better than a dose of American 'foreign culture' to soften up the masses?

The only modern building of any significance in Licheng Town was a large cinema-cum-theatre and it was here that the cultural life of the townspeople was about to be enlivened, if not enriched. It was all about the Chinese leadership wishing to appear modern and relaxed to their new Washington friends. The merry Xiao Wang, deputy to Li Hua, got us tickets for a showing of a new film programme, the first offering of Hollywood to penetrate China since the late 1940s. The Ministry of Culture had decided that the Chinese masses were ready for an ancient version of *Zorro*. Here at least the message was along acceptable lines – robbing the rich to give to the poor.

Far more confusingly, the very first foreign show broadcast nationwide by Central Television was *The Man from Atlantis*, a fantasy in which the hero (later 'Bobby' of *Dallas* fame) performs superhuman acts from the depths of the oceans where he presides as a kind of merman-king. Once a week I would make a point of wandering up to the classroom block of an evening where a television had been installed, to witness the credulous faces of my class of twenty-year-olds as they collectively soaked up this (true life?) drama from the world of the big noses. I never divined the Ministry's hidden purpose in allowing the hungry audience such nonsense.

In the middle of all this, to set the seal on new-found friendship, in early February 1979 China's supreme leader went off on his famous trip to the United States. Screened without commentary to an astounded television audience back home, the diminutive Deng Xiaoping was paraded nightly schmoozing with his new friend Jimmy Carter and assorted U.S. moneybags. Here he was at Simonton, Texas, at a rodeo, buried under a ten-gallon Stetson. There he was, taking tea and sandwiches in the palatial ranch-house style villa of a 'typical' American worker. And this was the week, too, that our local cinema, and no doubt every movie-house in the nation, chose to screen Yul Brunner in *West World*.

West World's story line has leading world statesmen invited to a subterranean lair in a Nevada desert crawling with rattlesnakes. Once there, their brains and organs are dismantled, to be replaced by robotic parts. Heads and bodies are then sewn up to create an end result indistinguishable from the human original. The robot 'leaders' are then despatched to their respective countries where they must do the bidding of an evil West World clique bent on ruling the universe.

This daft performance over, as we trooped down the concrete spittle-covered stairs of the cinema, I was all ears for audience reaction. Almost echoing my thoughts, though more literally, an elderly farmer grabbed my coat sleeves and proclaimed loudly:

'Probably that's what they'll be doing to old Deng.'

Truth parallels fiction: there is no doubt, looking back, that Deng's U.S. journey of 1979 marked the first real step in China's road towards China's incorporation into the global capitalist division of labour. This, then, was the strange and often forbidding atmosphere surrounding our second sojourn in China, down on the dusty plain of the Yellow River.

Right time, wrong place.

XVII
THE PRIEST'S STORY,
THE NUN'S STORY

SUMO WRESTLERS APART, Ken Craig was surely the largest person in the East. In profile, he put you in mind of a more inflated, a more florid Alfred Hitchcock, his rich and booming voice all of a part. To the Beijing locals of the mid-1970s, even the mousiest foreign devil was the object of amazement. As for Ken, his vast carcass evoked fascination and revulsion in equal measure. Whenever we took a stroll together outside the compound, it took just one rider in the bicycle tide to stare too long before the inevitable pile-up of whirling wheels and interlocked pedals.

Only a handful of times did we manage to get to Beijing from our posting on the Yangtze: as 'outside' foreigners we had to stay at the huge Soviet-era ghetto of the Friendship Hotel, the Youyi. This enclosed village of grey brick, walk-up four storey blocks was the corral for a diverse tribe of non-diplomatic foreigners.

We had mutual friends - the disreputable Maurice and Helen, thrown out of China for protesting against the disgraced ex-President Nixon's 'state' visit to the country. So Ken always felt his duty to take us under his ample wing. We did not mind. Ken was a phenomenon, and it was fascinating to observe him in his Youyi habitat.

Because of overindulgence in food and drink, the great man was regularly admitted to the Beijing hospital which ministered to the foreign community. Despite the urging of his doctors, Ken stoked and lubricated himself with obsessive deliberation. Unlike the other inmates of the Youyi, for whom a meal in the dining room was a chance for a gossip and most likely a moan, Ken preferred to eat in the privacy of his second-floor apartment. Three times daily, before the throng of Youyi residents arrived, an outsize blue tunic topped with Mao cap could be seen in rapid waddle towards the restaurant block. Enclosed by its carrying handle, the standard enamel food pannikin had three circular layers of lidded compartments. Ken's *fanhe* had five tiers, and he would scowl at the serving staff until each was well charged. His retreat over the desiccated Beijing lawn to the haven of his flat wasn't a pleasant sight. He would look neither left nor right, acknowledge neither friend nor foe, and summer or winter his taut purple mask would stream with the sweat of exertion and the anticipation of oral gratification to come.

China's central planning system meant that sometimes things continued to be turned out through sheer habit. Despite the constant railing against bourgeois influences, foreign-style alcohol was produced throughout the Cultural Revolution. The whisky was questionable, the gin convincing. And on the ground floor of the exclusive foreigners' emporium, the Friendship Store, it was usually possible to find a foiled and wired bottle marked with the three characters *xiang bin jiu* – Chinese champagne. Ken took full advantage of this inertia in China's production system. Our rare trips away from Nanjing were a release, and I was more than willing to join him for a binge.

In warm weather, Ken's band of fun seekers would gather around him on the broad steps of the compound's theatre. The impromptu party would settle down to a night of loud mischief, and soon Ken would be booming through his repertoire of operatic arias. As the evening wore on, out came Ken's adaptations of Chinese revolutionary ditties. My favourite was his version of the famous People's Liberation Army anthem, a tune inflicted

RICHARD KIRKBY

on us endlessly from the street loudspeakers. Ken's target was
officialdom, the words lampooning the Cultural Revolution's new
breed of fat cats, in their huge Red Flag (*Hongqi*) limousines:

*In my big black Hongqi racing past, driver faster, hoot
upon the horn!
From the workers, peasants, PLA, a new bourgeois element
is born.*

At such party time, with Ken in full voice, it was a brave soul
who tried to restrain him. When things got really out of hand,
and those attempting sleep in neighbouring blocks called up the
guard, a timorous posse of Foreign Expert Bureau minders would
wheedle the belligerent performer to his bed. On one famous
occasion, this was achieved only with the aid of a wheelbarrow.

Strangely, though Ken was officially just another foreign
expert, his bad behaviour did not meet with the usual disapproval.
There were no reprisals, and you only had to look as far as Ken's
curious political standing to guess the reason. Ken Craig was the
sole representative in China of the Communist Party of Britain
(Marxist-Leninist). In the absence of any alternative, Beijing had
decreed that this Maoist groupuscule was the chosen fraternal
party of the Chinese Communist Party. Membership of the CPB
(M-L) was indeed something of an exclusive matter. Chairman
Reginald Birch, 'great helmsman' of the United Kingdom, could
muster fewer followers than the average village darts team.
We could not quite get this across to our students, who would
enquire with shining eyes if we had ever had the good fortune of
glimpsing our Wise and Great Leader, about whom they had read
in the *People's Daily*.

Ken's special political cachet might have commanded awe
from Chinese associates, but it was bound to arouse the suspicion

315

of his fellow ghetto dwellers. In truth, most Youyi inmates took an ambivalent view of the man and his antics. They both admired him for his fluency in Chinese and apparent insider's knowledge of the world beyond the Youyi gates, and abhorred the excesses which they feared tarred all of them with the same brush. As for Ken, apart from his select group of drinking mates, he viewed the generality of his Youyi neighbours with disdain, even derision.

'Beyond reading *Peking Review*, they don't know a blind thing about the real China,' Ken would snarl. 'OK, we all moan about the cadres and how they treat us. But these people,' his podgy arm describing an arc over the stream of diners emerging from the hall,' these people are easily bought off by a bit of luxury, a special trip here or a seat at top table there.'

He was mostly right. And Ken would add his own special insult. 'They're just a bunch of silly sunshiners - there's no end to their slavishness to the bloody Chinese.' By 'sunshiner' Ken meant that they behaved as though every Chinese backside emitted a glorious light.

Hand-picked by China's embassies around the world, few of the rag-tag army of Youyi foreigners had more than a smattering of Mandarin. In contrast, Ken had somehow attained a frightening fluency. And he was forever hinting that his special standing allowed him into the inner sanctum of Party briefings. Despite his constant railing against the Mao system, I noticed that Ken himself was never slow to accept a ride in a Red Flag limo, to be whooshed off to the Great Hall of the People at Tiananmen for a gathering of True Comrades.

Another question that gave us some pause concerned Ken's nationality. The man affected a strong upper class English accent, was the ambassador-extraordinaire for the fraternal Maoist Party in Britain, and yet one day he asked me whether American passport holders now needed a visa to enter Hong Kong. Ken never explained this oddity of American citizenship but he did swear us to secrecy; it certainly would not have gone down too well amongst certain sections of Youyi society.

In those neurotic Beijing days of conformism, we did not let our own reservations about Ken put us off. Far from it - his wicked perspectives on sunshiners and officials were gleefully appreciated. As we got to know each other better, Ken began to reveal a little about himself. He spoke fondly of a Swedish mother, an accomplished opera singer no less, from whom he claimed his fine voice. His early years were in pre-1949 Shanghai; in Japanese-occupied Hong Kong he apparently ended up in the dreaded Stanley internment camp. What happened next is suffused in Oriental haze; at some point in the 1950s Ken entered the priesthood and for the next two decades he did the work of the Jesuits in the Far East and in Germany too. But in the late 1960s came Ken's Damascene awakening: as the Cultural Revolution raged, Ken abandoned the Jesuits for the Maoists. He darkly hinted that his induction into the Middle Kingdom was thanks to the Chairman himself. We let this pass – the idea of Mao Zedong getting mixed up with a lowly Hong Kong-based American priest was improbable, to say the least.

Of the colonising missionaries, it was the Catholics who had the longest lineage in China: almost four hundred years earlier, the great Matteo Ricci had set up shop in the Middle Kingdom and a succession of Jesuit priests served the Qing rulers, especially the Qianlong emperor. By the mid-nineteenth century, the Catholics had somehow become the greatest foreign landowners in the country. Among the myriad Christian intruders into China, it was they who aroused the greatest ire of the Chinese gentry. Catholic missions in particular were widely believed to be houses of child abduction, where the barbarian priests practised their odious arts, cannibalism included.

Of course, when the Communists took over in 1949, the Roman Catholics' organisational structures, its bishops and priests received especially severe treatment for their adherence to a foreign patriarch. Soon China's almost-quarter of humanity was firmly outside the reach of Rome, though even during the Cultural Revolution in some rural areas autonomous 'underground' Catholic worship survived. This was something successive pontiffs vainly hoped to rectify, and the Vatican became an enthusiastic member of the American-inspired anti-China bloc. In a country in thrall to its own semi-divine leader (Mao, that is) there was always going to be a problem with an alien figurehead in the faraway land of Italy. It was one shared by Ken. And as with all absolutist conversions, he reserved a special vitriol for his earlier incarnation, and given the chance, he would rage against the Church until I feared an attack of apoplexy.

There was a further aspect of Ken Craig which made his presence in Beijing extraordinary. Ken was gay. Yet in Cultural Revolution China, homosexuals were likely to be locked up, sent to mental hospitals; at the worst phase of mob rule they were put to death. In a half-hearted effort perhaps to protect himself, sometimes Ken would try to con me by pretending a loud homophobia. Remember that in those days, even heterosexual liaisons between foreigners and Chinese were absolutely taboo. I was aware of only a couple of cases where a few fleeting assignations occurred. In this atmosphere, gay love across the bamboo divide was beyond the pale. And Ken! A man of daunting dimensions and volatile demeanour? It smelt mighty fishy. Even worse: why on earth would Ken be involved sexually with his own *fuwuyuan* – the room servants – the very people who were trained to spy most closely on their foreign charges? Yet over the four years that we knew him, three of the white-jacketed Youyi room boys were successively introduced to us as 'special friends'. Knowing what I did of the dangers, I was aghast, and on one occasion I decided to challenge the big man.

'Ken, don't you think this is a bit dangerous, especially for the *fuwuyuan*?' I ventured. 'What do you think would happen to me if I started chasing one of the females around here? I'd be out on my neck in five minutes.'

'Not a problem, old chap. Xiao Li (or Xiao Wu or Xiao Zhang) has told them he's just spending time in my flat to 'learn English for the revolution'. Ken was mocking the hackneyed slogan which excused the new craze for English.

'Everyone's happy,' Ken added cheerily.

I was astonished when he proudly announced that he had managed to get his favourite of the moment into his own college, the Number 2 Foreign Languages Institute. This if true was a blatant case of *zou houmen* - back-doorism. Ken just laughed when I accused him of 'double back-doorism'.

The all-seeing authorities continued to turn a blind eye, political expediency no doubt the key. Still, in time-honoured fashion they did try to divert Ken. In the spring of 1979, we arrived from Shandong to hear strange rumours, and dumping our bags we rushed off to his flat. Ken greeted us with the broadest of smiles.

'Grand news, chaps – I'm to be married. My Institute's found me a quiet widow to darn my socks and keep my glass filled. Come and have a drink – look, I've got a couple bottles of the local piss in for you.'

Our congratulations probably sounded a little unconvincing, but that evening we went along with the usual carousing. With Ken and his political connections, anything was possible.

We were next in the capital some months on, and found a very different Ken. At first the whole marriage issue was simply avoided, and we did not like to enquire. But with a few beakers of gin in him, toasts were demanded to a lucky escape from a gold-digging harpie. Ken being a foreigner, the widow's relatives had quite reasonably suggested a foreigner's bride-price.

'Colour TV, Flying Pigeon bicycle, the whole bag of Friendship Store goodies,' Ken expostulated.

Mao had been gone for a couple of years, and old marriage customs were reasserting themselves, so this was nothing unexpected. But Ken played the ascetic communist, and he'd called the whole thing off.

'Better now than later,' I thought. In any case, when push came to shove, would the Chinese authorities really have allowed one of their fair daughters to be taken by this, the rudest of barbarians?

The madhouse of Chinese politics had a way of sweeping the unsuspecting foreigner into its schemings. Not long before, a group of old-timers, expatriates who had served the country since the early days, had been released from gaol. Their mistake was to associate with the wrong faction at the height of the Cultural Revolution. They had quickly found themselves out of their depth, and had paid a bitter price. I, too, was to discover that one could easily be caught up in Chinese intrigue. But it was Ken Craig's Beijing world which was about to be shattered.

Leaving Nanjing in early 1977, for eighteen months I worked on my research at the innocent-sounding Universities Service Centre. The USC was housed in an unmarked Art Deco villa on Kowloon's Argyle Street, right under the flight path of Kai Tak airport. The place was an Aladdin's Cave for the China watcher, its library brimming with Party documents smuggled over the nearby border. To the Centre came a steady stream of China experts from the U.S.A. and Europe, and a smattering of less easily identified characters too. The place was a magnet to Hong Kong's host of China watchers, not to mention spooks.

Amongst the visitors in the summer of 1978 was a matchstick-thin, bespectacled matron, well into her seventies, nicotine-grey hair done up in a loose-coiled bun. This was the chain-smoking Bridget. She would arrive at USC for the day, settle her wraith-like form in the corner of the lounge and stare out balefully over half-moon glasses. I thought I understood the type, though I still could not work out why Bridget should be hanging around the Centre. Yet the director was a tolerant soul, never known to turn anyone away, so there was nothing to stop Bridget leafing through the magazines and quietly ear-wigging on the lunchtime chatter. This was the moment when the dance of America-China friendship was in full swing, and normalisation of Beijing-Washington relations only a year away. A whole tribe of mainly elderly middle-class Americans were suddenly besotted with a prodigal China, urged on by a well-tuned Beijing diplomatic offensive which dazzled the receptive with Oriental mystique. The spectaculars of acupuncture anaesthesia, the stage-managed 'discoveries' of archaeological wonders, the luxury trips laid on for U.S. friendship groups went down like a dream. So I simply cast Bridget - I never learned her surname - in the mould of idealistic China lover. It did not really surprise me when she announced she was planning a grand mission - to commune with the real Chinese on the Mainland.

'These Hong Kong Cantonese aren't proper Chinese, you know,' she cackled. 'I'm going to go to and work in Beijing. That's the place to be, don't you think so?'

It soon became clear that Bridget's frequent visits to the Centre were aimed mainly at me. Hundreds of thousands of Hong Kong's new citizens had fled China, but generally they did not talk about their experiences. Hard to believe, but my own presence in Hong Kong after years in Mao's China made me something of a minor celebrity. Anyway, Bridget clearly thought I must be worth cultivating.

'You've got to help me get to China, you really have,' she

insisted. 'Couldn't you just introduce me to those news agency people who recruit foreigners for the Mainland?'

But it was tough living and working in China, and from the start, I had decided that helping Bridget get there would not be doing her a favour. More to the point, I just did not want to inflict her on China's eager youth. But her campaign was relentless, and eventually my desire to get the woman off my back overcame my reservations: I sent her off to the offices of the Xinhua News Agency in Happy Valley. Since arriving in Hong Kong I had maintained something of a relationship with Beijing's de facto diplomats in the British colony. But I knew Bridget had no chance of being sent to China, if only because the Chinese never took on elderly people who might die on them, and create a diplomatic muddle.

Bridget then disappeared as abruptly as she had arrived, and I was relieved that her chicken-clawed hand no longer tugged at my sleeve during Centre lunches, that her cigarette ash no longer spilled into my coffee. She quickly passed from my thoughts.

Making my own way back to China from Hong Kong at the end of 1978, I managed to get to Beijing in time to see the short-lived Democracy Wall in Beijing, where poster after poster demanded every conceivable reform of the Communist Party. And naturally, I was eager to catch up with Ken, for he was still holding court to a loyal band of followers at the Youyi. In the liberating atmosphere of the moment, even Ken had toned down his accustomed cynicism about the world. I could see that the big man now rolled along the corridors of the Friendship Hotel with a new confidence. No longer locking himself up to eat, he took his meals in the canteen alongside the other residents. Ken had always reviled his work unit, the Number 2 Foreign Languages Institute. To be fair, it did have a reputation as an odious place, and a regular chapter in Ken's tirades was reserved for his work leaders. But at last he had gone on to sweeter pastures.

'It was marvellous,' Ken exclaimed. 'Out of the blue, one morning one of those fucking great Hongqi limousines arrived at my Institute and swept me away to paradise.' He went on to relate how an immaculately dressed cadre stepped out of the car and demanded his presence.

'I am here at the personal command of Comrade Deng Xiaoping, 'and I am taking Comrade Craig to Beijing University,' mimicked Ken in mock-Chinese English. Beijing University – Beida - was then and perhaps remains at the pinnacle of China's education system, Oxbridge and Ivy League all in one.

'Even better,' sang Ken, 'At Beida, I've got a really congenial colleague - a little elderly perhaps, but a good companion.'

A few months later, I was in Beijing again from our new Yellow River home in Shandong. Not only had the Democracy Movement been nipped in the bud and all the exciting posters at the Xidan crossroads removed without trace, but Ken's new enthusiasm for life had quite evaporated too. He was back to his old seething anger - against the stupid, complacent Chinese, against the indifferent and politically-infantile foreigners in the Youyi compound, and above all, against a wicked and conspiring ancient chain-smoking American. She had broken cover one fateful morning, huddled next to Ken in the back of the Shanghai saloon which conveyed them from the Youyi to the Beida campus.

'Ken – I've got to tell you something! Back in the Ming dynasty, it took that great Jesuit Matteo Ricci years and years to breach the walls of Beijing. But I only needed a few weeks to sort things out, and here I am!' she boasted to her dear colleague.

'Bridget didn't realise that she was flaunting her missionary exploits to just the wrong person,' Ken declared, eyes afire. 'From that morning, of course, I refused to have anything more to do with the old hag.'

So the dreaded Bridget had made it to China and had somehow

got herself the most plum English teaching position in the whole country, too. 'She must have had some immaculately conceived references,' is all I could think. But I was truly shocked.

Like most Chinese, Ken's new masters at Beida thought of foreigners as one homogenous mass. They had no idea what the fuss was all about, and why they now had to send two cars to the Youyi each morning, one for Ken, one for Bridget. As for Ken, he had always crowed about the utter failure of the Roman Catholics' campaign to restore themselves to China after their expulsion by the Communists after 1949. Now Bridget's revelation unleashed from him an imaginative torrent of plots and conspiracies, in which the Catholic hierarchy and the Chinese Communist Party were equally entwined and equally treacherous.

Meanwhile, Bridget did all she could to ingratiate herself. Soon after the explosion with Ken, she begged for a transfer from the Youyi's island of comfort to the bleak dormitories of Beida's campus. Here, Bridget set about making herself available to the students at all hours. Even better, unlike Ken she seemed to have resources. Crate-loads of books, tape recorders and overhead projectors started arriving from Hong Kong. In short, Bridget had transmuted into a model and heroic foreign teacher. With his out-dated didactics and erratic performances in the classroom, this was a stage on which Ken just could not compete.

The Chinese New Year of 1979 loomed, and this being one of our two permitted holidays in the year, we managed to get permission to spend it in the capital. It was the talk of the Youyi that Bridget had been granted a rare exit permit for a couple of weeks.

'She's told everyone she's going to Italy for a holiday,' huffed Ken. 'There's no doubt about it – she's off to the Vatican to report to her overseers.'

Very likely Ken was right. But two could play at that game.

Swallowing his hatred for his former confrères, Ken too got his passport stamped and headed for Hong Kong, where he somehow engineered an audience with his old Catholic bishop. A happier Ken made his way back to Beijing.

'The bishop was none too pleased to learn of a rogue operator on his patch, I can tell you!' he gleefully reported. 'And the Bridget in question isn't just any old nun. For years she's been all over the Far East running things for her Order. Especially in Taiwan! She's just a deceptive old plain-clothes abbess, that's what she is.' proclaimed Ken.

'What are you going to do about it? 'I wanted to know.

'Isn't it obvious? I'm going to see to it that she's chucked out of China,' replied Ken with a triumphant flourish.

The great democracy debates, with their endless *dazibao*, had been stamped out. But this meant nothing to Comrade Craig as he set about plastering the Youyi and Beida walls with *dazibao* denouncing Bridget in particular and the Papist plot to take over the world in general. But all Ken's appeals to all his high-up Party people fell on deaf ears. Meanwhile, Bridget just kept on winning more friends and influence on campus.

Over the years, I had learned to anticipate paranoid reactions from Chinese officialdom about the motives of foreigners in China. Yet here was a strange indifference to Bridget, and her flagrant deception. Maybe after a decade of Cultural Revolution conspiracy chasing, the Chinese were just too weary of accusations and plots. Or just maybe the authorities were well aware of Bridget's 'mission' and were using it as a back-channel to Rome. Whatever, for poor Ken though, the failure of his righteous stand against the Catholic intruder marked the onset of his final decline.

Unbeknown to him, the Chinese intelligence people had indeed been roused by his appeals, and I wish I had been able to tell him the last part of the story, for it might just have saved him from himself. Though we spent a good few weeks in Beijing in the autumn of 1979, before and after the birth of our son, we did not see Ken at all. He was in hospital the whole time with a stomach ailment. Sadly, we were never again to meet, though after he removed himself from China I did make sure I heard about him from mutual Hong Kong friends.

With Jo heavily pregnant, we had reluctantly agreed to forgo our usual summer odyssey in favour of the strange seaside resort at Beidaihe. This place on the Bohai Gulf was where the highest in the land, including Mao himself, often spent the summer months, and all around were heavily-guarded compounds. Strolling one day on the beach, past the ghostly markers which still bore the inscriptions of the pre-1949 British Kailuan Coal Company, I was overtaken by a breathless man in an immaculate woollen cadre uniform. To my surprise, I recognised the slicked-back hair, fancy framed glasses and polished shoes of Comrade Zhang from Beijing. As the smooth-talking chief factotum of the Foreign Experts Bureau, who lived down a lane at the back of the Youyi compound, Comrade Zhang passed his time knocking on doors and weaving together the political and personal tittle-tattle of the resident foreigners. He was the Number 1 Official Spy and hardly cared to conceal the fact. On some pretext, I had once sought this man out at his home. I was curious about his reputation as neighbourhood snooper, as womaniser, and even as thief. A French family's bicycle had disappeared and someone had seen Comrade Zhang in town, blithely astride the machine. I thought he must be a man worth knowing.

'I have a very serious matter to discuss with you,' announced Zhang, omitting the usual pleasantries. 'Please come back with me now to your room for a little while.' Intrigued, I eagerly followed Zhang back to our chalet. He closed the door with exaggerated care.

'I have come to see you on the instruction of the Security Department of the State Council,' he grandly intoned. 'I have some information that you, Li Caide, recommended a certain old lady from America to work in China.'

How long had I known the woman? What was my relationship with her? When had I joined the *Tianzhujiao*, the Catholic church? How much money had I been paid? I tried to explain away my innocent involvement. But Zhang eventually realised he was getting nowhere; he rose to leave, threatening further discussions once we were back at the Youyi.

I could not resist a parting shot.

'You should remember that the Christians have two thousand years of secret organisation behind them. Your Communist Party has only had fifty years.'

Horrified by the very comparison, the speechless comrade slammed the door and the next day there was no sign of him at our Beidaihe compound. There was never any further interrogation, and whether the matter ended there, I neither knew nor cared. With our baby imminent I had other things on my mind.

The Bridget affair drove Ken Craig to make a second dramatic reversal. As suddenly and totally as he had renounced his Catholicism, now Ken turned his face against the Chinese Communist Party and all its works. With a heavy heart he decided he must leave China, and he wrote to me with his decision. The obvious place for him was Hong Kong, and I encouraged him to set himself up on Cheung Chau, the island where in between postings in Nanjing and Shandong. I had enjoyed a blissful two years. My informants on Cheung Chau were conscientious. For brief months, Ken heaved his sweating mass onto the Hong Kong ferry, finding work which was satisfactory neither to him nor, I fear, to the various language schools which took him on for his Beijing University credentials.

Ken's hostility to the Mainland regime was now total and implacable. On the final Guomindang National Day of his life – 10th October 1983 - he outraged the pro-China locals by draping a huge Republic of China flag from his balcony. But after the bitterness of the Beijing chapter of his life, Cheung Chau was something of a respite, and companionship even came his way in the form of a youthful islander.

As priest and then as Maoist disciple, Ken had pursued a life fuelled by alcoholic excess. It was obvious to all that Ken's immense frame was breaking down, and one day he failed to make it to the ferry. That evening he was airlifted to a Hong Kong hospital. But it was too late.

Ken's passing was lamented by his small circle of new admirers amongst the Cheung Chau crowd. But there were no relatives to mourn him and beyond his library of obscure works and a wardrobe of outsize clothes, nothing to show for his extraordinary life. As for Bridget, I know that she too spent some diplomatic time in hospital at the height of Ken's campaigning, but she soon returned stoically to her post. I see her even now in some book-lined Beijing retreat, nicotine-stained and indomitable, sermonizing Voice of America English to a select congregation of wide-eyed and grateful Chinese youth.

XVIII
VITAL BODILY FUNCTIONS

SEX WAS A MINEFIELD in Cultural Revolution China. I have mentioned *Red Azalea*, Anchee Min' account of the lives of her group sent down to the countryside. Youthful urges were brutally repressed, and in one case, willing lovers condemned to death. This kind of thing was confirmed to me more than once by friends who had shared the Red Guard life. Happily, as an alien on the fringe of the great Chinese masses my own experience of vital bodily functions was rather less harrowing.

The cultural offerings of Mao's China had no room for any human relationship other than revolutionary camaraderie. There was one glaring exception – 'foreign culture' in the form of North Korean movies readily permitted to the weary Chinese. Pyongyang and Beijing were close at the time, and it was not unusual to spot North Koreans in China on some obscure official business. Long after the Chinese had been allowed to dispense with their Chairman Mao badges, the giveaway was the Great Leader Kim Il-Sung's porky face on every lapel.

In an unguarded moment, a colleague joked that amongst all the world's peoples, only the Koreans found Mao's China a good place for a relaxing holiday. Yet in the realm of the silver screen lay a paradox. Like their Chinese counterparts, the North Korean film studios were expected to churn out patriotic epics of revolutionary bravado. But in contrast to the Chinese fare, Korean movies were laced with tear-jerking story lines which not infrequently turned upon the love between a man and a woman.

Our visits to the cinema or revolutionary opera were pretty

well obligatory in Nanjing. Just when we were looking forward to a peaceful evening, our minder would turn up and baldly announce 'You will go to see a show tonight'. We knew that to rebel would be an affront, so invariably we went. But we soon brightened up when a Korean film was on offer, and it was clear that the Chinese audiences just loved these creations even though the scenes depicting physical proximity between actors of opposite sexes were often crudely cut. Cultural Revolution China saw fit to censor – of all people - the North Koreans.

Indeed, the ultra-Puritanical society in which we were immersed embodied a host of paradoxical surprises. I was once strongly reprimanded by our Party overseer for touching a female student's forearm. I had momentarily forgotten that this part of female form carries sexual overtones; all I had been trying to do was get over a difficult point of grammar. We were a little taken aback that to the Chinese, no medical consultation was complete without a needle being wielded, and this was invariably to one's fleshy behind. Yet when I happened to pass by the ever-crowded clinic and the same young woman was offering her naked bottom to the nurse's giant syringe, not an unworthy thought seemed to cross the minds of the onlookers. I tried to remember this whenever my own hairy rump was laid bare for the delectation of passing colleagues and students alike.

Routine calls of nature were another case where vital bodily functions were regarded in a disarmingly unfamiliar way. I will not forget my first foray into a street latrine in Shanghai. This was in the early 1970s, when foreigners had not been seen for many a year – let alone their nether parts. The stinking concrete trough was perhaps fifty feet in length, and in an attempt to preserve some dignity, I chose a section free of immediate neighbours. As soon as I got into position, however, I found myself being flanked on both sides by a close line of squatters whose curiosity had got the better of them. I was fixed by two score eyes and a running commentary soon aroused general mirth.

The Chinese lavatorial experience often provided thought-provoking anthropological insights. And despite the ultra-Puritanism of Mao's China, bodily functions of a rather more alluring variety might also be conducted in a strangely matter-of-fact way. Official paranoia meant that we were never told of the comings and goings of other foreigners. But one day during our confinement in Nanjing's Dingshan we were pleased to find that there were new neighbours, a young couple from the 'fraternal revolutionary party' in Ecuador. With the dust of their long journey barely removed, the newcomers were assembled for introductory formalities by their minder, a timid grey woman of late middle age.

'Which size do you take?' was her straight-from-the-hip opening remark to the man. The new arrivals were puzzled. The woman pointed to the two children - a barely acceptable number for foreign friends to bring to China, the land of the one-child-family. She then waved at the man. When the penny dropped, there were gasps of astonishment and then embarrassed laughter. After all, Westerners did not start to talk about such intimate things in public until the AIDS virus arrived. I had indeed noticed that every downtown pharmacy had a counter where the goods were free. Around it, there was always a flurry of women, scrabbling through the poorly packaged *da* (large), *zhong* (medium) and *xiao* (small) condoms. Human nature being such and the central planners in Beijing characteristically unresponsive to consumer preference, of the 'small' variety a huge surplus always remained unclaimed.

When it came to the question of sexual liaison between East and West, a far less relaxed attitude prevailed. Life in China of the early 1970s was one of constant *yundong* – strident campaigns

331

to repudiate this or embrace that often incomprehensible political line. Like us, the Chinese sought diversions from the daily grind, and the unorthodox, the delinquent, the prurient were always compelling.

The non-event of the Suzhou dancer demonstrates the prevailing sexual hysteria. In 1976, the last year of Mao, a group of American political tourists had been so enthralled by a song and dance performance – part of their official itinerary – that they innocently invited the leading dancer for a sociable exchange after the curtain had come down. Since the performance had been staged in their Suzhou hotel, and official paranoia meant that no hostelry had any public meeting places available to foreign guests, the daring leading lady was seen entering the room of one of the Americans. I am sure nothing happened except a halting conversation over a cup of jasmine tea. Yet the thought of a lissom entertainer closeted with foreigners was too much for the authorities. The dancer was dismissed, and from the way it constantly returned to my own ears, the account of this non-event – ever more scandalous in the telling – must have reached a hundred million Chinese.

There was one tiny exception to the prohibition of sexual relationships between Chinese and foreigners. As a rule, the only foreigners in China in this period were distinctly middle class – diplomatic personnel, members of overseas friendship associations, and the like. And the only foreign proletarians who came into contact with the country were seafarers whose ships had business in Chinese ports. The port authorities made a great effort to lavish every attention on the visiting sailors and well-equipped seamen's clubs were found in every major port. These places were open to other foreigners such as ourselves, and we sought them out when in Shanghai and Qingdao, for they had the best canteen food anywhere in China. And it was strongly rumoured amongst the foreigners that the first class service to seafarers extended beyond the appetites of the stomach. In a gesture of proletarian internationalism, women could be provided too. There was, however, a small proviso: only those who could claim some Chinese blood were deemed eligible. It was said that the Filipino sailors were the main beneficiaries of this official pimping, for many are the descendants of Chinese settlers.

To be sure, sexual contacts with foreigners evoked fears of an invasive outside world, a theme deeply (and not unreasonably) embedded in the national psyche. Rapine, real and imaginary, was an integral element of the foreign aggression of the nineteenth century. But that only partly explains the widespread belief that Western foreigners (and Japanese too), whether male or female, were incapable of sexual self-control. There is even a Chinese character (*yin*) in the past used almost exclusively for the barbarian's lewd state of being. My wife heavily pregnant, I was only a little surprised when the University authorities suggested that they might arrange temporary relief. Not with a Chinese female, of course, but courtesy of another blameless and unsuspecting foreign resident.

'You and I are supposed to leap into bed together, now that Jo's pregnant,' I joked with the hapless Myumi, an unprepossessing Japanese school teacher who had just arrived at the University. Actually, we had a good laugh together about Li Hua's completely serious suggestion that she should be my concubine. We became friends, but that was it.

It was not really until the Cultural Revolution was truly dead and buried that foreigners began to learn that the inheritors of Mao's kingdom had vital appetites which are common to all humankind. A foretaste of what was in store came shortly after I had arrived at Shandong University. I was looking for the elderly, lame and definitely bourgeois intellectual who headed the department, in order to clarify some detail about my teaching programme. Professor Zhang was, we were told, partly disabled as he had jumped from a window in an attempt to kill himself and escape political harassment. I approached his office along the deserted concrete corridor, white enamel spittoon every ten yards, and rapped on the door. There were sounds, and I instinctively tried the handle, which did not yield. Inquisitiveness getting the better of me, I bent my head to a tiny scratch in the whitewashed glazing. The restricted line of vision allowed just one disconnected image - a rhythmically heaving naked buttock.

In a flash I was on my way, but amazement brought me back for a second glimpse. Was this really part of the shy retiring professor's anatomy? My curiosity was uncontrollable and I hung around at some distance until eventually someone emerged. It was not the rightful occupant of the room, but rather one of the powerful Party bureaucrats attached to our department - a man whose reputation for both indolence and malice had even reached my foreign ears. After a cautious interlude a second person came out. I recognised her as one of the more attractive members of our teaching group. It was the season of annual promotions.

With the Mao regime over and done with, by 1978 our requests to learn Chinese were at last being taken seriously. As it happened, the provision to us of a Chinese tutor was to leave us in pretty much the same state of ignorance of the language. But we did learn a great deal about the question of sex and the Chinese. Secluded association between foreigner and Chinese for any purpose was still considered highly risky, and the University authorities doubtless agonised over the choice of a suitable tutor. The search led unerringly to a middle-aged, podgy teacher of Chinese, who presented himself at our door in his bright blue polyester Sun Yat-sen jacket and an outsized cap under which his close eyes squinted shiftily. That cap was never to come off in all the months we had the dubious pleasure of Teacher Yin's instruction.

We had visions of a bald pate, with a single lank clump of hair sprouting from its pink apex. This was the image which fixed him from the first as 'Piggy', though it was some time before his porcine appetites would be fully revealed.

It was easy in those days of rigid uniform and standardised demeanour to spot a Chinese 'intellectual', and the new arrival just did not seem to measure up. We were quickly reassured, however, that in Piggy Yin we had an outstanding teacher, with as solid credentials as anyone might hope for. Not only had his parents been beggars before the communist victory, but they had also died shortly after it, and the orphan Piggy - it was respectfully announced - had been 'brought up by the Party'.

'Chairman Mao is my father,' Piggy proudly but enigmatically explained. In the ceaseless political campaigns, individuals with a background like this were pretty well immune from criticism. And the crucial issue for the University authorities in offering us Piggy was their own potential liability should something go wrong. We were being placed in a safe pair of hands. Even if he did succumb a little to the temptations, the 'sugar coated bullets' of we Western intruders, Piggy remained the surest bet.

To our surprise and enjoyment, it turned out that the Party's judgment of character was deeply flawed. It soon became very clear that if anyone ran the risk of moral corruption, it was certainly not Piggy Yin. Life in the Chinese provinces was not overburdened with excitements, and we soon came to relish every Chinese lesson as a minor adventure. The sessions would start routinely enough, Piggy's teaching material the usual pseudo-heroic stuff - the soldier who sacrificed his life by leaping into a raging torrent to save state property, the worker who was glad to be no more than a small cog in the machine. But the teacher's attention span proved somewhat less than his students'. Not far into the lesson, a point seemed suddenly to arrive when Piggy could no longer bear the boredom. His gaze would shift from the deadly revolutionary tract, his eyes glistening and protuberant in a pinkening face, his knees knocking together restlessly. Deep inside his many layers of winter underwear, something was very evidently stirring. Apropos of nothing, Piggy would now emit his only known words of English:

'Kee-ss, touch breast.'

This would be followed by a brief interlude of guiltily concerted attention to the Chinese text, Piggy all the while pressing himself against his retreating student, until he had practically shifted both buttocks from his chair to theirs.

Even more unexpected was Piggy's favoured catchphrase. *Ba tade kuzi la xia lai* ('rip her pants down'). Curiously, it was not uttered with any note of vulgar humour, but rather as fierce admonition. Once this point had been reached, all pretence of continuing the lesson was usually abandoned. Piggy would then start to pace the room, and with a practiced inevitability, settle on the pile of old American news magazines. This was 1979, and foreign publications remained out of bounds to ordinary folk. Most of our colleagues would show some furtive interest in the stories on world events, particularly as they impinged on China. But what interested our Piggy were the advertisements - especially the airline ads with their mildly suggestive but well-covered hostesses. His thrill lay in an unvarying little game of his own invention: he would insist that what was clearly female was male. Piggy's gratification came when he affected suddenly to notice that the person's upper body had certain unmanly adornments. It was then once again a case of 'Kee..ss, touch breast.'

Even without the socially difficult 'rip her trousers down' our Chinese made not a lot of progress. But we were delighted to keep Piggy on for sheer entertainment value. In any situation, sexually obsessive behaviour in a relative stranger would be rather astonishing. Under the circumstances of China at the time, it was a wonder.

But in due course, Jo decided that her own limits of tolerance had been reached, and if Piggy were to keep up his weekly visits to our apartment then I had better take over as the main 'student'.

By now, Piggy had abandoned the set course book in favour of what he called 'extensive conversation'. This consisted of regaling me with tales – probably more real than imaginary - of sexual exploits in the local community. There was the local official's wife who was seeing the Chinese equivalent of the window-cleaner (the lusty itinerant bean-curd seller, in fact). There were the four young female and four male workers who absented themselves from the shop floor in a local factory: after an extensive search they were all found naked, in a disused store-room. There were the by-now familiar stories of cadres who pressed favours from women workers in exchange for promotion.

On one occasion a crestfallen Piggy produced half-a-dozen black and white photos completely lacking any white. He had borrowed a friend's camera, and gone off peeping in the local park. What I was apparently meant to see were couples in various stages of advanced intimacy. Piggy just could not grasp why he had failed to record these exciting images. I explained, gently, that ancient Chinese box cameras do not really work after sunset.

One Wednesday evening, the appointed hour came and went, and no teacher. Long after we had retired for the night, there came a timid tapping at the door, and a shamefaced Piggy pushed his way in - eager and ready at this unheard-of hour to start the usual session. He breathlessly explained that while on the way over, some public security men had hauled him off to the neighbourhood police station for questioning. They were out looking for a rapist. Our initial thoughts were that perhaps just maybe, for once, the police might not have been too wide of the mark. But in reality there was something about our cumbersome little Chinese teacher which made him the most unlikely assailant, and we hoped that there was nothing sinister in his sudden disappearance.

For this turned out to be Piggy's last visit to our premises. Perhaps there was a simple explanation as to why our 'Chinese lessons' ceased so suddenly. But later, we realised that the privacy of our home had been compromised, our evenings with Piggy having a wider audience.

The thought of Piggy Yin and his expostulations still brings undimmed astonishment. The very fact of Piggy demonstrates a vital lesson: that individuality and independence of thought, however bizarre, are able to survive the severest straitjackets of politically-inspired conformity. We were strangely grateful for our Piggy Yin.

XIX
CHENGDU BY COINCIDENCE

Separate and remote from both the eastern Han heartlands and the wildnesses of Tibet, for Chinese and foreigners alike the great interior province of Sichuan has always held special allure. Only in recent history has the Sichuan plain become routinely accessible from the rest of China. This is a province known to the rest of China for its impenetrable dialect, its fiery cuisine, and, as my grandparents were to discover in the first decades of the twentieth century, its own deadly brand of warlordism. Only in the second half of the century did the province begin to draw closer, first by the long-mooted construction of the railway between Sichuan's capital Chengdu and the metropolis of Chongqing, and then by gradual improvements brought to Yangtze river navigation. High explosives became the answer to the worst shoals and skerries obstructing the great river's notorious cataracts, the Three Gorges.

Many a missionary memoir tells of the over two-thousand-mile odyssey from Shanghai up the Yangtze and Min rivers to the hidden world of Sichuan, the province's name meaning 'Four Rivers'. Indeed, the diaries of my own grandparents describe their anxious progress through the Yangtze Gorges over a century ago. Once, their craft was badly holed; they survived intact, but not their cabin trunks, the medical supplies for grandfather's clinic, and letters from home delivered to them downriver. Then, the Gorges could only be overcome with the back-breaking labour of half-naked trackers harnessed to long split bamboo tow lines, inching vessels up against the Yangtze torrents. My grandparents' journey upriver to the far interior could take many changes of vessel and many months. At Nanjing, Hankou, Wanxian, and Chongqing courtesy calls were made on mission houses, acquaintances renewed, provisions secured. The final part of the journey was an overland trek of several days, first over mountain passes and then onto the lush Sichuan plain. Joanna, my mother, was always proud that her Quaker father would rather walk alongside his chair carried on long bamboos, evoking in his half-starved opium-smoking bearers relief but also derision, for their face was being lost.

Sixty years after Joanna's birth, and amongst the first foreigners permitted on the river for years, I was to observe the same ragged lines of wiry men bent double on their narrow track along the precipitous cliffs of the gorges. Even in an age of diesel power, only straining sinews could win the day for the smaller craft. But now, of course, these trackers are gone for ever; the Gorges were inundated to create the world's largest reservoir, serving the controversial Three Gorges super-dam.

My upstanding mother, Joanna, after whom Bertolt Brecht might have named his 1943 play (*The Good Woman of Szechwan*) was born in a walled town of the province not a decade after the fall of the Qing dynasty. Even in her nineties, she still shuddered to recall the family's final retreat from occluded Sichuan. It was 1927, and revolutionists were on the warpath; Chengdu's European consuls ordered all foreigners to get downriver without delay. The natural hazards of their hastily prepared journey were bad enough, but on this last descent, once in stiller waters, their Yangtze steamer endured bullets flying from both banks. Joanna could still smell that bloody corpse lying against a hot ship's funnel. Perhaps a couple of the notorious Sichuan warlords were battling it out, or maybe it was just a side-play in the great anti-foreign nationalism which was sweeping southern China. Whatever, it was bad memories which kept Joanna away from China for the rest of her long life.

By the time I arrived in the Middle Kingdom, Mao's Cultural Revolution had placed Sichuan firmly beyond limits to the foreigner. We had heard many rumours of the turmoil which overcame the province during the first phase of the Cultural Revolution. In Beijing and Shanghai, the most lethal weaponry of the rampaging Red Guards was mortars fashioned from cast iron drain pipes. But in Chongqing, a key centre of China's heavy armaments industry, the young warriors got their hands on artillery, warplanes even. In most of the country, fighting had died away in 1968 when the People's Liberation Army was sent in to knock heads together, but in Sichuan the mayhem rumbled on for years.

Getting permission to leave our home base was always difficult. In our earlier posting of Nanjing it had proved well-nigh impossible, special occasions excepted. There were the highly restricted - but un-chaperoned trips allowed during the lunar New Year break, when our Party minders could be left happily at home with their families. On these journeys, we would face impressive bills for hotels and the unwanted guides who stuck to us leech-like until the final waving off. We had no choice but to follow their programmes of visits to factories, communes, neighbourhood committees and free time was non-existent. While most foreigners bridled against such impositions, I was able to put up with the endless 'brief introductions' and shop-floor tours as I saw it all as interesting background to my research into post-1949 China's strange urbanisation process.

We would encounter the same kinds of itineraries in our summer holidays, but at least the government had to pick up the extravagant bills. I relished these opportunities to see more, and observe the Chinese as politically-correct 'tourists'. Accompanied by a commissar from our work unit, we had journeyed to the famed pre-1949 Communist base areas - Yan'an in the Northwest and Jinggangshan in southern Jiangxi Province.

In our second posting, at Shandong University, political pilgrimage was no longer *de rigeur*, and the comrade from the University Party Committee did his best to paint a glowing picture of the pleasures of the Bohai Gulf resort of Beidaihe. This was, after all, he reminded us, where the Central Committee decamped every August. In the heat of a North China summer it was surely the best place to be. What the man could not mention was that the Beidaihe resort was the creation of the long-departed foreign devils and their (British) Kailuan Mining Company. In the early decades of the twentieth century, its summer residents were pampered colonial wives and children from the sweltering Treaty Ports, a tribe who, now in another age, we had no intention of mimicking.

From the official point of view, the calculation was that within the guarded walls of the Beidaihe compound, and corralled within a hundred yards of a beach bounded by rattan shark nets, scope for foreign mischief-making was limited. The downside for our cadres (and upside for us as far as Beidaihe went) was that there might be unwholesome fraternisation between the foreigners, herded together as we were from various corners of the land. Our neurotic minders were most anxious to keep us in the dark about street poster campaigns and noisy struggles in areas not our own. If this seems improbable today, hostile China watchers outside the country of the kind I encountered when working at a Hong Kong China research centre were always ready to feed on every tiny rumour coming out of the country. The overriding priority of every official was to keep their tame foreigners in happy ignorance of China's political squalls. And their methods were usually highly successful. The Bamboo Curtain was almost leak-proof.

RICHARD KIRKBY

It was early 1979. Mao Zedong had died over than two years earlier, and little by little, hidden regions of the country were opening up to select groups of foreign travellers.

The very human Li Hua, de facto chief of the University's foreign affairs office, and both our minder and fixer, was a breath of fresh air after the obdurate bureaucracy of Cultural Revolution days in Nanjing. Li Hua would often call by for a chat or an invitation to come to her home for a *jiaozi* supper. This time she brought extraordinary news.

'You've been invited with the Beijing foreigners to travel to Yunnan and Sichuan provinces,' she told us, hardly able to contain her excitement. 'Unfortunately President Wu won't let me go with you. Lao Guo will be the lucky one.'

Lao Guo was our genial and somewhat absent-brained minder; he would cause us few problems.

'How did you manage to get us included in the Beijing foreigners' group?' I enquired. No mean achievement in this land of Chinese walls. Li Hua merely smiled enigmatically. Our twenty handpicked companions on the tour would be drawn from the dis-united nations of government employees who inhabited Beijing's sprawling Friendship Hotel.

'Even better, you'll be the first foreigners for years to be allowed to travel on a Yangtze riverboat,' continued Li Hua. 'And the State Council will pay for everything!'

In Yunnan province we would go to the sub-tropical Xishuangbanna region, where the Mekong flows into Laos, and from where Burma is but a stone's throw. And we were also to be the first-ever foreigners on the fabled Chengdu-Kunming railway, joining Yunnan province to Sichuan. This extraordinary engineering feat was part of Mao's and Lin Biao's secret Third Front military defence network. I had seen a Party documentary about the Chengdu-Kunming: over half of its three hundred

343

kilometres consisted of tunnels and viaducts. Titillating rumour had it too that though the project had been completed some years before, anti-Mao saboteurs had kept it closed. The grand finale of our trip would be a river journey from Chongqing, through the Three Gorges of the Yangtze, and the just-completed giant Gezhouba locks to the gentler reaches of the great river. From there to Wuhan, where a couple of hours' flight would bring us home to Shandong.

My first impulse was to consult Joanna, my mother. Letters home were something of a hit-and-miss affair, the censors tending to mull over every sentence at their leisure. I took my chances on the creaky telephone system. You got hold of the city's only international operator well in advance, booked your call, and sat back and waited for the moment.

'Can you remember any names from the 1920s?' I yelled above the crackles. A long shot, but Joanna promised to consult her elder brother who remembered more, and dredge up some ideas we could work on. Her letter arrived with us in the nick of time. Four people were listed from a distant childhood on Chengdu's Green Dragon Street. The first had the name 'Lin Changcheng'; his family had lived within the foreign compound and Joanna remembered him as her playmate up until the age of eight when she'd left China. Then came the names of two men who with strong Quaker antecedents – in 1927, S.H. Fong was already in his thirties when the family left Chengdu; there was also the name of a much younger man, born about the same time as Joanna, who, it was known, had trained as a doctor. His family name was Yang. My mother's elder brother Henry had returned to China in the early 1940s with the Friends' Ambulance Unit, before the Communist Party took over, but that was the last time that anyone had had news any of the three.

The fourth person named in my mother's letter amused us: the family's *baomu*, nanny, always known as 'Wang-Wang'. The good lady was already in her fifties when my Rodwell grandparents and their family had left Sichuan, and my own journey to the province would be half-a-century on from then. So rather unlikely, to say the least.

We were conscious that to ask after the Chinese acquaintances of foreigners from the bad old days was not without its dangers. To them, not us. Foreign connections, however tenuous, at the very least brought a cloud of suspicion. Many had been persecuted for their irredeemable contamination pre-1949, and especially so if they had been involved with foreign churches. But we decided to risk it anyway, without naming any names. Further preparation before leaving Jinan was to fire off a list of wants to our leaders which would be passed via the Shandong foreign affairs office to their counterparts in Sichuan. In our humblest beseeching mode we submitted three requests for our stopover in Chengdu. With Joanna's letter and its four names in mind, our first was couched in deliberately vague terms. Could we please meet with some older citizens of Chengdu, the capital, who had memories of the foreigners in the 1920s and 1930s? Next, we asked to be allowed a special permit to go to a town some distance from the provincial capital to visit the family of one of our Sichuanese students who had innocently invited us to share a New Year dinner with his folks. Finally, and as a bit of cover, I threw in my routine 'urbanisation' request when allowed to travel - to meet with cadres from Chengdu's urban construction bureau.

The circuitous route to Chengdu was full of unscheduled surprises. For a start, Beijing had chosen that very moment to mount its preparations for a campaign to punish its erstwhile allies in war-weary Vietnam. We were flown from Kunming to an airstrip on the edge of the Yunnan plateau, from where we descended

345

by road towards the sub-tropical Xishuangbanna. Our bus was soon bogged down in the midst of huge military convoys oddly travelling both ways on the narrow and often steep highway. The sun had long since set by the time we reached our destination. China's February 1979 military build-up and its attack plans against Hanoi were, of course, being urged by new-found friends in the United States, ignominiously thrown out of Vietnam just four years earlier. So revenge by proxy was in the air. The last thing the Chinese government had reckoned with was that a bunch of awkward foreigners should witness the military preparations for an onslaught on its neighbour. Shortwave radio broadcasts I tuned into even a week later told that China was still denying any military build-up in the south. Foreign Experts Bureau heads must have rolled because of the bad timing of our trip.

To add to our minders' woes, we, the very first group of foreigners allowed into the Xishuangbanna region for decades, arrived in the midst of unprecedented street protests, the like of which we had never dreamt possible in regimented China. Under the guise of a patriotic movement to steel the new generation in revolutionary ways, back in 1968 Mao Zedong had ordered the rampaging youth out of the cities. Some tens of thousands of mainly Shanghai kids had been sent off to this far-flung corner of the empire. For us, this was a tropical paradise peopled by exotic non-Han, the main grouping in this corner of Yunnan being Thais and wild-looking Hanni people from the hills. But for the forlorn young exiles from China's greatest metropolis, it was a life sentence amongst an impoverished and often semi-hostile peasantry whose struggle for survival was difficult enough without the burden of extra mouths to feed.

After our long journey from a distant airstrip, we arrived in Jinghong, Xishuangbanna's capital. Our bus was pushing through knots of youthful slogan-shouters who were coursing up and down the main street. Jinghong was apparently without the usual 1950s Soviet-era hotel and we were comfortably accommodated in a charming villa – the cadres' guest house - a two-storey building with intricately-carved verandas set in a lush garden of unfamiliar tropical bushes.

Jo and I managed to sneak out before dinner to find out what was going on in Jinghong's streets. Normally, in public places people would avoid contact with dangerous foreigners, the youngsters on the street were all too eager to engage with us and declare their grievances. They were turned out in a way which contrasted sharply with the staring onlookers, the roughly-dressed inhabitants of the town. Indeed, these Shanghai kids had dressed up in their smartest Dacron jackets and trousers. What was more, they sported leather footwear - still a luxury in 1970s China. To emphasise their cultivated otherness, many wore their watch straps outside their jacket sleeves. Again, in those days few rural dwellers could afford a watch. All this yelled 'We don't belong here!' 'We want to go home!' 'No more years of labour in the mud of rice paddies and rubber plantations.'

A knot of young people surrounded us. 'We haven't got enough to eat, the locals do not like us. Sometimes the girls are ...'

Words failed our interlocutor, a young man who seemed to be something of a spokesman. He finished his explanation with a graphic indication of what had been done to some of his female comrades.

'Some of us managed to get to Kunming and we stopped the trains to the north by lying on the lines,' another piped up.

'What did the police do?' I asked. Not surprisingly one boy had been run over by a train, while several had been beaten and taken away.

Our absence from the guest house had, as ever, been noted and Lao Guo was sent out to retrieve us. After that, the officials more or less stood guard over our every moment in Jinghong. Yet everything in the town seemed to conspire against our hosts, all of whom in this land of 'national minorities' were unmistakably of the dominant Han majority.

After a mouth-watering dinner of fish, tropical fruits and vegetables, our group was ushered into the sultry tropical garden. On the immaculate lawn, white-jacketed staff were setting up a cinema screen and testing a projector.

'Now we will show you a film about how we Chinese care for our environment,' proudly announced Jinghong's Party secretary. The film makers' obvious intention was to show off their newly-found environmental awareness, their regard for the wildlife in the rainforests of Yunnan, but every time stalwart PLA soldier met terrified wildlife it ended with blood on the jungle floor. Like the Japanese who insist on killing whales 'for research', the PLA soldiers were finishing off pythons, monkeys and even a tiger or two in the interests of science. Ribald laughter and loud guffaws came from an unappreciative foreign audience.

Later, as we drove in our minibus to look at a rubber plantation, a smoking hillside came into view. It looked to me to be nothing other than traditional slash-and-burn agriculture - a practice which the cadres told us had been civilised out of the 'primitive' local decades before. I insisted on interrogating our flustered Jinghong Party secretary.

'These fires have been burning since before liberation,' he insisted.

With smouldering hillsides everywhere, as the cadre's explanation was relayed down the bus, peels of derisory laughter echoed back.

On the final day in Jinghong, we managed to miss the tour bus and took off on foot into the lush countryside. Soon we came upon a hamlet where the grim poverty of the broken-down hovels

- one of which we were invited to enter to drink white tea - hot water - was in shocking contrast to the cheery peasant dwellings we foreigners would normally be shown. And this was a Han settlement. Were conditions in Xishuangbanna's ethnic minority settlements far bleaker? In truth, when we visited a Dai village later obviously something of a model - but still - it seemed that they were far superior than those of that decrepit hamlet of poor Han peasants.

From Xishuangbanna, we were hastily returned to the province's capital, Kunming. There, matters went from bad to worse, at least for our Chinese hosts. Our appetites now thoroughly whetted for adventures on the Chinese street, we absconded from the official programme of kindergartens and factories so as to wander the rustic lanes lined with picturesque but crumbling wooden facades. We did not have to look very far for the next heterodox incident. In a wide avenue we ran into a milling crowd of several hundred, spilling out from the entrance to an enclosed compound. In an instant, two elderly men wearing white skull caps grabbed our arms and pulled us through the throng into the front courtyard of what appeared to be a traditional Chinese temple. Across the entrance hung a huge red banner, and my poor Chinese was able to make out that some kind of anniversary was being held - the 1408th year of some significant event. We were jostled by our guides into a side room to the side of the courtyard, where half a dozen men were seated on tiny stools. Strong hands forced us into two empty stools in their midst.

In charge was a middle-aged man with a sunburnt complexion, moustache, shiny dyed black hair, wearing a black woollen Mao jacket and smart black leather knee boots. He waved to a lad to bring tea - sweet tea in minute cups. Someone else set before us bowls of unleavened bread and with aromatic lamb keema. But the rapid-fire speech seemed to concern pigs rather than sheep. It had not occurred to us that this southwest corner of China could be an outpost of Islam. Yet now I vaguely recalled that in the mid-nineteenth century, Yunnan had seen a protracted Moslem rising against the ailing Qing empire; like the Taiping rebellion of south and east China, it had been put down with great brutality. We realised suddenly that the 1408 of the red banner must refer to the anniversary of the Prophet Mohammed's birth.

The day before, as our tour bus lurched through the busy streets, I had had noticed small *dazibao* pinned to lampposts and pavement walls - all identical and with the two characters *sha dian* in their heading. What was this *sha dian* – 'sand place' poster all about? I had hoped to have a closer look, but the answer now lay close at hand.

As people came and went from the cramped and airless room, the chief motioned to two hefty lads to take up positions in front of the door to the crowded courtyard. We were not sure we liked this development. Our new friends tried to reassure us with earnest smiles and whispers. The room went silent and the leader spoke:

'We want to tell our foreign friends something. The cadres came to our village of Shadian and ordered us to keep pigs.'

Now, I had had my own experiences working in a Jiangsu village for a time, and knew that one of Mao's little aphorisms was that every pig is a living fertiliser factory, capable of producing on average one whole tonne of muck a year. China was blessed with almost 150 million peasant households – a potential shit-pile of over 150 million tonnes. Perfectly sensible so far. When a *yundong* was unleashed to spread the pig-keeping dictum, it was with the usual dogmatic zeal, brooking no exception.

'We couldn't have pigs around because they're unclean,' continued the chief. 'They sent us Mao Zedong Thought Propaganda Teams. We listened to them but we still couldn't agree to pigs. Then they brought the militia, the *minbing*, and went to every household and ordered us to the Commune pig farm to get our pigs. We didn't go. Next they brought in the PLA, the *Jiefangjun*. It ended up with artillery fire on our village, and we still wouldn't have the pigs.'

The room stirred as memories were roused. The leader motioned for quiet and continued.

'Finally the soldiers came back to the village and hauled some of the men into the clearing where we thresh our grain, and used our own choppers to chop their legs off, above the knee, so they could no longer kneel to pray. In our area, more than four hundred died and lots of us were imprisoned, like this comrade here.'

He touched the arm of a man of about thirty, who launched into his own emotional story, with stark demonstrations of the tortures suffered in gaol. Our alarm at the man's account was mixed with our own fears. Just to know about such a thing could be dangerous. We tried to explain our need to leave, but were pressed back by many hands. More sweetened and un-Chinese tea was served. The chief then turned to us with a plea.

'Go to the Arab embassies in Beijing and let them know our story. And while you're there, we need Korans. We've only one left amongst us all.'

This was heady stuff and it was time to get out. We signalled our departure. Our two door guardians were joined by a couple of tall, moustachioed un-Chinese looking youths who hustled us out through the crowds and back onto the street. As we hurried in the direction of the hotel, we mulled over certain things which were said which appeared to implicate the recently deposed Chairman of the Communist Party, Hua Guofeng. It seemed that he had been involved in the Shadian events. In 1975, Hua had been appointed Minister for Public Security. and in 1976 he was anointed as Mao's 'chosen successor'. Mao's supposed imprimatur *Ni banshi, wo fangxin* ('With you I charge, I am at ease') was broadcast ad nauseam as proof of the legitimacy of Hua's claim to the Chinese throne. Could it be because Hua Guofeng, fellow Hunanese, was so brutally uncompromising in putting down the 'feudal splittists' of Shadian that Mao invested him with the supreme position of Party Chairman?

I had to wonder about the veracity of our Kunming informants about what had happened at Shadian. It was not until 2006 that I found corroboration in Roderick MacFaquahar and Michael Schoenals masterly work, *Mao's Last Revolution*. The initial point of conflict had been the refusal of the authorities to allow the re-opening of a mosque in the village. Things escalated and some of the Shadian protestors took to arming themselves before the PLA attack. According to the two authors' research, a large number of troops were used including a division from the 14th Corps, an artillery regiment and 'thousands' of local militia. The town was razed and 1,600 unarmed civilians of all ages were killed.

The amazing railway from Kunming over the high passes to Chengdu was something of an anti-climax. After the first dozen tunnels we felt that we had seen them all: rolling across yet another of the countless viaducts spanning deep gorges, it was impossible to appreciate their engineering splendour. We bedded down in our over-upholstered four-bunk 'soft seat' compartment and fell asleep to the gentle clickety-click of the rails. Awaking to grey whirls of mist, we found ourselves parked in a high mountain station looking down upon a valley filled with red smoke and noise. This, then, was the fabled steelworks of Panzhihua, implanted in the mountain gorges at huge cost as part of Mao's strategic plan against an expected Soviet invasion of China's coastal plains. Later that morning we halted at another station with a rather more magical name – Emeishan – above which towered the peaks of the most sacred of China's five sacred mountains. Our pleas for a detour here fell on deaf ears. Emeishan would remain closed to foreigners for some more years.

Our train descended gradually into the great basin of Sichuan, drifting by hamlets of half-timbered whitewashed farmsteads sheltering behind high groves of bamboo. More quickly than it seemed possible we had crossed the plain and were drawing into Chengdu station. As our party disgorged itself onto the low platform, the accompanying minders were introducing themselves with much obeisance to a bevy of cadres from the local foreign affairs bureaucracy. A rickety blue-and-white bus was awaiting, to take us to the newly re-designated foreigners' hotel, the Jinjiang, one of the typical, commodious creations for the Soviet engineers who had come to China in the 1950s for the First Five Year Plan.

Downtown Chengdu in the late 1970s retained a street atmosphere which my grandparents would have recognised. Two-storey terraces lined the city's narrow lanes where the newly-tolerated private traders hawked vegetables and mandarin oranges, jostling for space with the smoky woks of itinerant hot snack sellers. The Jinjiang Hotel was close to a large tract of such cityscape, set astride a wide avenue, at the city centre end of which stood one of the few giant statues of Mao Zedong still to be found in China. There was absolutely no trace on the ground, but we knew from our trusted *Nagel's Encylcopedia-Guide* that Mao's massive form stood where once was the gate of Chengdu's fourteenth century Imperial City, razed to the ground in a feudal-minded way in the frenzy of 'anti-feudalism' just a few years before.

The *Luxingshe*, the China Travel Service, generally arranged the foreign traveller's day in such a dense fashion that the chance of any untoward incident was minimal. Factories, communes, neighbourhood committees and 'scenic spots' by day gave way to mandatory performances of opera, acrobatics or political music hall by night. When finally returned tired-out to the hotel compound, it was to bed. Travelling in China at the time, if not quite an assault course, was certainly an obstacle race, with exhaustion the normal condition.

The familiar routine of those days was that within half an hour of arrival we would present ourselves to the local *Luxingshe* chieftains who were strictly *in loco parentis* until we were safely off their patch. Unlike in Western cultures, generally in China, the host is always in charge and the guest has few rights. Presentation of the boss's itinerary by a junior would be follow a standard formal welcome speech, to which the foreigners' group 'leader' would respond in kind, a ritual accompanied by smiles and mutual hand-clapping. The programme served up, the guests were invited to express their 'opinions and criticisms'. This was a bit of theatre - regardless of any humbly mouthed ideas (dutifully noted down by the junior) we knew we were observing a game. Deviation from the formal arrangements was rare indeed.

But now in Chengdu, something was different. There was no resort to the usual politenesses, and it was baldly announced that our two-day sojourn in the city was to be chopped by one day. Perhaps struggle-trouble was brewing in Chengdu, or maybe tales of our misadventures in Kunming and Xishuangbanna had gone before us. Or the excessive nervousness of the locals might simply have been because we were the first group of foreigners in town since the darker eruptions of the Cultural Revolution. The filmmaker Antonioni's chaotic progress through the Middle Kingdom a few years earlier had caused not a few travel officials' heads to roll, and recently there had been a national campaign against hostile foreign visitors.

So our Sichuan officials were anxious to see the back of this party of troublesome foreigners as soon as ever possible. We were left in no doubt that every one of us had to be on the early morning train bound for Chongqing. But for Jo and me, the odyssey to Chengdu had really begun years before. We just had to struggle for extra time. Rather than remonstrating, which would only confirm the stereotype of the blustering foreign devil, we managed to plead in a polite Chinese way. Until now on this trip we had deliberately not taxed our Shandong minder Lao Guo with any little problems. For one thing, he was clearly enjoying the rare delights of travel himself. But it was now time to put poor Lao Guo on the spot.

'Ask them if we can do the things on the list we sent them – to meet old people who might remember the foreigners here, to visit our student's home for a meal, to learn from Chengdu's city planners!'

'But the Chengdu comrades are in charge and I cannot say anything here,' Guo protested mildly.

Sure, that was always the case. In the inverted universe of Cultural-Revolutionised China, the pusillanimous 'intellectuals' found it hard enough asking anyone for anything. But with two insistent foreign devils snapping at his heels, there could be no escape. So Lao Guo assumed his most humble and smiley face and we marched him into the lion's den – the office where our hosts of the meeting were just congratulating themselves on an easy ride. Lao Guo said his piece. My heart sank as the travel supremos claimed no knowledge of our three advance requests. 'We'll look into the matter', was all we could get from them as we were shown the door.

The rest of that day was spent in dutiful pursuit of the official group programme. This took us first to the ancient Dujiangyan water conservancy system a few miles out of town. By no means an unwelcome bit of tourism: Dujiangyan is the prototype for all the superhuman efforts to conquer nature on which Chinese civilisation rests. What was odd was that we were offered very little commentary from our guides. It was impossible to fit this great endeavour from the Qin dynasty – several hundred years before Christ - into the bald political rhetoric of the present. As with all such wonders from the past for which today's regime found itself unable to take credit: the 'creative genius of the labouring masses' was always the stock message. In the fading blush of Maoism, we were left to wander amongst the ancient bridges and pavilions at Dujiangyan without a word of the obligatory 'brief introduction'. It was a pleasant morning.

Our entertainment that evening was a rendition of Sichuan opera at a down-at-heel theatre. The subtlety of the plot and the actors' stylised gesturing eluded us, but we were glad to be there. We had been ushered to the opera many a time, but this time it was different. In place of the updated model performances of the Cultural Revolution, politically choreographed by Mao's wife Jiang Qing, it seemed that the shows might be getting back to how they once were. The proscription of the old-style, 'feudal' Chinese opera was something, oddly, which resident foreigners had gained from. In Beijing's Dongdan district was a rickety old building which we called the 'opera shop'. Here the magnificent gold- and silver-embroidered wardrobes of China's most illustrious troupes – banished by Jiang Qing - were sold off for mere pennies. To this day, I have half a drawer full of torn-off sleeve borders, fur-lined caps and even a sheaf of fanciful choreographers' sketches. Now, in Chengdu, letting foreigners see the elaborate finery of tradition back on the stage for the first time for years was clearly charged with political significance.

In those days, public entertainments still kicked off in the very early evening, and much before nine o'clock, our bus drew back into the hotel compound. As our party made its weary way up the hotel steps, Jo and I managed yet again to slip off for a brief taste of reality - Chengdu at dusk. Venturing into the nearby park alongside the river, after a few paces we realised our mistake. Every willow-shadowed seat was occupied by couples in silent embrace. The post-Mao order was indeed proving an interesting one.

Our absence had, naturally, been noted by the hotel guardhouse, and five minutes after we got back to our room we were surprised by a gentle knocking. Lao Guo and a young man whom we recognised from the welcome meeting seated themselves in the overstuffed armchairs. We were not, for once, being told off. The atmosphere was relaxed, and as ever Guo wore his submissive smile.

'The Chengdu comrades have considered your demands and decided to give you special treatment.' It was always a difficulty that in Chinese there is only one word, *yaoqiu*, covering both 'request and 'demand'. Guo continued:

'Your visit to the village of Xiao Liu is not possible as it is in a place not open to foreign friends. Your two other demands will be met. But you must promise to leave Chengdu on time, with the group.'

Lao Guo brusquely informed us that we had to go on the official excursion the next morning and after lunch we would be excused from group activities. We were to go to our room and simply wait. The planners meeting would be routine, but just how our request to encounter folk 'who remembered the foreigners' would be dealt with we had no clue.

The following morning's programme was unusual: the official menu was completely devoid of factories, neighbourhood committees, kindergarten infants chanting 'I love Beijing's Tiananmen' - not a revolutionary committee in sight. Instead we were assigned a cultural trip, taking in the thatch-roofed compound where the Tang dynasty poet Du Fu was said to have lived. We knew little of classical Chinese poetry and our minds were occupied with the thought of what the afternoon would bring.

After lunch we settled down for a siesta. Mao's most ardent zealots had never dared challenge the right of every urban Chinese to indulge in a lengthy early afternoon snooze, and in summer work might not start again until three or even four. But now sleep eluded us. At a few minutes past the appointed, a breathless Lao Guo appeared at the door.

'They're coming,' he gasped. We peered down the dark tunnel of a corridor, gradually making out two white-gowned figures who seemed to be half-dragging a third body along the carpeted passage. Soon a very elderly man wearing goggle glasses and a cadre-style woollen peaked cap was being manhandled into our room. The two well-built nurses deposited him on the bed and then withdrew, leaving Guo and two CTS cadres in the room.

No one seemed to know what to say or how to proceed. The old fellow alternately peered bewilderedly round him and sank into a reverie all of his own.

The two Chengdu officials offered us no clarification, but merely took it in turns to yell, 'Hey, wake up! These *Yingguo pengyoumen* (English friends) have come to see you.'

After a while our visitor began muttering, and it wasn't in Chinese. He said simply, 'I'm Dr Fang. Very... pleased... to ... meet you.'

In my hand was Joanna's letter, listing the people we were to look out for over half a century after her family had left the city. The second name was indeed a 'Dr Fang', though spelt in the pre-pinyin style as 'Fong'. It had to be the self-same person, and my frustration rose as I realised that no sensible conversation was likely with the fragile old soul.

The minders evidently reckoned they had done their bit, and

retired to the armchairs. It was now to be left to me to interrogate our visitor. Crouching on the floor before him so as to meet his fixed gaze, I decided to try and communicate my grandparents' names by scrawling on the back of my notebook in large letters 'John Rodwell' – the name of my grandfather. But Dr Fang had slipped back into his doze then suddenly came to life.

'You look just like your mother,' he mumbled in passable English.

The cadres and Guo leapt to their feet and pressed around the old fellow.

'You know, I stayed with your grandfather's family twice in Derby, in Derby, in England – 1932.'

That was it. He was back into his dreams and it was obvious the ordeal should cease. The cadres yelled down the corridor and the two nurses reappeared.

Just as they were perfecting their grip on the old boy's shoulders, there came a firm knock at the half-open door, and in walked two people men in typical dress of the professional official, always recognisable by their badges of rank, the black plastic zip-up handbag. One was an angular fellow in his forties and the other, with the soft pink complexion peculiar to the Sichuanese, appeared to be about sixty. We were not surprised when our minders announced, smugly, that the new arrivals were from the city construction bureau.

Dr Fang had fallen back into his stupor, and the minders now signalled to the two hovering nurses that it was time to remove him. As they began to half-wrestle him towards the open door, I saw that the older of the two new arrivals was looking inquisitively at the old man and biting his lips. It was not always wise to reveal connections when a foreigner was around. Finally curiosity won the day he said quietly, 'What's he doing here?'

Guo, infected by our excitement, explained in rapid-fire

Chinese the circumstances had brought Dr Fang to our door, and the coincidence of his connection with my mother's family. He also mentioned Joanna's letter from England.

'Where is this letter?' boldly demanded our new acquaintance. I handed it to him and he seated himself on the bed and pored over the page with the list of four names. Slowly, his delicate Sichuan features reddened:

'I am the first person on your mother's list,' he declared in broken words. Her cursive script had led us all to think that we were seeking a Lin Changcheng.

'That is not *Lin*, it is *Liu*, and I am Liu Changcheng.'

We rose in disbelief and I took his two hands in mind and looked into his face.

'I was your mother's special little friend, her playmate, right up until she left Chengdu in – let's see – 1927. We were both seven years old at the time.'

Liu grabbed the letter again and announced: 'The third name is Dr Yang of the Medical College. He's still with us, and I know him well.'

At this turn of events, the minders shifted on their heels. Like anyone schooled in China after 1949, they had been brought up on a diet of patriotic spy stories in which coincidence often played some clinching role. They made to hustle the bowed figure of Dr Fang from the room again, but as they were doing so, Liu started to exclaim loudly. Guo could hardly contain himself.

'He says that he's brought up his family in the house in Green Dragon Street that was your grandparents' residence. He says that the little girl who became your mother lived there. And Mr Liu has just invited us three for lunch tomorrow.'

The travel office officials had missed this latter exchange. Now, as Guo explained the latest revelation, their mouths fell in disbelief. This was really one step too far. Sharp words were fired at Mr Liu, but the mild-mannered engineer stuck to his ground. Probably still a Christian after all these years, perhaps divine intervention was in his thoughts. How else to explain this coming together after fifty-three years, in a province of over one hundred million people which had gone through civil wars, the Japanese War, the Communist Party's revolution, mass starvation of the late 1950s and early 1960s, and countless political movements in which literally millions had been devoured in the revolutionary ferment?

From the mists of another age, my mother's cast of characters had risen before us like ghosts. The discussion about Chengdu's city planning and development with Mr Liu and his colleague now was gone through perfunctorily in an un-Chinese half hour.

Minder Lao Guo now excelled himself, begging – insisting, even - that we be allowed one extra day in the city. Even the *Luxingshe* duo seemed moved as they went off to report to their superiors. The afternoon passed quickly and our last evening in Chengdu was fast looming. Nervous, chain-smoking Guo stayed in our room, deep in discussion with Mr Liu. Just before the call for supper we had our answer. Yes, hard hearts at the provincial foreign affairs office had been melted. We were to have a stay of departure of twenty-four hours.

Qinglong gai in Sichuan dialect – Green Dragon Street – by 1979 had its former name restored after a politically-correct substitution of the Cultural Revolution., when I believe it was called *Shengli lu* ('Victory Street'). We were led by a smiling Liu Changcheng along a walled path off into a long compound. At the far end stood an imposing villa, built in what seemed a half-European and half-Chinese style, with typical Sichuan whitewashed half-timbered walls and a roof with pointed, devil-thwarting eaves. Liu led us around the back, and through the garden door we entered a largish room with some partitions off, the wooden floor oiled in that brown aromatic lacquer found in Chinese temples. Awaiting us was Liu's wife, a wiry bright-eyed woman with sparkling eyes and long, greying hair worn loose in a manner not usually seen in a woman of her age. She surprised us by introducing herself as 'Mary',

We were seated in cane chairs, and brought fine green tea and peanuts.

'This used to be your grandparents' kitchen and now it's our apartment,' Liu explained. 'Seven other families share this house, and in the Cultural Revolution there were several more families sent here,' he explained in his gentle tones.

I reflected that even my grandparents, modest Quakers that they were, whose children were forbidden to speak English so that they would integrate, must nonetheless have lived in some style.

A meal of many courses was put before us; while the occasion glowed with bonhomie, it seemed best for us to refrain from sensitive questions about how the couple had survived China's tumultuous years of struggle, both before and after the Communist Party took power. We could guess that in the years after 1949, as a family tainted by 'foreign religion' Liu Changcheng and Mary Xiao must have had a tough time. For them, the persecution must have started not with the Cultural Revolution's Red Guards, but back in 1957 when the Party had launched its first 'anti-rightist' offensive. Here was another Chinese irony: it was Deng Xiaoping who, obedient to Mao, had led the attack on the educated classes all those years before, and yet it was only through his feud with the latter-day Maoists that China was now slowly raising the Bamboo Curtain. Without the indefatigable Mr Deng we would not have been in the country at all, let alone in this far redoubt of Sichuan.

Liu Changcheng, number one name on Joanna's list, met us the following morning and took us to the former West China Union University (WCUU) campus, an ecumenical Protestant institution which my grandparents had had a hand in establishing and running. It was now the spacious campus of the Sichuan Medical School, renowned throughout China and coincidentally, where my second son William was years later to go under the knife for an injured leg.

We entered one of the four-storey residential compounds and were welcomed by the sixty-year-old Professor of Surgery Yang Zhenhua, Name Number Three on Joanna's list. Yang insisted that we call him 'Stephen'; just as for Mr Liu's wife, back in 1979 it was a bold rarity to hear Chinese advertising their pre-1949 foreign Christian names. Yang, we learned, was steeped in Quakerism. His father had been the first Chinese Quaker to get to England where, according to Charles Tyzack's *Friends to China*, '...he spent his time in Birmingham studying, not theology, as had been originally intended, but town planning, the Factory Acts, and 'building, on modern sanitary lines'.' As far as I am concerned, a sensible thing to do. Professor Yang, his surgeon son, was one of the thousands of 'returned scholars' of the early 1950s who left their comfortable niches in the West to help China build a new society. Unlike many of these returnees from North America and Europe, Yang Zhenhua had merely suffered the usual indignities, the lot of all 'bourgeois intellectuals', when the Red Guards were on the rampage. He, like Liu Changcheng, died in the late 1990s.

Along with the ancient Dr Fang, we had now encountered three out of the four people on Joanna's improbable list and fulfilled her mission in the face of monumental statistical odds. Coincidence or divine intercession as these latter-day Christians no doubt believed? All I can say is that on a further trip to this city, more remarkable coincidences beset me, so perhaps it is just something about Chengdu's *fengshui*.

With this, the new millennium, three decades on from my first visit, a few things have changed in Chengdu. Dr Fang, already half way to his heaven when we encountered him, lingered on until 1981. Only with Tyzack's publication of his comprehensive history of the Quakers in Sichuan did I appreciate the significance of our uncanny encounter with the second person on Joanna's list. Dr Fang Sixuan, or 'S.H. Fong' as he was known in my grandparents' day was born back in 1894; having attended the Friend's School in Chengdu, he then had the distinction of being the first graduate of the Quaker section of WCCU. In the early 1930s, Dr Fang actually became the President of the University, a position which he sustained throughout the Japanese occupation of eastern China when whole colleges from the east, including our very own Nanjing University, retreated to the interior and were somehow accommodated on the WCUU campus to the south of Chengdu's city centre. With the new government of 1949 demanding the expulsion of foreign religious personnel, Dr Fang had the delicate task of transferring the ownership of the University to the state. For the new rulers of China, he was just the kind of individual who was a likely target in the repeated political *yundong*. But against all the odds, he survived, and somehow the cadres of the provincial foreign affairs bureau had brought him to us. Whether this was witting or unwitting on their part, I will never know.

As a student of China's contemporary urbanisation process, I was only too aware that my mother's childhood residence had to be a piece of prime real estate. Since the early 1990s, China's cities have been torn asunder by an invasive and unstoppable land market; it was only a matter of time before the ageing villa on Green Dragon Street, near Chengdu's peak-value downtown district, would be razed in the frantic rush for profit. But the onslaught was not entirely unkind: Liu and his wife had been permitted to move to an airy two-storey home designed by Liu himself. The last time we met, he was complaining of his health but still sprightly, while from dawn to dusk Mary was taking in young aspirants on the piano.

Liu Changcheng, Mary Xiao, the Green Dragon Street house are all now memories. Joanna, my mother, outlived her childhood friend, but for some years they were able to make use of the great river of the Internet to rekindle their eighty-year-old but long-ruptured acquaintance.

Finally, I wrote earlier of Chengdu as a place of serendipity, coincidence. When William, second son born to Jo and myself, was invited to work in the headquarters of a Chinese company, it was by sheer fluke to Chengdu that he was called, and where he has settled down. Visiting the city in April 2014, along with young Sophie, my daughter with Louise, it was the unique panda reservation which came first on the itinerary. I was pleasantly surprised to find that China's conservationists have learnt something, at least, since that disastrous demonstration of their skills in Xishuangbanna which is related earlier in the chapter.

Next, William took us downtown to Green Dragon Street, where gleaming skyscrapers have now invaded the compound where once the small Quaker band of Chengdu forgathered, and where our family residence stood for almost a century. I was glad to have seen it in 1979, the exterior at least almost unchanged from the time of her childhood.

With a busy international airport, Chengdu is no longer isolated by the Yangtze Gorges. Today, almost a century after Joanna came into the world, dozens of flights a day connect the city to the rest of China, while British Airways will fly you direct from London to Sichuan's capital in just ten hours. Indeed, this is now a vibrant world metropolis, with numberless foreign residents and frighteningly, perhaps, the presence of hundreds of Western multinationals including half the US Fortune 500 companies.

Had they lived to witness Chengdu's transformation, I guess that old-timers Liu Changcheng, Dr's Yang and Fang (let alone my grandparents) would have been shocked and disoriented. But Number Two Son William loves it like it is. As for me, Chengdu will always be something of a magical place, arousing warm emotions, even despite my regrets about the disappearance of the low-rise, liveable cityscape which I found in 1979, and which my mother would have known in her distant Sichuan childhood.

XX
AN UNFINISHED TALE OF THE VENERABLE WEN

SOMEWHERE AROUND 2001 I chanced upon a *Newsweek* article about Jim. He had been tracked down to a retirement flat in Jinan, a city on the Yellow River. Though Jinan is the provincial capital of Shandong, when I was there in the 1970s it retained the air of a dusty, overgrown village. But the *Newsweek* man was not at all concerned with the ambiance of the place. His report rang with astonishment at the wiry octogenarian Jim, who at the least provocation would lurch raucously through every known verse of My Darlin' Clementine. He was a living American fossil.

In my day, some twenty years before the journalist's encounter, Jim had often sung to a different tune, one neither English nor Chinese but the vernacular Greek of the streets. For all his tumultuous decades in China, and even though he had never set foot in the land of his forebears, I came to see Jim as at heart a Mediterranean mama's boy.

In his twilight years, there was nothing that Jim liked more than to chew the fat, preferably over a bottle of strong liquor. With my own declaration of love for Greece, Jim and I made a pact, a Chinese 60-degrees-proof white-lightning pact. In our glazed minds' eyes, we would be seated under a bower of vines at a simple table. Between us would stand a rapidly emptying bottle of the some local raki, the corpses of countless Karelia cigarettes forming an ash-grey pyramid. Occasionally I would fiddle with my recording machine, over which flowed Jim's relentless reminiscences. Thus, in the most congenial way imaginable, I drew out Jim's strange life in the China of Mao.

At least I can claim that I have done my bit in terms of Jim's confessional. As a teenager I hitch-hiked across Europe to Greece and found myself on Samos, the lush Aegean island hard against the Turkish coast. Years later, in a moment of madness, I bought a decrepit townhouse on the isle. I always knew Samos would be a perfect place for Jim. The island's rich soil and ceaseless winter rain are ideal for the Muscat grape; indeed, none other than that great Byron had praised the Samian nectar. His palate coarsened by decades of Chinese *baijiu*, I guessed that for Jim the harsher distillations of Samos' co-op winery – the brandies and the tonsil-burning *souma* - would become his favourites.

Jim's other great companion through life was tobacco. There was a little farmer's tobacco on the island, even though under the enigmatic European Union rules, you could be fined for growing it. Strangely, in the closing years of the 19th century, Samos tobacco had the monopoly contract to supply the faraway Chinese imperial court. But of course, Samos had long since given up its eminence as the sole purveyor of 'Turkish cigares' to the Mandarins and eunuchs of Beijing's Forbidden City.

But I was on my own in Samos, just me and my laptop and those rickety chairs in an arbour of overgrown vines which enmesh themselves in our orange tree. In front of me were faded Chinese children's notebooks, illustrated with scenes from Madame Mao's model operas. In the unreal China of the 1970s, my diary had been as much a daily chore as cleaning my teeth. But the dense blue scratchings of my Hero fountain pen were deliberately illegible, as I could never assume that they were for my eyes only.

Jim has not made it to Samos. Memories were all that remained of former U.S. Army Private RA13009671 James George Veneris, aka Lao Wen, the Venerable Wen, captured by Chinese soldiers on

RICHARD KIRKBY

a freezing hillside in Korea in 1952.

I vividly recall my first sighting of Jim. It was 20th December
1978, and it was the official welcome banquet laid on by my new
employers at Shandong University. From sub-tropical Guangdong
to the dusty North China plain, that day I had crossed half a
continent. Landing at Jinan airport, I was whisked across the dusky
city and into the arid countryside, above which the University
loomed in the shadows of a huge 19th century Catholic cathedral.
No sooner had I dropped off my bags than with Jo alongside we
were screeching back towards the city. It did not do to arrive late
at one's own welcome banquet.

We pulled up at a restaurant with an array of neon around its
portals, glitzy refinements, long-banned but now all the rage in
the China of Deng Xiaoping. Standing to attention at the curtained
door of a private dining salon was a distinguished-looking tall
man in the fine grey woollen suit of a high cadre. I guessed that
this had to be the University president, Wu Fuheng. Behind him
hovered his rotund wife, professor of American literature, as well
as an attractive and smiling middle-aged woman. This I quickly
realised must be Li Hua, the Foreign Affairs chief whom Jo had
mentioned. Four grim-looking types dressed in cheap cadres'
outfits were already taking advantage of the Zhonghua cigarettes
that came with a foreigner's banquet. I guessed they were from the
University Party committee. 'Foreign friends' were still a novelty
in Shandong, though in this new post-Mao age with politics
supposed to be taking a back-seat, I had half expected to be free of
the ever-present cadres.

The strain of the long journey had eclipsed any thought of the
strange American whose presence had provoked my return to
China. Now, taking up the rear of the official reception committee
I noticed a Caucasian of medium height with deep smile-rifts

369

down his leathery cheeks, bottle-glass spectacles and a great quiff of silver hair, swept back, Elvis style. It still had not clicked when this out-of-place figure stepped forward, hand outstretched, and announced in rasping drawl, 'Hi, I'm Jim Veneris, Richard. My golly, I sure am glad to see you at last.'

The dinner commenced in low key, Jim maintaining an unnerving, steady eye contact through his thick and dusty lenses. From time to time, he looked as though he could restrain himself no longer, but long-ingrained Chinese etiquette got the better of him: on such occasions the host alone would be the one to initiate any conversation.

President Wu's obligatory speech of welcome came and went, the company rising politely to clink glasses. Now it was my turn to deliver as colourful a response as I could muster – 'journeyed over continents and the seven seas to be with you, a return to the great land of the Chinese', etc. All bonhomie and eternal friendship. By this point the three standard banquet beverages of red grape wine, beer and the local sixty percent-proof *baijiu* had begun to do their work. As was always the case at a formal banquet, the white-jacketed waitresses were conspiring to get the foolish foreigner pie-eyed. Every time you glanced at your three glasses, they were always mysteriously full to the brim.

My long day was suddenly catching up with me, and I started to wish I was tucked up under a warm quilt. But the proceedings were far from ending. No longer able to contain himself, Jim suddenly scraped his chair back and was on his feet. Gnarled hands grabbing the table's edge, he cast a beneficent glance around the assembled party, and proclaimed in a guttural American twang:

'I'd like to propose a toast to the great Chinese people who've struggled against the revisionist line ... er, under the wise leadership of Chairman Mao and Comrade Deng Xiaoping. *Ganbei, ganbei!*'

Jim's delivery was deep and rasping. As he warmed to his

RICHARD KIRKBY

theme, breathless bursts of hackneyed English were followed by rapid-fire renditions in Chinese. I could not help noticing that President Wu and his wife suddenly found they had spilt something on their napkins. The rest of the party seemed equally bemused. The Cultural Revolution was history - these were new times, with new tunes, and Jim clearly had not learned them.

His glass replenished, Jim rose to his climax:

'To the great Communist Party of China - my mother! To the Great Teacher and Leader of the Chinese people, Chairman Mao Zedong - my father.'

It was only two years since Mao had passed on, yet in polite political company such talk as this had already been cast aside. But Jim, after all, was a man whom history had got in the habit of leaving stranded. The table rose to a muted collective clink, followed by strained applause. The waiters were hovering with the banquet's piece de resistance, a large silver fish coated with fresh dill. Jim was given no second chance.

How on earth had Jim survived - first as a prisoner in the camps and later as one of the tiny number of foreigners who were natural targets for the slings and arrows of China's politics? Over the years, I have decided that his overweening impulse of self-preservation came from an ever-shifting identity: Greek boy in 1930s America, soldier in the Southern Seas, demobbed day labourer, infantryman in Korea, prisoner-of-war, honoured guest of the Chinese people, spy, turncoat, beast of burden (as he himself put it) in a Jinan paper mill, widower, divorced singleton. His final, present incarnation - as university lecturer - perhaps fitted him the most uncomfortably of all.

Raised in a coal mining area of Pennsylvania, at a tender age Jim had passed through the horrors of the Pacific War, only to volunteer again for the army. His backwoods home of Vandergrift

371

was mired in post-war slump and there seemed no other way out. The conflict in Korea to which he was despatched was a brutal maelstrom, way beyond anything experienced by the U.S. military in the Second World War. Very early in his deployment, Jim was seized by a platoon of Chinese forces, the famed Korea Volunteers. Contrary to all the GI's had been told, Jim's captors never did put that searing bullet through his skull. They merely dragged him to his feet, placed a rough cigarette between his trembling lips, and marched him unshackled down to an encampment by a frozen stream. There, Jim was told to sit cross-legged under the cover of some pines, alongside a few of his bedraggled comrades. The sounds of battle were already distant.

I never got to the bottom of what happened to Jim in the holding camps. Though he swore that physical abuse was not part of it, no doubt the Western POWs endured a harsh captivity. There are, after all, many testimonies of brutality. Even though we eventually became quite close, Jim remained silent on the subject. When the armistice came, the surviving prisoners on both sides were given a life-altering choice: to stay with their respective captors or return home. Along with a couple of dozen GI comrades, Jim forswore his country of birth and opted for the Middle Kingdom.

It was the early 1950s, the America of Joe McCarthy. A heart-searching anger was raised over the U.S. defectors, seduced somehow by the filthy slit-eyed Commies. The GIs' behaviour was aberrant, un-American, for surely no one willingly would sever themselves from the Land of the Free? It was meant to be the other way round, for heaven's sake. Those Godless schemers in Red China had somehow bewitched the honest sons of America. But there just had to be something too in the make-up of the turncoats which made them succumb to the Communists' blandishments. Whilst the newspapers shrieked 'Stool pigeons of the Reds', 'Brainwashed!', a popular magazine added 'low intelligence' to the reasoning. Psychologists meanwhile penned heavy papers: the defectors were victims of a mass illness, a kind of sympathetic hysteria.

'Our GIs were brainwashed,' the shrinks shrilled. This novel diagnosis, helpfully supported by the Chinese in their own use of the expression *xinao* (*xi*=wash, *nao*=brain), became the focus of much study. The Chinese had given their U.S. foes some good ideas. From that time on, the field of psy-ops warfare really took off in America. In our present, sad era of the 'war on terror', the deployment of mind-bending drugs, sleep deprivation, and other forms of brain disorientation has not remained the preserve of the Wicked Reds. If it ever was, that is.

In the years before the Cultural Revolution, any of the POWs who had undergone a change of heart was able to leave for home pretty well unhindered. As far as the Chinese were concerned, that is. They would be escorted to that single open border post where the People's Republic met Hong Kong, and handed into the care of the International Red Cross, who after exhaustive medicals would get them back home. But for several of the GI prisoners who took advantage of China's open door, things did not turn out to be so simple when they arrived home. While they might not have anticipated the welcome of heroes, the returnees had not bargained either for the hostility of their reception. The U.S. military sentenced several to many years behind bars.

With the McCarthy witch-hunts on the wane, twenty-one Americans who had rejected their homeland in favour of China were given dishonourable discharges *in absentia*. Unlike the early returnees, that seemed to be the extent of their punishment, and by the close of the 1950s, over half of the U.S. prisoners had turned their coats yet again and headed for home. Apart from the Americans, there was a large Turkish contingent who had stayed on: newly part of the anti-Soviet camp, the Turkish government had been pressured to supply a large number of foot-soldiers to the Korean cause. But the quirks of Chinese life proved too much for the Turks, and by the early 1960s, most had managed to get back home.

Thus in 1966 when the Cultural Revolution was launched, of the once-large Korean POW contingent from the United States, only two ex-prisoners remained in China: Jim Veneris and one Howard Adams. Some time in late 1950s, along with a few Turkish stragglers, the two Americans had been shifted from Beijing to the obscurity of a great Soviet-inspired paper mill in Jinan.

'What did you do in the mill?' I innocently enquired of Jim, thinking that he had probably been assigned to an office job in which his English might have been used in the designing of fanciful product labels. Or perhaps his work was translating foreign technical books.

'What did I do? Eight hours of each and every day I carried huge bales of old cotton shoes and straw brought in by the peasants and heaved them into these huge vats. Boy, it was tough, Richard.'

The Chinese have long memories, and it cannot have been easy to accept a British intruder such as myself. The old opium-running country was well known for its sins, its heaping of humiliation on the Chinese nation from the 1840s on. Nevertheless, I had always been accorded the honoured-guests-from-afar treatment. I was shocked by Jim's reply. So inured are we to the false security of our Western superiority that to contemplate Jim, White Man in the East, as manual labourer, lay quite beyond any normal realm of reference.

Yes, the Chinese nation for the most part cushioned our Jim and his POW comrades from the harshest experiences of life. The POWs nonetheless shared with their fellow workers the ordinary - but extraordinary - vantage point of the factory floor, the tenement block and the street. In their daily lives they were witness to the deeds both heroic and terrible which Mao inspired in the Chinese nation. By the time we became acquainted, Jim had been amongst the common people of China for the best part of a quarter of a century, a unique observer in a secretive land in turmoil and transformation.

The rich seam of Jim's everyday experiences was one not easily mined. Given a willing ear, Jim was capable of churning on for hours about ... well, Maoist dialectics, the price of cigarettes, almost anything. Yet to my broader, anthropological questioning, it was always 'What d'ya wanna know that for, Richard?' If my quest to tap Jim's brain for the banal, the everyday, seems a peculiar obsession, remember that after 1949 China was pretty well sealed off from prying eyes. The very impenetrability of the country nurtured a clique of intense watchers from the margins - journalists, spies and academics - who daily read the runes and whose theorising often rested on the flimsiest tittle-tattle. I admit I was amongst these constant seekers of the Real China. Our Jim was a unique witness of the Chinese street, and I was determined to capture his memories.

Relieved of their labouring jobs, the two remaining POWs Jim and Howard were expected to transmute into instant *zhishifenzi* - 'elements endowed with knowledge', the quaint Chinese expression immodestly rendered in English as 'intellectual'. The urbane Howard was lifted from the slurry of the paper mill to the local teachers training outpost, the Shandong Normal College. I visited him and his wife in their quarters a number of times, and Howard appeared to have made a seamless adjustment. As for rough diamond Jim, he was to surface in the far more rarefied corridors of the Foreign Languages Department of this, the prestigious provincial University. And it was here, of course, that our lives were thrown together. With two years of Hong Kong R&R under my expanding belt, and no thought of spending another day in the People's Republic of China, I could even claim that Jim played a decisive part in my destiny.

In late 1978, Jo and I had agreed to separate. To the delight of our Beijing minders who clung to us in the colony of Hong Kong, Jo decided to head north for Shandong; while I returned to Europe. We made no plans for our paths to cross. After just a few weeks, though, I was surprised by a distant voice on the phone.

Jo explained that yes, the Beijing Foreign Experts Bureau could just about claim that it had been true to its promise that in Shandong she would find a pristine foreigner-free environment. The official foreign population was nil – but a nil with a very odd exception.

'I'm being forced to eat with and to practically live with and prepare the lessons for a weird American and I don't think I can cope with him on my own.'

After the excitement of Hong Kong, I was finding that life in a market town in northern England was on the dull side. China beckoned, and I needed no second invitation. I was also, it must be said, missing my partner of over a decade. A few days later I was knocking on the door of the Chinese embassy in London's Portland Place and collecting a one-way ticket to Hong Kong, an impressive People's Republic entry visa decorating another page in my passport.

I already had enough experience of China to know that things are likely to happen to foreigners not because of what they have done, but simply because they are alien bodies in the great Chinese sea. So it was even with Jim. Our upright protector at Shandong University, Li Hua, could hardly hide a smile as she described how poor Jim - scarcely able to write a simple grammatical sentence - had been parachuted into a reluctant university English department.

It was October 1st 1976 and not long after Mao's demise and the arrest of his closest followers. Along with other long-time resident foreigners, Jim received his routine invitation to the annual National Day reception in Beijing's Great Hall of the People. Digesting the sumptuous delicacies of the banqueting chamber and after much mutual toasting and many a *ganbei*, Jim waited dutifully in line to be presented to the reception's official host, who happened to be China's Foreign Minister-in-waiting, Huang Hua.

Chinese Red Cross functionary: This is Lao Wen, our good friend who has been with us since the War to Aid Korea.

Minister: Ah, Lao Wen. We all know your name! And where do you live now and what do you do?

Jim: I'm a worker in the paper mill in Jinan that makes Double Happiness products.

Jim was about to add the proud company claim, namely that its Double Happiness toilet paper was the most eagerly demanded by our dear Hong Kong compatriots.

Minister: Hen hao – very good. So you're a technical translator in the factory?

Jim (with selfless expression, worthy of any labour hero): No, Minister, most of the time I carry heavy bales of cloth shoes and the like and shove them into the hot vats.

Thereupon, His Excellency turned to Jim's Red Cross guardian and rebuked him.

'This comrade can speak English. And Chinese too! He must be found a proper job where he can make his contribution to our Motherland. We must strictly adhere to Chairman Mao's wise policy of *Yang wei Zhong yong* ('Make foreign things serve China')

Mao had a penchant for aphorisms and everyone knew that this one. 'Make foreign things serve China' was normally rattled out like a charm, a protector of those senior Party people who wished for a little re-engagement with the outside world.

'Yes Minister, of course,' was the unavoidable but baffled response of Jim's Red Cross minder.

Shandong University simply had no choice in the matter.

The thing that surprised me most about the story of Jim's transmutation from coolie to intellectual was not the capriciousness of Mr. Huang Hua, so much as the very existence of the Chinese Red Cross. Mao's China simply did not entertain such foreign bodies. Yet I was forgetting the regime's neurotic, face-preserving compliance when it came to those few international compacts that it had signed up to. An instance of this was described to me, with much guffawing, by my runner friend Andy. It was Shanghai of the early 1980s, and the city had decided to show off its new worldliness by inviting foreigners to join a Marathon– the first ever staged in China. Eager to do the right thing, the organisers carefully noted all the rules of an international Marathon, amongst which was the idea that sponges be supplied to the runners at regular intervals along the route. So sponges there had to be. At every milepost, uniformed girls in lipstick, high heels and ra-ra skirts thrust jam-filled sponge cakes into the gasping runners' sweaty paws.

In my few years in China, I had lived through earthquake and flood and there had certainly been no Red Cross riding to the rescue. Puzzled, I looked up the text of the 1953 Korean Armistice, and found that it gave a hefty role to the Red Crosses of the various combatant nations. So there were no two ways about it – if Mao's China did not have a Red Cross, face demanded that it would have to create one. And it would have to be kept going just as long as there were Korean War POWs on Chinese soil. It was strange to imagine that in some obscure Beijing courtyard there was a bunch of Chinese cadres whose sole duty was to prove to International Red Cross headquarters in Geneva that they were upholding to the letter the terms of the Korean Armistice.

A few years ago there appeared an award winning novel about another POW of the Chinese called Jim - a book which I seized on with relish but soon put aside. With a grasp on reality so tenuous, Sid Smith's *Something Like a House* could, I suppose, be called a postmodern novel. What I found most implausible about the trials and tribulations of Smith's Jim – Jim Fraser – was the fact that his life seemed to be at the beck and call of a bunch of captors who reported to no one but themselves.

This was not how China worked, especially not during Chairman Mao's reign. Foreigners were a special tribe for whom some branch of the central bureaucracy always took charge. The Chinese state was all-encompassing, and in matters relating to foreigners there was no room for local autonomy. Beijing commanded and the foreigner's local work unit obeyed, *in* tight *loco parentis*.

Perhaps the most vital role of Jim's Red Cross was that it ensured he maintained a certain standard of living.

'I was well looked-after by the Party,' Jim would say.

Jim always got more ration tickets than his Chinese comrades. These vital tokens allowed him to get his hands on just a little more than usual of the three essentials: wheat flour, cooking oil, and cotton cloth. Unlike the northern Chinese population at large, he was also allowed a certain amount of coveted rice; when times were good, perhaps a bicycle or radio might be on the cards. In the early 1960s, with famine stalking the land, the extra food for the POWs meant that while many around them starved, they and their families managed quite comfortably.

The authorities always took extra special care of their POW charges. Keeping Jim and his family well-fed and clothed was the easy part; the nurturing and maintenance of 'correct thoughts' was, though, a relentless challenge, especially in the 1970s when the outside world might hear of this anomalous American and stray visitors to China might wish to meet him. No doubt a watchful eye was always kept, too, on Jim's associates, both at work and in the neighbourhood. And in what passed for Jim's more intimate requirements, his private life (insofar as any citizen had one), his overseers had to grasp a nasty nettle. Initially, any thoughts of marriage by the POWs were strongly discouraged - the Chinese have long held rather unsavoury views of the miscegenation kind. But a catalogue of 'woman incidents' involving the young and supposedly virile foreigners and Chinese womanhood eventually brought a change of tactic. Marriages with local women (the right type of local women, at least) were now sanctioned as a way of keeping the young POWs out of embarrassing trouble.

Of course, back in the 1950s, ordinary Chinese families would have been loath to hand their daughters to tainted foreign intruders. So the POWs were guided towards partners from amongst the more *lumpen* members of society – orphans, those with no surviving family, ex-prostitutes and the like. In the Maoist book, where one's political consciousness was considered hereditary if not genetic, women from the lower orders were held to be immune from corrupting influences. And this solution also took care of the problem of potentially embarrassing political targeting of the POWs in the endless *yundong*. Low-class girls were by definition above suspicion, offering a certain protection to their foreign spouses.

'I owe the Chinese people a lot, Richard – I was sent to study and learn Chinese properly in a top university, you know! And I didn't even graduate from high school back home!'

Jim described how a select group of the POWs were sent to Beijing's prestigious People's University and enrolled on a tailored course of political education, Chinese style. After a painful couple of years, Jim could at last struggle through the *People's Daily* and get the gist of the lectures. He proudly showed me a lined notebook full of spidery but neat copperplate. This was his college dissertation. 'The Greatness of our Two Peoples, the Chinese and the Americans' did not perhaps promise profound insights but still, it was a considerable achievement for the unlettered Jim.

Was this college interlude meant to prepare Jim for a more elevated work assignment? If so, the plan came to nothing, for not long after he had left the People's University, the Cultural Revolution broke upon the Chinese nation. The general hysteria meant that Jim bore the drudgery of the factory floor as both a badge of honour and a suit of armour, for there was nothing better designed to deflect criticism than hard physical graft.

It seemed that wherever I happened to be on the campus I could never escape Jim's unmistakable 1930s stage voice. 'How yuh doin', buddy?' 'Where yuh headin', boy?' It did not take long before I was inveigled to his lair, a cell some twelve feet by eight. On its concrete floor Jim would set up his little stove and prepared for an ingestion of smoke. China had certainly taught Jim to be big on smoking. His mates at the paper mill used to boast that using the paper they had produced they could roll the longest and fattest smokes in town. By the time I arrived, when his stash of Lucky Strikes was only rarely replenished, the most outrageous cheroots would dangle from Jim's lips.

As for Jim's beloved coffee, he always seemed to have a little sack of precious beans, an exotic luxury unknown to ordinary folk. With a vigorous crushing of a precious measure in an old enamel mug, Jim would set to fanning the embers of his briquette stove. This standard, smelly device found all over China, known as the 'economy stove', was nothing more than a steel drum with a hole at the bottom for the ash and draught and an aperture on the top to put the circular briquettes in and let the heat out. After an age of contemplating the smoky pan of water and coffee grounds, we would enjoy together the gritty, thick beverage - highly sweetened in the style of Jim's Greek youth.

As I got to know Jim, it seemed that his new life as English instructor was only mildly daunting. But he did at least recognise his limitations and I soon got used to his daily ruminations on the unfathomable mysteries of English grammar. Of an evening, when the coffee had been drunk and the air was thick with tobacco smoke, Jim would take from his locker a lurid bottle of local hooch and we would settle down to an erratic tutorial on the mysteries of present participles and gerunds.

Jim's students, knowing better than their Foreign Minister that his presence before them was a farce, would bait him with grammar queries. The poor man had not a clue. I racked my brains in explaining things to poor Jim, but it was no good. After a while, it was 'Richard old buddy, couldya just explain that noun thing once more?' He tried, he tried until his brow was deeply furrowed, but Jim was the rat on the treadmill of English grammar. Lao Wen, as the students knew him, would survive the two long hours of the standard lesson by sheer chutzpah, by never staying on the subject in question. His classes complained of his constant digressions, but I guess Jim felt he was acquitting himself well just so long as English emanated from his lips. At least he was blessed with the gift of the gab and if anyone was capable of an endless stream of consciousness it was Jim. Energized by his sheer classroom survival, he would sometimes want to go at it for another two hours. His students had other ideas.

Catching up with me in the corridor of the teaching block, Jim would painfully back-slap me and announce 'I gave them good ol' bullshit today, Richard.'

Jim was an affable soul, and he relished the life of *renao* - the popular Chinese notion conveying 'conviviality', 'warmth', generally many bodies.

'Apart from the *yundong*, Richard, it was good at the paper mill and I liked the place where we lived too,' he told me, not quite complaining at his new lot. I assumed that somewhere there was also a family, but Jim was not forthcoming.

In his previous incarnation as an ordinary worker, which he felt had been cruelly wrenched from him, he would gather in the evenings with a group of mates in the gateman's hut of his apartment block. Endless game of cards would be punctuated by much shooting of the breeze and sipping from battered brown-ringed enamel mugs. Green tea in summer and warming *baijiu* around the brazier in winter. With his authentic Shandong accent and all the habits of the locals, Jim was so much part of the furniture that people had almost forgotten he was not truly one of them. Now in his new life on campus, things were very different. Battered by the Cultural Revolution and nervous of further punishments, the university types surrounding him were hardly the life and soul. In a word, *renao* was glaringly absent.

Most single employees of a work-unit would be accommodated in grim dormitories, many to a room. I suppose the University thought they were doing Jim a favour by putting him in its guest hostel, its *zhaodaisuo*. Every self-respecting work unit of a certain size had one of these establishments. A unit's *zhaodaisuo* was more than a place to sleep: it was a shop-window designed to impress visitors from the outside world. The travelling cadre could usually look forward to a little haven of luxury amongst the often-desolate landscape of urban China. Uniformed *zhaodaisuo* girls chosen for their looks delivered thermos of boiled water for tea, the beds had clean sheets with embroidered silken covers, while canteens served the local delicacies, none of which demanded one's precious ration tickets. Ordinary mortals almost never had the chance to travel in those days. But back then, in a more rigid China, there seemed to be endless opportunity for cadres of a certain rank to get around the country, 'comparing experiences' with other work units. A well-appointed *zhaodaisuo* was considered essential.

Shandong University's *zhaodaisuo*, however, was a soulless and miserable affair and did nothing for the reputation of the place. Its layout was reminiscent of an old-fashioned North China caravanserai, only without the bustle and noise. The University's *zhaodaisuo* was a single storey brick and concrete structure thrown up in the 1950s and bearing no signs of any attention since. Along its length were the cell-like guest rooms which opened out onto a central courtyard, a long rectangular pit full of weeds and muck. At the far corner of the rectangular inner compound was a washroom with troughs of rough concrete. Summer or freezing Shandong winter, only cold water came out of the taps. Adjacent were more troughs – this time low slung and smelly, for the inmates' evacuations.

Some distance from the *zhaodaisuo's* arched entrance was the students' canteen block, where the residents would find the geyser for their boiling water which they carried back in enormous vacuum flasks encased in split bamboo. Our own luxurious accommodation with its front door, reception rooms, a separate bedroom and study - not to mention running water and clanking steam radiators - was a thousand *li* away from Jim's rough barracks.

A couple of the cells had just been converted into a kitchen-cum-dining room, for exclusive use of we foreign arrivals, and twice daily we would trek over to the depressing reception building. The new facility was the closely-guarded turf of Lao Zhao, our portly and florid cook. Just as at the hotel in Nanjing years earlier, until we protested that our stomachs were learning

RICHARD KIRKBY

Chinese ways, Lao Zhao thought to concoct for our delectation great piles of inedible animal flesh in what he imagined was the Western style. His pride and joy was a vast new refrigerator; it was soon clear that Lao Zhao held to the belief that this magic box would keep dead things fresh forever.

One day we found our jolly chef helping to reverse a Liberation lorry through the *zhaodaisuo* portals. Lao Zhao pointed to its load: dripping away in the Shandong spring sunshine was a huge block of ice with pink and grey bits deeply embedded.

'*Li xiansheng, daxia laile!*' ('Mr Li, the prawns have come!') he beamed.

I watched with sinking heart as the driver took an axe from his cab and chopped off a great hunk from his cargo. These were our long-promised tiger prawns, landed at Qingdao far away to the east, and sent up country especially for the Shandong foreigners. We could not argue with the truck's other cargo – crates of the famous Tsingtao (Qingdao) beer. We had been agitating for a consignment of this, the champagne of Chinese beers, and had been upset that it was denied us, even though Qingdao was *our* port in *our* province.

The icy prawn crush went straight off the truck into the bottom compartment of Lao Zhao's fridge. Unfortunately our chef had not reckoned with Jinan's power cuts. For a week, sweet-and-sour prawns, prawns fried with garlic, prawns in batter with their little tails sticking out were an exotic addition to our diet. But to paraphrase Chairman Mao's dialectics, little by little the delicious crustaceans turned into their opposites. By the third week, the mush of prawn fragments escaping from Lao Zhao's magic box was beyond even our politeness to accept. Not so for Jim. As our privileged dining companion, he persevered until the pungent end.

'I've been in this country most of my life, Richard, and I can eat

385

just about anything they care to serve up,' he explained. His iron stomach he put down to the Shandong habit of a *hors d'oeuvre* of several raw garlic cloves.

Our cook had a scrawny kitchen helper. Of inestimable age, Lao Wu was never seen without both her grease-caked cap and an unlit fag-end which hung from her toothless gums. Our appetites were hardly assisted by Lao Wu's thoughtful method of keeping the food warm while she carried it from the kitchen. She would cover the smeared, thumb-printed bowls with a filthy rag – the self-same rag she employed in the wiping of hands and ever-dripping nose. She would whip this off with the flourish of a conjuror revealing the rabbit. Jim delighted in ingenuous flirtation with Lao Wu, and his delight at all the food she set before him was genuine.

After a short while, the powers-that-be decided to downgrade Jim and he was denied the privilege of Lao Zhao's cuisine. This certainly improved my own digestion, for Jim demanded constant attention. Poor man, he now had to join the other *zhaodaisuo* guests as they trundled over to the University canteen with their enamelled food carriers. There, they were doled out the basic nourishment which constituted the students' fare – a couple of steamed bread *mantou* on top of some watery mixture of cabbage leaves with vague traces of meat. But at least he enjoyed himself in the food queue, chatting on to anyone who would listen and causing ripples of laughter when he came out with some preposterous Shandong slang.

On one occasion Lao Zhao excelled himself in the kitchen, with dish after dish of steaming delicacies. Out of the blue, that great figure of linguistics and literary criticism Ivor Armstrong Richards, teacher of William Empson and contemporary of F.R. Leavis, turned up at the University, complete with Beijing minders.

Amongst European men of letters, Richards was a rare bird, for in the early decades of the twentieth century he had shown a deep interest in the Chinese and their language.

Back in 1979, Shandong University was not the obvious destination for a British Council literary itinerary. The luminary's arrival in our backwoods station was a mystery. There was a connection, it was true, but it was tenuous. Our silver-haired President Wu had attended Harvard in the 1930s, and Richards was also a regular Harvard visitor, teaching there in 1931-2, so perhaps some acquaintance was imagined.

The makeshift dining room, with its greasy, dark concrete floor and flaking whitewashed walls, all under a naked 40-watt bulb, was the unlikely setting for Lao Zhao's banquet in honour of one of the Western world's most celebrated literary figures. The meal passed with some difficulty, Richards putting up a valiant effort but often slumping at the table and clearly out of it; his erudite wife covering up by keeping the small-talk going. The Chinese arranged their tours with relentless efficiency and even the young and fit were apt to droop after a few days. Closer to ninety years of age than eighty, Ivor Richards was seriously flagging.

I suppose it was to make up the numbers that Jim was invited along, but it was a strangely subdued Jim. Overawed by the company, his customary calls to hail the Great and Wise Leader Chairman Mao, the Party and eternal friendship were not heard that night. Half way through the proceedings, Jim and I had to unceremoniously manhandle the honoured guest along the open corridor to the *zhaodaisuo's* frightful privy. Richards released a pathetic stream, and what I shall never forget was its hue of long-brewed tea. Lao Zhao had excelled himself that night, our Jim had behaved with exemplary restraint, but poor Richards never recovered from his Shandong sojourn. Sadly, he only just made the return journey to England, to die in his beloved Cambridge.

Whether there was a connection between Lao Zhao's prawns and Ivor Armstrong Richard's demise, I really cannot say. But as memorable that night as the illustrious guest was a glimpse of a sober, thoughtful and very adult Jim.

It was a long while into our acquaintance, before Jim started to tell me about his family life in China.

'I had a good first wife,' Richard. 'She was a nurse, and how she nursed me!'

In the 'three bad years' of the early 1960s, when much of China was semi-starving, Wife No.1 was in the habit of bringing home extra rations, and especially an unidentified but delicious kind of meat. He smiled as he recollected his enjoyment of rare animal protein – stir-fried, sweet and sour, whichever way.

'D'ya know, I could hardly move this hand because of arthritis, and little by little after I'd started eating that meat again I was cured. Yeah. One hundred percent.'

'What on earth was it?' I enquired.

'That's what I asked my wife, but she was a bit mysterious about the whole thing, Richard.'

Eventually Jim cottoned on. No.1's best friend was a midwife and his exotic meat ration came from her. When my own son Yongshan came into the world a few months after this conversation, I was not at all surprised when the old woman who was present as an auxiliary scrabbled up the rich, liver-like afterbirth into an aluminium food carrier, U.S. army pattern, and placed it inside a huge fridge. Apparently the stuff had many uses, not least of them the anti-flu vaccine which the university clinic would deliver to my bared buttocks each autumn.

Wife No.1 was undoubtedly the love of Jim's life and his time with her was brief. After only a year or two of happiness he lost her to tuberculosis.

Wife No.2 was a rather different proposition.

'She has a great class background. She's from a family of real beggars,' Jim announced, his eyes gleaming through his bottle lenses with political correctness.

I thought Jim was joking until I remembered that we were in the land of nature first and nurture second.

'Yes, but what was she like?' I persisted, scarcely able to keep a straight face.

Jim's muttered expletive-filled response left no doubt that impeccable though her class background might have been, No.2 was a woman of the lowest and most devious character. This was a tough admission for Jim - people of such humble origins were meant to be genetically incapable of wrongdoing.

Later, fuelled by a few beakers of white lightning, Jim ranted freely about No.2. He had her down as the worst kind of gold-digger, thick-skinned enough to take the jibes which went with being married to a big-nose foreigner, cunning enough to enjoy all the material advantages of his Red Cross status. In Mao's China, divorce was rare and it tended to be strictly on grounds of political incompatibility. To 'draw a clear line' between oneself and one's ideologically dodgy spouse was a well-worn path, but one closed to Jim.

To No.2, however, it was the easiest recourse, for a foreigner was by definition irredeemably suspect. That is how she was able to get rid of Jim while hanging onto his worldly goods, his workers' apartment and, most wounding, their two children. The bust-up with No.2 had happened only shortly before my arrival, and hence Jim's lone status on the campus. Running battles were continuing over Jim's rights of access and he had returned to the *zhaodaisuo* pale and angry, regaling me with the latest affronts.

One day, a tearful Jim hammered on the door of our quarters. It seemed that his ex had done a runner, taking their girl and boy with her. From dawn to dusk, Jim tramped the streets of Jinan searching in vain for his beloved children, returning to his bare cell in despair. Poor Jim then appealed to every official in Shandong who would listen to him. There were many empty promises and many false leads. So Jim jumped on an overnight train to Beijing and headed for the Red Cross HQ. His minders made all the right noises but did nothing. Someone tipped him off that No.2 had connections in the provincial public security bureau, and they had helped hide the children in faraway Shaanxi province. By the time I left a few months later, Jim was still bereft of his offspring. Some years and another marriage had to go by before he was reunited with them.

As a confirmed collector of the People's Republic's secrets, I burned with curiosity about Jim's political survival in China. After all, he was almost the only foreigner who had witnessed from the bottom-up a quarter century of tumultuous events in the People's Republic. But the normally garrulous Jim was not giving any hostages to fortune. It was not that he denied himself a few politically safe banalities. Once, I tried to find out what he had been up to in the 1958 Great Leap Forward, when Mao's mass mobilisations were legion, and the 'backyard furnaces' set up in every urban work-unit in a hapless effort to produce a metal bonanza in the land.

'We made our own furnace, Richard, and d'ya know, my job was to chuck in sacks of ancient bronzes, old swords and coins and the like to produce metal for new guns,' he chuckled. Beyond this amusing desecration, about the Great Leap I could get nothing more out of him.

As for the first part of the Cultural Revolution, when the Red Guards were rampant and rabid accusations being thrown hither and thither, Jim would let on little. He did once reveal that his workmates in the mill were jealous of him, creating some small trouble and perhaps a little 'cow-penning' for him too. The 'cow-pens' were the impromptu prisons set up within work-units, where suspects were sent for days, months or even years of humiliation.

Oh yes – there was one other small matter revealed on an unguarded *baijiu*-lubricated night. The Vietnam War was raging, and Jim had been sent to the south – was it to the border province of Yunnan or perhaps to Hanoi itself? - to broadcast insurrection to Uncle Sam's troops. Though he probably had little choice in the matter, I warmed to Jim for doing this. Come the sober light of day, I was made to vow to keep my mouth shut; it would be tricky for Jim if his subversion became known to the U.S. authorities.

On that score, I was surprised that through all the anti-U.S. campaigns and the ultra-xenophobia of the Cultural Revolution, the arch-Chinese patriot Jim had never entirely thrown in his lot with the People's Republic. It was this that made me realise that behind Jim's endless proclamations of loyalty to the Chinese revolution there lurked a self-protective and even cunning calculation. Most of the other dozen or so Beijing-based foreigners, the 'intellectuals', who in the early 1950s opted for the People's Republic had renounced their original citizenship. Had Jim done so, however, he would no longer have been under the tender care of the Red Cross. An enormous loss to material security.

'When my kids grow up, they're gonna have U.S. passports!' Jim once told me. He well knew that if he lost his own American citizenship, this could never be.

As I listened to Jim's eulogies over his adopted country, the old question of brainwashing would never quite go away. His constant mouthing of the rhetoric was one thing, but I never could bring myself to believe that anybody could truly lose the capacity for independent thought. Perhaps I am naive about human nature, but Jim's face to the world was so open-hearted, and appealingly childlike. Surely, I pondered, he could still distinguish between truth and untruth? If that were so, as an ever-available target for the countless political campaigns, guile had to be there too, buried somewhere below the surface. My time in China had taught me that for people who were natural targets, punished in successive political campaigns from the mid-1950s on, dissembling had become an essential survival skill. It was quite possible to learn to say the right thing, if not always to do it, without any actual brainwashing. Like millions of others in the possible line of fire, what drove Jim was an instinct for survival.

Gradually, I came to understand Jim as a generally harmless opportunist; but I was to get a taste of the underlying guile myself.

A nasty habit in China in those days was the *xiao baogao* – the often spiteful and vengeful 'little report' to the authorities. Such things often had impacts which were far from little. During China's shocking attack on Vietnam in early 1979, I vehemently expressed my opposition. It is now said that in the brief campaign, China lost over 50,000 dead and wounded. Many of the soldiers were from Shandong, and Jim and I mulled over the rumour that local boys were coming back in coffins, bullets in their backs. In the face of the battle-hardened Vietnamese, the callow PLA boys had turned tail, only to be shot by their officers. Someone reported my 'anti-China' views up the line, and I suspected Jim. Indeed, years later on a trip to England our open-minded Li Hua, de facto chief of the University's foreign affairs office, confirmed Jim's betrayal of me, one which a few months on was to hasten my departure from China. Since another 'spy', Sam Ginsburg, the Russian who had taken Chinese citizenship in the early days had also reported us for these illicit opinions, Li Hua's disclosure did not make me feel any different towards Jim. I knew that his behaviour was what years in China had taught as necessary for survival.

And yes, deviousness apart, Jim did have huge cause for

gratitude, for loyalty to the China which had nurtured and fed him, educated him, and cared for his family too. At the beginning of it all, on 28th November 1950, was that cataclysmic moment. Jim and his comrades had been told that the Commies would show him no mercy, and when the PLA boys stumbled into Jim's cave he fell to his feet and pleaded loudly for his life. The bullet was never fired. If Jim harboured blind loyalty, it came from that infinitesimal moment, the point of his rebirth, his brain's reprogramming.

Somehow, Jim had persuaded the U.S. Interests Office in Beijing, the precursor to an American embassy, to issue him with a passport, and in 1976 he broke his quarter-century of exile. From the Chinese point of view, this was a peculiar time to let him go, as 1976 was a year of unceasing tumult. One by one, the most eminent leaders of the revolution went to their graves, mass opposition surfaced for the first time, the most destructive earthquake the modern world has ever seen struck Tangshan, and to cap it all, following Mao's death in September, the Cultural Revolution leaders fell in a palace coup.

Unlike us in Nanjing, Jim had been lucky to miss all the intense politicking around these events. I guess Jim's overseers in Beijing calculated he would be more use in the United States than in China, and with his children left behind, the risk of his doing a reverse defection was minimal. After all, his Beijing case officers had had a quarter of a century to analyse their charge, and so by the time he was sent off to America they were pretty sure of their man. Risks had to be taken, as China was desperate to push forward its diplomatic offensive. It was now years after Nixon and Mao had shaken hands, and yet recognition by Washington and a seat on the UN Security Council remained elusive.

But Beijing had not been idle in stealthily building up a head of steam in the U.S. The idea was to woo receptive Americans, for decades denied anything but negative news of China, with the true wonders of the mysterious Middle Kingdom. In the United States of the 1970s there seemed to be an endless appetite amongst the liberal educated classes for Oriental exoticism, this skilfully exploited by Chinese diplomats nurturing of friendship societies in every major city. China's quasi-diplomats in Washington would shower them with *China Reconstructs* and *China Pictorial*, periodicals carrying persuasive stories of a peaceful and happy people labouring to improve their lives under the wise leadership of the Party. Celebrities such as Shirley MacLaine, the ageing Hollywood star, embraced China with bizarre enthusiasm, The 'magic' of China's acupuncture anaesthesia and spectacular archaeological finds, well advertised by museum exhibitions which travelled Europe and North America, lent an added gloss. At the political level, the apparent egalitarianism of Maoism – in education, in rural health with the 'barefoot' doctors, had strong appeal to an educated American public sickened by racism and strife at home, not to mention the never-ending horrors of the Indochinese wars. School teachers, doctors, lawyers signed up enthusiastically for China 'study tours', organised by the mushrooming chapters of U.S. -China Friendship. And Jim was to play an unwitting but significant role in all of this.

'I'd only planned to go home for a month or so, Richard, but once I arrived I was grabbed by the Friendship people. They asked me if I'd speak at their meetings, and I agreed. Before I knew what had happened, I was on a tour throughout most of the States, and I hardly saw my mother at all.'

Jim was to perform on dozens of stages in half of all the States. As elsewhere in the world, there had been no first-hand news from China for a generation and people flocked to hear him. It was clear that our Jim had the pull of a fairground freak. Yet I am certain of one thing: his tales of life in China were always rosy, and no beans were ever spilt on the darker episodes of life in the People's Republic. Starting with the 1957 witch-hunt against 'rightists' and continuing in an almost unbroken line until Jim's year in America, those grim times had lasted two decades.

In this opacity, Jim was no different from the other foreigners who had survived China since the 1950s. While he himself had escaped incarceration, many of the small Beijing contingent had ended up in gaol for quite some years. Yet as China started to open up in the late 1970s and such individuals took to holding court to inquisitive Western visitors, it was rare for an adverse word about Mao's China ever to pass their lips. I am sure that an emphasis on the 95 percent positive would have been Jim's line exactly, though with audiences naturally given to scepticism, I would loved to have witnessed how he managed to carry it off. For carry it off he certainly did, and there was no end to the demand for Jim's instructive lectures on the wonders of his adopted country.

Away from the snake oil, it was Jim's off-stage experiences in the country of his birth which put one in mind of that innocent abroad, the eponymous 1950s film hero in *The Adventures of Hiram Holiday*. In the late 1950s, the surreal show appeared on our English TV and as a small boy I remember being in raptures of laughter. For a start, Jim's very manner of speech seemed to be straight from some old Hollywood movie. His renditions were deadpan, with an absence of both irony and self-parody. With the *baijiu* white lightning flowing and as Jim described his travels, I was soon rolling in the aisles.

Jim had, in effect, been away from America since the late 1930s. His youth had been spent in a very different country, the white divided from black America of Roosevelt and Truman. In 1976, in his first day of wonderment in New York, Jim walked and walked, eyes popping from their sockets. He was thirsty and he dodged into a Harlem dive for a beer, and found himself seated at the bar alongside a line of black drinkers. Coming down the line was what Jim took to be a large cheroot, and having sized up this strange apparition of a whitey in their midst, his neighbour generously passed it on. This reminded Jim of home – the paper mill – where the boys would vie to make the largest roll-up out of home-grown tobacco and waste paper. Jim did not think much of the handiwork and promptly screwed the smouldering object into the nearest ashtray. A stir went through his new acquaintances. Another reefer came down the line, and again Jim squashed it flat in the ashtray. The next thing he knew he was hot-footing it for his life.

'I just thought I was doing them a favour – that they wanted me to stub out their cigarettes. Why do you think they got wild at me?'

Jim's iconic tour for the China Friendship people occasionally plunged him into hostile territory of a different kind. One night he was holding forth to an enraptured audience in a community hall somewhere in the Midwest. Suddenly a man at the back started barracking and screaming.

'Coward, traitor, Commie! You won't get out of this town alive,' was his parting shot as he was hustled out of the hall.

Unruffled, Jim went on with his eulogy on the people's communes and the barefoot doctors. The next morning, his host was putting him on the Greyhound for the next venue when Jim remembered the dire threats of the night before.

'What about that feller who was hollering at me last night?' he asked. 'I thought he'd be here to send me off .'

'Oh, you're still here but it was him that died,' came the reply. 'He got so worked up over you that he had a heart attack, right there outside the meeting hall.'

Jim's progress brought him in due course to California. It was there that the hounds of media and publishing made a concerted attempt to nail him. As Jim had moved slowly westward, it seemed that so had a thin, slicked-haired character who popped up at half a dozen of his meetings in as many States. Back in Oregon, Jim had actually collared this fellow as he made his way out of the meeting hall.

'You spying on me then? 'Jim was angry – the U.S. authorities had, after all, promised to leave him alone.

'You got me wrong, Mr Veneris. I wanted to hear you, again and again. And I want to make you an offer – there's a check for one million dollars made out to you, and its waiting in my hotel room.'

Despite his love of the limelight, Jim had shied away from interviews on local TV and radio, though there had been plenty of offers - lavish hotel rooms and meals, unspecified expense accounts. Now, apparently, he was being promised a king's ransom for his life's story. Jim must have realised that if he told one tenth of what he knew, he would never be allowed back into China, and he might face a prison cell in the U.S. too.

'I told him I wasn't interested,' Jim loftily replied.

In San Francisco, the local China lobby put him up in quite a nice hotel. The first evening, Jim was relaxing over a drink and found himself talking to a friendly man called Dave who insisted on buying the next of many more beers. Dozens of speaking engagements had left even Jim exhausted, and with no fixed end for his trip to the States yet in view, he was determined to have a week or two off.

'Dave told me he was on a tour of California, looking at real estate prices for his boss and it would be no trouble if I came along,' he explained. Dave would show him Hollywood, and that holy of holies, Nixon's house. The great Tricky Dicky whom Jim regarded as his saviour and the majority of the Western world regarded as a shyster-par-excellence. And Dave promised to show him the rest too, from A to Z. Jim was charmed. The next day they set out, and Jim being Jim, he soon fell to talking about his time in China. Dave paid for the motel rooms. Jim kept on talking into the night. Dave drove here there and everywhere, for a week. Jim kept talking. Dave soon found Jim's weak spot, and fed him daily from hamburger stalls washed down with a Coors.

Finally, the day came when the two pals should part.

'Dave was really good. He went to the trunk and got me this thing.' Jim's eyes sparkled as he pulled an orange Frisbee from the bottom of his locker.

'I asked him, 'What's that – a hat for my wife?' Of course, now I know that it's a kind of flying saucer game.'

'One thing, Richard, that did puzzle me,' he went on. 'Under his jacket and kinda on his belt he had a whirring machine, that he kept messing with. What do you think that could've been?'

Well, I wonder.

Towards the end of my time in Shandong I saw little of Jim. I had my own problems and he certainly had his. His students were playing him up. Wife No.2 was playing him up. And out of the blue he had sustained a serious injury too.

Jim had started on a daily routine of stress-relieving vigorous, directionless walking. Not as young as he once was, on one such sortie, he fell while leaping a farm ditch, badly breaking a leg. Happy relief from the classroom at last. Jim faced several months in a wearisome hospital ward, but it was not anything like as cheerless as the University *zhaodaisuo*. Here, Jim had a captive audience drawn from his own adopted culture – the Chinese working class. In those days, Chinese hospital wards were unapologetic havens of smoking, and my role in Jim's life was reduced to delivering cartons of Lucky Strikes which a friend had sent me from Hong Kong, along with back copies of *Time* magazine. We never had the

398

chance of another long conversation, for soon I was embroiled in a political farrago and forced to leave the country in a hurry.

Two years after I had beaten a hasty retreat from Shandong I was back. It was 1982, and in the course of a British Academy-funded research trip to China, I was surprised to receive a telegram from our Foreign Affairs supremo Li Hua, mysteriously delivered to my Beijing hotel. Could I spend a few days in Shandong to meet old friends, all expenses paid?

My second arrival in Jinan was marked by a welcome banquet rather more muted than my first, four years earlier. For a start, there was no Jim in sight, no loyal toasts to the late Chairman Mao. Even the habit of plying foreign guests with *baijiu* seemed to have passed. The reason for my invitation soon became apparent: my unorthodox flight from Shandong in 1980, soon to be revealed.

With the University's unexpected apologies ringing in my ears, and a pocket full of Renminbi which they thrust on me as compensation, I was eager to look up my old friend, Lao Wen.

In the two years since I had last seen him, Jim had not rested on his laurels. He proudly introduced me to Wife No.3, a demure widow, a botany professor, no less. Such an incongruous but eminent spouse meant an apartment in the No.1 Compound reserved for high academics and Party leaders. Jim was now ensconced in the very building with its clanking steam radiators where Jo and I had spent our Shandong days. The lonely discomforts of the *zhaodaisuo* were a distant memory. But if ever there was a marriage of convenience, pressed on both partners by well-meaning but misguided advisers, this was it. Jim was a hard-drinking, hard-smoking proletarian and he was an obvious daughter of what the Maoist had reviled as the 'bourgeois intelligentsia'. Jim seemed strangely subdued. We had a good few cups of tea, a shot or two of *baijiu* for old time's sake, and I left Jinan and Jim for the very last time.

In the early 1980s, Jim and I exchanged letters a couple of times, and then there was silence. Years later, the next sounding on Jim Veneris was that piece by the canny *Newsweek* reporter who somehow ran him to ground. The most astonishing thing I learned from the article concerned Jim's state of marriage. Apparently, at the time of the interview, Jim was living comfortably in a three-bedroomed Jinan apartment along with the mother of his children. For a moment, I was off-balance. Surely this was not the gold-digging ex-beggar, Wife No.2, who twenty years earlier had made off with his children? Not to mention his foreign-acquired treasures? The reporter failed to mention Jim's third marriage to the timid professor of botany. For once perhaps, tact had probably got the better of Jim. Since things had come full circle, I guess that Jim and No.2 must have just deserved each other.

I have not given up on Jim; in fact from time to time I send off an airmail letter to his last known address. I trust the Chinese post office - they have long experience in knowing exactly where everyone is. But the years have slipped by, and even the great trouper Jim may by now have succumbed to them. I keep that table under the spreading Samos vines, just in case.

XXI
BORN IN BEIJING

I AM NOT SURE I should be writing this. It seems disrespectful to Yongshan's mother, who carried him all those months and then suffered the sublime torture of his birth. Yet of all my China adventures of the 1970s, the delightful novelty of fatherhood has a special place. As does the strange manner in which Yongshan entered this world.

China in the final dramatic phase of the Cultural Revolution had confined us first to the Nanjing Hotel and then to a well-guarded and isolated guest-house, a former prison no less. For myself (no doubt for Jo, too), the eighteen months we had spent separately in Hong Kong was a welcome release from an enforced bonding. From the dreamy magic of Hong Kong's Cheung Chau island, Jo headed north to Shandong, and I returned to a sepia England. But Barnard Castle, that market town in County Durham with its fantastic chateau, the Bowes Museum, where my father was lately director, had little to keep me. So I sleep-walked back to China.

To we alien bodies, Shandong at the end of the 1970s finally revealed a country actually populated by human beings. Not quite a normal country, but one in which a conversation about the price of cabbages could at least proceed without being misconstrued as political allusion. Gradually, the Chinese nation was starting to breathe again. And our posting to Shandong was to be invested with new life too, as within a day of my arrival in late 1978, Jo and I resumed our long-adjourned relationship. Nine months on, the unusual birth of our son, Yongshan, was to bring ill-health to Jo and after she had been obliged to leave China to seek treatment, my isolation made me a focus for the political schemers.

Neither Jo nor I knew much about babies, so we asked our friends to mail us a small library of DIY manuals, and these were to prove their worth right through to the grand finale in that hospital delivery room. Attentively chaperoned by the good Li Hua of the University foreign affairs office, Jo's pregnancy proceeded happily and without alarm. When the time came to choose where the baby would be born, we were eager to demonstrate our local loyalties. Li Hua urged Jo to seek the comforts of a Beijing establishment, but Jo insisted that what was good enough for Shandong womanhood was good enough for her. Until, that is, she was taken on a tour of the maternity ward and delivery room at the big hospital in Jinan, capital of our province. Both were caked with grime. The ward itself was a repository for boiler coal, no doubt quite sterile, but a heap of the stuff was piled up by the beds where she would lie.

To Li Hua's evident relief, Jo decided that safety came before any notion of proletarian solidarity and arrangements were made to install her when the time came in Beijing's Capital Hospital, the famous *Shoudu yiyuan*. The government's smattering of foreign employees were, after all, exotic creatures and invariably looked after by the finest doctors in the land. Maybe that is why Yongshan's birth at the Capital Hospital turned out to be so unforgettable.

Over the years since 1949, street, personal and institutional names had been enthusiastically re-jigged in line with political prejudice. Indeed, at the height of the Cultural Revolution traffic lights were briefly changed: red, emblem of revolution, was designated as 'go' rather than 'halt', with all the consequences which one might imagine. The Capital Hospital was not spared, for it had ignominious origins which merited special attention. Formerly the Peking Union Medical College, it had come into being in the early years of the twentieth century; then, it was run by a cocktail of missionary groups, mainly American but with a smattering of British ones too. Even worse in the eyes of the Communist Party when it at last grasped power, back in 1915 that arch-player in global finance, and some say in global financial conspiracy too - the Rockefeller Foundation - had assumed control of China's most prestigious medical institution. So under undiluted Chinese rule, it was renamed simply 'Capital Hospital'.

By mid-July when the semester ended and Jo was already heavy with child, departing the dusty furnace of the north China plain seemed sensible. In the past, we had always strenuously argued against ghettoisation at Hebei province's old colonial resort of Beidaihe. We wanted to travel, to see those little corners of China that the government had deemed available to inquisitive 'big noses'. But now, putting aside our usual objections we conceded that a seaside holiday was the most plausible option. Beaches were boring and one might be just anywhere, but at least the seaside would be a safe place for Jo, and I would be able to have a summer of swimming - something I had sorely missed throughout my time in China. So we agreed to Li Hua's plan for us, delighting our good minder, who otherwise herself could never have dreamt of being allowed within a hundred *li* of this hallowed resort of China's top leaders.

Past the still-ruined city of Tangshan, near which three years earlier we had narrowly escaped the cruel earthquake, we left the Northeast mainline with its gigantic freight trains thundering through one upon another and were transported in a bus of ancient vintage to the Beidaihe No.1 Sanatorium, an extensive but enclosed compound sloping to the seashore. Amongst the pines and shrubberies nestled a couple of dozen well-maintained European-style villas set around an airy modern restaurant block. We were soon installed in the ground floor of a fine apartment where a bevy of handsome attendants were ready to serve our every need. These underlings were clearly excited to have a secondment by the sea from their posts in Beijing's ghetto for foreigners, the Friendship Hotel.

As ever that summer, but firmly out of our sight, the Party Central Committee had also decamped to Beidaihe. The highest in the land, including Mao himself, had long enjoyed the secluded seaside villas behind high walls, the well-tended gardens leading down to pure white beaches lapped by a tepid Bohai Gulf. Leaving the compound and strolling through the nearby countryside, I was to gawp through high metal fences at vast halls with neo-classical columns and pediments, the leaders' home-from-home. It was, incidentally, from his Beidaihe redoubt that Mao's second-in-command, Lin Biao, was said to have made his traitorous exit in 1971 in a Trident aircraft, crashing in the grasslands of Mongolia. Yet the Revolution had left Beidaihe's reputation for spectacular seafood undimmed. I could just see the Party's old boys cracking those Beidaihe crab claws in the dexterous way of the Chinese.

That year, 1979, perhaps half of the Beijing Youyi foreigners had opted for Beidaihe – we recognised a few from our brief visits to the capital over the past five years. And there were at least as many Chinese, mostly elderly. To be housed cheek-by-jowl with real Chinese people was a bizarrely novel experience, for the customary apartheid was absent. Above our rooms lodged an elegant elderly Chinese woman, along with a handsome man in his forties with an unusual aquiline nose whom we took to be her son. We soon heard that our upstairs neighbour was Wang Guangmei, widow of Liu Shaoqi, the man reviled by the Maoists as 'China's Khrushchev'. Before the Cultural Revolution, Liu had come second only to Mao in the pecking order; he had been left in prison a decade earlier to die a painful death. The Party had obviously decided that Beidaihe was to be a step towards the land of the living for his surviving family members.

Opposite our villa was the temporary home of the Syrian doctor, George Hatem, Ma Haide as he was known. Hatem was celebrated for his 1950s campaign to eradicate China's endemic venereal diseases. On occasions, we sipped tea and swapped small talk in the garden he shared with another survivor of the 'ten years of chaos', the renowned artist Li Keran. As it happened, Jo had noticed a peculiar skin lesion across her abdomen and Hatem concluded – wrongly as it turned out – that there was nothing to worry about. The weeks at Beidaihe passed pleasantly, with evenings spent cracking the crab claws and marvelling at the lemon meringue pies of a restaurant in the nearby village. With their faded inscriptions of a once-famous German patisserie established a century earlier in the foreign concession area of Tianjin, the tea cups and saucers spoke of a forgotten age.

Beidaihe's fantasy time was all too soon over, and we were back in Shandong for the new semester.

Suddenly – far too early – Jo's waters broke. According to our handy manuals, this was not supposed to happen, at least not unless the birth was imminent. No time was to be lost, and Li Hua and Jo were on the next Beijing train. There, they were sent to separate quarters in the sprawling Friendship Hotel, Jo expecting to be whisked off to the Capital Hospital at any moment. Meanwhile, back in Shandong, I continued negligently with my teaching duties. The plan was that I would hop on an overnight train to Beijing as soon as the birth was imminent. But communications with the capital were erratic, the only available phone being in the little gatehouse of our No.1 Compound which required the frayed wires to be held together before it would function. No one had told me that when telephone wires are in use, live electricity flows. And frustratingly (and worryingly) it took an anxious week of electrocution before the order finally came to make a move. Unusually, I was allowed to board a night train with no minder in tow, and eight sleepless hours on, in the great bustling plaza in front of Beijing station, I found a taxi and sped towards the hospital.

It was not far. The Capital Hospital stood at the end of a quiet road which led off the south end of Beijing's still-unglittering equivalent of Oxford Street, Wangfujing. The hospital had been created in the early years of the twentieth century in a grandiose palace style, but its red-lacquered pillars and green tiling now looked weary. I mounted the concrete steps to the portico, and within, the palace image quickly dissolved. The familiar damp concrete floors, the walls lined with benches interspersed by white enamel spittoons being made good use of by the many patients who had wandered from their wards in a variety of bandages and bed-dress.

I found Jo in a private room on the first floor, with a window which looked out over the entrance. And I had arrived just in time – this was no false alarm. Jo was tucked up in an old-style hospital-bed, and being administered to by an ancient female whom I took to be a nursing auxiliary. Though the mother-to-be appeared to have only minutes to go, I was surprised that this attendant's chief concern seemed to be nourishment.

'Ni yiding yao chi shenma,' the woman insisted.

But to eat something, as the woman was demanding, was the very last thing Jo had in mind. In between the deep panting of labour, she grimaced and the woman retreated, soon to reappear with a large bowl of battered prawns in a sweet sauce resting on a mound of rice.

'Women have to keep up their strength,' the old lady said with a smile.

Having missed my dinner the night before, as well as breakfast, it was I who gratefully downed her offering.

From across the corridor came blood-curdling screams. Fortunately Jo was too far gone to register these unhelpful noises from the delivery room. Midnight came and went. The screamers had temporarily fallen silent, while Jo was becoming ever more discomforted. The attendant hovered nearby, wringing her hands and muttering. I was beginning to wonder what should happen next when a tousled male head peered around the door, hesitated, and then entered. In came a pleasant-faced character in his forties, an 'intellectual' type, bespectacled and wearing a wrinkled gown of grey-white which partly obscured a faded jacket. Green army trousers were finished off by dun-coloured laceless plimsolls.

'I'm Doctor Lang Jinghe,' he said softly in Chinese, as he advanced gingerly towards the foreign apparitions. 'I'll be looking after you,' he added unconvincingly.

With this he left the room. No examination, then, though I had read enough in our baby manuals to know that nothing could proceed until the cervix was properly open. And there was only one way to judge that – the magic four-finger test. Jo's moaning and writhing was ever more disturbing, and now getting quite wound up myself, I went off into the corridor to seek the doctor. Our old nurse pointed to a room opposite – the one where the screams had now started up again. Dr. Lang was obviously back in the delivery room and had his hands full.

After what seemed an age, he reappeared by Jo's bedside and took her pulse. I signalled to him that he might have a good look to see if the time was ripe. No – off the doctor went again. This time I pursued him, almost dragging the foreigner-shy fellow back into the room.

'Foreign women are the same as Chinese women,' I half-yelled in Chinese. But still nothing. Then after what seemed an age, a decision. The auxiliary and another nurse rolled Jo off her bed and shuffled her into the delivery room where she was hoisted onto a plastic-covered bench. Meanwhile, I managed to grab a gown from the corridor, and despite weak protests from the women, in I went after my partner.

My distrustful eyes were fixed now on the doctor, who was making a great show of scrubbing up at a corner basin. I registered with subdued amusement that he had changed his footwear for some black galoshes.

'Why that?' I thought, until my shoes squelched and looking down I saw, numb to emotion, that they were covered in pools of congealing blood.

Holding Jo's hand tightly, I prayed that something would happen. Dr Lang hovered, left the room, reappeared, went out again. But nature was asserting itself, and Jo was evidently pushing hard between breaths. Next time the doctor returned, I ushered him over in a shoulder grip, all the while mouthing 'fingers'. He backed off in horror and then seemed to relent. Four fingers were inserted, but into the orifice from which no baby has ever emerged.

'Babies come out of foreign women from the same place as your Chinese women,' I shouted. But poor Dr Lang had done as much as he dared. It was the same old story - a mistake with a foreigner could cost someone in Dr Lang's position their job, or worse. Better to do nothing.

Suddenly I noticed a development - I could now see a dome shape slowly enlarging, to the size and appearance of a small coconut. But progress halted. For an age - it seemed like an hour but must have been far less - there was no change. I thought back to those DIY baby books and knew that if this went on there was danger of brain damage.

I swore at Dr Lang, pointing to a tray on which various instruments were shrouded in grey cloth. What we needed was a scalpel. The doctor appeared to come to his senses. With shaking hands, and with me almost directing him, he made the necessary incisions. At the moment when I least expected it, Yongshan shot from his mother like a cork from a popgun. The scalpel was wielded once more, this time on the umbilical cord. The old women had reappeared. Mumbling to herself, one of them picked up the slime-covered little body and went through the routine of inversion and shaking. There came a robust cry, and I exploded with laughter. Before I knew what was happening, the baby was wound into yards of white swaddling, for all the world like a little Egyptian mummy. I laughed hysterically again.

But I had quite forgotten the final task. Now Dr Lang was a changed man and appeared in complete command. Standing in still concentration over Jo, he was waiting for some mysterious event. After an anticlimactic minute, out tumbled the afterbirth. I was intrigued, for the stuff had the consistency of a heap of liver on a butcher's slab. Until, that is, the doctor started scrabbling through it as though he was searching for pearls, whereupon it broke down into a gooey mass.

By now, I was more the interested observer than panic-stricken birth partner. The man opened a large, American domed-topped refrigerator of Art-Deco vintage. Each shelf was crammed with oblong aluminium food containers with fold-over handles, recognisably ex-U.S. army. Into one of these he quickly scooped the afterbirth. I was wondering what all this was about when I remembered that the anti-flu injection which the clinic administered to my backside each autumn was a product of China's delivery rooms.

It was only at that point that it occurred to me to ask, 'Boy or girl?'

We were back at our temporary Beijing home, the Friendship Hotel. There, a ghetto stalwart, Aussie Pauline, took us in hand

and as the baby routine set its ways, I began to fall in a big way for fatherhood.

The British Embassy officials were surprised when we knocked on their door. They had no idea that any of their nationals were in Shandong. That was our careful design – all kinds of suspicions might have been aroused if contact with diplomats had been maintained. When Yongshan's Chinese birth certificate was exchanged for a British one, he became Jonathan; he has always enjoyed the quizzical looks of border guards when they scan his passport for 'Place of Birth'.

But Shandong again beckoned, a depressing prospect after the many comforts of Beijing (cheese and yoghurt, lemons even), and, of course, the companionship which we craved in our lonely outpost. Our trepidation was well-founded, for the Shandong locals had firm ideas on baby treatment. Li Hua's ancient mother led the granny pack, charmingly baking from dough a painted tiger figure to guard Yongshan's cot. The moment we were out of the room, an old girl would be trying to smother the poor little creature in more layers of padded cotton. When the elders brought in a couple of bricks and inserted them either side of Yongshan's head to mould a flat cranium 'so he would find a wife more easily', we drew the line.

Far more serious was the line drawn under Jo's health. Dr Lang's behaviour and my inexperience in the delivery room had brought on a prolapse, for which the Shandong remedies were unsavoury. Against both of our principles, we petitioned for an early return for Jo and Yongshan. By Christmas 1979, doting Yorkshire grandparents were celebrating Jo's and baby's 'return to civilisation'. But it turned out that Dr Hatem had been badly mistaken when he had examined her in the balmy heat of Beidaihe. Jo went under the knife twice, for her now-huge skin lesion. For myself, I felt duty-bound to see out the semester. That was a decision which proved to be unfortunate.

Unlike his grandmother who left China aged seven and for whom bad memories meant no return, after much equivocation Jonathan finally - and happily – set foot again in the land of his birth. Three-and-a-half decades after his traumatic entry into this world, he was to find a China quite unlike the country his parents had known in the 1970s, and yet one which was curiously recognisable from the many tales he had endured in his Liverpool childhood.

XXII
NOT QUITE FRAMED, OR THE
FATE OF THE MUSK DEER

SEALED AS I AM BETWEEN greying sheets in the common ward of this Hong Kong hospital, I am programmed for sound rather than sight. The clunking progress of a gnarled orderly is one I anticipate uneasily: at least once a day he does his rounds, a grim reaper pushing before him a battered aluminium coffin trolley. Somewhere up the ward there comes a dull thump as his latest cargo is carelessly loaded. Once, I raise myself and catch the curious eye of the coffin-steerer, who nods conspiratorially.

In the cot to my left lies a wizened dark-skinned gnome, a fisherman in the last stages of bodily rot. I am the alien intruder from a remote colonial over-class, and as a gesture to my white skin someone sees fit to line the floor between our beds with green-wicked bottles of air freshener. With his weeping family by his side, I am swept by embarrassment at the insensitivity of whoever decided to do this. The coffin man will soon be coming even nearer.

My arrival in the dying ward of a Hong Kong public hospital I owe to the good Dr Huang. 'If you think you're having an attack,' she advised, 'make sure you tell the ambulance that you want to go to the University hospital, the Queen Mary, where you foreign devils get the best free treatment Hong Kong can offer.'

What Dr Huang was unaware of was that patients off the street were sent to the hospital's teaching wing on even days of the week. On odd days they ended up on the sink-wards along with the indigent, the most hopeless cases. And I had managed to fall ill on Queen's Road Central on a Wednesday. So there I was, wondering what on earth was going to happen to me next, no lifelines to the outside world.

But matters were to end more happily than for most of the inmates of Ward 7. My numerous heart tests all proved normal, and on the fifth day the overworked youth doing the ward rounds hovered impatiently over me.

'We cannot find anything wrong with you,' he said accusingly. 'You can leave, now!'

I was left in no doubt that were I a local I would have felt the sharp edge of his tongue. Still, as the Chinese saying goes, 'better to be cursed as a malingerer than to be wept over as a corpse'. The transition from prone patient-hood to medically certified fitness was not at all easy, but I had my orders. The timeless un-world of my hospital bed was soon exchanged once more for the thronged pavements of Hong Kong's Central district.

My unrewarding medical experience had its birth on the dusty shores of the Yellow River, far to the north. At that uninviting department of English at Shandong University, one of my few duties as a so-called foreign expert was to coach a new postgraduate student. I got on with Lin from the start. I liked his uncharacteristic forward behaviour which betrayed none of the cringing deference which students were inclined to visit upon their teachers, especially their foreign ones. Lin and I were both in our early thirties and we seemed to hit it off. It would be excellent, I thought to myself, if we could somehow arrange regular contact beyond our formal teaching sessions. This would be an absolute first for me: a give-and take, pretty well normal relationship with a Chinese person.

Lin shone with the most important life skills demanded by the

Chinese reality: he was a practised networker, a schmoozer even.

'But how are you going to persuade the University foreign affairs office that you can come and see me in my home?' I asked him.

'That's no problem for me,' replied Lin in his competent English. 'Your boss, Li Hua, is already a friend of mine and I'm sure she'll agree to me having extra tutorials.'

And this she apparently did. Lin and I would retreat into the back room of our apartment with my stash of coveted Peony cigarettes and one of those bottles of clear fiery liquid which he had chosen for me in the nearby booze shop. Yes, even China at its most turbulent and puritanical didn't deny the benefits of alcohol. Very soon Lin and I were the closest of pals, confidants in the raw spirit of *in vino veritas*.

For those who have not lived through China at its most paranoid, its most xenophobic, it is difficult to appreciate what a revelation all this was to me. Over the previous six years, my relationships with Chinese individuals had been almost exclusively correct, formal, and distant. Foreigners were, after all, a high-risk species, and anyone dealing with them would be foolhardy to overlook the dangers. My new pal, though, started to drop by our apartment as would any friend back home. We would enjoy a drink, and the conversation would range quite naturally over events and personalities in the world beyond our door. Looking back, it was the heady, demob happy post-Mao era, and my guard dropped far too far. After a few weeks with Lin, it had sunk without trace, as had significant quantities of the fiery local *baijiu*.

During our first stay in China, the radical faction's 'revolution in education' was still in full swing, and when the universities re-opened in the early 1970s, our worker-peasant-soldier students were supposedly recruited because of their political merit. In 1978, this dubious qualification no longer held sway. China was sorely missing its educated elite, and entrance to university by examination – denounced so recently as a bourgeois device – was reinstated. Though would-be candidates had to gain the consent of their enterprise leaders, by past standards this was meritocracy at work. The new entrance exams were open to most comers, even those with 'bad' family backgrounds, those with a dash of *chusheng buhao* ('birth not good').

Under the new rules, you just had to be clever enough at passing the highly competitive tests. Our Lin was very sharp indeed; more important, he was powerfully motivated. Only through success in his studies might he stand a chance of ending his exile from Shanghai, where his child was growing up hardly knowing she had a father.

I was intrigued by all my Chinese acquaintances' backgrounds, and especially their experiences during the long and turbulent years of political strife. But almost always my reticence – my fear that I might goad them to a dangerous indiscretion - got in the way. Now, three years since Mao Zedong's death, I thought I might get some unvarnished and more personal reflections. What, I enquired, had my new friend been up to when the Red Guard phase of the Cultural Revolution was at its raging height?

'Oh, I was just a young student at the Shanghai Foreign Languages Institute, and I didn't do much really,' Lin replied. This disappointed me a little, as Shanghai was one of the few places where the disorder of Mao's upheaval was turning at one point into something really interesting - ordinary citizens actually began to take power away from the bureaucrats.

'How about the great workers' movement in Shanghai and the famous Shanghai Commune?' I asked.

'Don't ask me about that, Richard,' he quickly responded. 'I just had a nice time dancing and singing around the place, that's all.'

'Dancing and singing while the whole world around you was marching to revolution!' I admonished with a smile. But I knew enough to read between the lines on this one. Most work-units, and certainly the renowned Shanghai Foreign Language Institute where Lin had been a student, had their own shock 'culture' troops, who also doubled as tormentors.

'So you were an activist in your Institute's Mao Zedong Thought Propaganda Team,' I said, spluttering through this mouthful. Lin grinned widely, and changed the subject.

My next line of probing centred on Lin's life since leaving Shanghai. After 1968, a large segment of China's urban youth had been sent out of the cities, to 'learn from the poor and lower-middle peasants' as the cliché had it. Two years of lawless Cultural Revolution meant that the huge cohort of young people approaching school-leaving age presented the regime with a logistical headache, and now with the rampages of the Red Guards, a public order nightmare too. This was the swollen generation, conceived in the years of the fledgling People's Republic, when stability reigned and couples celebrated it enthusiastically under their quilts. By the late 1960s, these extra millions were ready for work, and China's cities were incapable of supplying millions of new jobs. No wonder that Mao conceived the *shang shan xia xiang* ('Up to the Mountains, Down to the Countryside') programme of mass rustication, dressing it up in slogans of proletarian rectitude and patriotic duty.

I was curious to know about Lin's sending-down experiences.

'Hah, I wasn't sent to a village like the rest of my classmates,' said Lin. 'I volunteered for a tougher assignment and was sent to an Army Farm.'

RICHARD KIRKBY

'Sent' was, as it turned out, a rather loose interpretation of the facts. More like 'sentenced', for Lin described a brutally tough military-run camp on the scratch-poor dusty plains of southern Shandong. Rising before daylight, he would be force-marched to twelve-hour shifts gouging out canals, throwing up railway embankments and levelling fields. Think of those 1960s newsreels of the Chinese 'blue ants' moving mountains with nothing more than mattocks, shovels and handcarts. Yet here we were now, with Lin in comfortable student mode; I found it hard to visualize this suave character in selfless sacrifice for the masses. And why had he left his wife and baby in a city to which he would almost certainly never be allowed to return? These were the days of strict migration controls, putting the great metropolis of Shanghai particularly out of reach to anyone who had lost that city's *hukou* – its vital household registration.

'Was this all for punishment or did you really volunteer?' I wanted to know, but did not need to ask.

'I didn't have to do labour for the whole time I was in the countryside,' Lin said by way of reply.

Lin's salvation from hard labour had been as sudden as it was unexpected. One fine morning, scouts arrived from the local county education bureau, announcing that they needed him as an English teacher. High politics were at work: by the end of the 1960s, fierce skirmishes on the frozen border rivers to the north had finally put paid to China's dealings with the Soviet 'Elder Brother'. Not long after, the previously unthinkable happened: Richard Nixon, a man who had made his reputation as a rabid anti-communist, arrived at the gates of the Forbidden City, bearing tribute to the Chinese Communist Party. In an Orwellian manoeuvre, Beijing was suddenly lauding the old enemy, the U.S.A., as the best of friends, and the new partners set about constructing a fearsome

417

alliance against the Soviet Union.

Engagement with the outer barbarians of the West demanded language skills, and almost overnight Russian was abandoned as China's first foreign language. Hence that bizarre slogan 'We learn English for the revolution' which decorated the walls of my draughty classroom at Nanjing University, where back in the mid-1970s I had encountered my first class of ex-Red Guard.

It was at this grand juncture that word went out that anyone who had any grounding in English had to be put to work for the new cause. Jim Veneris, the ex-POW at the University, was another one of those caught up in the fever for English.-learning. So Lin's tough Shandong army regimen was exchanged for a teacher's life in a commune-run middle school. An unbelievable stroke of good fortune. It was from this new launch pad that Lin began to plan his long march back to Shanghai, to his family.

'When I heard that Shandong University would be holding entrance exams, I persuaded my school bosses to let me have a go,' explained Lin. 'It only took a bottle or two of the best Maotai.'

Lin was referring to China's most sought-after sorghum-based liquor from Guizhou. He sailed through the exams, and in no time at all here he was - one of the five postgraduate students enrolled on the newly-created Masters programme in English literature. In the China of the 1980s, a university degree of any kind was a rare commodity. A higher qualification in the newly-fashionable English virtually guaranteed a university teaching job.

'All I have to do now is be a good student and just get through the course,' proclaimed Lin rather too airily. And - he might have added - pray for Shanghai, the ultimate mountain to climb.

Lin's sanctioned weekly visit to our premises very soon became twice-weekly. And after a month or so, his characteristic tap on the front door might come at any time, even deep into the evening when wholesome Chinese were supposed to be tucked up in bed. I began to be seriously concerned that my new friend might be accused of over-associating himself with the foreigner.

Over a smoothing bottle of hooch, I broached this sensitive subject.

'Won't you be in trouble if you come here too often?' I enquired.

'*Meiyou wenti*,' no problem, claimed Lin. 'You two are China's trusted friends - and the Party Secretary has given me permission to come and go whenever I want.'

So Lin had somehow got himself *carte blanche* to enter the hallowed No.1 Compound. I assumed that this had involved skulduggery – indeed, I spied him once scurrying past our door in the direction of the University Party Secretary's home, clutching newspaper-wrapped bottles. Lin, as we have seen, was good at this kind of thing. So I quickly forgot my worries and decided simply to enjoy the luxury of his company.

Our camaraderie flourished, and as spring gave way to another searing North China summer, little by little the frontiers of our often-inebriated sessions widened. Lin blithely disclosed all the latest rumours - favouritism and fornication even – implicating the high-ups in the local bureaucracy. He willingly borrowed our 'dangerous' imported newspapers and lapped up tales of the world we had left behind.

Like all those brought up in Mao's China, Lin had curious notions of Western life. On the one hand, Chinese in the know were becoming ever-more aware of the worldly riches of many Western societies. On the other, the English primers still being issued even to university students described a Dickensian Jim, an unemployed London docker, who pored over the works of Chairman Mao in his garret while his little boy roamed the streets selling matches. I was disappointed that Lin could never truly understand my world. But it was important to me that he was proclaiming an apparently genuine egalitarianism; alongside my own unorthodox socialist leanings, I felt him to be a kindred spirit.

One day in early summer 1979, Lin bounced into the flat and announced that he wanted my support in a new study plan. His supervisor, the elderly professor of modern American literature, was not long rehabilitated and was desperate to make good on the years remaining to her. Lu Fan's surprising strategy was to marshal her new postgraduate flock in an assault on the works of Saul Bellow. Why the obscure Bellow? The way things were in China, it may have been a choice which was purely spurious. Perhaps some U.S. diplomat had come by and left a few books in the guest house which the Security had picked up and delivered to the University. This is how it was in those days of hunger for anything from America. Anyway, Lu Fan's strategy was to be the first to achieve an unassailable monopoly of Bellow. The first task was to translate whichever of his novels she could get her hands on, and that is where her retinue of postgraduates could be useful. Later, when the field had developed a little, critical commentaries could be penned, to be placed in resurrected Chinese journals such as *Foreign Literature*.

Lu Fan was not alone. This was to be the route to resurgence for many of those elderly languages academics who nursed the burning ambition to rise again from the obscurity which the Cultural Revolution had forced upon them. Needless to say, though her five willing slaves would do all the work, Lu Fan's name, and her name alone, would appear on any Chinese Bellow publications.

I had suffered quite a few excruciating evenings trying to fathom obscure, allusion-ridden Bellow passages which poor Lin had been ordered to translate for his supervisor's greater glory. We had both had enough.

'I don't want to just translate the Professor's stuff, Richard. I can't survive three years eating Bellow. How about translating George Orwell into Chinese?'

So Lin was proposing to be the monopoly owner of the dangerous Orwell? Yes, I would be a willing conspirator. No hesitation at all.

Much later, I realised that it must have been me who first mentioned the name George Orwell. There was no way that Lin could possibly have stumbled across it on his own. By the time that the Soviet Union and China were in bed together in the 1950s, Orwell had been declared an un-person by Stalin himself; the Russian tutors of the new post-Liberation generation of Chinese intelligentsia in the 1950s naturally made no reference to him. Orwell's sympathies for the Soviet state, such as they were, had died on the battlefields of the Spanish Civil War. Back in late 1976, while still in Nanjing, with Mao Zedong gone and the sudden arrest of his closest comrades, I had rashly lent a copy of Orwell's *1984* to our trusted Party Secretary Duan of the University's English section. Devouring the book overnight, this liberal-minded man (today enjoying his retirement with a collection of ancient Chinese bronzes) just could not believe that its author had passed from this world without witnessing Mao's reign in China.

I urged my friend to act quickly, for any number of China's hungry foreign literature mafia might be having similar thoughts of become the Orwell monopolist. What was more, I could be the instrument of Lin's plan, as my younger brother had just written to let me know that he had moved in above a Norwich bookshop.

'I can just nip downstairs and get you any book you want,' he had explained. 'Tell me what you'd like.'

You bet!

A few weeks later, a heavy package arrived from England, apparently unmolested by the Public Security. Lin was now the proud commander of what was probably the very first complete works of George Orwell to reach the shores of China. On the face of it, I had done no wrong, for there was no specific ban. China did not work like that. But for the coffin being thoughtfully constructed for me, this was the first nail.

I was soon innocently blundering towards Nail Number 2. The protests and street debates conducted via *dazibao* ('big-character posters') had been a familiar part of our Nanjing years. The *dazibao* had a long history, but it was the Cultural Revolution which made it a key weapon of political warfare. Ripping down one's opponents' insulting posters and replacing them with one's own was perhaps a substitute for real violence, though plenty of that went on too. By mid-1978, Deng Xiaoping had finally climbed back onto the pedestal of power, having twice been knocked from it in the previous decade. Much *dazibao*-ed against himself, Deng deliberately used the pent-up forces for change to express itself in a national *dazibao* campaign. For a brief few months, a long brick wall bordering a central Beijing street called Xidan became known as 'Democracy Wall'; here, countless *dazibao* were posted and milling, excited crowds denounced the 'conservative' anti-Deng forces in the Party. I happened to get to Beijing myself to linger by the famed wall. Once Deng Xiaoping had consolidated his comeback, and exposed his Party enemies to the full blast of public criticism and lampooning, he simply changed the rules of the game. By late 1979, Deng declared that *dazibao* would no longer be tolerated accept at a few tame official sites.

Not long after the banning of this traditional mode of protest, I found myself in the uncomfortable position of authoring my own *dazibao*. And in the context of China's politics it was more than a little inflammatory.

Our compound was reached from the gates of the main University campus along a stretch of what passed for the town's main street; a few hundred yards further on was the No.2 Compound which housed the more lowly staff. All of us had to use this road to reach the campus gates. Already by 1979, China's famous rural collective enterprises were beginning to flourish. One such used our thoroughfare as a transit route between its various workshops. In the China of three decades ago, motor vehicles were in short supply. Most rural communes had a few hand tractors which were as often as not used as road transport – the two-wheeled tractor units hitched to homemade carts. All day long, convoys of these vehicles with their over-laden appendages would charge along our road in the unsteady hands of shaggy-haired peasant youths sporting mirrored sunglasses. As they dodged the potholes, a good part of their load - a nameless grey ash – would be shed upon the road.

The relentless north winds of winter swirled and eddied the thick deposits and a short walk would stiffen hair and soil clothes. Spring and summer rains would produce a grey morass through which we poor pedestrians would struggle to and from the classrooms, invariably arriving grey-splashed and discomforted. And this was not all: the ditches flanking the road were clogged with the stuff and were a breeding ground for all manner of nuisances. Our disgusted colleagues complained that the many efforts to raise this environmental malaise with the local satraps – the Licheng County Party committee - had come to nothing.

Indeed, this was just one element in the quarrel with the local bureaucrats: regular power cuts on campus were explained to me as the County committee's malicious needling of the lily-livered intellectuals. The Shandong provincial government had been petitioned, but so far no remedies had transpired.

One day Lin arrived with a proposition which, as a daily victim of the dreadful road, I was all too eager to entertain.

'You told me that you had a Masters degree in city planning, so you're a real expert. One word from a big nose is worth a hundred from a Chinese,' he said. 'We all want you to write a *dazibao* about this road. Don't worry – you can do it in English and I'll enjoy translating it and making the poster.'

The University authorities, he assured me, proposed to display my work in the customary spot, just inside the campus gates.

'But this isn't the usual place any more, because *dazibao* are against Deng Xiaoping's new *guiding* – his rule banning them,' I objected.

'Oh, don't worry about that, Lao Li,' Lin replied. 'Your *dazibao* will be different, I promise you.'

I was fired up and, setting about my task, I quickly forgot my concerns. By the time dawn broke, I had produced what was nothing less than a diatribe. My final outburst against the despoilers of the road was a demand that the County bosses be punished if they failed to mend their ways. Lin came along in the morning and I proudly delivered my handiwork for his translation and scholarly calligraphy.

Days passed into weeks, and yet no poster made an appearance at the University gates. Lin seemed to want to avoid the subject.

'The leaders have decided to put up your poster somewhere else, don't worry,' was all I could get from him. The matter soon passed from my thoughts.

A month or so later, several of my teacher colleagues came up to thank me for my good work. Perhaps, I thought, the University had sent off my protest to the provincial authorities as a kind of petition. Whatever, I was informed that the Shandong Party people were about to sort out this 'contradiction among the people'. Sure enough, a delegation of well-dressed cadres soon appeared on the road outside our compound. Over several days, I noticed the group of a dozen hanging around the campus. At our canteen up at the Reception Centre they were being wined and dined by the University's leaders in the next room to ours. Finally, the cadres donned their amusing Chinese short rubber galoshes and wielding picks and shovels, they made a much-photographed show of shovelling muck from the ditches outside the campus gates. The real job was then completed by a resentful gaggle of University cadres, rudely ejected from their office slumbers.

I knew in my bones that this was not going to be good news for me, the interfering instigator of the clean-up. It just so happened that Shandong's provincial leadership was the most unreconstructed of all China's, for at its head was the one-legged Bai Rubing. Bai had been an early joiner of the Party – in 1927. As head of the Shandong Provincial Party Committee, he was also on the Central Committee – a very big shot. Reputedly a close associate of the Party's widely-hated and now-deceased secret service chief, Kang Sheng - also a Shandong man - Bai Rubing was the only provincial chieftain to have survived the Cultural Revolution. In Chinese terms, it turned out, I had as good as declared myself his public critic. Thus arrived Nail Number 2 in my coffin.

More unwitting self-incrimination – Nail Number 3 - was not far off. In the summer of 1979 with son Yongshan well on the way, Jo and I were sent to the famed resort of Beidaihe a day's train journey north-east of Beijing. Bathing within the safety of shark nets, we dined each evening at the town's Kiessling's cafe where incongruously, coffee, lemon meringue pie and fresh crab sandwiches were served up on the faded, chipped cups and saucers bearing the company name. How they'd survived the Red Guards was a mystery.

One of the villas in our secluded compound was given over to a group of ancient artists who had been victimised in the decade-long purges. Amongst them was a Cantonese painter, known in pre-Cultural Revolution days for his slightly risqué paintings of willowy ladies. In tow was his mysterious daughter – a cropped-haired beauty in her late twenties. Often when I ventured down to the shark nets to bathe she would waylay me; despite the taboo against unsanctioned contact with foreigners, especially of the opposite sex, the young woman begged me to teach her to swim. I thought 'what the hell! The problem was that swimming lessons demanded that I sometimes judiciously placed my hands upon her floundering body. Not the done thing in China. Later, whilst wandering post-prandially along a sweet-smelling path down by the sea, suddenly the young woman was by my side. You can imagine my astonishment, and lack of resistance, when she tugged me off the path and planted a clumsy kiss on my lips and declared her love for me and her hatred of her life-sentence to proletarianship.

She told me that the Party had ordered that redemption from her 'bad birth' could only be gained if she spent her life as a production line worker in a Beijing radio factory. She clearly hated her life. But the poor girl's notion that I could be her saviour was sadly misplaced. Like many aspiring young Chinese women of the time and since, I suppose she imagined that the foreigner had the power to whisk her into a kinder world.

Back on campus, I regaled a wide-eyed Lin with tales of the illustrious Beidaihe elite, mentioning also those odd encounters with the artist's daughter. Later I felt some strong twinges of self-loathing at my alcohol-induced lack of discretion with Lin. I knew that even in 1979, such matters could bring disaster to the individual concerned. But it never occurred to me that this Beidaihe non-event would be turned sharply against me.

The late autumn of 1979 found us on a Jinan-bound train with our new-born son Yongshan. We were expecting to settle back into the teaching routine and see through the remaining year or so of our contracts. Unhappily, Jo had been subjected to some rather odd medical intervention in the Capital Hospital, and as a result she was not in good shape. The University authorities agreed that she and our baby should be allowed to leave China early, while I would soldier on until the end of my contract the following spring. So I waved mother and son farewell at Jinan airport, and returned to a lonely apartment, the winter nights drawing on and the dust-laden winds swirling across the arid Yellow River plain.

Yet for many Chinese, this was a time of release, the tight societal bonds of Mao's era rapidly unravelling. An outcome of this was a real spate of lawlessness, the like of which had not been seen for a generation. Whispers reached my ears of gangs on the prowl, of muggings and break-ins. Lin continued to arrive for his evening sessions, bringing lurid tales of robbery and bloodlust. And what was more, he claimed of hearing of rumours that my own premises – in local imaginings stuffed with foreign-made goodies - were high on the list of the malcontents. I was pretty astonished when Lin begged me to conceal in a handy place an ornate, evil-looking Dai dagger I had acquired as a souvenir on the trip to Yunnan. In drunken jest, and really just to shut him up, I let him put the fearsome weapon under my bed. We both practiced lying prone and reaching as quickly as we could for the dagger. I soon forgot it was there. But Nail Number 4 was now well in place.

My next venture along the rocky road to villainy was brought on by some silly imaginings.

While firmly being a politico and never inclined to hippy-dom, as a child of the 1960s, I could hardly escape a passing partiality towards the various delights of *cannabis sativa*. And China was a land where the distinctive feathery hemp plant grows as a roadside weed. This intriguing scenario was, unhappily, to beckon on Nail

Number 5 in my baleful coffin.

In our first stay in China, ordinary tourism was unknown, and our only chance of going anywhere really distant and interesting was if Chairman Mao had been there before us. Supreme amongst the sites of political pilgrimage was the Chairman's birthplace, Shaoshan in Hunan Province, an unavoidable destination during my first visit to China in 1973. Like millions before us, we gaped during the permitted thirty seconds at a rather handsome cottage, definitely a rich person's cottage, which the shrine-keepers explained was the abode of the impecunious Mao family. How could it be anything else?

During our second summer break at Nanjing University, we swept south through Jiangxi Province in a convoy of dust-encased Shanghai saloons, arriving finally at the mountain redoubt of Jinggangshan. This was the sanctuary of the remnants of the Communist forces driven from the Yangtze cities by the massacres of 1927. As Leon Trotsky had warned it would, the so-called leaders of China's 'bourgeois revolution', the Nationalist Party, had turned on their erstwhile leftist allies and with the enthusiastic help of organised crime, the Triads. The British secret service, amongst other imperialist powers had ensured a ready supply of weaponry; tens of thousands of workers and intellectuals were slaughtered in a matter of days.

The year before, we had been to Yan'an, an even more revered shrine of the Revolution. Here, in the crumbling loess hills of the Northwest, Mao's bedraggled forces of the epic Long March had established their military and political headquarters. Despite encirclement and blockade, first by the Guomindang and later by the Japanese invaders the communist forces had survived to fight their victorious battles in China's Second Civil War.

At both holy sites, Ya'nan and Jinggangshan, Chairman Mao had obviously moved around quite a bit, and we political pilgrims were expected to relish each and every hut and cave where he had spent the night. Always, straw sandals were tucked under the simple beds, while desks were always strewn with books and pens to show Mao's tireless devotion to study and war-planning. The young guides – usually rusticated female Red Guards from Beijing - intoned their word-perfect eulogies. For them, a rural exile to Yan'an was actually the supreme honour. It was all very fascinating, as much from an anthropological point of view as from the tales of triumph over adversity.

The tour routine, the dedicated note-taking at every stop, was relieved in a rather bizarre way. We soon noticed that behind every former Chairman Mao billet was a lush garden of hemp. Much later, while at Beidaihe, even at a lonely cliff-top pavilion on the Bohai Gulf (a spot where Mao happened to have dreamt up one of his most famous poems), we were wafted not by the fresh sea breeze but rather by that characteristic slightly sickly aroma. We had started taking bets on how quickly we could spot the weed. Not difficult: at each and every house once inhabited by Mao in the decades of struggle was planted a hemp garden. Often enough, Jo and I managed to distract our chaperones whilst one of us nipped round the back to stuff our green canvas 'Serve the People' bag with the delicate fronds.

As a tiny part of my relentless struggle for the real China I just had to find out what the official line was on cannabis. Yet subtle raising of the matter amongst colleagues drew a blank. So I was forced to pursue the matter more obliquely. The first thing my research turned up was that my Chinese dictionary entry for the generic word hemp also offered the meaning of 'anaesthetic'. This was encouraging, as it immediately conjured 'healthy'– in contrast to the tedious 'bad-for-you' that was the official response back home. From my sly enquiries, I knew that ordinary pharmacies would stock cannabis derivatives, alongside all the other strange bits of animal and vegetable matter which to the untutored appeared to be nothing other than sweepings from the forest floor.

My first thought was to just go down the street and buy a few grams over the counter. In reality, there was no way that I could ever get away with this: in any public place we would within seconds garner an audience of dozens, even hundreds of gawping bystanders, one or two of whom would be bound to be police-informing busybodies. I could hardly stand there and demand in my best Chinese 'A *liang* of your best *dama*, please'.

But I was still determined to discover whether or not the Chinese had the idea of using the stuff as a recreational drug.

My answer finally came during that summer stay in the officials' seaside resort of Beidaihe.

The balmy evening ride from the compound to the nearest town and its various interesting eateries was by an ancient hole-riddled shuttle bus. At a certain point on the short journey a distinctive whiff would waft through the glass-free windows.

'It's a lovely evening and I'd like to walk back to the compound,' I chanced at the vehicle's security minder.

'But you are our foreign friend and we must take care of you,' was the stock response. I ignored it and slipped off the bus while he was getting a light for his cigarette. I intended to enjoy the illusion of freedom which a stroll back to the encampment would induce.

Arriving at the aroma point, I found half a dozen locals, each balanced on his tiny bamboo stool and absorbed in an unfathomable but noisy card game. From their ragged white singlets and multi-patched blue shorts protruded the delicate sun-browned limbs of China's working masses. These were definitely poor folk and my enquiries produced the gruff reply that they belonged to a fishing brigade of a nearby people's commune. My arrival had put them off neither their card game nor their giant-size reefers. But I just had to have it out with them, and I issued what turned out to be more of a frontal attack than I'd had in mind.

'Why are you smoking *mafei?*' I asked.

The unusual situation of communicating with the masses without a minder present had scrambled my Chinese and instead of the word *dama* for cannabis, I had accused them of smoking morphine. Not surprisingly, the neutral mood switched to one of tight-lipped frowns: morphine and heroin were regarded as ills of the long-gone 'old society'. Their illicit use was almost unknown in post-1949 China, and no doubt any drug abuse would have attracted the severest punishment. I realised my error as soon as the word had left me and after copious mutterings of '*duibuqi*' – 'apologies' - the atmosphere lightened.

'Here, try it yourself.' To the raucous amusement of his friends, one of the card players thrust towards me his clumsy cheroot and I took a modest puff.

But I still had not fathomed how it was that my companions were sitting there openly indulging in the exotic narcotic.

'Please tell me why you're smoking this stuff,' I asked in my best Chinese tones. I was becoming an embarrassment and the guy who had lent me his reefer decided it was time to send me packing:

'Look, we're poor peasants and fishermen and tobacco costs money. We used to able to grow a bit in our gardens but the Party doesn't like this anymore. So we're forced to make do with this roadside weed.'

I inwardly grinned at the thought that our minders would have been far more exercised about this admission of poverty than the open use of what we back home regarded as an illicit drug. After all, the cornerstone of Cultural Revolution self-advertising was the well-being of the countryside, nothing less than the complete eradication of the poverty of old. And the foreign affairs cadres did a good job: the average foreign political tourist to Mao's communes generally came away with a glowing impression.

Learning from the poor peasants, the fisher-folk of Beidaihe, when I got back to Shandong I decided on a little harvest of my own. I was tipped off that the best hemp grew on the slopes of the nearby Qianfo Shan, which after the ravages of the Red Guards could no longer boast the thousand Buddhas of its name. It was Saturday afternoon – the start of our weekend - I propelled my gearless Flying Pigeon bike through Jinan's dust-ridden industrial zone in the direction of the modest hill, and soon found myself on a scruffy slope with a few broken steles and pillars scattered around.

The hillside was indeed blessed by copious stands of two-metre tall hemp plants, and a bumper harvest was promised. A group of elderly locals, out for a saunter, stood amazed at the sight of a foreign devil with reddish curls half-hidden under a broad-rimmed straw hat, slashing inexpertly at the thick stemmed plants with his borrowed sickle. I peddled victoriously home with a full sack of green fronds tied to the rear carrier.

Back in England I had once been spun an implausible tale by a dope aficionado: the marijuana farmers simply course through their fields of ripe plants clad in leather aprons with built-in kangaroo pouches. The sticky mess from the flowers is then scraped off the apron, compacted and solidified to produce the familiar light or dark brown hashish. My own plan, however, I thought to be more scientific. In the entrance lobby to the flat we had a bottle-gas kitchen burner.

From Widow Wang upstairs I borrowed a huge cast-iron saucepan and spent the afternoon shoving the leaves and stalks into the bubbling olive-green mess. This turned gradually to a brown slush, which I persisted in boiling down until its consistency appeared to be something like the stuff one could buy on the streets of London. When I had dried a lump out on the radiator and tried to smoke it in my little Chinese peasant pipe, the effect was ....nil. My labours had produced nothing more than a dirty inert sludge. The atmosphere in the flat was a different matter though - kitchen and corridors were unmistakably alive with a heady vapour. Undoubtedly the wrong kind of hemp. When Lin turned up that evening I tried to explain what I had seen on my visits to Mao's former residences, and what I was now getting up to. Stupidly, I had now added drug abuse to my unseen catalogue of sins, and with my tales of Mao's gardens, a dangerous dose of *lèse majesté* too.

The final and sixth nail was now hovering above my coffin. With Jo and son Yongshan safely back in Yorkshire, the number of resident Westerners in a province of seventy million had dropped back to six. I was originally meant to stay on another year, but now I was allowed to revise my contract so I could leave Shandong some time after the Chinese New Year of 1980.

Lin no longer needed much excuse to call as every Chinese knew that empty spaces bred neuroses. To the cadres, the unpredictable, mercurial foreigner spelt trouble and it was best that someone kept an eye on him. One evening my friend burst into the flat and gushed out a wild proposal. Some weeks before, I had innocently shared with him a postcard from Hong Kong from John Dolfin, the Director of the Universities Service Centre. JD mentioned how a friend of the sender – a member of a European royal house and a Tibetologist - had been allowed an official trip to the still-closed city of Lhasa. There, a tame Tibetan dignitary had taken it into his head to present the prince with a lump of deer musk. The prince, perhaps short of a few dollars, had disposed of the gift in Hong Kong.

To the Chinese, deer musk is medicine, believed to be magically effective against certain cancers. Its potency is said to be so great that even a tiny amount taken near a pregnant woman will cause her to abort. As for the little animal that produces the stuff, it is almost impossible to domesticate and 'milk'. The gland containing the precious accretion - a hairy lump on the underbelly about the size of a crab apple – is cut out and the creature dies in order to give up its treasure. In the high valleys of the eastern Himalayas, the poor musk deer, like all large fauna, was becoming a rare sight. The great Chinese diaspora had made sure of that, for the super-rich of Hong Kong, Taiwan and Singapore had already pushed the musk price to astronomical heights: in that year of 1979, musk was, weight for weight, about six times more valuable than gold. Not surprising, then, that my friend's joking admonition 'Don't forget to bring the musk' was bound to go round and round in my head.

We had happily proposed that our new-born son would have Lin as his godfather. Lin came up with an idea: after selflessly serving the Chinese people, we were returning home to a tough economic situation, with the newly-elected Thatcher government already beginning to lay waste to Britain's traditional economy.

'Now that I'm little Eternal Mountain's godfather, I must help you,' Lin solemnly proclaimed.

'What have you in mind,' I enquired.

'You will have musk,' Lin mysteriously replied.

In fact, Lin's plan was all worked out. On my part, I had to put in a request to pay a brief Chinese New Year visit to Hong Kong before finally leaving for home. I should take with me a quantity of the stuff, and the proceeds could then be invested for our son, Eternal Mountain's future. Lin was quick to point out that there were no laws against any of this. The trouble was, there were few laws at all, and legality depended on the day of the week. Whatever, the little scheme appealed both to my naughty streak and to my gambling instinct, and if Lin was game, so was I.

'We're lucky. A cousin of mine works in a pharmacy up in Wanxian on the Yangtze, and he can easily get hold of musk.'

I knew where Wanxian was – our Yangtze vessel had made a stop there that very year on our way downstream from Chongqing. Wanxian sounded a likely place where musk might be brought down from the mountains to the west. The plan was that every so often, Lin's cousin would 'relocate' a few grams of the precious substance. For safety's sake it would not be sent directly to Lin in Shandong: a little cunning was demanded, and Lin would despatch my money to his wife in Shanghai via the normal post office remittance route. She would send it on to Wanxian and the musk would come back by the same route in reverse. I thought it all sounded very plausible.

Accordingly, a couple of weeks later, and on every payday for three months, Lin came to me for a wad of hundred Renminbi notes; he would soon re-appear with a conspiratorial grin, and extract from the inside pocket of his faded green army tunic a despatch receipt. We would then retire to the bathroom to perform the little drama of disposal of the evidence: fingers to lips, he would ignite the slip of paper and drop it into the pan, whispering to me to flush away the ashes.

Nineteen seventy nine was a defining year in China's opening up to the outside world. The consummation of full diplomatic relations between Beijing and Washington on the first day of that year meant the arrival on shining red carpets of droves of Americans - tour groups, business people and students and academics. This was all regarded with some wryness by us old timers, inured as we were to daily struggles with the bureaucracy over issues mostly trivial.

Now, in late January 1980, the New Year festival was nigh. In two weeks I was due to leave for Hong Kong. Exit and re-entry visas had been arranged by the reliable Li Hua, and return flights to the staging post of Guangzhou booked. Lin was to deliver the goods a few days before my departure.

Normalisation of relations in 1979 between Beijing and Washington brought a contingent of Americans to China who knew little or nothing of the daily struggle which for years past had assailed resident foreigners. U.S. China scholars had been denied access to the country for fully three decades, in many cases an offense against their sense of entitlement to go anywhere in the world and ask any questions they wished. Now, high-up Chinese officials were suddenly available for academic discussions, and no research topic seemed closed to the newcomers.

Frankly, I was jealous. I had been beavering away on the quiet with my research on post-1949 urbanisation with little help and usually subtle obstruction from officials. Worse, for the Americans who wanted to travel, restrictions to closed areas were largely lifted and they could go to places we had only dreamed of. All very galling, and to cap it all, the latest Hollywood movies were flown in for private screenings for China's new best friends.

I had not bargained for our University's own quota of Americans. There were two arrivals, and it was Norma Diamond of the University of Michigan who became my nemesis. Norma Diamond was a China anthropologist of repute, and she was hell-bent on burnishing her academic credentials by being the first foreigner to conduct village fieldwork in post-1949 China. Her focus was a settlement in eastern Shandong which in the 1930s had been a research base of a celebrated Chinese anthropologist. Of course, after 1949 even for Chinese academics there was no room for such bourgeois studies of village life: rural society could only be interpreted through the prism of 'Mao Zedong Thought'.

Unbeknown to Norma, the village she wanted to focus on

now lay within a military zone, an absolute no-go area. Foreign Affairs supremo, Li Hua, did not get on with this new, demanding foreigner either:

'I feel trapped!' she told us. 'The PLA commanders are very obstinate and so is Norma Diamond. What shall I do?'

Of course, Li Hua was unable to let the American herself know about the problem – it was all a 'military secret' which she was prepared to entrust to Jo and me only. Festering on campus, moaning that her precious study-leave was being frittered away, Norma found an ally in American literature Professor Lu Fan, wife to the University President and Li Hua's undeclared rival. Later I was to find out that there had long been bad blood between the two women: Li Hua had played some part in a denunciation meeting of Lu Fan at the height of the Cultural Revolution.

Our paths crossed with Norma's twice daily in the dignitaries' new restaurant block, where her complaints about the fare ('not like Chinese restaurants back home') were unceasing. And this despite the University having dug up a couple of cheery chefs who in the distant pre-1949 world had served up omelettes, steaks, French fries and sponge cakes to the U.S. Navy in Qingdao.

One day when we were sitting down to our lunchtime meal, *a propos* nothing Norma Diamond loudly threw a comment across the table that was as shocking as it was sudden:

'You know that man from the Foreign Languages Department who you're always hanging around with? Well, he's working for the Security.'

I just about gagged on my Qingdao-style chicken Kiev and my heart missed several beats.

'How, who......what?' I spluttered.

'Oh', she said. 'Professor Lu Fan told me to let you know.'

I am sure that this unusual information came Norma's way in the expectation that it would be conveyed to me subtly, in the

Chinese way. Small hope of that. Absolute disbelief overwhelmed me. My heart was racing. I just could not take in the fact that Lin, to whom I felt closer than my closest friend anywhere, could possibly be in the business of betrayal. I dashed out of the dining hall; I just wanted to find Lin and have him reassure me it was all some great misunderstanding.

As luck would have it, as I ran towards the teaching block, my heart thumping, I spotted Lin striding diagonally over the sports ground, deep in thought. I changed course to intercept him. Lin stared at me distantly as I blurted out in breathless jerks what I had just heard. He remained impassive. It is true that a cultural trait of the Chinese is to respond to tension by grinning, and now a forced smile came to Lin's lips:

'Richard, why should you believe a single word of that loud-mouthed American woman?' he said.

Through luck rather than presence of mind I had not mentioned the source of the allegation, though I suppose Lin put two and two together. Without another word, off he strode, leaving me prone in the middle of the sports field, wondering what on earth to do next.

I was never to set eyes upon my erstwhile friend again.

If all was as it now appeared, the plotters would hate being foiled at the eleventh hour. The first thing to do was a minute check on the place where Lin had suggested I conceal the musk-cache – the tubular frame of my old rucksack. In the days that followed, I carefully shoved a straightened coat-hanger through each unscrewed tube. I was convinced that even if I did not take the musk from Lin – and of course I now had no intention of doing so – the Security would plant the stuff on me anyway. Their set-up had taken months to prepare, and it seemed unlikely that they would just abandon their plans.

That evening I skipped dinner, went early to bed, and fell

to a fitful slumber from which layers of consciousness became entwined in a strange tap-tapping from outside my window. My watch showed just after midnight. The thought that it must surely be Lin brought me to keen wakefulness. Here he was with some simple explanation; I rushed to unbolt the door. But in the darkness of the porch was a short figure, its upper body swathed in a black woollen shawl. Immediately the apparition pushed the door shut and shoved itself by me. Then it spoke, and I recognised immediately the throaty tones of Professor Lu Fan, wife of the University president, and Norma Diamond's mentor.

Without any of the usual fuss, Lu Fan led the way into the living room and plonked herself down, shawl and all, in one of the heavy armchairs. I, still in pyjamas but too taken aback either to feel the cold or any impropriety, seated myself opposite.

With not a hint of the usual Chinese temporising my visitor waded in:

'Why has my student Lin been coming to your flat so often and what has he been saying? You must tell me the truth, Richard,' she insisted.

The normal assumption was that work-unit bosses – and I was well aware that Lu Fan was a member of the University's Party Committee - were already in possession of one's innermost secrets. Even in the relatively liberal climate of Shandong in 1979, Jo and I understood that our daily lives continued to be scrutinised, our mail obviously opened and resealed, and we guessed that the phone at the gatehouse was tapped too. Yet Lu Fan's interrogation seemed genuinely in search of answers.

'I'm frightened,' she said. 'If my husband and I don't know what's going on, who does?'

In those pre-AIDS days Lin and I had once theatrically engaged in a blood-mingling oath of secrecy which I had no intention of breaching. Yet any hesitation I had in betraying my friend was quickly out of the window. Oddly, I still feel ashamed that I broke my word so freely. But it was the profound shock of the previous day which had quite turned me inside out. In less than a minute I had blurted it out and Lu Fan was privy to the whole saga of the musk.

Now it was my turn to be surprised, for Lu Fan seemed overcome by a bitter energy which was causing her to writhe on her seat. Back in 1967, she reminded me, she and her husband had provided the rampaging Red Guards with perfect targets. There was not much that could be done to protect such perfect examples of the 'bourgeoisie' as two professors of American literature. Of course, they lost their jobs and were sent to be 'educated through labour' in the deepest countryside. The couple were well aware of the fate of others like them in Shanghai's educational institutions. Lin, she said, had actually been one of the most prominent and loathed of the Shanghai rebels and had played a leading part in the persecution and untimely deaths of a number of staff at the Foreign Languages Institute. Some had been close colleagues of Lu Fan and her husband. And that is why Lin had been sent for punishment at an army farm, while normal young rabble rousers were customarily assigned to rural people's communes.

It was only after Lin arrived at the University to be her graduate student that chance conversations with Shanghai literary friends made her realise he was one and the same Lin, the erstwhile student leader who had terrorised the Foreign Languages Institute. But there was nothing for it. Under the new meritocratic entry rules, Lin was a legitimate student and her only role was to nurture his studies.

At this point, I recalled Lin's protestations about a quiet Cultural Revolution. I was very good at dancing for Chairman Mao,' was always his cryptic comment, before changing the subject.

I was now desperate for Lu Fan's explanation of what Lin was up to.

'I've no idea, Richard,' she explained, 'but it must be something to do with you!'

Li Hua had told her that when she had needed to visit the Provincial Public Security recently on some trivial matter, she had been surprised to spot Lin in an adjacent room deep in conversation with someone. He was talking animatedly, as if to an equal. Later she spied him at the end of a long corridor, standing at a window where people who had been out on official trips could reclaim their expenses.

'But what official business could a mere student possibly be involved in?' Li Hua had asked Lu Fan.

Yes, I now recalled that a couple of weeks before, Lin had indeed disappeared from the campus for a few days. He had told me that he was going off to a place in southern Shandong to make a courtesy call on his old friends from army farm days. And I had actually missed him.

Lu Fan went on: 'Li Hua has a good friend in the Public Security who found out for her that Lin's *bao xiao* - his expenses reclaim - was for visiting Beijing. But the policeman was too frightened to say any more.'

Li Hua always impressed me by her powers of persuasion, usually accompanied by a handsome smile. She was a skilled operator and had many contacts, high and low.

Lu Fan then went to ponder aloud. 'How could it be that neither I nor my husband know anything about a problem with you, Richard?'

The couple were both at the apex of the University's Party Committee and yet they had no inkling of anything untoward. Normally, anything the Public Security had on someone, especially a rare foreigner, would be a matter for the Party apparatus.

'It must be this musk business,' I told Lu Fan.

'Yes, Richard, you have been very stupid,' she replied. 'Someone is trying to make an example of a foreigner, for sure, and it seems you're the one.'

And then she added with a shudder: 'Perhaps Lin is spying on me too.'

The elderly professor, still draped in her dark shawl, appeared deathly worried, and I guessed it wasn't just on my account. A 'leftist' plot in Shandong could end her new lease of life once and for all.

Lu Fan slipped through the door as wraith-like as she had arrived and was swallowed up by the shadows of the compound. As all possible scenarios rushed through my brain, sleep was out of the question. Pangs of paranoia were deepening and they were by no means delusionary. The dark exchange with Lu Fan, oddly the most 'normal' exchange I had ever had with a Chinese official, had thoroughly frightened me. I pondered on whether there was going to be anyone out there who could help me. Throughout the remainder of that night I found myself reaching under the bedstead to feel the reassuring hilt of my huge Dai dagger.

The following days were a blur. By chance, a short time before these events I had pushed myself into a rather belated and lackadaisical fitness drive. It was all that fat pork and sweet-and-sour prawns which Lao Zhao, our rustic chef, had insisted were the right of every foreign friend. My plan was a daily jog around the University sports field. But I had not had any real exercise for years, and a couple of days before my nasty shock, I had felt a certain tightness of chest during my jogging session, followed by shooting pains to my fingertips, which would not go away. I knew enough to suspect a possible heart problem. The tensions that now beset me surely made the discomfort worse, and a couple of days later Li Hua took me to a consultation with Shandong Province's most eminent heart specialist.

RICHARD KIRKBY

Dr Wu was a wiry balding chain-smoker in his fifties; his role in life was to minister to the usually imaginary ailments of the gerontocratic chieftains of the Province's party and military organs. Dr Wu was the proud owner of a brand new toy, still in its box – a portable Japanese electrocardiogram which some visiting businessman had no doubt 'donated' to the leaders. As befitted his first-ever foreign patient, the magic box was now inaugurated. Before I knew it I was immobilised by a tangle of probes and wires, and the printer was spewing out reams of graphs. Dr Wu studied these for a minute or two and approached my shackled form with a victorious smile: his machine showed that I definitely had something badly wrong with the bit of my heart which his dictionary described as the myocardium.

It may seem odd, but this was actually an excellent turn of events. In those days, a little conspiracy ran through urban China, one aimed at eking out the miserably short holidays. Whatever their job, an employee who claimed to be unwell would rarely be cajoled into returning to work. That conspiracy happily seemed to extend to me. Or perhaps the official reaction was occasioned by fear, for those in command had long decreed that all effort must be made to prevent a foreigner dying on Chinese soil: such an occurrence could raise all kinds of sticky problems. No one questioned Dr Wu's diagnosis, and when Li Hua suggested that as soon as possible I should get back to my own country for proper treatment I almost hugged her on the spot. Instead of a short trip to Hong Kong and back, I would be going there en route for home. A Houdini-like escape from that coffin was in prospect.

If getting out of China was difficult for citizens of the country - back then, they were still swimming to Hong Kong over shark-infested Daya Bay with their shirts stuffed with ping-pong balls - it seemed hardly much easier for a foreign employee of the government. To

443

jump through all the hoops in the ten days remaining before New Year was asking the Chinese bureaucracy to perform miraculous feats. No fewer than three vital permits were required for one's release into the world. For a tense few days I was faced by a logjam, each vortex of officialdom demanding prior sight of the others' permits before issuing their own. But suddenly all Catch 22's dissolved. Meanwhile the University carpentry shop had knocked up five large crates and I busied myself with sorting and packing our possessions.

My overwhelming thought was that to save their plot, my unseen enemies would plant something on me. I started to stick hairs on the door jambs and drawers whenever I was out. It might have been better not to have done so, because each time I returned home some of these tell-tales were missing.

Though my daily search of the tubes of the rucksack yielded nothing, I was convinced that whoever was behind the conspiracy would try to get me as I left the country. A plan formed in my mind: I had to have a witness on my long journey to the Hong Kong border. Not long before, a quiet New Zealander in her early thirties had arrived to teach at the Shandong Normal College. One evening I escaped the compound and pedalled over to Caroline's college.

'Have you ever seen Hong Kong?' I asked her. 'There's nothing like it, especially at Chinese New Year, what with the fireworks, the dwarf mandarin trees everywhere, the bustle!'

After all, I went on, the holiday was hers to do what she wished, and it would be so dreadfully tedious to stay in boring old Jinan

'I know the place well, I continued, 'and I'll be happy to be your personal guide.'

Caroline would have run a mile at the merest hint of cloak-and-dagger and naturally, I did not mention the real reason I wanted her alongside me. Anyway, she was easily convinced and started

RICHARD KIRKBY

to make plans with her work unit.

Finally all was in place. The green University Liberation truck lurched out of the No.1 Compound gates in the direction of distant Qingdao and the Ocean Shipping Company, my roughly-hewn cases bouncing this way and that. Only thinking now of preserving life and limb, I cared not whether I ever saw them again. I said a muted farewell to my few friends at the University, and with no sadness whatever at leaving Shandong, I was seen off at the city's airport by Li Hua. I had contrived to leave on the same plane as Caroline and wondered darkly if the plotters had rumbled my self-protection scheme.

Four hours in the air and we were landing in the balmy southern metropolis of Guangzhou, the staging post for what then was still, amazingly, the primary way in and out of the Middle Kingdom. We took a taxi, as planned, to the main centre city hotel, the White Swan, one of the tallest buildings in the land. Over breakfast the next morning both of us recounted similar nocturnal events. Telephone calls with no one there except once, when a male voice asked for Caroline, repeated knocking on our doors which we opened onto an empty corridor. Someone was keeping a close eye, and seemed bent on intimidating us.

The dreaded morning had arrived. A new system of border crossing had just been introduced for travellers to and from Hong Kong. It was no longer necessary to walk over that old Shenzhen River bailey bridge, with its succession of stinking freight cars loaded with squealing pigs. Now you went through border formalities at Guangzhou railway station, to be sealed into a train which ran non-stop to Hunghom Station in Kowloon. We approached the ranks of makeshift border control booths and the moment had finally arrived for Caroline. My palms sweating, I whispered to her to watch me ever so closely. It was my turn, and I stepped forward towards the booth occupied by a green-

445

uniformed officer of the new border guard brigade, his eyes half obscured by a Russian-style over-sized peaked cap. I shuffled my passport through the booth's ellipse of badly cut glass, trying my hardest at a facial set of pure nonchalance. After an age of expert one-handed flicking, the young guard reached for his stamp and brought it down loudly on my visa.

I walked, and was exhilarated. Caroline passed though with equal ease. We lumbered down the concrete ramp leading towards the platform, where a train was disgorging a throng of New Territories farmers on their way to spend the New Year in their ancestral villages in Guangdong. Caroline gasped as a gnarled woman sidestepped her, a huge colour TV on one end of a shoulder pole, balanced by a treacly brown roast pig on the other.

I could restrain myself no longer and motioned Caroline to be seated beside me on a concrete wall in sight of our still-emptying train. I garbled out my story, or at least the final episode of the musk. She sat there open-mouthed and said not a word. It was time to board, and as the train sped south towards the Hong Kong border and the New Territories, Caroline sat silently, staring ahead. Finally she turned to me:

'You can forget showing me the sights of Hong Kong,' she said testily. 'You've just been using me.'

The train drew to a halt and my chaperone stepped ahead of me onto the platform of Hunghom station and disappeared into the crowd.

I was back in Hong Kong, back to safety. My chest heaved with exhaustion and relief, and I collapsed against a pillar as streams of heavily-laden travellers milled past me on the platform. I had worked out in advance what my next move should be and eventually got to my feet and found a bank of public phones.

I dialled the number of my hoped-for protector, the good

446

Dr Huang. Dr Huang had arrived in one of my intermediate level classes at the British Council language school, where I had taught before going to Shandong. We had struck up an unlikely friendship, based in part on the fact that I was the only foreigner she had come across in Hong Kong who knew what life was like in what was always quaintly called 'the Mainland'. Dr Huang had managed to get to Hong Kong after the Cultural Revolution as it was her original home, her artist father having moved to the British colony back in the thirties. A woman of middle age and twenty years my senior, she had been working in a Beijing hospital before allowed out to re-join her Hong Kong family. As a 'foreigner' from Beijing, Dr Huang became an unlikely trophy for the young Cantonese office workers who formed the bulk of my student group. When weekend barbecue trips were arranged to my island home of Cheung Chau, it was always Dr Huang who was the stalwart organiser.

Despite my relative youth, I was forever going to be regarded by her as her teacher. Chinese tradition meant that it was Dr Huang's duty to look out for me and as a medic, particularly to concern herself with my health. Within a hour she was with me, and driving me in her little Toyota to her workplace, the Baptist Hospital in Kowloon where I was smuggled me through the lobby and into a lift. We arrived at the cardiac unit where I was stripped of my clothes and told to run up and down a set of steps. Dr Huang then attached me to a magic machine which spewed out reams of graphs. After that, I was wheeled down to the hospital pharmacy and issued a clutch of different drugs. We then drove through the harbour tunnel and on through North Point, to the brand new vertical city of Taikoo Shing. My old 'foreign expert' pal Shanghai Susan had recently rented a 24th floor flat there, and this was where I was to rest up until fit for the flight home.

Some days later, I was walking along Queen's Road East in

Central and was felled by a sharp pain in my chest. Bystanders called an ambulance, and that is how I ended up in the dying ward of the University of Hong Kong's Queen Mary Hospital - where this convoluted tale began.

Dr Huang finally nailed my 'heart attack': it turned out to be nothing more than a trapped nerve in my neck which responded immediately to the anti-inflammatory medicine which she managed to filch from the hospital pharmacy.

I was soon on my way to England, to be reunited with wife and baby. But there was no way I could keep away from China, and two years later, in the summer of 1982, I was back. The British Academy had signed an agreement with the Chinese Academy of Social Sciences, and for the first time I could officially present myself as a *bona fide* researcher. After a tough apprenticeship to China, the urge to produce the definitive study of urbanisation in the People's Republic was stronger than ever; now that China was once again publishing national statistics and even a clutch of new academic journals stuffed with relevant information my goal seemed attainable. It was a research trip which yielded good results.

Shandong University somehow got to hear of my visit, for out of the blue I had a phone call asking me if I would pay them a visit. I did not feel entirely comfortable with the idea of returning to the scene of the crime, so to speak, but with all expenses offered and a couple of spare days in my Beijing programme I agreed to go. At Jinan station I was met with open arms by Professor Lu Fan and Li Hua; just like old times, we went straight to Li Hua's campus cottage for a homely dinner. Walking back along the dusty lanes of the town, Lu Fan told me that I was due at a meeting arranged for the following day.

I knew it had to be about my unorthodox departure from the

University two years earlier. With some trepidation - and a bad head from the fire-water of the previous night - I got myself to the appointed office in the Foreign Languages department to find only my hosts of the day before. They seemed no less relaxed, and my fears melted.

'We've been asked by the University to return to you the money which Lin stole from you,' announced Li Hua as she took from her little black plastic cadre bag the familiar brown envelope of paydays past. Embarrassed, I shoved it into my pocket without opening it. Lu Fan then continued with what was clearly a prepared speech.

'After you left for Hong Kong, Lin ran round the campus shouting that he'd exposed a foreign spy.'

She went on to describe how he had even posted notices listing my crimes – drug addiction, indecent behaviour with Chinese women, counter-revolutionary activities, opposition to China's war with Vietnam, and conspiracy to smuggle precious Chinese medicines.

'But how did he pass off his own involvement in getting the musk?' I wanted to know. The explanation Lin had offered was just a little far-fetched. Li Hua smiled as she explained:

'Do you remember that huge dagger you got on the trip to Yunnan? Well, Lin said you'd threatened to kill him with it unless he did everything you told him, and he lived in constant terror of you.'

Lin had been allowed to finish his Masters degree, though I am sure it was painful Bellow rather than Orwell who was the subject of his dissertation. Then to everyone's amazement, when he graduated the bureaucrats who controlled job allocations gave him a plum position in impregnable Shanghai.

'But...' I objected, 'what's so good about that? Lin got just the reward he'd been promised?'

Yes, Shandong's education supremos did believe Lin's heroic tale – or at least, they were forced by someone to appear to believe it. But that was far from the final act. A few months after his triumphant return to Shanghai, Lin was deposed from his college lectureship and, as Lu Fan put it, 'punished for his crimes'. And he had been made to hand over every last *yuan* I had given him for the musk shipments. Oddly, the cash was still in one of my envelopes.

I tried my hardest in the next months and years to discover what form Lin's punishment had taken. To this day, Li Hua who survives in a Qingdao flat where she lives with her daughter flatly refuses to say. I can only think that as with other notorious Red Guard leaders, scores were settled with Lin, and after a perfunctory trial he was taken to some wasteland where in time honoured fashion the back of his neck awaited a single bullet. Decades on, the wad of *yuan* notes returned to me in 1982 remains untouched in some bottom drawer in my home.

There was something more from Li Hua, but that had to wait a few years. In 1995, our Shandong mentor was permitted to leave China to attend a professional conference in London. By that time, Chinese nationals – Party members included - on official business abroad were no longer required to keep their distance from foreigners. They were even allowed to accept their hospitality as house guests. It was over a decade since Jo and I had last seen our warm Shandong mother figure, for that is how we always thought of her, especially during the period of Jo's pregnancy when she had been a great source of support. We were pleased to be able to return a little kindness and Li Hua happily accepted an invitation to Liverpool.

After a day or two I thought it a good opportunity to take our guest out for a more intimate chat, so we headed north towards the lush dales of the Forest of Bowland. I decided it would be fun to get Li Hua into a country pub: Chinese people of her generation had been warned that English pubs were Dickensian dens of vice which they should never enter. Li Hua gazed about her at the brass knick-knacks on the wall and the reproduction hunting prints and relaxed into her bangers and mash. We drove on to the nearest town, and in the unlikely setting of the ramparts of Clitheroe Castle, my companion started to reminisce. My ordeal with Lin was unforgettable, but I had no idea how serious things had been.

'As soon as you arrived at the University I started getting messages from the Shandong Public Security to watch you carefully, Richard. But I didn't believe you were a bad man so I just treated you as our guest,' Li Hua told me.

'Why should they have been concerned about me?' I asked, amazed.

'It was something the Jiangsu Provincial Security had told them about you, about the fact you were a trouble-maker and probably a British spy when you were in Nanjing.'

As we walked along the ramparts, high above the town, my thoughts turned to the tumultuous events of Nanjing in 1976, when we had taken part in the anti-government uprising at Qingming festival; a year later our sinful label had been removed and unwittingly, we had become 'heroes of the revolution'. The Jiangsu Public Security had later been forced to eat humble pie, to lose face by returning our confiscated photographs. Then, when we arrived a year or so later in Shandong, Jiangsu had apparently done the dirty and warned their colleagues in Shandong against us – or against me, to be accurate. So even after its official ending, the Cultural Revolution was still rumbling on beneath the surface.

Li Hua then reminded me of several trips she had made to Beijing shortly before I had left Shandong. I well remembered her unexplained disappearances to the capital, at a time when it was not easy to get permission for a junior Party cadre to travel there.

'I was ordered there by the Security Section of the Foreign Experts Bureau, Richard, because of your so-called spying!' She was driven to an obscure building where she was confronted by a surreal display. Dozens of blown-up black and white photos were pinned to the walls, showing me in various settings and occasionally in conversation with persons unknown.

'I was shocked, amazed, to see you there!' she told me. 'And I spent a long time telling them - trying to convince them - that you weren't what they thought you were. In fact they promised to take the photos down after that, but next time I was called to the Security, I found even more.'

Li Hua was no longer her smiley relaxed self as we slowly coursed the high castle walls.

'I was really frightened, not only for you but for me and my family too, because we'd always been so friendly to you both,' she said.

The mood passed and we found a place for a cup of tea and a scone. Our friend then launched into an account of a trip we had made together back in 1979 to Taishan - Mount Tai - when she had indulged my mountain-climbing passion. With the distance of time, what Li Hua now told me was more hilarious than worrying.

'Didn't you notice at the guest house in Tai'an, where you stayed before you set out to climb, there were four men, each in the kind of clothes which policemen think are not uniforms? There were two in the each of the rooms on either side of yours. You must have been blind,' Li Hua giggled.

She went on to remind me that as we struggled up the mountain, the foursome kept pace with us the whole day. When we stopped for a rest, so did they. When we speeded up, they did likewise. There they were again in the hostel at the top of the mountain, lodged on either side of us. Well, climbing the over

5,000 feet of Taishan in a day is a hard push, and I had not taken too much notice of my companions on the pilgrim trail. Famous Chinese mountains are normally crowded places. But yes, when I had looked at the pictures I had taken of the climb, I had found it odd that four similarly-dressed fellow pilgrims in shiny street shoes, Mr Plods were lurking in the foreground throughout the ten-hour ascent.

Li Hua then started going on about those awful electrocardiographs, proof of my Shandong 'heart attack'. She was famously one of life's schmoozers and wherever we went she seemed to greet people. And in those days in China, whom you knew was vital. The medic who had examined me – Dr Wu, chief provincial heart specialist – was already an important addition to Li Hua's opportunistic network of acquaintances. She explained that Wu was no friend of the radicals, for he had been persecuted in the Cultural Revolution, so he was willing to help sabotage any plot against me. Dr Wu had simply faked the ECGs. A bad heart was going to be my passport to freedom..

Fakes? 'If only I'd been told,' I remarked ungratefully. 'Then I wouldn't have had that painful week in a Hong Kong hospital.'

'It was the Party Secretary of Shandong Province, Bai Rubing, who'd planned the operation against you with the deer musk,' Li Hua told me with a serious expression. 'He thought catching a foreigner doing bad things would be a great idea because he hated Deng Xiaoping's' Open Door policy. And it was your criticism of the Party Committee in your *dazibao* protest poster which had got them angry in the first place,' she explained.

I knew that the one-legged Bai Rubing was the last remaining provincial Party Secretary from Mao's time. I had always well understood that eternal ambivalence towards the outside world and its representatives was likely to turn into xenophobia when times were hard. The propagandists were always going on about the 'struggle between the two lines' and when it came to attitudes towards the Foreign Other, the formula fitted. In the higher echelons of the Party, you were either against opening up to the foreign world or you were cautiously for it.

By the late 1970s, the openers-up under Deng Xiaoping were in charge. But a residue of leaders around Mao's former bodyguard Wang Dongxing, the ex-mayor of Beijing Wu De, and a few recalcitrant provincial leaders such as Shandong's own Bai Rubing, had apparently conspired to arrest the new 'Open Door' surge. Their simplistic tactic was to discredit it by proving the perfidy of the foreigner. Far from the embassies and news agencies of Beijing, I had presented myself as an ideal fall-guy.

Thanks to my protectors, I suffered no lasting damage. Li Hua and the powerful Lu Fan along with her University President husband had confounded the plotters. I harbour no ill feelings towards Lin, who did what he had to do under huge duress. Yet to this day, I still shudder at the thought that while I escaped it, Lin, my first bosom friend in China – the godfather of our Beijing-born son - may himself have shared a similar fate to those gentle creatures of the high Tibetan passes, the timid musk deer.

Acknowledgements

LIKE THE ARTIST CARVING away at a piece of sculpture, shavings and chippings littering the studio floor, much has been cast aside in the making of this book. And so it is with my acknowledgement of those many individuals who both smoothed the way during my time in 1970s China, and who played a part in its creation.

Of those I do name in this brief note, first and foremost comes my then-partner Jo, who at my reckless urging launched herself from a secure niche into the great unknown of the Cultural Revolution. Most of the episodes described below were shared ones. And self-evidently, it was Jo who bore the burden of pregnancy and childbirth in an often unpredictable and comfortless environment. In this, all eventually turned out well: decades on, our first-born Jonathan is to be thanked, especially for keeping his obtuse father on-track with the technical essentials of writing in this digital age. Speaking of children, William and Sophie are fondly acknowledged for their encouragement, and for their inspired choice to become the fourth generation in the family to engage with matters Chinese. My partnership with Louise, mother of Sophie, has coincided with the long maturation of this book: she has always readily supplied encouragement and wise appraisal, and for her presence behind the scenes, I am truly grateful.

The Nanjing chapters may read as though there was a complete absence of human warmth in our daily lives. It would be wrong of me not to qualify this impression. A handful of our colleagues in those years certainly went beyond the call of duty in their kindness to us and, at risk of invidious exclusions, I would mention the names of Yang, Yu, Qian, and Lin (*aka* Duan in the book), all of whom became erudite professors in later, kinder times. If they ever get to see this work, all of them will know who they are. Our Nanjing period was also made more bearable and amusing by Renée and François and their three daughters, with whom a lasting friendship was forged. In Shandong (1978-80) we were fortunate to fall into the hands of an enlightened (and lovely) university foreign affairs supremo whom I have called Li Hua. She too, and her children, will know who she is.

Kendal friends and near-neighbours Chris Tribble and Sue Maingay are offered my gratitude not merely for advice on matters technical, but more vitally for their unfailing generosity in the face of my family's complicated domestic routines.

Finally, a fulsome word of thanks to my publisher Graham Earnshaw - an assiduous and punctilious taskmaster indeed; with an intensive few months of back and forth behind us, he has guided me towards a far better end.

About the Author

 Richard Kirkby was born in Yorkshire, into a farming family with very strong China antecedents, and was educated at a Quaker school, at Bristol University and at the Architectural Association, London. Unlike many of his peers, he remembers the Sixties, when he was heavily involved in student politics. In the early 1970s, he spread his wings to Cultural Revolution China, with a quest centering on China's development model of massive industrialisation with little of the usually attendant urban squalor. He taught English at Nanjing University from 1974 to 1977, an experience enriched by spells of labour in rice paddies and a factory machine shop. After Mao Zedong's death but with China still in troubled times, he moved to Shandong University in Jinan city. Since 1980, the author has been a consultant on the Chinese economy, a director of a China firm, a writer of academic tracts (starting with his 1985 book *Urbanisation in China*, which is considered a foundation work in the field), and a broadcaster. In the 1990s, he exchanged his barefoot academic status for a fully shoed one at Liverpool University, directing a China research institute. In the city's Chinatown, he oversaw the creation of a ceremonial archway. He now focuses on Chinese art and the classical guitar, as well as fell walking in his home territory of the Lake District. He is married to museologist Louise Tythacott; his children are the fourth generation in his family to get the China bug, William living in Chengdu and Sophie studying at Nanjing University.